# Who's Who in
# Early Medieval England

# Who's Who in Early Medieval England
## (1066-1272)

*being the second volume in the*
*Who's Who in British History series*

## CHRISTOPHER TYERMAN

### Series Editor:
### GEOFFREY TREASURE

SHEPHEARD-WALWYN

First published in 1996 by
Shepheard-Walwyn (Publishers) Ltd
Suite 34, 26 Charing Cross Road, London WC2H 0DH

*British Library Cataloguing in Publication Data*

Tyerman, Christopher
Who's Who in Early Medieval England (to 1272).
— (Who's Who in British History Series)
I. Title II. Series
942

ISBN 0 85683 091 7 cased
ISBN 0 85683 132 8 limp

Typesetting by Alacrity, Banwell Castle, Weston-super-Mare
Printed in Great Britain by BPC Wheatons Ltd, Exeter

# CONTENTS

*For Elizabeth, Edward and Thomas*

# GENERAL INTRODUCTION

The original volumes in the series *Who's Who in History* were well received by readers who responded favourably to the claim of the late C. R. N. Routh, general editor of the series, that there was a need for a work of reference which should present the latest findings of scholarship in the form of short biographical essays. Published by Basil Blackwell in five volumes, the series covered British history from the earliest times to 1837. It was designed to please several kinds of reader: the 'general reader', the browser who might find it hard to resist the temptation to go from one character to another, and, of course, the student of all ages. Each author sought in his own way to convey more than the bare facts of his subject's life, to place him in the context of his age and to evoke what was distinctive in his character and achievement. At the same time, by using a broadly chronological rather than alphabetical sequence, and by grouping together similar classes of people, each volume provided a portrait of the age. Presenting history in biographical form, it complemented the conventional textbook.

Since the publication of the first volumes of the series in the early sixties, the continuing work of research has brought new facts to light and has led to some important revaluations. In particular the late mediaeval period, a hitherto somewhat neglected field, has been thoroughly studied. There has also been intense controversy about certain aspects of Tudor and Stuart history. There is plainly a need for fuller treatment of the mediaeval period than was allowed for in the original series, in which the late W. O. Hassall's volume covered the years 55 B.C. to 1485 A.D. The time seems also to be ripe for a reassessment of some Tudor and Stuart figures. Meanwhile the continued requests of teachers and students for the series to be reprinted encourages the authors of the new series to think that there will be a warm response to a fuller and more comprehensive *Who's Who* which will eventually include the nineteenth and early twentieth centuries. They are therefore grateful to Shepheard-

Walwyn for the opportunity to present the new, enlarged *Who's Who*.

Following Volume I, devoted to the Roman and Anglo-Saxon period, two further books cover the Middle Ages. The Tudor volume, by the late C. R. Routh, has been extensively revised by Dr. Peter Holmes. Peter Hill and I have revised for re-publication our own volumes on the Stuart and Georgian periods. Between Edward I's conquest of Wales and the Act of Union which joined England and Scotland in 1707, the authors' prime concern has been England, with Scotsmen and Irishmen figuring only if they happened in any way to be prominent in English history. In the eighteenth century Scotsmen come into the picture, in the nineteenth Irishmen, in their own right, as inhabitants of Great Britain. It is hoped that full justice will be done to Scotsmen and Irishmen – and indeed to some early Welshmen – in subsequent volumes devoted to the history of those countries. When the series is complete, we believe that it will provide a comprehensive work of reference which will stand the test of time. Nowadays when so much historical writing is necessarily becoming more technical, more abstract or simply more specialised, when textbooks seem so often to have little room to spare for the men and women who are the life and soul of the past, there is a place for a history of our country which is composed of the lives of those who helped make it what it was, and is. In contributing to this history the authors can be said to have taken heed of the stern warning of Trevor H. Roper's inaugural lecture at Oxford in 1957 against 'the removal of humane studies into a specialisation so remote that they cease to have that lay interest which is their sole ultimate justification'.

The hard-pressed examinee often needs an essay which puts an important life into perspective. From necessarily brief accounts he may learn valuable lessons in proportion, concision and relevance. We hope that he will be tempted to find out more and so have added, wherever possible, the titles of books for further reading. Mindful of his needs, we have not however confined our attention to those who have left their mark on church and state. The man who invented the umbrella, the archbishop who shot a gamekeeper, a successful highwayman and an unsuccessful admiral find their place among the great and good. Nor have we eschewed anecdote or turned a blind eye to folly or foible: it is not the authors' view that history which is instructive cannot also be entertaining.

With the development of a secure and civilised society, the range of characters becomes richer, their achievements more diverse. Besides the soldiers, politicians and churchmen who dominate the mediaeval scene there are merchants, inventors, industrialists; more scholars, lawyers, artists; explorers and colonial pioneers. More is known about more people and the task of selection becomes ever harder. Throughout, whether looking at the mediaeval warrior, the Elizabethan seaman, the Stuart radical or the eighteenth century entrepreneur, the authors have been guided by the criterion of excellence. To record the achievements of those few who have had the chance to excel and who have left a name behind them is not to denigrate the unremarkable or unremarked for whom there was no opportunity to shine or chronicler at hand to describe what they made or did. It is not to deny that a Neville or a Pelham might have died obscure if he had not been born to high estate. It is to offer, for the instruction and inspiration of a generation which has been led too often to believe that individuals count for little in the face of the forces which shape economy and society, the conviction that a country is as remarkable as the individuals of which it is composed. In these pages there will be found examples of heroism, genius and altruism; of self-seeking and squalor. There will be little that is ordinary. It is therefore the hope of the authors that there will be little that is dull.

GEOFFREY TREASURE
Harrow

# PREFACE

When younger, I believed it possible to write academically respectable history for a general reader. It has been a suitably humbling experience to try my own hand at it. Whatever the result, it has taken far longer than I, my editor, Geoffrey Treasure, or my publisher, Anthony Werner, hoped or imagined. To them I extend warmest thanks for their patience and encouragement. My intellectual debts will be obvious from the books listed for further reading and to those expert or interested enough to read between the lines. My mistakes as always are my own. I acknowledge the kind permission of Oxford University Press to quote an extract from *The Life of Christina of Markyate*, edited and translated by C. H. Talbot, 1959. There would not have been any book, however slowly written, without the often unconscious help and sustaining vibrancy of my family. My dedication is to those who have for such a long time put up with me, this book and so much more.

C. J. T.
Oxford
January 1996

# INTRODUCTION

One of the most beguiling aspects of English history is its apparent continuity. That modern institutions can be traced from ancient origins has proved both the making and the undoing of the study of early England. The monarchy, the treasury, chancery and Exchequer, parliament, the courts of Common Pleas and King's bench, shires, the universities of Oxford and Cambridge: their antiquity and survival have lent a comfortable sense of wholeness with the past; a positive incitement to argue that in continuity lies the uniqueness of the English experience. Such impressions are illusory. In the period covered by this book, the central fact of English political history was dislocation and disruption. The verdict of Hastings was final, indeed a fateful day in William of Malmesbury's phrase. There was no Anglo-Saxon Restoration. However, there was nothing inevitable or providential about this. The consequences distinguished English experience both from the immediate past and from that of neighbouring countries. Twelfth century historians such as William of Malmesbury or story-tellers such as Geoffrey of Monmouth peered into the distant past precisely because of the lack of continuity. This was more than a literary problem. Whereas the kings of France could trace their ancestry and rule back to the tenth century, their title and provenance secured by custom, habit and history, the kings of England owed their position to the accident of war, a bloody and chancy conquest, a rude, drastic and, as it turned out, permanent interruption of English history.

Politically, England was redirected by a new French governing class which, for more than a century, maintained wide and deep links with northern France. Conquering landowners imposed their will through coercion and the visible monuments of military power: castles. Church-life was similarly colonised, the new cathedrals resembling the secular stone towers in proclaiming a new dominant order that owed little or nothing to the Anglo-Saxon past: even the saints buried at Canterbury were weeded out to suit the continental interlopers. The language of government and justice became Latin and French. Even though the numbers of French-born settlers in England cannot have numbered more than a few thousand in a population of a few million, as rulers their impact on certain features of culture and society was profound. At the most basic level of language, the Norman Conquest of 1066 and the Angevin inheritance of 1154 left its marks. Today English-speakers eat beef and pork, not cow and pig: medieval meat-eating was the preserve of the well-to-do, of social superiors who spoke French, not the peasants who herded the animals and spoke English. In justice, as the greatest English medievalist of all, F. W. Maitland, acutely observed, 'almost all our words that have a definite legal import are in a certain sense French words'. The ruled adopted the words of the rulers. They also adopted their names. It was a matter of fashion not demography that from the late eleventh century English parents increasingly used French names for their children. The consciousness of the Norman Conquest as a caesura in English history was recognised in 1272 when a new king, named after the Old English royal saint Edward the Confessor, ascended the throne not as Edward IV, but Edward the First since the Conquest.

Yet Edward's father, Henry III, possibly eccentrically, was devoted to Anglo-Saxon saints (he named his second son Edmund after a ninth century royal martyr). 1066 did not usher in a completely new world; there was exchange, synthesis and continuity linking 1066-1272 with the years before. Twelfth century law books explicitly looked back to the Laws of the Confessor. The economic and social substructure of manor and parish was unaltered even if the vernacular and vocabulary changed from Anglo-Saxon to Latin and French. Contact was confirmed by inter-marriage and bi-lingualism. Many children in the French ruling class had English wet-nurses and nannies. The Norman yoke was maintained by men who had been reared on English nursery rhymes. For the majority of the population, the agrarian workers who lived in various states of legal and economic servitude, the impact of the new aristocracy was limited to harsher exactions. Their language and that of manorial courts and peasant tenures remained English. Beneath the elites who have left records and largely hidden from view, during the two centuries after the Conquest English continued to be spoken, slowly re-emerging as a literary language, famously in the late twelfth century poem *The Owl and the Nightingale*. By the end of Henry III's reign, even some official pronouncements were published in the native vernacular.

Even so, throughout the period, to be *literatus* meant knowing Latin. French, increasingly a learnt, second language for the aristocracy, was a sign of social distinction. Both allowed Englishmen wide, easy and regular access to and participation in European cultural, religious and intellectual developments in philosophy, canon law, education, religious orders, crusading, art, banking and architecture. English responses may have been provincial compared to Paris or Rome, but only in geography was England insular. Just as England attracted foreigners, so Englishmen took their place in a genuinely cosmopolitan Christendom: one of them, Nicholas Brakespeare, even becoming pope.

The landmarks of this period were monuments neither to national vitality nor foreign enslavement, yet, unlike those of pre-Conquest England, they are more accessible to us: Domesday Book, the Exchequer, the martyrdom of Thomas Becket, Richard I's crusade, Magna Carta, the Provisions of Oxford, Simon de Montfort's parliament, the foundation of the universities of Oxford and Cambridge. Each has been etched into the national consciousness in a way that Anglo-Saxon precedents have not. Some recognisable themes of national identity were sketched in this period. But this poses a problem. Such resonance for later observers is frequently wholly at odds with the contemporary reality, a difficulty compounded by the nature of the surviving evidence which tends to be enigmatic, opaque and hardly ever neutral or objective.

The most obvious limitation is that we know almost nothing individually and little collectively about the vast majority of the population. Although by the end of the thirteenth century peasants begin to appear in the political and legal records, there are few if any pieces of direct evidence as to what they thought except through opinions and attitudes ascribed to them by others. Archaeology, manorial accounts and law suits can trace their physical existence, but they have no authentic voice of their own. Inevitably, concentration in this book has been on those whose lives can be traced, but without implying any view of historical causation. Therefore, those included in this volume are from the ecclesiastical and secular elites. But the pitfalls of evidence remain. Narrative history was written in profusion by monks, canons or secular priests but usually to the sound of grinding axes. Private letters survive usually because they were collected for a purpose other than biographical. History is written by the victors; legal records by the officials of the court. Writing was becoming increasingly important, but nobody wrote without a purpose. Written evidence cannot be taken at face value; but neither can it be ignored or deconstructed in the blender of post-modernism. Evidence is all the historian has to connect with the actuality of the past: there seems little point using it to indulge the present.

If the past, more specifically the distant past, is a world that is lost, a foreign and alien country, the historian can, at least, attempt to observe what contemporaries thought of themselves. Here the evidence is suggestive, not necessarily by its content but by its nature, tone or form. We can see how the fierce corporate loyalty of monastic chroniclers infected their views of the doings of popes and princes. The lives of kings are depicted as morality tales. The preambles to royal documents point to ideologies of monarchic authority. The stories of Arthur hint at a more oligarchic, baronial vision of a world in which king and noble share power. Illustrations in manuscripts reveal vivid social stereotypes, with power clearly delineated and shared between church and state ruling a peasantry by turns drudges, oafs, destitute recipients of charity or rebels. The imagery of devout patronage is matched by those of war and brute force, order with chaos, but the chaos existing within a frame, both artistic and providential. Impersonal typology rather than portraiture predominates.

Images closer to individuals and their assessment of themselves are found in the seals of the great magnates. Commonly they depict themselves as mounted armed knights, a reminder both of the cultural centrality of the martial ethos and chivalry and of the recognition that the basis of the authority of the

English nobility was military conquest. As late as the reign of Edward I, a story went the rounds of the earl Warenne, who, on being asked by what warrant he held his land, produced a rusty sword saying 'this is my warrant! My ancestors came with William the Bastard and conquered their lands with the sword and by the sword I will defend them from anyone intending to seize them'. On one of Simon de Montfort's seals, the earl is shown as a huntsman, riding to hounds. There were few aspects of the lives of medieval nobles more obsessive than hunting which occupied enormous amounts of their time. Hunting was more than a rich man's hobby; it was part of his culture, way of life, and expression of his status, skill and breeding, an assertion of his exclusivity.

The seals and tombs of kings are equally instructive, of what they shared with their magnates and the crucial differences. Royal seals have the king on one side as a knight; on the other he appears robed in majestic state, a hierophant dispensing order and justice under God. In death, too, kings emphasised their quasi-sacral office. Even the grandest of their subjects, such as William Marshal in the Temple Church in London, are portrayed on their tombs as knights in armour. Yet the earliest surviving effigies of kings, those of Henry II and Richard I at Fontevrault Abbey in Anjou, John at Worcester and Henry III in Westminster Abbey, show the king robed like a bishop. The unanointed could not aspire to such status. The king's divinity may have caused political wrangles, but was iconographically unchallenged. At least the propaganda of social hierarchy was consistent.

The years 1066-1272 were formative. Before and after there were English kings; during them there were kings of England whose outlooks were essentially French, Norman then Angevin. Increasingly, the interests of the monarch diverged from those of their more powerful subjects who, by the mid-thirteenth century, had little feeling for France. When Henry III relinquished his claims to his ancestral lands of Normandy and Anjou in 1259, royal policy was reconciled with political reality and the ambitions of the barons. By then, too, the political nation had expanded beyond the king's companions and the great lords and churchmen, to include wealthy and assertive burgesses, knights and gentry. Between 1258-65 there emerged the first populist political movement in English history under Simon de Montfort. Thereafter, no government could ignore the non-baronial. Montfort's defeat ensured that leadership of this self-styled community of the realm would remain firmly with the Crown, its agents and law courts in which a Common Law, available to all freemen, was administered by royal justices.

It was a far cry from the violence and insecurity of the generations after the Conquest. Any impression of an ordered progression to a harmonious and united polity is grossly misleading. No royal succession was uncontested until 1272. There were three major civil wars, between 1139-53; 1215-17 and 1263-7. An archbishop of Canterbury and a bishop of Durham were murdered. Kings were excommunicated; church life interrupted by papal interdict. In 1194 and 1213, England was declared a vassal state to, respectively, the Holy Roman Emperor and the pope. By accident the verdict of Hastings was not seriously challenged after 1070, but dynastic stability continued elusive. As late as 1216, another radical change of ruling family — Capetian French for Angevin French — was a distinct possibility.

However, away from politics, this period saw steady change. This was a period of economic growth. The population increased as did the size and diversity of the economy. Agricultural wealth was based on cereals and wool. There were signs by the later thirteenth century of pressure on natural resources and peasant tenancies from the growing number of people. As the economy expanded, the lot of the individual villein may not have improved; it may even have got worse. Some historians have seen the years 1180-1220 as a time of massive inflation, in its own way matching those of the sixteenth century and 1970s. If prices, especially for the government, rose, there is no demonstrable depreciation in wealth. England was prosperous in 1272 and, like 1066, most people had little or no share in it. For those who did, there were more markets and more bankers. The urbanisation seen since the tenth century continued unchecked. In almost every way, 1066 made no effective impact on the basic unit of agrarian organisation, the manor.

Parallel to this were changes in the church and religious life. Investment by lay patrons in the creation and sustenance of parishes and parish churches may have been given an impetus by the newly endowed lay aristocracy after 1066. Certainly they indulged in the expensive fashion of stone churches. The spiritual lives of parishioners remained stubbornly or comfortingly conservative, but the administration of the clergy and dioceses were widely overhauled. The aftermath of the papal reform movement of the late eleventh century led to a greater awareness and promotion of the differences between the secular clergy and the laity, a more severe insistence on the spiritual qualities of the priest being manifest in a privileged status. Fuelling this was the penetration of canon law and the elaboration of church courts. Clerical attitudes were informed by the wider study of theology spreading from Paris to Oxford. The spiritual life of the church was provided with new models of simplicity in new monastic orders in the twelfth century and the friars of the thirteenth. Even so, the number of monks and regular clergy, far greater in the thirteenth century than the eleventh century, was still a tiny fraction of the population, their influence hard to judge, but almost certainly exaggerated by the preponderence of evidence they themselves provided.

Conflict between church and state, a staple of so much historical writing, is something of a misnomer. Laymen drew no clear line between the material and the supernatural. Relations of patrons with churches or monasteries remained close, prudentially so for both parties. The church was part of lay society in a manner unfamiliar since the sixteenth century. Indeed, one of the habitual complaints of medieval reformers was that the church too much followed the grain of secular life. At the highest level, apart from the few spectacular disputes, relations between bishops and the kings were pragmatic, not heroic. Rivalries within the church, between bishops, cathedral chapters and monasteries, were far more virulent than any clash between church and state. Indeed, there emerged in the thirteenth century in some clerical circles a view that the main threat to church life in England came not from the king but the pope.

Ecclesiastical insularity coincided with a growing feeling of distinctive national identity. 1066 to 1272 witnessed the fracture and reforging of Englishness. This was not a revival of Anglo-Saxon independence after foreign subjugation, what could be called the Ivanhoe theory of English history. Instead, the conquest and rule by foreigners and the interaction between the native and the alien over many generations created a distinct and self-conscious culture and self-image, recognisable alike to peasant and prince. To observe English history without the European context and contribution is to see *Hamlet* without the Danes.

What weight in such developments should be given individuals is hard to tell. The aim here is to place a few of those whose lives can be traced in their surroundings, both masters and victims of circumstance. No doubt there are some who should have been mentioned who are absent. Equally, the choice of others may baffle. The hope is that, from these biographies, an image of the period is revealed that does it justice on its own terms. All periods attract clouds of myth. By studying a few individuals, it is hoped some of this fog may be dispersed. It is impossible to be definitive about the past, especially a period so remote: the sources do not permit. But something of the diversity of the period can be sketched by looking at the lives of those prominent at the time. By reducing the past to a human scale, recognition may be easier. However distant, the people themselves encourage the effort to understand.

**England: The Shires c. 1085**

*North Sea*

Newcastle

Durham

ST CUTHBERTS LAND

UNSHIRED LANDS ANNEXED TO YORKSHIRE

YORK

Lancaster

York

BETWEEN RIBBLE & MERSEY

LINCOLN

CHESHIRE
Chester

Lincoln

DERBY

NOTTINGHAM

STAFFORD
Derby

Nottingham

Shrewsbury

Stafford

NORFOLK

SHROPSHIRE

Tamworth

LEICESTER

Leicester

Norwich

Thetford

WARWICK

NORTHAMPTON

HUNTS

CAMBRIDGE

SUFFOLK

WORCESTER

Warwick

Huntingdon

Bury St Edmunds

HEREFORD

Worcester

Northampton

Cambridge

Ipswich

Hereford

Bedford

BEDS

Colchester

Buckingham

Hertford

Gloucester

OXFORD

BUCKS

HERTFORD

ESSEX

GLOUCESTER

Oxford

MIDDLESEX

London

BERKS

Reading

Rochester

Sandwich

Bristol

WILTS

HANTS

Guildford

Canterbury

KENT

SOMERSET

Salisbury

Winchester

SUSSEX

Dover

Taunton

Southampton

Lewes

DEVON

DORSET

Exeter

Dorchester

Launceston

CORNWALL

*English Channel*

0  10  20  30  40  50 miles

xix

# England and Northern France

*North
Sea*

Newcastle
Durham
Richmond
York
Chester
Lincoln
Nottingham
Shrewsbury
Lichfield
Stamford
Peterborough
Norfolk
Coventry
Ely
Worcester
Warwick
Cambridge
Bury
Hereford
Colchester
Gloucester
Oxford
London
Bristol
Rochester
Bath
Canterbury
Salisbury
Winchester
Dover
Hastings
Pevensey
Exeter
Dorchester

**FLANDERS**

*English Channel*

**PONTHIEU**

Amiens

Bayeux
Rouen
Jumièges
Caen
Lisieux
Évreux
Coutances
**NORMANDY**
Paris
CHANNEL
ISLANDS
Mt. St. Michel
Avranches
Martain
**ISLE DE FRANCE**
Dol
Pontorson
Fougères
Rennes
**MAINE**
Le Mans
**BLOIS**
Orleans
**BRITTANY**
Angers
Tours
**ANJOU**
**TOURAINE**

0   20   40   60   80   100 miles

**POITOU**

# THE ROYAL DYNASTY OF ENGLAND
## 1066-1272

William I
(*k.* 1066-87)

Robert Curthose
(*d.* 1134)

William II
Rufus
(*k.* 1087-1100)

Henry I
(*k.* 1100-35)

Adela

Stephen
(*k.* 1135-54)

William
(*d.* 1120)

Matilda
(*d.* 1167)

Henry II
(*k.* 1154-89

Henry
('The Young King')
(*d.* 1183)

Richard I
(*k.* 1189-99)

Geoffrey
(*d.* 1186)

John
(*k.* 1199-1216)

Arthur of
Brittany
(*d.* ?1204)

Henry III
(*k.* 1216-72)

Richard of
Cornwall
(*d.* 1272)

Eleanor
= Simon de
Montfort
(*d.* 1265)

Edward I
(*k.* 1272-1307)

Monarchs are underlined

# LIST OF ILLUSTRATIONS
# & ACKNOWLEDGEMENTS

The author and publisher wish to thank the following for permission to reproduce materials in their care and possession. Where requested, shelf marks are shown after the name below.

L'Abbaye Royale de Fontevraud for illustration nos. 9, 10, 12, 15
La Ville de Bayeux for illustration no. 3
The British library for illustration nos. 1, 6, 7, 11, 21, 22
The British Museum for illustration nos. 8, 16
The Bodleian Library, Oxford for illustration no. 2
Chetham's Library, Manchester for illustration no. 13
The Master and Fellows of Corpus Christi College, Cambridge for illustration nos. 17, 18, 20
The President and Fellows of Corpus Christi College, Oxford for illustration no. 5
The Provost and Fellows of Eton College for illustration no. 4
The Dean and Chapter of Westminster Abbey for illustration no. 19
The Dean and Chapter of Worcester Cathedral for illustration no. 14

1. William I (MS Cotton, Domitian A II fol. 22)
2. Lanfranc (MS Bodl. 569, fol. 1r)
3. Odo of Bayeux
4. William II
5. Henry I
6. Stephen (Seal no xxxix. 10 obverse)
7. Robert of Leicester (Seal HARLEY Charter 84.H.19)
8. Henry of Blois
9. Henry II
10. Eleanor of Aquitaine
11. Thomas Becket (MS Cotton, Claudius B II, fol. 341)
12. Richard I
13. Hubert Walter
14. John

# WHO'S WHO IN
# EARLY MEDIEVAL ENGLAND

**WILLIAM I**, known as the Bastard or the Conqueror (*c*.1028-1087; duke of Normandy 1035-1087; king of England 1066-87) exemplified with unsurpassed clarity a favoured theme of medieval writers, the unexpected turns of Fortune's wheel. He overcame adversities of birth, circumstances and opposition to seize the most glittering prize of the century and to die the most feared and respected ruler of his age. His deeds resounded through Europe and remain to this day a source of controversy and debate, of admiration and horror. If in no other respect, the accession of a duke of Normandy and his heirs to the English throne fundamentally altered the perspective of English politics by opening an inescapably intimate continental dimension which formed a major theme of English history for the next few centuries and provided the chief distinctive feature of post-Conquest English history.

Born the illegitimate son of Robert the Devil, duke of Normandy and Herleve, daughter of Fulbert of Falaise, allegedly a tanner, William was recognised in 1034 by the Norman magnates as heir to the duchy on the insistence of his father, who was about to embark on a pilgrimage to Jerusalem. Robert's death in Asia Minor on his return from the Holy Sepulchre in 1035 provoked a long and bitter struggle for power within and beyond the ducal dynasty during which ducal authority crumbled and from which William himself barely escaped with his life. It is said that his guardians were less fortunate: two were murdered; another poisoned and a fourth, the seneschal Osbern, killed in the very room in which the young duke was sleeping. William's survival largely depended on the assistance of Henry I, king of France, whose intervention culminated in the defeat of the anti-ducal rebels from Lower Normandy at Val-ès-Dunes in 1047. However, in the face of continued internal dissent, the rise of a hostile Anjou to the south and a change in French policy, William's

1

*William I with the symbols of authority, the crown and sceptre*
(From the Chronicle of Battle Abbey)

position was precarious until a French invasion was repulsed at
Mortemer in 1054.

William's subsequent consolidation of control over both
church and magnates depended crucially upon military success
and his consequent ability to reward loyalty, attract support and
punish opposition. Northern France, a patchwork of competing
lordships and conflicting claims of allegiance, offered considerable scope for a vigorous and well-organised power. Between
1054 and 1064 William extended his influence and authority to

Ponthieu, the Norman Vexin, Brittany and Maine. A Flemish alliance was achieved by his marriage (*c*.1051) to Matilda (*d*.1083) the diminutive but forceful daughter of Baldwin V, count of Flanders. William also allied with the counts of Boulogne. This network of alliances proved vital when William planned his invasion of England. Norman expansionism was considerably assisted by the chance of the deaths of Henry of France and Count Geoffrey Martel of Anjou in 1060. Both had been hostile to William's advances but were replaced respectively by a sympathetic minority government in France and a succession dispute in Anjou.

William, as all medieval rulers, relied for his success on cooperation with leading landholders and the church. The Norman military aristocracy was of recent creation and heavily dependent on ducal patronage. The church was dominated by prelates appointed either from the ducal and other noble families (such as William's uncle Mauger at Rouen or his half-brother Odo at Bayeux) or by ducal appointment (such as Lanfranc of Pavia at Bec and Caen). William's skill lay in identifying mutual self-interest: lands and military activity for the lay aristocracy; ducal patronage for ecclesiastical reform, endowments, buildings and the fashionable Truce of God movement for churchmen. The Truce of God movement, supported by William's government as early as 1042, required knights to swear to keep the peace for specified periods and to police that agreement, if necessary by taking arms against transgressors. For William this was a highly convenient combination of political control, social cohesion and ecclesiastical authority all under ducal protection.

The eleventh century saw acquisitive lords and knights from Normandy seek their fortunes far beyond the confines of the duchy, in the eastern Mediterranean, southern Italy, and England. William's great-aunt, Emma, a daughter of Duke Richard I, married, in turn, Ethelred the Unready (king of England 978-1016) and Cnut (king of England 1016-35). Her son by Ethelred, Edward, spent his exile after 1016 at the Norman court and after becoming king himself in 1042 he introduced a number of Normans into England, notably his nephew Ralph the Timid as earl of Hereford and Richard Champart of Jumièges successively as bishop of London and, briefly, archbishop of Canterbury. Whether the childless Edward offered William the inheritance of the throne in 1051-2, as Norman propagandists insisted after the Conquest, must remain speculation. Despite some evident falsehoods in the Norman version, it is possible that Edward took the opportunity of the disgrace of the powerful Godwins to cement an Anglo-Norman alliance and solve the chronic uncertainty over the succession. However, other sources, no less partisan and unreliable than the Norman chroniclers, tell different stories. Perhaps it is worth noting that in 1051-2 Edward had a number of male relatives closer in blood than William; that William was far from secure in Normandy; that it would have been gross political folly for Edward to close options so soon and so completely; and that, despite later Godwin special pleading and Westminster Abbey hagiography, Edward himself could have expected to have heirs, especially as he had just put aside his first wife presumably in the hope of a second, fruitful marriage. If an attempt is made to reconcile the various accounts, Norman, Scandinavian, Godwin and non-Godwin English, then Edward must appear the most eccentric, foolish and politically profligate and devious ruler in English history, promising his throne to anybody, indeed everybody, as whim and circumstance dictated. The fact is that there are no trustworthy sources for the period leading up to 1066. All are to some extent wise after the event and concerned to justify or explain or refute. Above all, the Norman writers, William of Poitiers and William of Jumièges are apologists determined to establish William's claim. But as they wrote after 1066, their interpretation cannot, as many modern historians have done, be taken at face or perhaps any value.

What can be suggested is that by 1064 William was interested in the succession to England as a natural further extension of his power, especially as he could — and did — assert a dynastic claim. Edward may actually have been trying to secure William's support for a non-Norman inheritance by sending to him Godwin hostages and then, in 1064, Harold Godwinson himself, the leading magnate in England. It is clear from Norman and English written sources, and the Bayeux Tapestry (perhaps devised under the patronage of Odo of Bayeux at Canterbury, a suggestion lent some support by its similarities to the account of

1066 by the Canterbury monk Eadmer) that the 1064 embassy of Harold was a diplomatic triumph for William. Eadmer even records Edward's sharp displeasure at the turn of events, an image perhaps preserved in the Bayeux Tapestry's cringeing figure of Harold reporting back to an admonishing Edward. According to the Norman sources, Harold had sworn to be William's man and to help him secure the English succession. Whatever the truth, just as he confidently insisted on the legitimacy of his rights to overlordship in Brittany, the Vexin or Maine, William portrayed himself as believing in his absolute right to the English throne, a posture lent subsequent validity by friendly propagandists, supported by the verdict of events.

On hearing that Harold had been crowned king of England after Edward's death (January 1066), William began elaborate preparations. In a series of councils he attracted the support of his nobles. He publicised his claim at the Papal Curia, emphasizing the oath-breaking of Harold and the irregularities of the English church, which would be grist to the slow, sure-grinding mills of the holier-than-thou, purist elite then in control of the papacy. He received the blessing and a banner from Pope Alexander II, a signal, as he saw it, of the justice of his cause. Throughout, William laid claim to what modern historians call the moral high ground: at Hastings he wore a necklace of holy relics. His patronage of militant clerics and the Truce of God movement bore spectacular fruit.

William's wealth, reputation and carefully laid diplomacy attracted lords, knights and mercenaries from all over France and, it was said, beyond. Throughout the summer of 1066, ships were built and fitted in the Channel ports; equipment and horses were gathered. Modern assessments of the scale of William's enterprise tend to be conditioned by the weight of evidence. Yet, as we do not have much information about earlier amphibious operations, which, in English history, go back at least to Edwin of Northumbria's attack on the Isle of Man in the 620s, we should be wary of investing William's preparations with a uniqueness which may only be apparent because of the surviving evidence. Angles, Saxons, Jutes, Franks, Danes, Swedes and Norwegians, all had invasion fleets. Was William's so different?

William had not only isolated Harold diplomatically, but had also probably been in contact with Harold's brother Tostig and Harald Hadrada who were themselves planning an attack on England. A bloody crisis was inevitable, the tension being heightened by the appearance of Halley's Comet in the spring of 1066. In August William assembled his fleet in the River Dives, but contrary winds, and, perhaps, knowledge of English defences, delayed his sailing. The fleet was transferred to St Valéry on the Somme whence, at dusk on 27 September, it embarked for England, arriving, unopposed and intact, at Pevensey the next morning. The English defensive forces in the south had been disbanded on 8 September, as William probably knew, and Harold was in the north, having just defeated and killed Tostig and Hadrada at Stamford Bridge (25 September). The ensuing campaign showed William's skill and his luck in equal proportions. Establishing a fortified base at Hastings, William proceeded with the normal medieval tactic of concerted pillaging with the intention of drawing Harold to precipitate action. It worked. Arriving with a hastily levied army, Harold offered battle immediately. The battle of Hastings, fought on Saturday, 14 October 1066, left Harold and his brothers dead, his army destroyed and the road to London and the crown open. William had barely survived the battle himself, but he acquitted himself well as a field commander in what was his first pitched battle in sole charge (Henry I took the lead at Val-ès-Dunes and William was not at Mortemer). The rarity of set-piece battles is a feature of warfare in this period, some great warlords, for example Henry II of England (1154-1189), never fighting any battles at all. Hastings reminds us why.

After a cleverly conceived and ruthlessly executed campaign of devastation, William forced the submission of the surviving English magnates, led by Aldred, archbishop of York, the legitimist claimant, Edgar Atheling and the earls Edwin and Morkere. The military *fait accompli* was sanctified on Christmas Day, 1066 when William was hallowed king of the English in Westminster Abbey, a scene of reconciliation and acceptance, William being attended not only by his French companions but also his English nobles and bishops. By adding an arc to the crown of Edward the Confessor, a sign of almost imperial pretentions, William indicated the grandeur of his designs in the British Isles.

The manner in which William held his kingdom was as impressive as the way in which it had been won. Between 1067 and 1075 a succession of rebellions were dealt with firmly. In one nine month period in 1068 the new king subdued Exeter, parts of the West Country and Midlands and York. The northern rising in 1069, when native earls allied with Scandinavian invaders, led to a winter campaign of deliberate cruelty. The so-called Harrying of the North lasted three months (January- March 1070), embraced parts of Wales, Lincolnshire, Yorkshire, Teesdale, Chester and Stafford, and left areas of Yorkshire wasted for a generation. Calculated violence was a noted and consistent instrument of William's policy. Twenty years earlier he had ordered that thirty-two citizens of Alençon have their hands and feet cut off, ostensibly because they had jeered at his illegitimacy, but more probably to encourage loyalty from this vital frontier town in southern Normandy. By the end of 1071, the Danish fleet had been paid off and Hereward the Wake flushed out of his base at Ely. William's regime fell heavily on French as well as English, but its effectiveness was not in doubt, as witnessed by the suppression of the 1075 revolt of the French earls of Norfolk and Hereford in the king's absence.

Although there was little threat from Wales, the king of Scotland, Malcolm III Canmore, eagerly fished in the troubled waters of English politics. In response, in 1072 in an effort to secure his northern frontier as he had his northern subjects, William launched one of his most remarkable campaigns. In a classic demonstration of the use of concentrated military aggression in pursuit of political advantage, William marched his army, shadowed by a fleet, up the east coast as far as the Tay where, at Abernethy, a cowed Malcolm was forced to come to terms. This, as all William's military success,was based on the employment of disciplined troops, mainly household knights and mercenaries, mobility and castles, such as those at Hastings, Exeter, Dover, London, Newcastle, Warwick and York built variously as part of aggressive military strategy, as focal points for controlling an occupied country and as centres of administration.

From 1072 William could concentrate on France, in particular

his ambitions in Brittany, Maine and the Vexin. Defeats at Dol
(1076) and Gerberoi (1079) at the hands of Norman rebels, the
disloyalty of his brother Odo and his eldest son Robert
Curthose, placed William on the defensive in his later years,
which makes his achievements in England the more remarkable.
With interests so far flung, William had to rely on a small
group of faithful magnates, men such as his half-brother Robert
of Mortain, William FitzOsbern, Roger of Beaumont, Bishop
Geoffrey of Coutances and Archbishop Lanfranc. Their consistent support says much for William's ability to inspire loyalty.
After the risings of the late 1060s and the execution of Earl
Waltheof in 1076 for complicity in the 1075 rebellion, attempts
to reconcile the surviving English lords were abandoned. By the
end of his reign power and property had shifted wholesale from
Englishmen to Frenchmen or Normans. The Domesday Survey
of 1086 recorded only 5% of the land held by members of the
families of pre-Conquest owners, not all of them English, and
only two Englishmen, Coleswein of Lincoln and Thorkell of
Arden, held land directly from the king. The church presents the
same picture. After 1070 many English bishops were dismissed
and no new Englishmen were appointed. William and his archbishop, Lanfranc, introduced reforms in ecclesiastical law and
diocesan organisation based on continental models.

The tenurial, aristocratic and ecclesiastical revolution was
sweeping and profound, but it was consequent on the replacement of English with French landlords and the new interests of
the rulers rather than on any deliberate or accidental alterations
of the structure of society, landholding or law. William did not
introduce a new system of 'feudalism'. English thegns had held
land in return for military service for centuries, their obligations
becoming more regulated as the demands of central government
became more effective. If William and his successors introduced
a more precise method of assessing obligation, *servitium debi-
tum*, and the so-called knights' fee, that was because of their
need for defined resources to support their wars. The technology
of war in pre-1066 England was not so very different from that
in pre-1066 Normandy, as shown, for example, in the Bayeux
Tapestry and descriptions of thegns' military equipment contained in Old English law codes. The new rulers were careful to

assert that their land was held in all respects in the same way and with the same rights as those enjoyed by their English predecessors. Even the great Oath of Salisbury (1086), seen by some historians as demonstrating the feudalisation of England, can be compared with the general oaths imposed by English kings over the previous century. What undoubtedly changed, not immediately but inexorably, was the idiom describing and defining tenurial relationships among the landed elite and, in a similar process, the language and articulation of the law. An early example of French management of an English system of rule is found in the record of the Penenden Heath inquiry (c.1072) into the rights in Kent of Archbishop Lanfranc and Odo of Bayeux. Although the case involved two leading tenants of the king, it was heard in the traditional English shire court. Although the presiding justice was the Norman Geoffrey of Coutances, he called upon the legal knowledge of the deposed English bishop of Selsey, Aethelric: English law in a French context. What affected the French rulers was suitably rearticulated. What did not, namely the activities of the mass of the population, for example the manorial system, continued to develop as if Hastings had not been fought.

In 1066 England possessed a mature structure of government, administration and law, in most respects the superior to those of France and Normandy. William always insisted that he was a legitimate English king who respected English customs as surely as any of his predecessors. He wanted England to exploit not to change. Many historians have claimed that the Normans 'modernised' England. Recently, however, it has been observed how incompetently the new rulers managed traditional mechanisms of royal control, for instance the shire system and the coinage. Certainly, William's chief concern was less to understand the intricacies of English administrative habits than to obtain money in order to enhance and protect his position, especially in France. This desire attracted contemporary accusations of avarice and extortion. But, as the last crisis of his reign illustrates, William was no simple-minded thug.

At Christmas 1085, faced by the prospect of a huge Danish invasion and a fresh continental campaign, William and his advisors ordered the compilation of the Domesday Survey, which appears to have had the dual purpose of identifying the bases for innumerable disputes over possession of land and of reassessing income from property preliminary to a new, increased land tax. The resulting Domesday Book, although overtaken as an immediate administrative weapon by William's death, stands as a unique monument to English governmental tradition and Norman political initiative, and provides information unparalleled for any eleventh century kingdom. At Salisbury, on 1 August 1086, William, about to depart for Normandy, extracted oaths of loyalty from his tenants-in-chief and their followers (one source says their knights; others their tenants).

Such harnessing of clear perceptions of political and fiscal needs with vigorous military and administrative action is typical of William's role. If not all his ambitions were achieved, if Maine and the French Vexin remained outside his grasp, if luck had played a vital role throughout his career, William's achievements remain stupendous. Determined, energetic, ruthless, William possessed a personality and practical intelligence which, more often than many rulers in history, allowed him to dominate his contemporaries and to control his destiny, from the precarious life of a hunted bastard to the most powerful position in western Europe. William's success transformed the political map of Europe and the course of English history. The Norman Conquest gave English politics a fresh context, English government and law a different language, English society a new ruling class, and English culture an additional perspective.

William himself was impressive in manner and, on the evidence of a surviving bone recovered after the desecration of his tomb during the French Revolution, tall (c.5ft 10ins). Contemporary physical descriptions are almost entirely formal, although he may have had a noticeably harsh voice, and, like so many medieval aristocrats, have run to fat. A man of at least conventional piety, he was an active and generous patron of the church. He died at St Gervais near Rouen on 9 September 1087, his final illness possibly resulting from a riding accident suffered during a characteristically vicious attack on Mantes. Active to the end in pursuit of his interests, William was a man who seized his opportunities with unrivalled vigour, and, as many contemporaries said, with unrivalled cruelty as well. Whatever judgment is made on the nature and extent of his influence on his time and his new kingdom, whether he is regarded as cypher or architect, William the Conqueror was and is one of the most notable figures in English history.

D. C. Douglas, *William the Conqueror,* 1964.
D. Bates, *William the Conqueror,* 1989.

**EDGAR ATHELING** (*c*.1057-*c*.1125) was the son of Edward the Exile (*d*.1057) and so the grandson of Edmund Ironside and great-grandson of Ethelred the Unready. There is some evidence that Edward the Confessor, his great-uncle, intended Edgar to succeed him as king of England in 1066. After the death of Harold II at Hastings he was chosen as king by the remaining English magnates in London, but was soon forced to submit to the victorious William of Normandy. For the rest of his career, Edgar fulfilled the frustrating and ultimately barren existence suggested by his cogomen: an atheling was a member of a noble or royal family with a claim to the throne. By virtue of his position as the male heir of the House of Wessex, Edgar enjoyed patronage and hostility beyond his deserts, by turns an exile and a boon companion to the great. A rootless, restless, charming and feckless man, he had the personal qualities to attract supporters and lead troops, but neither the experience nor aptitude for political success. His career was a wheel of fortune which never reached the top. Initially accepted at William I's court, Edgar, with the rest of his family, fled to Scotland in 1068, where his sister Margaret married King Malcolm III. After the Treaty of Abernethy (1072) between Malcolm and William I Edgar was again on his travels, to Flanders and France, where Philip I hoped to use him to foment trouble against William. Soon reconciled with William, Edgar received some small estates in England, a place at court, a pension of £1 a day (which he casually exchanged for a horse) as the price of political emasculation. During this period, Edgar may have formed his attachment to Robert Curthose, whose character and career matched his so well. In 1086, Edgar was allowed to raise a force of two hundred knights to fight in southern Italy. On his return he was established with lands in Normandy where Curthose was now duke

(1087), only to be expelled from them in 1091 as part of a treaty between Curthose and his brother William II, who evidently found Edgar's independence as unsettling as had his father. However, Edgar's Scottish connections proved useful to William Rufus in his attempts to destroy the hostile regime of King Donalbane (1094-7), and in 1097 Edgar was put at the head of an English-sponsored invasion of Scotland which placed Edgar's nephew, also called Edgar, on the Scottish throne. Despite his family's hold on Scotland and Henry I of England's marriage to his niece, Matilda (1100), Edgar remained excluded from political power. In 1101-2, he, and one of his English supporters who had been with him in Scotland, Robert FitzGodwine, went to the newly captured Holy Land. Back in Europe, Edgar once more found himself on the losing side when he supported Curthose at the battle of Tinchebrai (1106). Thereafter, Edgar lingered on in obscurity, a relic of an increasingly irrelevant past, a curiosity, perhaps, to a generation in which Edgar's freelance adventurism had little or no place.

D. C. Douglas, *William the Conqueror*, 1964.
F. Barlow, *William Rufus*, 1983.

**LANFRANC OF PAVIA** (*c*.1010-1089; archbishop of Canterbury 1070-89) by circumstance and skill was one of the most influential archbishops of Canterbury. After the Norman Conquest, his political alliance and personal friendship with William I reset the pattern of Church/State relations which, despite a few well-publicised exceptions, were characterised by cooperation. Lanfranc maintained the intimacy between king and archbishop which had been established by Dunstan and Edgar a century earlier. Jealous of his authority within the church, where his concentration on rights and canon law bred episcopal arrogance and rancour, when the ecclesiastical and secular worlds met Lanfranc saw his role as the king's adviser, not challenger or competitor. He expressed this policy succinctly, the Latin giving a flavour of the clarity and vigour of his mind: 'contra preceptum regis nil rogare et nil iubere praesumo' ('I cannot take the responsibility for giving any directive or order that is contrary to the king's instructions').

*Lanfranc*
(A Norman depiction c.1100)

In 1070, William I engineered the deposition of Archbishop Stigand, ostensibly on the canonical grounds of irregular appointment and pluralism, but in reality because of Stigand's suspect loyalty. The king's choice of successor was risky yet understandable. Lanfranc was an ageing monk and scholar whose administrative and political experience had been confined to the world of Norman monasteries. Yet, as abbot of the ducal foundation of St Etienne at Caen, he was an intimate of William's household and family. From William's perspective, Lanfranc offered the moral integrity of a monk; the personal devotion of a friend; and the clarity of intellect and purpose of a lawyer. Although Lanfranc was never really at home in England, he effectively managed to mould the English church as he and his master desired.

Lanfranc's early career was not one which suggested his later hierarchical eminence. In the early eleventh century important

Western European bishops were usually from the ranks of the high nobility and, except in tenth century England, tended to be secular clerks, not monks. Even in England, the habit of appointing monks as bishops was waning in the decades before the Conquest. Lanfranc, from an urban professional background, had begun his career as a student of law in northern Italy. About 1030, he crossed the Alps into Burgundy and France where he seems to have studied and perhaps taught the traditional trivium — grammar, rhetoric and logic — before settling to teach at Avranches c.1039. Around 1042, Lanfranc underwent a conversion and joined the religious community at Bec where, despite his complaints about its lack of eremitic rigour, he stayed for twenty years, from c.1045 as prior. During the 1050s he resumed teaching, his interests still centred on law, grammar and rhetoric, traditional subjects to which he contributed little that was not soon superceded. Although he engaged in controversy, attacking Berengar of Tours' views on the Eucharist in the 1060s, Lanfranc as an academic, as later as a churchman, was a conservative. Unlike his successor as prior of Bec and archbishop, Anselm of Aosta, Lanfranc did not engage in the higher flights of speculative philosophy or theology. However, as an expert in canon law, Lanfranc was concerned with ecclesiastical discipline and the moral standard of the clergy. In this he was in tune with contemporary church reformers who enjoyed the support of Duke William and made him a suitable candidate in 1063 for the abbacy of the duke's Abbey of St Etienne, the so-called Abbaye-aux-Hommes, at Caen.

As in Normandy, Lanfranc's policies in England were those of an old-fashioned reformer, looking to a partnership with the secular ruler to achieve an improvement in the organisation, manners, morals and buildings of the clergy. In his insistence on legal precedent and rights, Lanfranc had much in common with the reformers who, in the late 1040s had captured the papacy, their vociferous campaign against the abuses of simony, lay investiture and clerical marriage reaching a crescendo during the pontificate of Gregory VII (1073-85), after whom the movement is commonly known. But on the issue of authority and the subjugation of temporal to spiritual power, Lanfranc parted company with the Gregorians who wished to enforce fealty from secular rulers and subservience from the ecclesiastical hierarchy. Thus in 1080, Lanfranc was not prepared to agree that the king of England was, by virtue of the payment of Peter's Pence, an annual gift to the pope, a papal vassal. Equally, within the church Lanfranc respected the pope's position, but not without qualification. As he wrote to Pope Gregory: 'I am ready to yield obedience to your commands in everything *according to the canons*' (my italics). Throughout his reign, Lanfranc maintained mutual support with the king and the independent rights of Canterbury.

Lanfranc's rule of the English church mirrored and sustained the secular conquest of the country. Like the king, he pursued his rights through law and, failing that, violence. In 1088, when meeting resistance from the monks of St Augustine's, Canterbury to his nominee as abbot, he dispersed some of them, imprisoned others and had one publicly flogged: 'thus did Lanfranc enforce obedience, and so long as he lived he broke down the opposition of the rest by dread of his name'. He presided over an almost wholesale exclusion of Englishmen from the highest posts in the church: not one native was appointed to a see during his nineteen years at Canterbury. He sponsored the introduction of continental monastic practices, and even some foreign monks. Where William built castles, Lanfranc encouraged the construction of new cathedrals which in their size and austere regularity of design were visible symbols of the new order in church as in state. Using the model of his abbey at Caen (and importing stone from there too), Lanfranc rebuilt his own cathedral in the 1070s on a grand scale, dedicated to Christ Himself. At Canterbury, he disparaged English saints, removing their relics from the cathedral and their names from the calendar of feast days. Even St Dunstan was demoted in this fashion and he thought so little of local sentiment that Archbishop Elphege, murdered by the Danes in 1012, only narrowly avoided a similar fate. Some of his early predecessors and other saints from the heroic age of the Conversion Lanfranc moved to his new foundation of St Gregory's which thereby was lent an instant, potentially lucrative, if spurious aura of venerable sanctity. At the very least there was an intrusively abrasive quality about Lanfranc's behaviour. As the Canterbury monk Eadmer (who revered Elphege as a 'holy martyr') commented, Lanfranc was 'a somewhat unfinished Englishman' (*quasi rudis Anglus*). In this he was just like most of the others who ruled the kingdom after 1066.

Yet if he had little time for English customs, he was unflagging in establishing what he saw as the traditional rights of his office. Claiming primacy over all Britain, in addition to English prelates he consecrated, either personally or by delegation, Irish and Orcadian bishops. In 1072, he secured a papal judgement acknowledging the supremacy of Canterbury over York, although this failed to resolve what became one of the longest running ecclesiastical feuds in Europe. The method of establishing Canterbury's primacy shows Lanfranc at his most characteristic. The case was heard at a council presided over by the king, held at Winchester, at which Lanfranc, the lawyer to his core, produced an impressive array of evidence, including chronicles, Bede's *Ecclesiastical History,* and papal privileges (possibly forged for the purpose).

Canterbury's temporal rights were not neglected either. At the famous trial at Penenden Heath (1072 or, possibly, 1075/6), Lanfranc not only made good his claim to certain estates in Kent against Odo of Bayeux and others, but also, in the words of one account, 'vindicated afresh the liberties of his church and the customary jurisdiction which he was entitled to exercise' over his lands. The judgement effectively recognised the immunity of Lanfranc's lands from the scrutiny of royal officials.

In ruling the church, Lanfranc was equally keen to establish a legal basis, often agreed at church councils, of which he held seven. At Winchester in 1072, apart from the dispute with York, issues of the church calendar, simony, wandering clergy and monks, treason and an instruction to secular priests to say masses for the king (an extension of tenth century English practice) were discussed. The Council of London in 1075 was the largest of the reign chaired, in the absence of the king, by Lanfranc himself. The main business was the transfer of sees, usually to towns, a sign of both political necessity and the growing urbanisation of England: Sherborne to Old Sarum; Selsey to Chichester; Lichfield to Chester; Dorchester-on-Thames to Lincoln and North Elmham to Norwich. Characteristically, justification for these removals was found in precedent and canon law. The latter also provided the basis for decisions on pastoral care; discipline of the clergy; good order within monasteries; lay marriage customs, and, even, prohibitions on white magic : 'the bones of dead animals must not be hung up anywhere as a charm against cattle-disease'.

However, despite such admirably reformist procedures, it is salutary — and very far from the Gregorian ideal — to note that the removal of spiritual pleas from secular to episcopal courts 'according to the precepts of the holy canons' was ordered by royal writ. All that Lanfranc achieved was in the context of royal power. Whatever independence he had in church matters was delegated from the king, a situation typical of both England and the continent over the previous century and more. What was different was Lanfranc's insistence upon legal, canonical precedent and his grip of the church structure expressed through patronage, regular meetings with his fellow bishops and occasional church councils.

Much of this successful exercise of archiepisopal *auctoritas* depended on Lanfranc's own personality and his willingness to identify his interests with those of the king. At least twice, in facing down the serious rebellion of 1075 in the king's absence and in the securing of the succession of William II in England in 1087-88, his active political support for the monarch was crucial. His loyalty, on a public level, is understandable. One great advantage Lanfranc had as archbishop was that he had no independent network of influence, patronage or power. He had no family or landed connections in the Anglo-Norman nobility. He was unaffected by faction as all he had came from the king's favour. Thus isolated, Lanfranc, as has recently been written, 'could only be the king's man'.

That he embraced this position with enthusiasm cannot be doubted. He was one of the few men that William I trusted and cherished: on one occasion Lanfranc was forced to rest and submit to a medical regime 'on the king's orders'. No less important was his concept of obedience and hierarchy. At the trial of the rebel bishop of Durham in 1088 against William II, Lanfranc adopted a position entirely at odds with Gregorianism: 'We judge the bishop not as a bishop but as a vassal, as we judged Odo of Bayeux [in 1082] . . . by his original breach of faith and by accusing the king's magnates of deceit the bishop has lost the safe-conduct which he has invoked'. This outburst provoked spontaneous applause from the king's barons who shouted 'Seize the bishop! The old bloodhound's right!' For Lanfranc, the right order of the world was one which recognised the importance of the secular ruler in maintaining peace: that was not a function of a monk. Early in the 1070s he summed up his view: 'While the king lives we have peace of a kind, but after his death we expect to have neither peace nor any other benefit'. Lanfranc saw temporal things as ephemeral, papal pretentions to dominate the world no less transitory than those of princes.

From the sources, Lanfranc does not emerge as a particularly warm or attractive personality. He was apparently uninterested in the spiritual life of the laity, more concerned with legally proper forms of administration and organisation. His contempt for local English cults is revealing. Even his apparently generous gesture in allowing women who had fled to nunneries 'for fear of the Normans' to re-enter the world and marry was dictated by pragmatism and an acknowledgement of the legal as well as emotional fragility of vows made under exceptional compulsion. To Lanfranc's obsession with legality and rights and his creation of an ambitious, able but self-conscious episcopal elite has been attributed one of the least creditable yet most tenacious aspects of the post-Conquest church; the endless round of infra-ecclesiastical litigation and bickering over shares in the church's chest of temporal wealth, jurisdiction, status and power. Lanfranc could be cruel and, if not necessarily vindictive, then sternly unyielding. Small wonder he and William I got on so well. Yet although he contributed much to royal government, for all his forensic intellectual skills and his legal clarity of language, he kept his independence. Unlike Geoffrey of Coutances or Odo of Bayeux, he was never a glorified member of the king's administration. He rarely even witnessed royal charters.

The apparent contradictions of medieval monks who adopted public roles are probably impenetrable to modern observers. Yet for all his worldly prestige, wealth and power, Lanfranc's monastic vocation was central to his personality and, hence, his effectiveness. Unlike some famous medieval holy men, he did not flaunt his spirituality. Neither did contemporaries accuse him of hypocrisy. He belonged to a generation of monks less self-consciously obsessed with their own virtue than their successors. He reconciled his public labours and private faith through a sense of rectitude which could be unforgiving but was untainted by self-righteousness. In England he was able to avoid the posturing of the continental Investiture Contest partly because he achieved what the militants of Gregorianism missed entirely. He was able to see that necessary political action for the benefit, as he saw it, of God's church was not dependent on the constant scrutiny of first principles which owed nothing to accepted precedence, custom or efficiency. If anything, his legacy to the church in England consists of a pragmatic and independent appreciation and application of universal canon law which encompassed both royal control and ecclesiastical autonomy.

M. Gibson, *Lanfranc of Bec,* 1978.
H. Clover and M. Gibson, *The Letters of Lanfranc,* 1979.

**REGENBALD** (*fl.*1050-67; *d.* after 1086) was the head of Edward the Confessor's writing office, in effect, and possibly in name, his chancellor. He seems to have continued in this office under William I until replaced in 1067, in which year the new king confirmed all his previous holdings and added some estates formerly held by Harold II. Regenbald still held extensive benefices and property in 1086 when he was described in Domesday Book as *canceler.* A clerk, who under Edward the Confessor enjoyed the status although not the office of a bishop, his retention of land suggests he may have done the new regime some service as an agent of administrative continuity. His wealth and power in 1066 reflects the growth of a central royal writing office whose professionalism was reflected in the well-fashioned writs of the last Anglo-Saxon kings, an administrative tradition exploited and extended by the Norman rulers. His estates in 1086 indicate that the Norman tenurial revolution had limits. Regenbald, perhaps originally German, had another qualification to be an adhesive tenant. He was vicar of Bray. His acceptance of the changing governments of the 1060s merely foreshadowed his two more notorious successors, Simon Aleyn, who survived the religious upheavals of the 1530s to 1560s, and

Francis Carswell, who trod delicately through the ecclesiastical minefields of late Stuart and early Georgian England. Aleyn was supposed to have denied being a turncoat: 'I alwaies kept my Principle, which is this, to live and die the Vicar of Bray', the exact sentiments attributed to Carswell in the famous eighteenth century song. Regenbald would have recognised their achievement.

S. Keynes, 'Regenbald The Chancellor (sic)' *Anglo-Norman Studies*, x, 1988.

**WALTHEOF** (*d.*1076) was the last of the Old English earls to survive under William I, his execution for treason in 1076 marking a significant stage in the aristocratic and tenurial revolution which followed 1066. Younger son of Earl Siward of Northumbria, Waltheof became earl of Huntingdon probably in 1065. As one of the few English magnates not from the Godwin faction, he accepted and was accepted by William I, witnessing royal charters and remaining loyal to the new regime until in 1069 he joined with the Danes in their invasion of Northumbria. He was prominent in their capture of York, hoping, no doubt, to be restored to his father's position. This opportunism is perhaps more characteristic of English magnate reactions to the political turmoil of 1065-70 than any supposed national feeling. However, the revolt and invasion were defeated by William I's winter campaign of 1069-70. It is a measure of William's insecurity that when Waltheof submitted in 1070 he was restored to royal favour and, in 1072, added the earldom of Northumbria to his holdings. To bind him more tightly to the Norman dispensation, William gave him his niece Judith in marriage. But in 1075, Waltheof was implicated in the largely French revolt led by Ralph, earl of Norfolk and Roger, earl of Hereford. Despite his lack of military action, his confession, apparent contrition and the support of Archbishop Lanfranc, Waltheof was executed on 31 May 1076.

The king's motives are obscure. Waltheof was the only prominent Englishman to be executed in the reign. Perhaps his removal was part of William's justifiably nervous response to the problem of controlling Northumbria. It may have made sense to take the chance to remove a potential — and proven —focus of northern discontent. Yet Waltheof's heirs were not harried, one daughter marrying David I of Scotland (1142-53), another Ralph IV of Tosny, a leading Norman baron.

Waltheof is a significant reminder that the period around 1066 was transitional, with no necessarily definite beginnings or endings. Waltheof adapted to the new order, falling foul, it seems, of the ambitions and schemes of others, not least of parvenus Frenchmen. He married into the new elite, yet embodied the old. Heir to both English and Anglo-Danish traditions, it was he who completed one of the most celebrated of Anglo-Saxon blood-feuds. In 1016, Uhtred, earl of Northumbria was murdered by a northern nobleman called Thurbrand. He was, in turn, killed by Uhtred's son and successor, Ealdred who was himself slain by Thurbrand's son, Carl. Waltheof's mother was Ealdred's daughter and he avenged his great-grandfather and grandfather by massacring a number of Carl's sons.

Waltheof himself was buried at Crowland Abbey where, as did many martyrs to royal policy in the middle ages, he found posthumous fame in a cult which, by the mid-twelfth century, was venerating him as a saint. Yet his career in the north shows that not far beneath the measured tones of Norman propagandists or the efficient gloss of English bureaucratic procedures simmered the violence of Dark Age epic.

F. Stenton, *Anglo-Saxon England,* 1943.

**WULFSTAN OF WORCESTER** (*c.*1010-1095; bishop of Worcester 1062-95), was the last surviving pre-Conquest bishop who, while revering the traditions of Anglo-Saxon episcopal monasticism, actively supported the Norman regime. Unlike some contemporaries and modern historians, Wulfstan saw no contradition in this. A patron and preserver of English learning, he sent a favoured pupil, Nicholas, to study under the rigorous Lanfranc at Canterbury. Wulfstan was son of one of the bishop of Worcester's servants. After education at Evesham and Peterborough Abbeys, he returned to Worcester where he spent most of the rest of his career. Ordained when a member of the household of Bishop Brihtheah (1033-38), he soon abandoned his secular living at Hawkesbury and returned to Worcester to become a monk. In the cathedral priory he rose to become prior. When the pluralist Aldred of York was induced to give up the diocese of Worcester in 1062, Wulfstan was the unexpected choice as his successor. Perhaps his appointment was not so surprising: steeped in Worcester tradition, Wulfstan continued to fight for its privileges long after 1066. As a diocesan bishop, he was conscientious and efficient, seeing his role as extending beyond the focal points of monasteries. Capitalising on the recent extension of the parochial system, Wulfstan perambulated his diocese, preaching and personally supervising baptisms and confessions. In this, he was in step with continental practices and his episcopate suggests that the well publicised discrepancy between England and the rest of the western church was somewhat exaggerated. With his colleague Aethelwig, abbot of Evesham, he not only accepted the new dispensation after 1066, but convinced William I of his loyalty. Probably it was this as much as any apparent holiness or efficiency which enabled him to survive the purge of Anglo-Saxon bishops in 1070-72. A trusted associate of Lanfranc, he repaid the Anglo-Norman state with energetic service. In 1075 and 1088 he supported the king against rebels and rivals. His posthumous reputation depended heavily on his legacy at Worcester, which produced at least two considerable historians in the following century, Florence and John, and his biography written in English by Coleman, Wulfstan's chaplain. Coleman's Life was given wider circulation on being translated into Latin by William of Malmesbury for whom Wulfstan was an emblematic figure: a holy Englishman, noted for piety and simplicity, who recognised and embraced the virtues of the French conquerors without disclaiming his inheritance. Of Wulfstan's local status there was no doubt. A cult sprang up at Worcester soon after his death and he was canonised in 1203. In 1216, King John, in extremis, chose to be buried at Wulfstan's shrine in Worcester cathedral. John may have wished to be identified with a national, English interest against the rebels who had sought assistance from Prince Louis of France. After Edward the Confessor, whose shrine at Westminster was inaccessible to royalists in 1216, Wulfstan represented the best known and most respected example of English sanctity. But Wulfstan was more. He was no solitary monk yearning for escape from his episcopal duties. While remaining true to his self-denying vocation, he cared not just for the laity but as keenly as any twelfth century legist Wulfstan was determined to secure the rights and privileges of Worcester. In pursuit of this policy he commissioned a Cartulary from Hemming, a Worcester monk, of documents crucial to the defence of Worcester property and estates. In this Wulfstan was a link between the fierce corporate ecclesiastical identities of the tenth and twelve centuries.

E. Mason, *St. Wulfstan of Worcester,* 1990.

**ODO OF BAYEUX** (early or late 1030s-1097; bishop of Bayeux 1049/50-97) was one of the most powerful men in England in the twenty years after the Norman Conquest. Although famously ambitious, ruthless and energetic, Odo's position depended on his half-brother, William the Conqueror. To him Odo owed the immensely lucrative see of Bayeux when he was still a teenager. After playing an active part in the Conquest, Odo was granted the strategically important earldom of Kent as well as vast estates throughout England which, by the 1080s, were worth over £3,000 per annum, making him the richest tenant-in-chief in the kingdom. In the king's absence, Odo regularly acted as one of his deputies in England. Unlike other magnates, Odo travelled the kingdom settling, ostensibly in the king's name, small land disputes, of which there was no shortage in the messy aftermath of conquest. His motives were hardly altruistic, his intervention in land tenure becoming notorious. As a man and a politician Odo acquired a bad reputation for luxury, vice and cruelty. Viewed objectively, he was both wealthy and efficient: he reorganised the diocese and extended the chapter at Bayeux; he proved a vigorous military commander in the north of 1080; and he increased the yield from his own demesne in England by 40% in twenty years. However, his power relied entirely on royal favour. Unlike the prince-bishops of the Rhineland, he had no real independence. In 1072, he lost claims to lands in Kent against Lanfranc by the judgement of a royal agent. In 1082, for reasons still obscure, but possibly connected

*Odo of Bayeux (left) conferring with*
*William the Conqueror and Robert of Mortain*
(From the Bayeux Tapestry *c*.1080)

with Odo's continental ambitions or his support for William's impatient eldest son, Robert, the king decided to destroy his brother. He was arrested and spent the rest of William's reign a prisoner at Rouen. Although restored by Rufus, Odo rebelled in 1088 with other members of the 'old guard'. His defeat led to the final confiscation of his English lands. His last years were spent on the continent, presiding over a thriving cathedral community at Bayeux. In 1095, he cut an incongruous figure at the Council of Clermont, at which Urban II proclaimed the First Crusade. Odo embodies much of what the reforming popes detested: lay appointment; secular office; a love of material wealth and power; a layman in all but dress and, perhaps, education. Nonetheless, Odo, seeing his favoured nephew lose his grasp on Normandy to Rufus, joined Robert on crusade. Odo got no further than Palermo, where he died early in 1097 while visiting a Norman soul-mate, the tough, successful adventurer Roger, the Great Count of Sicily. Odo's career touched greatness but ended in failure. His lasting achievements came from his local power: his endowment and building at Bayeux; his probable sponsorship of the Bayeux Tapestry, almost certainly embroidered in Kent; and, above all, his patronage of gifted secular clerks from Bayeux who went on to scale the heights of church and state, including three archbishops of York (Thomas I, 1070-1100; Thomas II, 1109-1114; Thurstan 1114-1140); William of St Calais, bishop of Durham (1080-97), the compiler of the Domesday Book; and Ranulf Flambard, Rufus's feared chief minister. They formed a fitting epitaph for a man described a generation later as 'more given to wordly affairs than spiritual contemplation'.

D. Bates, 'Odo of Bayeux', *Speculum*, 1975.

**ROBERT OF MORTAIN** (*c*.1031-90), half-brother of William the Conqueror, became the wealthiest subject of the English crown in the generation after the Conquest. The second son of the Conqueror's mother, Herleve and Herluin, vicomte of Conteville, Robert was appointed by William count of Mortain in south-west Normandy around 1055. Robert's elevation was part of William's policy of creating a close network of loyal nobles, often related to the ducal house, with and through whom William controlled his duchy and, later, was to conquer his kingdom (Robert's full brother, Odo, was bishop of Bayeux). Robert's prominent part in the invasion of England was remembered in his depiction in the Bayeux Tapestry advising William with his brother Odo after the landing at Pevensey. Both at Hastings and during the often difficult pacification of England 1066-69, Robert proved an effective military subordinate to William. His reward was massive. By 1086, with almost eight hundred manors from Sussex to Yorkshire to Cornwall, as well as valuable castles, such as Pevensey, Robert was the greatest secular landholder after the king and the church. Together, his and Odo's estates were worth £5,000: the next richest lay holdings were valued at c.£750. However powerful his grip on his vassals, William preferred to keep power in the family. This presented problems; both his brother Odo of Bayeux and son Robert Curthose openly rebelled. Unlike the restless Odo, Robert of Mortain made little individual mark on events. He spent much time with his half-brother in a career, until 1087, conspicuous by its loyalty. In 1087, Robert persuaded the dying king to release Odo from prison and was probably one of those who insisted that Robert Curthose succeed to Normandy. Although initially accepting William Rufus as king, in 1088 Robert threw in his lot with Odo and Curthose. He held Pevensey for the rebels, withstanding a six-week siege by Rufus in person. After his submission, he was pardoned but withdrew to Normandy to die. Robert emerges dimly from the records, the least colourful or defined of a family of striking personalities. He seems to have been on close terms with both his brothers and to have harboured a soft spot for Robert Curthose. Alternatively, he wished to preside over his lands free from superior exactions, an independence fostered perhaps by his paternal inheritance (it was in his father's monastery of Grestain that he was buried), and later offered by the policies of Odo and the character of Curthose. Only the accident of his mother's liaison with Duke Robert I elevated this child of provincial aristocracy to the greatest heights of the Anglo-Norman baronage. In the eleventh century at least, nobility could be acquired by favour and fortune, not just by blood.

**GEOFFREY OF COUTANCES.** Geoffrey de Mowbray, bishop of Coutances (*d*.1093; bishop 1048/9) was one of William the Conqueror's closest advisers. From a prominent Norman family, before 1066 Geoffrey played a leading part in the ecclesiastical reforms patronised by Duke William. In the early 1050s he visited Rome and, in an early display of his talent for secular business, raised money for a new cathedral from the Hauteville rulers of southern Italy, who had originally come from the Cotentin. By 1066 an intimate of Duke William, he accompanied the invasion of England, was present at Hastings and at William's coronation at Westminster on Christmas Day 1066 when the acclamation Geoffrey led caused a near-riot. Although retaining his Norman see, Geoffrey spent much of William's reign governing England. He was especially prominent in settling major land disputes, for example at Penenden Heath in 1072 (re. lands claimed by Lanfranc) or Kentford in 1082/3 (re. lands claimed by the abbey of Ely). These involved important political interests and the need to establish formal continuity of possession between current claimants and their English predecessors before 1066. Such shows of legal propriety legitimised individual tenures specifically and Norman rule in general. Geoffrey also attended all major lay and ecclesiastical councils in England and Normandy during William's reign. In 1069 and 1075 he helped crush rebellions, brutally on both occa-sions: in 1069, prisoners were mutilated; in 1075, each had his right foot cut off. Geoffrey's dedication to William was rewarded with massive estates. In Somerset alone, Geoffrey received almost eighty manors and, by 1086, he was one of the top ten wealthiest magnates in England, with as many as two hundred and eighty manors. After William's death, he joined Odo of Bayeux's revolt against William II in 1088. When this failed, he unsuccessfully tried to ingratiate himself with the new king at the council which condemned his fellow rebel the bishop of Durham. Faced down by Lanfranc's hostility, he withdrew to Normandy for the rest of his life. Geoffrey was one of a close-knit group of friends and advisers who made the Norman Conquest possible in 1066 and thereafter. Great though his rewards were, his power depended upon the king's favour. The unity, coherence and survival of the Norman achievement in England were forged by such bonds of loyalty responding to authority.

D. C. Douglas, *William the Conqueror*, 1964.

**WILLIAM FITZOSBERN** (d.1071) was a military adventurer on a grand scale. The son of Osbern the Seneschal, one of William the Conqueror's murdered guardians, he became a close friend and steward of the duke. At the Council of Lillebonne in 1066 he urged the Norman barons to invade England and later played a leading role in the campaign, according to the twelfth century writer Wace commanding the right wing at Hastings. His importance was signalled by the vast English estates with which he was rewarded, notably in the Welsh Marches. Within six months of Hastings FitzOsbern was earl of Hereford and, with Odo of Bayeux, viceroy of England during William's absence in Normandy (March-December 1067). Heavily engaged in defence and assault against the Welsh, he assumed a task vital to rulers of the English since the seventh century. FitzOsbern set about his responsibilities with particular vigour and acumen. He became notorious for his generosity to his knights, lavishing special legal immunities and large wages on those who served him, this dispersal of treasure incurring, so William of Malmesbury two generations later claimed, the disapproval of the king. To reward his knights further, he settled many of them on lands previously belonging to the church. Uninhibited in exploiting his power over laity as well as clergy, he built a number of castles, for example at Clifford, Wigmore and Chepstow, with local forced labour. Such a policy was merely a continuation of earlier public obligations to contribute to the construction of ramparts which had been fully employed by rulers at least as far back as Ethelbald and Offa of Mercia in the eighth century. Now it provoked a revolt by an English dissident, Edric the Wild, in Herefordshire who allied with Welsh princes. Two years later, in 1069, FitzOsbern helped King William suppress the Northern insurrection and dealt with more trouble from Edric. He attracted further hostile comment from ecclesiastical writers by apparently advising a financially hard-pressed king in 1070 to seize treasure from the English monasteries. The main source for FitzOsbern's life, Orderic Vitalis, is torn between admiration at his material success and disapproval of his methods. Of the former there was no doubt. At Christmas 1070 he was in Normandy helping administer the duchy. Early in 1071 he was sent to Flanders to protect the regent, Richildis, and her son, Arnulf, the young count (and William I's nephew), against a rival claimant, Robert 'le Frison', Arnulf's uncle. To secure FitzOsbern's aid, Richildis offered him her hand in marriage. The air of chivalric romance was caught by the contemporary observation that FitzOsbern travelled to Flanders 'as if to a game'. If so, it proved fatal. He was killed in the decisive battle with Robert 'le Frison' at Cassel in February 1071.

FitzOsbern's dramatic career showed that the immemorial skills of warrior and warlord remained as central to the success of William the Conqueror as to that of any of the great fighting kings and heroes of the early Middle Ages. Whatever their political or administrative talents, which now seem rather less compelling than once they did, the French invaders of 1066 secured their conquests by violence, often crude and extreme. But it should be noticed that FitzOsbern secured his military support by rewards of cash and privileges as much as by grants of land: he relied on a paid host , not a 'feudal' levy in the classic sense. His life also suggests that in the eleventh as in other centuries, there was only a fine line separating art and nature: a murdered father; personal bravery; cruel conquest; great wealth and friendship with the great won by the sword; international fame for arms; a dowager in distress; the offer of marriage as well as power; and a death in the defence of a widow and orphan. Compared to the images manufactured by Norman apologists for King William himself, FitzOsbern may appear a throwback to a nastier, more vicious age. Yet in achieving great power and transforming his destiny through the exercise of military strength and the expenditure of large sums of money, FitzOsbern and his master, ruthless opportunists both, had much in common.

D. C. Douglas, *William the Conqueror*, 1964.

**HEREWARD THE WAKE** (*fl.*1060-70) was a Lincolnshire noble and outlaw who became a popular figure of legend in the twelfth century. At some date before 1066, Hereward fled his lands in south Lincolnshire, banished, according to local tradition, on his father's petition by Edward the Confessor as a troublemaker. After the Conquest, his lands were distributed to newcomers, for example Oger the Breton. This may have supplied the motive for Hereward's brief career of Fenland banditry. Leading his own gang, he joined the invading Danes under King Sweyn when they seized Ely in 1070. Although Ely became the focus of what the one version Anglo-Saxon Chronicle (later kept locally at Peterborough) described in terms of a general uprising, Hereward had his own interests to pursue. A former tenant of Peterborough Abbey, he led a raid which looted the abbey, perhaps in revenge for the new French abbot's refusal to restore Hereward's estates. After Sweyn had come to terms with King William and withdrawn, Ely continued to hold out into 1071, its resistance attracting some distinguished Anglo-Danish opponents of the Norman regime, including Morkere, formerly earl of Northumbria, and bishop Aethelwine of Durham. Starvation and self-preservation finally led to the rebels surrendering to the king, but not before Hereward had broken out to escape with some followers. Although apparently reconciled with William, it seems that he was subsequently killed by other Frenchmen, possibly nervous lest he made good any claims to their newly acquired property. What is more remarkable than this career of violence and failure is the rapid elevation of Hereward as a local, later national hero. By 1140, at Ely, Peterborough and in Gaimar's *Histoire des Engleis*, Hereward's deeds were recorded in detail and romanticised. That the reality was more prosaic is suggested not only by the raid on Peterborough but by the evidence of Domesday Book concerning conflicting claims to lands supposedly held by Hereward before 1066. Personal vendetta; the opportunities offered by the Conquest for outlawry and self-advancement; the coincidence of individual ambition with foreign invasion and national rebellion are all involved in Hereward's story showing that, in its earliest years, the Norman Conquest was neither as neat nor as secure as it later appeared. 1066 added to rather than initiated violent tenurial disputes and local rivalries. Hereward, described in the admittedly hostile Peterborough *Gesta Herewardi Saxonis* as 'cruel in act and severe in play', was an outlaw to Edward the Confessor as well as William the Conqueror. He became, however, a figurehead in the sentimental tradition of English resistance: by 1200, local Fenlanders were naming their sons after him. Unlike his surplanter as the symbol of anti-French English solidarity, Robin Hood, Hereward not only existed but actually did do some of the things claimed for him. (His nickname, 'the Wake', means watchful.)

J. Hayward, 'Hereward the Outlaw', *Journal of Medieval History*, xiv, 1988.

**HERFAST**, (*d*.1084; bishop of the East Angles 1070-1084) was possibly the first royal servant to be called chancellor, in 1069. A Norman clerk, he was witnessing ducal charters from 1060. Sometime after the Conquest, perhaps in 1068, Herfast was appointed to head the royal writing office, in succession to Regenbald, who had served Edward the Confessor as well as William I. As chancellor, Herfast made no obvious innovations: for example, the English vernacular in royal writs was retained. In 1070, he received the East Anglian bishopric which was then sited at Elmham but which he moved to the more prosperous centre of Thetford. His episcopate was notable for a strenuous contest with the abbey of Bury St Edmund's over the monks' immunity from the bishop's jurisdiction. The dispute, which concerned the vital interests of both wealthy abbey and impoverished diocese, drew a testy rebuke for Herfast from Archbishop Lanfranc: 'Were you to devote less time to gambling and games of chance, to read the Bible for a change and to learn some canon law . . . you would cease to argue with your mother church'. This attack reveals less about Herfast's relaxed morality (he may have been married and was reputed to have fathered a son) than of the widening gulf between old style curial clerks and the new intellectual puritans, a divide which transcended any supposed contrast between 'backward' English and 'progressive' Normans. Herfast was as much a creature of court life and the traditional habits of aristocratic clergy as the disgraced Stigand and, as such, hardly less offensive to the stern reformist Lanfranc.

**MAURICE OF LONDON** (*d*.1107; bishop of London 1086-1107) was one of those public servants whose private life, although notorious and scandalous, scarcely interrupted his successful career. A Norman by birth, he was appointed archdeacon of Maine as part of William the Conqueror's annexation of the county after 1063. He became William I's chancellor c.1078, an office he held until his appointment to the see of London in 1086. Evidently an efficient organiser, he reconstructed his cathedral of St. Paul's on a lavishly grand scale. His legal experience failed to prevail, however, in 1094 when he unsuccessfully contested Anselm's right to consecrate the parish church of St. Mary's in the archbishop's manor of Harrow. In 1100, he played a central role in the succession of Henry I to the throne after the sudden death of William Rufus, crowning the new king only three days after his brother died. His influence in royal administration is reflected here and in the earlier rise to dominance of his protégé, Ranulf Flambard. Like Flambard, Maurice, even though not in full priestly orders until shortly before his consecration as bishop, was a libertine, his pursuit of women attracting considerable monkish condemnation. Apparently, Maurice justified his sexual exploits by claiming that, on medical grounds, they were essential to his health.

GUNDULF, (?1024-1108; bishop of Rochester 1077-1108) was typical of the ecclesiastical administrators introduced after the Conquest, earning himself an equal reputation for saintliness as a champion of monasticism and for efficiency as Archbishop Lanfranc's business manager and supervisor of the construction of the Tower of London. Born in the Vexin and becoming a clerk in Rouen cathedral, he vowed to become a monk after a difficult pilgrimage to Jerusalem, entering Bec c.1060, at about the same time as Anselm. There he soon became the protégé of the prior, Lanfranc, whom he followed to St. Etienne, Caen in 1063 and to Canterbury in 1070. In England, Gundulf acted as Lanfranc's proctor and helped run the new archbishop's estates. Rewarded by William I and Lanfranc with the see of Rochester in 1077, Gundulf continued to be closely associated with the fortunes of Canterbury, providing the ecclesiastical administration during the archiepiscopal vacancy 1089-93. In 1095, he refused to disown his fellow Bec alumnus, Anselm, at the Council of Rockingham, but in general he remained loyal to the king. He undertook building work at Rochester Castle for William II, in whose cause he defended it during the civil war of 1088. In 1100 he witnessed Henry I's Coronation Charter and, in Archbishop Anselm's absence, baptised the king's son, William, in 1103. Like his mentor and patron Lanfranc, Gundulf saw no contradiction in the power of Church and State. He used his evidently considerable skills as an organiser to the benefit of his diocese. In tune with earlier eleventh century thinking, the secular canons at Rochester were replaced by sixty monks with an independent endowment and new conventual buildings. Rochester Cathedral was rebuilt as was the shrine of St Paulinus, Gundulf's most famous predecessor and, like him, a foreigner who got on well with kings. At the episcopal residence at West Malling, Gundulf erected a tower, an indication, perhaps, of the constant anxiety for security which characterised the first generation of French conquerors.

It is, however, for his involvement in the construction of the White Tower in London that Gundulf is most remembered. At about the time he was promoted to Rochester, Gundulf was appointed by William I to supervise work on 'the great tower of London'. His precise role is unclear. Although being described a decade later as being 'very competent and skilful in building in stone', and having commissioned a number of construction projects, civil, military and ecclesiastical, it is unlikely that Gundulf was himself an architect. For instance, there is no evidence to link him with Colchester Castle (completed by 1087) which appears to have been designed by the same architect as the White Tower, although on an even grander scale, Gundulf probably acted in a financial and administrative capacity, although he supervised building at close hand, lodging in the London house of one Eadmer the Lefthanded. Perhaps Gundulf had gained experience of construction work during his time at Caen which saw the building of both St. Etienne and its sister house Holy Trinity. Yet, although castles were a commonplace of the Conquest, there was nothing quite like the White Tower or Colchester in England or on the continent. Four-square to the ground, they are unlike the donjons of northern France, such as that at Falaise. It has been suggested that the apsidal chapels built out from the walls indicate a function beyond the purely military. The White Tower was built for what it remained, a royal palace as well as a stronghold, an idea confirmed, perhaps, by William II's need to provide a wall around it in 1097. For centuries, the White Tower acted as a centre of government, a respository of archives and, as no doubt it had been intended by the Conqueror, a symbol of power.

Gundulf emerges vividly as the archetypal administrator-bishop from two separate sources, an early twelfth century *Vita* and the contemporary collection of Rochester records, the *Textus Roffensis*. Combining lacrymose piety with a knack for business, Gundulf was a monk of the world. This duality, so common and so essential in effective medieval bishops, finds expression in Gundulf's dying words, reported in his *Vita*: 'Thanks be to God for giving me such wealth that I can help the poor and still leave my successor enough to cover his expenses even if he has to support thirty followers.'

H. M. Colvin *et al.*, *History of the King's Works*, i, 1963. M. Rudd, 'Gundulf of Rochester', *Anglo-Norman Studies*, xi, 1988.

THOMAS OF BAYEUX (archbishop of York 1070-1100) was a member of a remarkable ecclesiastical dynasty: his brother Samson became bishop of Worcester (1096-1112); one nephew, Thomas, was archbishop of York (1109-1114); another, Richard, was bishop of Bayeux 1108-1133). The family owed much to the patronage of Odo of Bayeux, whose influence almost certainly lay behind Thomas' appointment to York. The son of Osbert, a priest, and Muriel, he and his brother Samson were sent by Bishop Odo to Liège, presumably to complete their studies. Before his elevation to York he had been a canon and treasurer of Bayeux. By 1070 he seems to have become one of William I's chaplains. His had been the well trodden high road to ecclesiastical preferment. However, Thomas's tenure of the archdiocese was no sinecure. In particular, he had to cope with two intractable problems: externally the assertion of York's independence from the primacy of Canterbury; and internally the restoration of the church's finances and administration.

Although the status of York as a subservient archbishopric was anomalous in Western Christendom, neither Lanfranc of

Canterbury nor, even less, William I were prepared to concede the point. Politically, subjugation of York was one part of William's policy of subduing the north and reducing the prospects of local particularist support for any invader or rival claimant. For the same reason in the tenth century the kings of England had attached York to the see of Worcester and entrusted both to loyal West Saxons. William's and Lanfranc's way was ostensibly more legalistic. Thomas waged a stern but unavailing campaign to establish the equality of York as a metropolitan see. After expressing reservations before his consecration by Lanfranc in 1070, he urged his claims to autonomy at Rome when he and Lanfranc went to collect their *pallia* in 1071. In 1072, a council at Winchester found in Canterbury's favour and Lanfranc had his primacy and right to York's profession of obedience upheld. The archbishop of York was left with only Durham as a suffragan (Carlisle was not founded until 1133). Royal pressure not canon law or precedent determined the judgement; the papacy significantly failed to ratify the position. Indeed, the dispute rumbled on, occasionally flaring into spectacular, if often petty, rows, until the Reformation. The archbishop of York still cannot wear his pontifical robes in the southern province, a lasting legacy of the Norman political and ecclesiastical settlement.

Within his province, Thomas met with more success. At York he organised a chapter of secular canons and introduced a system of prebends (ie. lands and revenues owned by the cathedral but specifically attached to support individual canonries), no mean feat given the poverty and disruption of cathedral finances and personnel. The arrangement, although in tune with continental practice, contrasted with the monastic chapters of many southern cathedrals which Lanfranc, a monk, continued to support, not least at Canterbury itself. Indeed, the monk's customary disdain and suspicion of the secular priest may account for an edge in Lanfranc's relations with Thomas. It is possible, for instance, that Thomas, in common with many contemporary clerics, was married. The professional celibate would not approve. Yet as well as being a skilled administrator, Thomas was no philistine: a noted musician and patron of scholars, he was remembered by Hugh the Chantor a generation after his death as having rebuilt York Minster and restored the fortunes of a shattered diocese.

G. Aylmer and R. Cant, *A History of York Minster*, 1977. F. Barlow, *The English Church 1066-1154*, 1979.

**WILLIAM WARENNE** (*d.*1088) was one of those followers of William of Normandy who made their fortunes by the conquest of England. The younger son of Rudulf of Varenne in Normandy (*d.*1074), he distinguished himself in ducal service as a very young man in the early 1050s. After the ducal victory at Mortemer (1054) he received estates in upper Normandy, but it was only after the English invasion that he attained the front rank. He fought at Hastings and was rewarded with lands which by 1086 extended into thirteen counties, most notably strategically important estates in Sussex centred round Lewes. By the end of William I's reign he was one of the dozen largest individual landowners in England. He repaid his debt with vigorous loyalty in both England and France. In 1075 he played a leading role in supressing the revolt of the earls of Hereford and Norfolk. After the Conqueror's death, Warenne supported William Rufus in 1087-88 against Robert Curthose and Odo of Bayeux. Rufus encouraged his service by creating him earl of Surrey in 1088. The same year Warenne was seriously wounded by an arrow in his leg at the siege of Pevensey and died at his foundation of Lewes Priory on 24 June 1088. Warenne's career was more than meteoric. A younger son of an obscure minor Norman nobleman, he had risen through conspicuous loyalty to his lord to become not only one of the richest men in one of the richest kingdoms of Europe but also the founder of a dynasty which, powerful, wealthy and influential, survived as earls of Surrey until 1347. Warenne's foundation at Lewes (1078/80) was the first Cluniac house in England, another sign of the Conquest's effect on establishing institutional as well as personal links across the Channel. Warenne's success depended on the traditional chivalric virtues of loyalty, bravery and prowess in arms. His life illustrates the stupendous prizes and the personal dangers on offer to those who joined the conquest of England. It was appropriate that Warenne's direct descendent, John de

Warenne, earl of Surrey (1231-1304), when challenged in 1278 by royal commissioners to produce title to his lands, produced an old rusty sword declaring 'Here, my Lord, is my warrant (*warrantus:* a pun which no doubt appealed to the somewhat intractable sense of honour of the time). My ancestors came with William the Bastard and won their lands with the sword, and by the sword I will hold them against all comers'. Earl John won his case. William of Warenne would have approved.

**ROGER OF MONTGOMERY** (*d.*1094), first earl of Shrewsbury, created one of the most powerful and strategically important lordships in post-Conquest England. The son of a Norman *vicomte*, he first appears in the army of Duke William in 1051-2. Probably only a few years younger than the duke, thereafter he enjoyed William's special confidence. In the early 1050s he greatly increased his estates by marrying the forceful Mabel, heiress to the extensive lordship of Bellême. Although closely involved in planning the invasion of 1066, Roger remained in the duchy to help the administration of the Duchess Matilda. It was only the later romances of Wace that put him at Hastings, a tribute to his subsequent fame and reputation. In 1067, however, he accompanied William to England where he received huge estates in Sussex and Shropshire. By the end of 1074, he was titled earl of Shrewsbury. His administration of his Marcher lands provide an insight in how the Conquest was secured. Roger had a more or less free hand. Before 1066, there had been no crown lands or royal thegns in Shropshire: by 1086, apart from Roger, there were only five other lay tenants-in-chief in the whole county. To support him, Roger gave out land to men already his vassals in Normandy with whom he set about building castles (as at Shrewsbury and Montgomery) and extending his power into Wales. Orderic Vitalis, whose father, Odelerius, was Roger's chaplain, described the earl as wise and prudent 'a lover of justice, who always enjoyed the company of learned and sober men'. His English subjects were as unimpressed as they were unfavoured. The citizens of Shrewsbury complained that they still had to pay the same level of geld after the castle had been built as before, perhaps because of the loss of houses incurred in its construction, let alone the forced labour. Roger's rule was effective and ruthless; his authority based on ties of personal allegiance; a network of castles; successful protection from the Welsh; and brute force. In many ways he remained a conqueror and exploiter rather than a settler. But he left his mark on the Marches, in his castle mounds and the perpetuation of his name in the Welsh town and county of Montgomery. As J. Le Patourel wrote, Roger's career 'shows what was possible in Norman society during the eleventh century'.

**WALKELIN OF WINCHESTER** (d.1098; bishop of Winchester 1070-98) was William Rufus's chief minister in the 1090s. Although not on the intimate terms of advisers such as Robert of Meulan, Walkelin was prominent in the king's council, often heading witness lists to charters and writs, and seems to have had charge of the king's financial affairs, in which he worked closely with Ranulf Flambard. It was said that Rufus's incessant demands for cash finally killed him. A Norman, royal clerk of William I and canon of Rouen, whose brother became abbot of Ely and nephew bishop of Hereford and archbishop of York, at Winchester Walkelin was typical of the new continental episcopate appointed by the Conqueror. Initially hostile to the local tradition of monastic chapters, his attempts to secularize Winchester were thwarted by Lanfranc and, despite the anomalous position of a secular clerk presiding over monks, came to be regarded with affection by them. In 1079, he began to rebuild his cathedral on a grand scale in monumental romanesque: austere, regular, massive, a statement as much about the new secular order as religion. Much of Walkelin's work survives, in the nave and transepts. As bishop of Winchester, Walkelin was in a position to oversee the main royal treasury houses in the city's castle. Additionally, he acted as a royal commissioner in both secular and ecclesiastical matters: in 1089 he dealt with the restive monks of St Augustine's, Canterbury; in 1095 he investigated the rights of Herbert Losinga, bishop of Thetford/Norwich; in 1096, he led a judicial circuit of the South-West to hear royal pleas. At court his authority grew in the early 1090s. After the death of Bishop William of Durham in January 1096, Walkelin was the dominant figure in the administration of England, organising the geld of that year and acting as regent in Rufus's absence in France in 1097. Although he did not work alone, some historians have seen in Walkelin's activities the origins of the office of Chief Justiciar. This seems to be an exaggeration. Walkelin was the king's main administrative deputy, not his Prime Minister.

F. Barlow, *William Rufus*, 1983.

**ROBERT LOSINGA**, *i.e.* the Lorrainer (*d.*1095; bishop of Hereford 1079-95) was a distinguished mathematician, computist, chronologist and astronomer (*i.e.* astrologer). An unusual choice as a post-Conquest bishop, he was neither a royal clerk nor a Norman monk, his experience being of scholarship not administration. To England and his diocese, Robert brought a range of influences. Notably, he rebuilt Hereford cathedral on the model of Aachen and attempted to popularize the eccentric chronological system of the Irish recluse Marianus Scotus (*d.* 1082). (This added twenty-two years to the AD calculation.) Robert sent a copy of Marianus's *Universal Chronicle* to his friend Wulfstan of Worcester in 1082, where it was incorporated into the cathedral chronicle, and himself wrote a commentary on it, wrongly described as *Excerpts* from Marianus, in 1086. This included a uniquely contemporary description of the Domesday Survey then in the process of being conducted. Perhaps Robert's greatest fame came from his study of the stars, by which he claimed to have successfully predicted the future, famously when he declined to set out for the consecration of Lincoln Cathedral in 1095 because he rightly foresaw it would not take place. It is possible that Robert also introduced the western, two-dimensional abacus into England, thus facilitating the computing revolution which transformed royal and baronial auditing in the following century, the abacus being a chequered cloth which gave its name to the Exchequer. It is likely that Robert's brand of cosmopolitan learning would have reached England regardless of the Conquest, but the employment of Robert reveals how closely England was drawn into movements of European culture. Rather than his acknowledged skill at computing time and numbers, where his high reputation despite gross error made him a model of academic achievement, perhaps

Robert's main attraction to William was his expertise as an astrologer. If so, Robert was not alone. The Conqueror's doctor, Gilbert Maminot, bishop of Lisieux (1077-1101), a scholarly sybarite who spent much of his time gambling and hunting, was also a *sagax horoscopus,* a learned astrologer. Medieval monarchs were nothing if not superstitious; they greatly favoured those who convinced them that divination was a science.

**OSMUND OF SALISBURY** (*d.*1099; bishop of Salisbury 1078-99) was probably a distant relative of William the Conqueror whom he accompanied to England as a chaplain. From c.1070-78 he was the king's chancellor, head of the small writing office which drew up royal documents, mainly charters and writs. Described in the Northamptonshire Geld Roll (*c.*1070/78) as the king's *writere,* it is even possible that during his chancellorship he was effectively the sole court scribe, the rest of the writing for the government being farmed out to cathedral and monastic *scriptoria.* Certainly, William of Malmesbury later described Osmund as bookish who, even as bishop, 'did not disdain writing or binding books'. In his time as Chancellor, Latin fully replaced English as the sole official language of government. Following almost invariable custom, Osmund's reward for his services came in the form of a bishopric. At Salisbury (what is now Old Sarum), he built a new cathedral and reformed the cathedral chapter, installing a hierarchy of officials and thirty-two secular canons. Osmund does not appear to have played a very prominent part in national or ecclesiastical politics. However, he was closely involved in planning Domesday Book, probably being a commissioner for the survey of South-Western counties, now contained in the so-called Exon Domesday which may have been written at the Salisbury *scriptorium.* Of even more lasting significance was his institution of new orders for liturgical services, the so-called 'Use of Sarum', a compilation designed to establish uniformity of worship. Whether or not it was introduced in response to the reluctance of English clergy to adopt Norman styles of chanting, the Sarum Use, with emendations especially in the thirteenth century, came to dominate the liturgy of the English church for the rest of the middle ages.

When Osmund was finally canonised in 1457, the work he had started almost four centuries before had left an indelible mark on the religious life of his adopted country.

**WILLIAM OF ST CALAIS** (*d*.1096; bishop of Durham 1080-96) was trained under Bishop Odo at Bayeux, the Anglo-Norman administrative Sandhurst. Unlike many of his colleagues, William became a monk, his first offices being prior of St Calais in Maine and abbot of St. Vincent-des-Près at Le Mans. He caught the eye of William I as a diplomat, but his experience of a frontier province may have influenced the king's decision to appoint him to the see of Durham in 1080 after the murder of Bishop Walcher. A conscientous and efficient diocesan, in 1083 he introduced monks to Durham cathedral, thus founding a priory which remained a centre of scholarship and learning until the Reformation. If pious, William was also intelligent and ambitious. By the end of William I's reign he was a leading royal servant. Largely on manuscript evidence which associates the scribes of Domesday Book with the Durham *scriptorium*, it has been suggested that William was in overall adminsitrative charge of the Domesday Survey. There are other references to William of St Calais's concern with the details of which baron owned what, and it may be significant that every writ of William II referring to Domesday Book is witnessed by Bishop William. He was thus probably responsible for one of the most remarkable governmental achievements of the age. The absence of returns from north of the Tees, William's diocese, might also suggest his involvement as a relatively neutral organiser.

The Domesday Survey was conducted between Christmas 1085 and 1 August 1086. The kingdom was divided into seven circuits, each with its own commissioners, who were deliberately not drawn from local landowners. To reduce fraud, a second batch of commissioners was despatched shortly after the first to check the declarations. The material collected concerned the extent of holdings, ownership and revenues, calculated in terms of tangible assets such as mills, ploughs, ploughteams and labourers. The commissioners asked three further questions: what was the estate worth and whose was it a) '*tempore regis Edwardi*' (*i.e.* in the time of Edward the

Confessor, 1066); b) when the present owner took possession; c) in 1086. The information was collated under counties, arranged by tenants-in-chief, *i.e.* those who held their lands directly from the king. Thus each county entry would begin by listing the holdings of the king, then the archbishop/bishop, then the leading barons and so on.

In fact Domesday Book is three separate texts:

1. The Exon Domesday, which covers the south-western counties, seems to be an early draft of material collected by one group of commissioners and is organised by tenants-in-chief and then by counties and not, as the others, vice versa;

2. Little Domesday, which contains a fair copy of returns from East Anglia;

3. Great Domesday, apparently a final, condensed text, covers all England south of the Tees except East Anglia and the City of London. The scale of the enterprise is only matched by its monumental result. Domesday was an apt nickname as the survey established, or sought to establish, title to land to which government officials referred for over a century after. Medieval rulers frequently surveyed their holdings, usually for fiscal reasons. In spirit, therefore, Domesday is not unique. But in size, detail and deliberation it stands alone as a towering monument to Anglo-Norman administrative skill. For it was a non-racial product. The main scribe of Great Domesday was, given his penchant for anglicising place names, most likely English. But the guiding force, William I, and the executor, William of St Calais, were French.

One mystery surrounding Domesday is its purpose. It has variously been interpreted as a tax book preparatory to a new assessment of the land tax or a more efficient collection of the old; a schedule on which new feudal and military obligations could be calculated; a statement of ownership of land which confirmed title or provided the basis for the settlement of tenurial disputes; or an immediate reaction to a political crisis (the threatened Danish invasion) in which landowners cooperated in the assessment in order to curtail royal misuse of the right to billet troops. What can be said is that potentially Domesday Book had fiscal and tenurial application and must have had considerable magnate approval for the survey to be completed so quickly. It is intriguing, however, that for all its bureaucratic grandeur, Domesday was still-born. It existed, and exists, and was, and is, used as a mine of information. But it led to no obvious political or fiscal initiative. In part this may have been because its originator, William I, died in 1087. It may also have been because the minister most closely responsible, within fifteen months of the Conqueror's death, was on trial for treason.

On his accession, William II, says the *Anglo-Saxon Chronicle*, treated Bishop William 'so well that all England went by his counsel and did exactly as he wished'. This was hardly surprising if the bishop had the evidence of Domesday at his disposal: knowledge is power. However, during the civil war of 1087-88 between William II and his brother Robert Curthose and their uncle Odo of Bayeux, Bishop William deserted the king and refused to fight against the rebels. His reasons are obscure as he seemed to have got on well with Rufus, supplying smooth talk for a tongue-tied monarch. The king's reaction at what he saw as treachery was commensurately vigorous. The bishop was arraigned for treason at a royal court at Salisbury on 2 November 1088. The king, vocally supported by Archbishop Lanfranc, insisted that William was being tried as a secular lord: his ecclesiastical position and office were not in dispute. William, ever nimble in debate, adopted the mantle of Gregory VII, claiming canonical immunity from secular prosecution or trial, arguing that he could only be judged by fellow bishops or the pope. Lanfranc dismissed such posturing as irrelevant. William forfeited his temporalities and went into exile, possibly to the court of Robert Curthose. Lanfranc's rejection of William's arguments may have been prompted by disbelief at this royal clerk's sudden conversion to clerical immunity, which, ironically, William may have derived from Lanfranc's own collection of canon law. But this early example of the clash between royal and ecclesiastical jurisdiction reveals that the English clergy were traditionalists: unlike advanced Gregorians they continued to recognise the practical distinction between the spiritual and temporal spheres.

It is perhaps a sign of William's ability or Rufus's magnanimity that the bishop was restored to favour in 1091 and resumed his position as one of the king's closest advisers. In 1095, at the Council of Rockingham, he led the bishops in their repudiation of Archbishop Anselm, accusing the primate, unblushingly despite the events of 1088, of polluting his fealty to the king. William evidently chose arguments that would serve his immediate turn, and would, no doubt, have agreed with Winston Churchill that consistency is a mark of mediocrity. But the violence of his attack on Anselm lost William the support of the barons: he was, perhaps, too clever by half. He died on 2 January 1096, appropriately enough at the king's court at Windsor, for his career was crucially bound up with the government of the first two Norman kings. Yet he never neglected his diocese. Under his auspices, a new cathedral was begin in 1093. He thus lays claim to have been the begetter of two of the most impressive surviving monuments of his age: Domesday Book and Durham Cathedral.

J. C. Holt, *Domesday Studies,* 1987.

**HUGH, COUNT OF AVRANCHES, and EARL OF CHESTER** (*c.*1047-1101) presents the world of the eleventh century nobleman in its full diversity. A violent military adventurer, a student of vice and self-indulgence, he was a friend of Anselm. Profligate with his income, he was a patron of monasteries. His household contained a bunch of rowdy thugs; it was also cultivated, even pious. Nicknamed 'the fat' or 'the wolf', Hugh died in the habit of a Benedictine monk. If contemporaries saw a contradiction, they have left no sign. Hugh, the son of the count of the Avranchin in western Normandy and nephew of William the Conqueror, probably fought at Hastings. Early in the 1070s he was granted palatine powers over a wide area of the northern Welsh Marches centred on Chester within which, except for church lands and pleas, he, not the king, was sovereign. This grant allowed Hugh complete freedom to establish, by force, French control over the northern frontier with Wales and to penetrate along the coast of North Wales towards Anglesey. Hugh was outside royal supervision, a law unto himself, a tactic copied with the Montgomerys in Shropshire. Taking full advantage of his opportunity, he campaigned relentlessly against the Welsh, extending his power to Bangor, where he established a bishopric in 1092, and Anglesey. Beyond the English frontier, however, his authority could only be sustained by castles, garrisons and repeated raids which, in turn, provoked continual resistance and rebellion. On its fringes, the Norman Conquest remained a messy affair. Elsewhere, Hugh was one of the leading magnates in the Anglo-Norman realms, inheriting Avranches from his father in the 1080s and, by 1086, holding land in twenty counties outside Chester. In the succession disputes after the Conqueror's death, he supported William II and Henry I. Hugh acquired a foul reputation: vicious; violent; addicted to gambling and sex; and so greedy 'that, weighed down by a mountain of fat, he could hardly move'. He was also generous, which explains why his household was always crowded with many as debauched and sybaritic as he. But there was another side. Hugh was, according to Eadmer, an old and close friend of Anselm whom he persuaded to come to England in 1092 to supervise the installation of a community of monks at St Werburgh's Chester. Open-handed to 'good men, clerks as well as knights' as well as bad, he employed a Norman clerk, Gerold, who took upon himself the moral instruction of his fellow courtiers, using admonitory stories from the Bible and, no doubt more popular, stirring tales of Christian warriors and 'holy knights'. In such a raucous atmosphere of passion, carnality, militarism and piety, was nurtured the mentality which, in Hugh's lifetime, generated the Crusades. The knights who, in 1099, stormed Jerusalem and massacred its inhabitants, some of them Hugh's relatives and friends, shared this heady brew of self-righteous, self-pitying extremes of hedonism, brutality, guilt, obligation, spirituality and remorse.

**ROGER BIGOD** (*d*.1107) was one of the tight-knit group of second-rank Norman nobles who did well out of the conquest of England. Prominent in the Calvados region before 1064 as an under-tenant of Odo of Bayeux, he rose in ducal and royal service to become, by 1086, one of the leading barons in East Anglia, holding wide estates to which he added Belvoir by marriage and Framlingham by grant of Henry I. His territorial fortune was based on his service in the royal household, where he was a close adviser and agent for the first three Norman kings, and the propitious circumstances of post-Conquest politics. Much of his honour in East Anglia was carved out of lands previously belonging to the dispossessed Archbishop Stigand, his brother Bishop Aethelmar of Elmham and the disgraced Earl Ralph of Norfolk. A royal justice 1076-9 and regularly sheriff of Norfolk and Suffolk, under Rufus — if not before — Roger was one of the king's stewards. Usually in attendance on the king, he regularly witnessed writs but was also sent out to the provinces as a justice or commissioner. Apart from a flirtation with the cause of Robert Curthose in 1088, he remained conspicuously loyal to Rufus and Henry I, for whom he continued to act as steward and to witness charters. The adherence of such men was vital to the Norman kings. Through them central business could be conducted and localities controlled. Small wonder they were well rewarded. Roger established a dynasty which dominated East Anglia, from the 1140s as earls of Norfolk, until 1306. Roger's byname and the subsequent family name was derived from a word (*bigot*) meaning double-headed instrument such as a pickaxe: a tribute, perhaps, to Roger's effectiveness as a royal servant; certainly an apt image of one who worked hard both for his masters and himself.

F. Barlow, *William Rufus*, 1983.

**SAMSON OF WORCESTER** (*d.*1112: bishop of Worcester 1096-1112), a chaplain to William I and William II, was claimed by V. H. Galbraith in 1967 as the compiler and scribe of the so-called Great Domesday Book, the surviving fair copy of the survey of 1086. A Norman of noble origins, son of Osbert, a priest, like so many administrators of the first and second generations after 1066, Samson was a protégé of Odo of Bayeux, becoming a canon and treasurer of Bayeux Cathedral. In royal service by 1074, he apparently declined the see of Le Mans in 1081 saying that he was a man of this world not the next. Although having been married and still only in minor orders, Samson was appointed by William II to the bishopric of

Worcester in 1096: a striking, and possibly deliberate, contrast to his saintly predecessor Wulfstan. Samson was at the centre of a remarkable ecclesiastical dynasty: his brother Thomas of Bayeux was archbishop of York (1070-1100), as was one of his sons, Thomas, (archbishop of York 1109-1114); another son, Richard, was bishop of Bayeux (1108-1133). This scale of preferment for one clerical-administative family is impressive but not unique; it was matched if not surpassed by the rise of Roger of Salisbury and the Le Poers under Henry I. Samson was one of those secular minded ecclesiastics so mistrusted and vilified by the reformers clustered around the late eleventh century papacy. According to William of Malmesbury, Samson was an '*antiquorum homo morum*' a man of the old school. Although personally given to the pleasures of the flesh, particularly food ('a veritable sink of eatables' in William of Malmesbury's phrase) Samson does not seem to have been a bad bishop. However, recent scholarly opinion denies his authorship of Domesday, not least because there are inconsistencies and errors in the valuation attached to one of Samson's own estates, Templecomb (Somerset), by the scribe Galbraith sought to identify as Samson himself. Whatever their other shortcomings, Norman curial officials and landowners were unlikely to make mistakes of that sort.

J. C. Holt, *Domesday Studies,* 1987.
F. Barlow, *The English Church 1066-1154,* 1979.

**WILLIAM II** (*c*.1060-1100; king of England 1087-1100) has attracted more personal opprobrium than most English kings. His relatively brief reign has tended to be recalled for his morals, bad language, viciousness and dramatic death, not for his achievement in mastering the Anglo-Norman lands and, from inauspicious beginnings, becoming one of the most feared and respected rulers of his time.

William was the third, but second surviving, son of William the Conqueror. His red face as much as his hair earned him the nickname Rufus. Unlike his eldest brother Robert Curthose, the younger William remained conspicuously loyal to his father during the family conflicts of the 1070s and 1080s: he was wounded at Gerberoi (1079) fighting against a rebellious coalition led by

Curthose. His reward was designation as heir to England by the Conqueror on his deathbed in 1087, even though William had previously received no lands or titles. Seizing his opportunity with speed, William was crowned by Archbishop Lanfranc at Westminster on 26 September 1087, only seventeen days after his father's death at Rouen. Curthose, supported by his uncle Odo of Bayeux, refused to accept the division of the Anglo-Norman lands and disputed the succession in England. But after a short, vigorous campaign in 1088, Rufus suppressed opposition in England, in the process establishing his reputation as an effective warrior.

Between 1090 and 1096, Rufus bent his energy to consolidate his kingdom and reunite the Anglo-Norman dominions. He regularly invaded Normandy and, by vigorous military action and a skilful use of money, he managed to occupy or gain the allegiance of large parts of the duchy. In 1091, in alliance with Curthose, he ousted his younger brother Henry from the Cotentin in western Normandy, but from 1094 he and Henry cooperated against Robert. William's task was made easier by Curthose's failings as a ruler. An ineffectual politician, Curthose was unable to control his self-interested nobility. Instead, he fell back on a rootless charm and a name for bravery: he was no match for William. In 1096, the First Crusade provided unexpected relief for Robert and opportunity for William. In return for a mortgage of 10,000 marks to pay his brother's crusade expenses (raised in England by a heavy and unpopular tax of four shillings to the hide), William received the whole duchy for three years in pledge. From 1096 *de facto* duke of Normandy, Rufus had reunited his father's possessions with much of the Conqueror's skill, determination and opportunism.

In England, apart from the civil war in 1088 and a revolt by the Mowbrays in 1095, Rufus's main concern was the protection of his frontiers. He campaigned against the Welsh (1095 and 1097) and Scots (1091) and in 1092 Cumbria was annexed. In 1097 Rufus was behind the establishment of Edgar as king of Scots who then acknowledged him as overlord. However, France continued to be Rufus's main concern as he attempted to make good his father's claims to the Vexin (1097-8) and Maine (1098 and 1099). Rufus's ambition ranged widely.

*William II*
(From the reverse of his seal 1091/2: the king as warrior)

With his bullish and seemingly limitless self-confidence, some even thought he aspired to the French crown itself. He certainly cut a rather more impressive figure than the obese and lethargic King Philip. A characteristically bold plan to annexe Aquitaine in the same manner as he had acquired Normandy, through a mortgage for the count of Poitiers departing on crusade, was thwarted only by Rufus's death on 2 August 1100 when he was killed by a stray arrow while hunting deer in the New Forest.

The king's sudden death was a political sensation and a

moralist's dream. No respector of ecclesiastical privileges, William in death attracted the censure and hostile comment that few dared address to him in life. To die without time to confess or repent sins was seen as particularly awful in the Middle Ages, a judgement of God. Lurid stories filled with blood-curdling omens were soon embroidered around the fatal hunt. The reality was probably more chaotic than dramatic. Hunting accidents were commonplace: William's own brother, Richard, had been killed in the New Forest c.1070 and a nephew, a bastard of Curthose, had suffered an almost identical fate to William's only three months earlier. Some historians have smelt conspiracy rather than divine retribution in the king's death. Its timing was opportune for Henry, Rufus's younger brother, to seize the throne before Curthose had reached Normandy on return from his crusade. The man who most probably fired the deadly arrow, Walter Tirel of Poix, was a connection of the Clares who were close adherents of Henry. What we know of Henry suggests that he stopped at little that stood between him and his ambition. Cruel, violent, unsqueamish and unscrupulous, in fact just like Rufus, Henry, who happened to be one of the king's fellow hunters, certainly took full advantage of the situation. But beyond the circumstantial there is no evidence of premiditation: Henry's chance was fortuitous, not planned. Of that, contemporaries were more or less unanimous.

One cause of the suspicious, hostile, sanctimonious and scurrilous accounts in ecclesiastical chronicles of Rufus's life and death was his relationship with the Church. Not only was his quarrel with Archbishop Anselm of Canterbury notorious, but his concerted exploitation of church land, especially during deliberately prolonged episcopal vacancies (during which time the king enjoyed the bishopric's revenues), earned him the posthumous dislike of clerical writers, ever fearful for their collective and corporate rights, privileges and, always, income. The confrontation with Anselm has received so much attention largely because of the work of Anselm's biographer and companion, Eadmer. It is worth noting, however, that despite the later clerical disapproval and condescension, Rufus never lost his grip on what he regarded as his Church. Some writers, such as Orderic Vitalis, evidently preferred a vigorous if brusque ruler to the inept drift of a Curthose, even if strict canonical immunities suffered. The conflict with Anselm was unusual, if predictable. In 1088, Archbishop Lanfranc had sided with the king in deciding that the bishop of Durham, William of St Calais, a rebel sympathiser, should be answerable in the royal court as a tenant-in-chief and not be able to claim clerical immunity or appeal to the pope. This was Norman convention. Anselm himself was only too willing to cooperate with royal power: in 1096, for example, he and Rufus combined to prevent some monks of Cerne Abbas from illegally setting out on crus-ade. In principle, Anselm had little objection to working with the monarch. However, his over-precise academic intellect made him a tactless, over-fastidious and undiplomatic coadjutor of a king who suffered fools marginally better than those he deemed muddle-headed or obstructive. From William's point of view, Anselm was both. Their relations were fraught from the beginning, when, in 1093, a dangerously ill William had, in fear for his soul, forced a reluctant Anselm to become archbishop. Much of the antagonism was based on personal and local issues: the archbishop's military contribution; whether the archbishop or king had the right to decide which of two competing popes to recognise; and the right of the archbishop unilaterally to appeal to Rome. Although failing to oust Anselm at the Council of Rockingham (1095), Rufus managed to force the archbishop into exile in 1097 to the king's considerable financial and political benefit. It may be significant that none of Anselm's episcopal colleagues saw fit to share his exile: the dispute was between the king and archbishop, not State against Church. Up to his death, Rufus was the clear winner.

The ineffective eccentricity of Anselm was the familiar consequence of the don in politics. Rufus relied, as had his father, on more practical sons of the Church to effect his policies, men like Bishop Walkelin of Winchester and Ranulf Flambard, whom he elevated to the see of Durham in 1099 as reward for outstanding (some would say infamous) service in filling the king's coffers. But he was unafraid to destroy the unfaithful, as he showed when he broke his father's minister William of St Calais, bishop of Durham, in 1088.

Rufus's reign was marked by heavy financial exactions

commensurate with the scope of his political and military designs. National taxes, such as those of 1094 and 1096, were required to pay for constant war and the Normandy mortgage. It is possible that, in 1096 at lease, the information gathered in Domesday Book (1086) was employed to increase revenue. Local justiciars extracted as much as they could from royal rights and dues in the counties. More notoriously, the profits of vacant bishoprics were ruthlessly exploited, although only two vacancies, Canterbury (1089-93) and Durham (1096-99) were in royal custody for more than a couple of years. His dealings with abbacies were equally a matter of profit and patronage. Yet, despite the injured hostility of ecclesiastical chroniclers, Rufus was no tyrant. He surrounded himself with a loyal group of administrators, nobles and household companions. He consulted, as well as employed, his magnates, as over the 1096 tax, for it was on them that the king relied to fight his wars, to govern his country, secure his justice and collect his taxes. Testimony to his political as well as financial success is found in his achievements and his contemporary reputation. Abbot Suger of St Denis, writing a generation later, acutely described William as 'magnanimous', 'prodigal with the treasures of England, a brilliant recruiter and paymaster of soldiers'.

However, English chroniclers, from Eadmer to William of Malmesbury, Orderic Vitalis and Henry of Huntingdon, developed an increasingly unflattering portrait of a foul-mouthed, loutish homosexual; an almost demonic character for whom few good words could be found; an oppressor of the Church whose death was a blessing and whose burial without ceremony or prayers just deserts. Of his bad language there are so many references as to be credible (his favourite oath being, somewhat obscurely, 'By the Face of Lucca' — a reference to a popular Italian icon of the time). All chroniclers note his blunt manner of talking, which matches a career driven by a practical intelligence as much as fierce energy. The earliest observer, Eadmer, noted that William's court in 1094 was crowded with effeminate young men, parading girlishly long hair, mincing walks and flirtatious glances. Predictably, Anselm, although interested, was unamused. William of Malmesbury added a quarter of a century later details of elaborate and garish shoes and tight-fitting clothes. Such stories were coupled with dark mutterings about the king's own sexual habits. When Anselm, in 1094, proposed holding a Church Council to condemn sodomy, William refused. But it was only many years after his death that explicit accusations of homosexuality were levelled against William himself. Much of the surrounding disapproval can be explained by an odd cultural barrier between France and England which amounted to little more than different fashions. As early as 1077, William of Poitiers had recorded the Norman astonishment at the English habit of men wearing their hair long, something only women did in macho Normandy. The association of long hair with degeneracy and moral turpitude was pursued by a Council at Rouen in 1096 which publically condemned long hair. This obsession has had a remarkably tenacious hold on the English aristocracy and their imitators by no means extinguished even today.

It is probable, therefore, that the chroniclers, uniformly monastic, were voicing prim, prudish, perhaps prurient dislike of a fashion they regarded as alien or out of date but which William and his courtiers had adopted rather ostentatiously: an English Conquest, perhaps. That Rufus was content if not eager to go his own way cannot surprise. After all, he is one of the very few whose first title was that of king: he had no previous claim to a lordship, earldom, county or principality. What is more remarkable was his failure to marry. Although his brothers left marriage until relatively late (Curthose at forty-seven; Henry I at thirty-two), for a monarch not to make provision for legitimate offspring is exceptional. The only clear parallel to Rufus's behaviour is remote: Aethelbald, king of Mercia and overlord of southern England (716-757). Otherwise the only adult monarch bachelors or spinsters since 1066 are Elizabeth I and Edward VIII, and he married as soon as he could after abdicating. It is possible that William was homosexual. Unusually for his family, no bastards are attributed to him. Given the manner of his death, the rumours of his life and the interests of his successor, it is understandable that writers coloured their accounts. William of Malmesbury depicts Rufus as a short, pot-bellied, red-faced braggart with long, combed fair hair who, despite these obvious physical disadvantages, nonetheless insisted on wearing the gaudiest of the latest male fashions. Whatever the truth, William Rufus left few observers indifferent. Although it is impossible to be certain how, he made a powerful impression on those he encountered. His actions reveal him as a man of extraordinary, if occasionally undisciplined, energy, singular determination and exalted ambition. His career exudes self-confidence of a high order. But there was more to him than blustering activity. One July afternoon in 1099, while dining at Brockenhurst in the New Forest (another source has him hunting), he learnt that his garrison at Le Mans was under siege. He immediately set off towards the coast and, despite stormy weather and reluctant ferrymen, landed unscathed in Normandy at dawn the next day ready to raise an army. Such speed of reaction was, to say the least, unsettling to his opponents and cheering to his supporters.

Rufus effectively harnessed the resources of England to pursue deliberate policies of consolidation and aggression in France and the English marches. If he was impatient and tolerated no opposition, he was also remarkably successful in achieving his designated ends. Much of the responsibility for the permanence of his father's conquests and the scope of his brother's dominance can be credited to Rufus. The anecdotes about him make him more vivid than either. Begun in 1097, Westminster Hall, which in spite of evidently hasty construction stands to this day, was, at 240 feet by 67 feet 6 inches, by far the largest secular building in western Europe. It is typical of its builder that when he first saw it, William Rufus complained that it was too small.

F. Barlow, *William Rufus*, 1983.

**ANSELM** (1033-1109; archbishop of Canterbury 1093-1109) was one of the most original thinkers of the western middle ages. By using reason and logic, his proofs of the existence of God and the importance of the Incarnation for the first time went beyond the traditional Scriptural and Patristic foundations of Christian theology. He wrote not just to confirm but to convince. Anselm's talents were not restricted to academic speculation: forty-six of his forty-nine years as a monk were spent in administrative or political positions, as prior, then abbot of Bec, and archbishop of Canterbury. His life is unusually well-documented in a biography written, much of it during his lifetime, by a close companion, Eadmer of Canterbury.

Born of noble parents in Aosta in northern Italy, his youthful desire to become a monk clashed with his status as an only son who was expected by his father to inherit the family estates. In the late 1050s he left Italy in search of education and vocation. In particular he was attracted by the reputation of another ex-patriot Italian, Lanfranc of Pavia, who had settled in Normandy. In 1060, Anselm became a monk at Bec, where Lanfranc was prior. He had earlier rejected the idea of entering the great Burgundian monastery of Cluny because its emphasis on reciting the liturgy — a sort of eternal choir-practice — left little time for academic study. In 1063, Anselm succeeded Lanfranc as prior of Bec; in 1078 he was made abbot. Although concentrating on study and teaching, Anselm presided conscientiously over his institutional responsibilities. At Bec, scholarship and administration walked hand in hand: it is no coincidence that so many of Anselm's pupils went on to positions of high responsibility in church and state, Bec becoming the Sandhurst of the Anglo-Norman church militant. On Lanfranc's death in 1089, Anselm appeared as his obvious successor to many, not least the monks at Canterbury who had already made him an honorary member of their community. William II was, however, in no hurry to fill the vacancy until, in March 1093, he fell seriously ill. It happened that Anselm was at court. In what appears to have been a coordinated ploy by some of William's lay advisers and the bishops, William was persuaded to appoint Anselm archbishop if he wished to recover. The advantages to both church and state of having a new primate, preferably in the Lanfranc mould, were obvious: leadership for the church; control for the state. Anselm regarded the prospect with horror: he protested his age; his loyalty to his vocation and monks at Bec; and, rather disingenuously, his lack of aptitude for secular affairs. He may also have been wary of the irascible and volatile temperament of the king. The courtiers, barons and bishops would have none of it. He was manhandled into the royal presence and the crozier forced into his clenched fist. As he put it, after his hurried consecration, 'you have yoked together in the plough the untamed bull and the old and feeble sheep'. As archbishop, Anselm was by no means as inept as he pretended. By denying the validity of his initial appointment, he managed to negotiate terms with William for six months before finally doing homage and fealty to the king in September 1093. The central issue was property: Anselm accepted the archbishopric only after William had agreed that all lands held by Lanfranc in 1089 should be restored. Legalistic and plain-speaking, Anselm did not behave in a sheep-like manner. Relations with the king deteriorated as the two men found themselves incompatible and unable to reach agreement on anything without argument. Although the disputes concerned perceptions of royal and archiepiscopal rights, the essential conflict appears to have been personal and temperamental: a foul-mouthed, aggressive, self-confident king and a silver-tongued, prim and obstinate prelate. Events early in 1094 were typical. Anselm offered a gift of £500 to support William's projected campaign against his brother, Robert, in Normandy. When the king demanded more, Anselm withdrew the offer completely. Anselm continued to send out contradictory signals. He was willing to put the question of recognition of Pope Urban II, one of the conditions of his acceptance of the archbishopric the previous year, on one side, yet publicly condemned the vices at William's court; proposed a church council to discuss sexual morality; and challenged William's policy of holding abbeys vacant. The king was by turns angry and dismissive. The pattern continued the next year. Anselm was eager to receive his pallium from the pope in Rome, but this required recognition of Pope Urban II, rather than the anti-pope, Clement III, or, as William I and William II had preferred since 1085, neither. Anselm did not deny his fealty to William but placed more weight on his allegiance to Urban, given when abbot of Bec. The matter was discussed at a council at Rockingham in February 1095. The bishops, led by William of St Calais, bishop of Durham, tried to bully Anselm into accepting William's authority over papal recognition. There were threats of deposition. The barons, ironically, took Anselm's part. The deadlock was resolved by a royally initiated compromise with the help of a papal legate, Walter of Albano. William recognised Urban II; confirmed Anselm in office and favour (*i.e.* the king would refrain from harassment: anything more positive was out of the question). Anselm, faced with papal support for the king, had to accept traditional royal rights over the church. In return, he received the pallium the legate had brought.

Anselm's agreement to the compromise of 1095 suggests a more pragmatic strain than Eadmer would allow. Once the issue of principle was settled, Anselm fell in with royal policy, even to the extent of accepting the military command of Canterbury and eastern Kent in the face of a projected invasion by Robert Curthose. It is understandable that this episode was ignored by Eadmer. Conflict broke out, however, again initially on a secular matter. William was furious at what he considered to be unsuitable and poorly trained knights provided by Canterbury for his campaigns in Wales in 1097. For his part, Anselm was increasingly angered by William's refusal to countenance a church council to reform morals. In the fact of royal hostility, Anselm insisted on being allowed to appeal to Rome. William took this as braking the 1095 agreement and presented Anselm with a choice: either swear to abide by English customs and never again appeal to the pope or go into exile. Anselm, almost happily, chose the latter, hoping perhaps that, once at Rome, he could resign his office.

What was at stake between Anselm and William II was neither the prerogatives of the newly reformed papacy, nor the freedom of the English church from secular tyranny. At issue were the rights of the see of Canterbury regarding lands, political influence, moral authority and secular obligations. Above all, perhaps, at the heart of the problem was Anselm, a tender conscience backed by an adamantine will. Unlike Becket, however, Anselm never identified his own cause with that of the church as a whole. His exile was solitary — no bishop shared it — and personal. In many areas, he had no quarrel with traditional practices and fully acknowledged the rights of the king, except where they conflicted with his principles or his see's interests. Long taken as a champion of the papal side in the Investiture Contest between lay control and ecclesiastical independence, Anselm was nothing of the sort. His acts were political, but his vision was not. He did not see himself as belonging to any terrestrial party.

If Anselm hoped to be relieved of his duties by the pope he was disappointed. His presence added lustre to the increasingly self-confident papal curia. In 1098, at the council of Bari, he debated the nature of the Procession of the Holy Ghost with Greek theologians and was present at the Council of Rome in April 1099 when the most extreme decrees prohibiting lay investitute were promulgated. This was a ticklish issue for Anselm, as he himself had been invested with the staff of office, if not the ring, and had sworn homage and fealty to the king, both of which were condemned at Rome.

Anselm returned to England after the death of William II in 1100. Soon he was in difficulties again. Acting in accordance with the Rome decrees of 1099, he refused to pay homage to the new king, Henry I, for his Canterbury lands, even though, as the king insisted, it was customary. This time, the problem was not Anselm's personal fastidiousness, but his loyalty to the pope. On one level, Anselm worked well with King Henry I. He officiated at the king's marriage in 1100; he was allowed to hold his reforming council at London in 1102; and, while the pope was considering his case, permitted Henry to invest bishops. There was not the personal bitterness with Henry as there had been with his brother. Unfortunately, circumstances and Anselm's logic made a compromise difficult to broker. It was his obedience to Rome, not any hostility to lay investiture, which conditioned his actions. As a Benedictine monk, obedience was central to his understanding of the religious life. For Pope Paschal II (1099-1118), any retreat from the 1099 decrees would weaken his position in the struggle against the German king, yet he was reluctant to alienate Henry I. For Henry, abandoning control of episcopal appointments could, quite literally, put his power over England at risk, so great were ecclesiastical land holdings. For Paschal and Henry, the issue was political; for Anselm it was of principle. The final compromise agreed at Bec (1106) and confirmed in London (1107) outlawed lay investitute while allowing episcopal homage. Additionally, and for the king, crucially, royal approval of elections was permitted. Anselm was perfectly content with this. Free elections had never held much appeal to him: he had been chosen by the king and confirmed by personal agreement between them. He had, more or less, chosen his successor at Bec. For Anselm, good men not good procedures were what mattered. Thus fealty and homage were permissible, as neither contradicted the priestly office, whereas lay investiture did: how could a layman grant a cure of souls? Anselm's final years were marked by close co-operation with the king, for example over the creation of the diocese of Ely (1109). His identification with his see, a dominant *leitmotif* of his episcopate, he retained to the end. One of his last public acts was to insist that the archbishop-elect of York acknowledge the supremacy of Canterbury. Discipline and obedience were the hallmarks of Anselm as thinker and monk. What made him a controversial archbishop was that he had his own often highly individual scale of allegiances. Above all was his conception of what he owed to God. This high idealism proved inconvenient to friends and foes alike.

As archbishop, Anselm cannot be judged a great success. His obstinacy had engineered a change in procedure, without altering the substance of the political relationship between church and state. His absences had done little to protect and nurture the interests of the monks at Canterbury, as some of them noted. His influence on affairs was personal. According to Eadmer, a man of lively wit and robust conversation, his clarity of mind impressed, exasperated or annoyed all who encountered him. He possessed to a fault the donnish habit of discovering intractable problems of principle behind apparently innocent situations. Yet — another donnish fad — he found public affairs irresistible. He may not have been a willing politician; he certainly was not an effective one. But Eadmer fails to persuade when he has his hero declare 'I have shunned all wordly business': God's purpose for the military commander of Canterbury in 1095 was more complicated than that.

What is unquestionable is his stature as a theologian, the more remarkable as some of his greatest works were composed amidst the distractions of abbatial and archiepiscopal affairs. His thought revolved around the ontological proof of God and His nature *i.e.* because it is impossible to conceive of that which does not exist, the idea of a perfect God must, of necessity, imply the existence of such a God, as is argued in the *Monologion* (1077). This is inductive, taking the conclusion, 'I believe in God', and working back to the proof of the reality of the statement. In the *Proslogion* (1078), he demonstrates the same point from a different, deductive direction, beginning with the statement 'there is no God' which, Anselm argued, is self-contradictory as it implies the idea of a God as a being 'than whom no greater can be conceived'. Thus, Anselm did more than re-affirm God's existence according to Christian texts: he relied on reason and logic. In *Cur Deus Homo* (*c*.1095-98), he went further. To show that the claims of Christianity were specifically valid, consistent and without flaw, he demonstrated the necessity of the Incarnation as the only means whereby Man's debt to God could be discharged and Man redeemed. Throughout his theological works there runs a clear line of concise reason and precise argument, supported by a lucid Latin style. Anselm was no free-thinking rationalist. He wrote that men might obey the teachings of the Church. Reason depended on faith, not *vice versa*: 'I do not seek to understand that I may believe, but I believe that I may understand, for this also I believe, that unless I believe I shall not understand'.

But there was another side to Anselm. As a monk at Bec, he showed an intense devotion to Christ, the Virgin Mary, saints and other monks. His *Prayers and Meditations* and his friendships with pupils reveal a passionate, occasionally tortured nature, the human emotion which drove him to explain the mystery of God to his fellow men. His personality comes down the centuries, that of a lively, charming, considerate, but intellectually tough, uncompromising and rather intimidating tutor of the best sort, a friend to his pupils rather than their inquisitor. His intellectual reputation has never dimmed. He was in Dante's *Paradiso* among 'the spirits of light and power in the sphere of the sun'. His contemporaries, particularly at Canterbury and at court, were perhaps somewhat more equivocal in their reactions. Eadmer, to still criticism, had to append lists of his miracles to his biography in the 1120s. Anselm was not the stuff of martyrs; to many he must have seemed a nuisance. It is intriguing that his canonisation had to wait until 1494 and the rather unlikely auspices of the Borgia pope, Alexander VI.

R. W. Southern, *St Anselm*, 1963.

Eadmer, *Life of St Anselm,* ed. & trans. R. W. Southern, 1962.

**RANULF FLAMBARD** (*c.*1060-1128; bishop of Durham 1099-1128) was one of the most powerful and controversial figures of the reign of William II. His actions and personality excited resentment, admiration and anecdote. His character and reputation are suggested by his nickname, 'Flambard': flamboyant, fiery, glittering, scorching, prompting William of Malmesbury's pun, 'a torch of iniquity'; definitely dangerous to know if he were against you, but a generous benefactor to family and friends. His work for William Rufus earned him the obloquy of ecclesiastical commentators but his monks at Durham remembered him with affection. The remarkable attention lavished on him by contemporary writers suggests that Ranulf was not easy to ignore. Ranulf is one of the few people of his generation (barring saints) for whose personality there is plentiful and plausible evidence. From the excavation of his tomb, it is possible to know what he chose for his episcopal staff and ring and even what he looked like. Five foot nine tall, he had a short, broad head, a strong jaw and sloping forehead: witnesses thought him good-looking.

The son of Thurstin, an obscure parish priest in the diocese of Bayeux, Ranulf was probably introduced to the royal court by Odo of Bayeux. By 1086, as well as a royal chaplain, he had become keeper of the king's seal, working under Maurice the Chancellor. Already Ranulf had amassed lands, houses and churches across southern England worth about £30. For Ranulf, royal employment was always a means to profit. It is characteristic that when Maurice, now bishop of London, reputedly denied him a deanery, Ranulf looked elsewhere for patronage. Precisely what tasks he performed for William I is unclear, but it is likely he was involved in producing and executing royal writs, and hence in legal business and finance. By 1087 he may have had experience in what became one of his specialities, the administration of vacant churches on behalf of the crown.

After 1087 Ranulf rose rapidly in the household of the new king. The two men were of a similar age; neither, in the words of R. W. Southern, 'can be called respectable'; they shared a certain exuberant enjoyment of life. Although Ranulf was always a servant, and their relationship never reached the intimacy of that between Henry II and Becket, they got on well. In his unceasing search for money and the exploitation of royal rights, Rufus had, in Ranulf, an agent as predatory as himself.

Within the royal household, although never holding any office other than royal chaplain, Ranulf soon emerged as a key administrator. Regularly witnessing royal writs, in 1093 his name appeared immediately after the bishops and chancellor; in 1096, his name headed the witnesses to a writ ordering tenants of Worcester to pay a relief to the king. It may be no coincidence that these years saw an increased use of the writ for communicating royal orders to the localities, there being a substantial fine of £10 imposed for non-compliance. Throughout William II's reign, Ranulf witnessed more writs than anybody else (35), but he acted as part of a team of officials, including the grand curial bishops William of St. Calais of Durham and Walkelin of Winchester, and the household servants: the chancellors William Giffard and Robert Bloet; the stewards Eudo and Haimo; and Urse d'Abitot. Ranulf's dominance was, perhaps, exaggerated by later chroniclers searching for a scapegoat for Rufus's harsh ecclesiastical exactions, but Ranulf did emerge in the 1090s as the king's leading man of business. In part, this was because he was unafraid to appear in public on his master's behalf, as in 1093 when he appeared at Canterbury to serve a writ on Anselm on the very day of the archbishop's enthronement. Ranulf was also able to roam across a wide area of royal administration, unhampered by any formal designated duties, when, in 1097-99, he acted as one of the regents left in England during the king's absences.

Contemporaries were in no doubt about his power, calling him 'justiciar' and *totius regni procurator*, titles later applied to Henry I's chief minister, Roger of Salisbury. The two areas beyond the royal household in which Ranulf was most active were finance and the law, both liable to provoke hostility and publicity in equal measure. Although Orderic Vitalis portrayed Ranulf as measuring England with a rope in his eagerness to reassess royal dues, most evidence comes from the exploitation of existing feudal incidents, such as reliefs, and the exploitation of the church. As bishops and abbots technically were tenants-in-chief of the king, during vacancies the crown had the right to administer the church's lands. That this was profitable, and that William to some extent manipulated his rights by delaying appointments, was widely recognised, even if exaggerated, especially when compared to the similarly lucrative secular custodies which, affecting lay lordships, failed to incite the chroniclers' corporate wrath. Ranulf was appointed administrator of Ely Abbey possibly by William I. During Rufus's reign he was involved in the custody of Ramsey; New Minster, Winchester; Christ Church, Canterbury; and the bishopric of Worcester in 1095. Between 1096 and 1099, Ranulf made £300pa as custodian of the see of Durham. Other abbeys which fell under Ranulf's frankly commercial control included Thorney, where he ordered a re-assessment of services (presumably upwards), and Hyde Abbey which he sold to a close associate, Herbert Losinga, in 1090. It is small wonder that Ranulf was seen by monkish chroniclers as a rapacious asset-stripper.

Called by some the king's *placitator* or advocate, Ranulf was equally heavily engaged in the endless litigation involving land rights and jurisdiction. Whatever else, the Norman Conquest and subsequent land settlement had left uncertainty and, as Domesday revealed, a host of disputes, many involving the crown. Part of Ranulf's job was to travel the realm in pursuit of royal claims. This line of business took Ranulf to Canterbury in 1093 and Bury St Edmunds in 1095; in 1096, he toured Devon and Cornwall asserting royal rights to lands in a manner which looked back to the circuits of Odo of Bayeux under the Conqueror and forward to the itinerant justices of Henry I and Henry II. Ranulf's handling of suits demonstrated that medieval royal justice usually meant deciding cases in favour of the crown, its friends and its allies. Justice was neither neutral nor blind. As with ecclesiastical and secular custodies, the currency of civil law was property; so were the profits, to king, to Ranulf and to his associates. Ranulf, as the king's representative, could intimidate or favour litigants.

It is hardly surprising that such a vigorous royal servant should be feared. However, he was resented because he was a *parvenu* who lined his own pockets. Whether or not in 1094 he took a cut of the money he received from the fyrd of Hastings in lieu of military service, he certainly exploited his custodies and amassed a fortune in lands, revenues and ecclesiastical preferment. Archbishop Anselm called Ranulf a prince of publicans, implying that he exploited royal taxes for his own advantage. By the late 1090s, Ranulf enjoyed a string of lucrative benefices across southern England, as well as canonries at Salisbury, London and Lincoln. These last perhaps indicate a network of old government hands with whom Ranulf had worked, including the three former royal chancellors, Bishops Osmund of Salisbury, Maurice of London and Bloet of Lincoln. Ranulf also took care of his family, including his own sons, his brothers and nephews for whom he worked hard, and with some success, to place throughout the Anglo-Norman church. However, the gravy train of government service had a precise destination. Hitherto wholly dependent on royal favour, in 1099 Ranulf bought himself independent power and position with £1,000 for the bishopric of Durham. The *arriviste* had arrived.

Just as suddenly, Ranulf's career as royal minister was ended with the death of his master on 2 August 1100. Within a fortnight, Ranulf was arrested, deprived of his bishopric and sent to the Tower of London, earning himself the distinction of being the first political prisoner to be incarcerated there. His fall was primarily symbolic. In tune with his coronation Charter of Liberties, Henry I was trying to distinguish his regime from that of his predecessor in order to garner the widest support for his coup. Ranulf, more than any of Henry's subsequent favourites, a man 'raised from the dust', was expendable, whereas, for example, his former boss, Maurice of London, or Rufus's last chancellor, William Giffard, were not, and were received into Henry's favour. Ranulf's reaction to adversity showed his mettle. In February 1101 he escaped from the Tower (later romancers said by rope) and placed his services at the disposal of Robert Curthose in Normandy in attempting to unseat Henry from the English throne. Ranulf may have acted as one of Curthose's leading advisers for the invasion of England in 1101 which led to the inconclusive Treaty of Alton, but was probably unimpressed by the quality of his new master. Once peace had been agreed, there was a reconciliation with Henry which restored Ranulf's bishopric and his English lands. An unspoken condition seems to have been that Ranulf stayed in Normandy as a double-agent for Henry in the methodical campaign to annexe the duchy. He visited his see only occasionally, as in 1104 for the translation of relics of SS Cuthbert and Bede, despite his apparent doubts as to their authenticity. Meanwhile, he exercised his energies in administering the diocese of Lisieux, which he attempted to convert into a family sinecure, first for his brother, then his son.

After 1106, and the successful conquest of Normandy by Henry I, Ranulf returned to Durham for good. No longer the king's protégé, materially in reduced circumstances, Ranulf set about organising the monastic priory at Durham which his predecessor, William of St Calais, had founded. Inevitably, as in most medieval cathedrals, there were disputes between bishop and chapter over money, in this instance over the income from priory lands to be used to pay for the building of the great new cathedral church. The row emphasised the straitened circumstances of the northern diocese. The idea of the wordly former civil servant cloistered with his monks inevitably gave rise to ribald stories. On one occasion it was alleged the bishop provided a lavish meal of food normally forbidden the monks served by waitresses in tight fitting clothes; Ranulf sat back watching the brothers' surreptitious glances at the women and chiding them for their hypocrisy. In fact Ranulf was generous to his monks and relations were normally good. Ranulf's business acumen brought stability to Durham's finances; he attracted scholars to his household, including the future archbishop of Canterbury, William of Corbeil. He was a friend and benefactor of the influential and respected local hermit, Godric of Finchale. In Durham and the surrounding area, Ranulf was remembered with affection. There is a flattering portrait of him in a later twelfth century Life of St Godric by one Durham monk; another recalled: 'that was our golden age, under Ranulf our bishop'.

That Ranulf was heartily disliked by many cannot be denied. Yet hatred and condemnation were often tinged with respect, as in the story of his escape from kidnap and attempted murder by Thames pirates when keeper of the king's seal or in the account of his daring escape from the Tower. He lived life to the full. Handsome, intelligent, witty, he was an attractive figure, fond of clothes, food, drink and sex. His attempted seduction and failed rape of his wife's niece Theodora in 1114 has become notorious because his intended victim later became the well-known hermit, Christina of Markyate. Yet after he had become a bishop he provided for his wife Aelfgifu by respectably marrying her off to a prosperous man in Huntingdon. He neglected neither her nor his children. In the eleventh century, for able children of humble parents like Ranulf, the only hope of advancement lay either in the church or in especial skill at martial butchery. Inevitably religious vocations could be affected or strained. Yet in all the calumny heaped on Ranulf, nobody accused him of hypocrisy, for which he was perhaps too honest, too aware of human weaknesses, both excellent credentials for his role as royal extortioner. Ranulf's sins were venal and venial. To compensate for social insecurity he sought to establish a dynasty. He understood that to be great a man had to be generous, as his household and monks as well as his family discovered. He fascinated even those whom he terrorized. The monk Simeon of Durham, who knew him, summed up his quality: 'impatient of leisure, he went on from labour to labour, thinking nothing done unless new enterprises pressed on the heels of those already accomplished'. To this restless energy was allied acute intelligence and organising genius. His career had a wider significance than that of Rufus's henchman. Again in the words of Southern, 'the great line of administrators who fashioned and finally destroyed the medieval system of government in England begins with Flambard'.

R. W. Southern, *Medieval Humanism*, 1970.
F. Barlow, *William Rufus*, 1983.

**ROBERT**, nicknamed **CURTHOSE** (*c*.1053-1134; duke of Normandy 1087-1106) twice failed to make good his claim to the English throne. The eldest son of William the Conqueror, he had been designated count of Maine in 1063 and duke of Normandy in 1077-8. Impatient for power and easily led by dissident Norman barons, from 1078 he persistently rebelled against his father. Nevertheless, on his deathbed, William confirmed Robert's succession in Normandy, leaving England to his more capable son William Rufus. Between 1087 and 1088, Robert and his allies made a concerted but unsuccessful bid to wrest

England from his brother. Thereafter, his rule in Normandy was constantly undermined by William and his youngest brother Henry. In 1096, having mortgaged his duchy to William for 10,000 marks, he departed on the First Crusade, during which he won for himself glittering fame. On his return he found William dead and Henry installed in England. Once again, his invasion of England failed, terms being agreed at Alton in 1101. In 1106, Henry exploited his growing political advantage in Normandy, defeating and capturing Robert at the battle of Tinchebrai. Thereafter, Henry held his brother in comfortable but close confinement. It was said that Henry mitigated the harsh treatment usually meted out to his political prisoners in deference to Robert's status as a former crusader. Most of Robert's captivity was spent in Cardiff Castle where, according to tradition, he learnt Welsh and composed at least one poem, on a tree he could see from the window of his cell. His threat to Henry I was maintained by his son, William Clito (d.1128). Robert was a poor ruler, vain and malleable. He was, however, a fine warrior, who once wounded his own father in battle at Gerberoi (1079) and earned such fame on crusade that even in his lifetime chroniclers invented improbable deeds of valour and spread the false story that he had been offered the crown of Jerusalem in 1099. His legendary deeds were enshrined in stained glass by Abbot Suger at St Denis. As an effective, disciplined ruler, Robert was a failure, but as a military leader and companion, he won renown, a paradox central to many political tensions of the period.

C. W. David, *Robert Curthose*, 1920.

**ADELA OF BLOIS** (?1062-1137) was a daughter of William I and his wife,, Matilda of Flanders, and the mother of King Stephen (king of England 1135-1153). In 1080 she married Stephen, count of Blois and Chartres. She appears to have played an active role in the administration of her husband's lands, regularly witnessing his charters. A noted bluestocking, among her friends were two of the leading intellectuals of her day, the canonist Ivo of Chartres and Anselm. Having inherited her father's appetite and ability to rule, Adela persuaded her popular but weak-willed husband to join the First Crusade in 1096, assuming the regency of his counties herself. Her role was not nominal, Hildebert, bishop of Le Mans commenting that 'in you . . . is all that is needed to steer the ship of state'. Her husband was less fortunate. Although in charge of the central funds of the Crusade, Stephen deserted at Antioch in 1098, understandably enough in the face of overwhelming odds. Unfortunately for his reputation, the crusaders survived and succeeded in capturing Jerusalem in 1099. According to Orderic Vitalis, Adela was unamused by a disgraced husband, 'mocked by almost everyone'. She waged a sustained campaign of bullying and moral blackmail that extended into their bedroom where, between intercourse, she would urge Stephen to think of his reputation and return to the Holy Land. In the end, her nagging worked and Stephen departed East once more in 1101, to meet a satisfactorily noble death at Ramlah the following year. No longer a coward's wife but more congenially a hero's widow, Adela continued to rule Blois-Chartres until 1107 when she formally transferred authority to her son Theobald. Nevertheless, she maintained her network of active political contacts, not least with her brother, Henry I, who lavished patronage on another son, Stephen, and appointed a third, Henry, bishop of Winchester, the richest see in England. Adela retired in 1120 to the abbey of Marcigny-sur-Loire, where she died in 1137. By all accounts a forceful personality, Adela's qualities were not uncommon among women aristocrats, although more often they found an outlet in the running of nunneries. Adela's secular career, as *de facto* ruler of one of the most powerful principalities of northern France for more than a decade, is exceptional, testimony to the power of breeding as well as to her own determination. Although married to a French count and living to see a son crowned king of England, she significantly chose to be buried beside her mother at Caen under an inscription 'Adela, filia regis'. She was always the Conqueror's daughter.

**WALTER TIREL III** (*fl.*1100), lord of Poix, was notorious in the early twelfth century as the man who shot dead William II king of England during a deer hunt in the New Forest on 2 August 1100. His repeated and strenuous denials of responsibility made under oath to Abbot Suger of St Denis, chief minister of Louis VI of France, suggest that public infamy was as intrusive and tenacious as it is today. Castellan of Pontoise in the strategically important Vexin between Normandy and the lands of the king of France and related by marriage to the powerful Anglo-Norman Clare dynasty, Walter Tirel received lands from William I and was a close friend of William II. All contemporary accounts attribute William's death to a stray arrow, a hunting accident. Most, including William of Malmesbury, the Worcester chronicler and Orderic Vitalis, name Walter Tirel as the unwitting culprit. It seems likely that he shot the arrow that missed a deer and killed the king. He certainly fled the scene immediately afterwards. Some modern conspiracy theorists have used this to support their reconstruction of a plot hatched by the Clares and William's brother, Henry. It is true that Henry was present on the fatal hunt and grasped the opportunity to sieze the throne. For him, the circumstances and timing of his brother's death were convenient, but probably fortuitous. William Rufus was not the first to die by accident in the New Forest. His brother Richard had been killed hunting there c.1070 and a nephew, also called Richard, had met a fate eerily similar to the king's in May 1100. Walter Tirel was not a scapegoat or a fall-guy. Subsequently, he neither suffered retribution nor enjoyed preferment. But to kill a king, even by accident, was an uncomfortable burden for a boon-companion to bear. As his confessions demonstrated, Walter Tirel was less concerned with the schemes of men than with the opinion of his peers and the designs of God.

**HENRY I** (1068-1135; king of England 1100-1135) was one of the most effective and successful of all English monarchs. It is no coincidence that he was also one of the most ruthless, violent and vicious. According to Henry of Huntingdon, writing after his death, his public virtues of wisdom, military success and wealth were complemented by private vices of greed, cruelty and lust. A demanding patron and a frightening enemy, Henry constructed a royal dominance over England that was more than personal; one that was recalled with awe, respect and, in the civil war under his successor, even nostalgia; one that provided the basis in propaganda and in fact for the rule of his grandson,

Henry II. The cost of Henry's achievement was great: to the noble houses he ruined; to the dynastic rivals he destroyed; to the subjects, lay and clerical, he taxed with unsurpassed ferocity; and to himself. He was as stern and cruel as his father, the Conqueror; as energetic as his brother Rufus; but he was more suspicious of those around him than either. More than one contemporary chronicler recorded Henry's fearfulness and acute anxiety: fear of those whom he had made suffer for his ambition; anxiety lest his success turn to ashes. However harsh his actions and self-confidently lordly his official pronouncements, Henry appears to have understood the cost of success and the fragility of his achievement. He suffered from nightmares and at times feared being murdered in his own bed.

Henry's career cannot be viewed solely in an English perspective. The unifying factor of his life was his ambition to secure for himself as much of his father's Anglo-Norman inheritance as possible. Between 1087 and 1100, this meant balancing his interests between his competitive elder brothers Duke Robert of Normandy and King William of England. On Rufus's death, it required a determined and unending struggle to establish control and authority in England, then Normandy against rival claims and baronial hostility. The pursuit of security in France led to long absences from his kingdom; just over 50% of his entire reign: from the Summer of 1111 to his death at the end of 1135, the proportion rose to 67%. The effect on England, however, was direct through the king's demand for men and especially money to finance his diplomacy and wars. These requirements were the engines which drove the notable developments in English government organisation, financial management and legal administration which marked Henry's reign.

The fourth surviving son of Wiliam the Conqueror, although the only one born after 1066 (thus *porphyrogenitus*, a point emphasised in his later propaganda), Henry may have been intended for the church. There is some evidence that he understood Latin. It is unlikely, however, that he could write, the nickname 'Beauclerc' being a thirteenth century invention. The eulogising William of Malmesbury claimed Henry had been introduced to the liberal arts when young and had obtained learning 'by snatches', although the chronicler admits that the king 'never read much in public and displayed his skills sparingly'. The death of his second son, Richard, in 1075 may have persuaded the Conqueror to keep his youngest son available for secular lordship. Even so, the old king declined to grant him land (Rufus was similarly denied). On his deathbed, when he disposed of Normandy to Robert and England to William Rufus, the Conqueror bequeathed Henry the substantial sum of £5,000, but no property. (This memory may have prompted Henry, on his own deathbed forty-eight years later, to leave his son, Robert of Gloucester, an even greater sum of money.) Henry had to make his own way. In the 1090s the opportunities lay in Normandy where Henry built up a significant lordship in the west of the duchy. Henry's prospects were determined by his relations with his brothers. In 1091, when they combined against him, he was temporarily deprived of the Cotentin, Avranches and Mont-St-Michel. From 1092, however, Henry, now established at Domfront, threw in his lot with Rufus in his attempts to increase his power in the duchy between 1093 and 1096. After Robert mortgaged the duchy to Rufus to pay for his crusade in 1096, Henry was rewarded with Coutances and Bayeux. Thereafter Henry appears loyal to Rufus, an intimate at his court. His choice was dramatically vindicated. He was in the New Forest with the royal hunting party on 2 August 1100 when Rufus was fatally wounded. Because he was present, Henry was able to seize the opportunity and the crown.

Although not the most glorious passage of Henry's life, the 1090s were formative. Forced to live off his wits as much as his birth, Henry gained experience of war, diplomacy and the subtler political arts of managing men, winning people to his cause, exploiting the weaknesses of rivals and calculating his own long-term advantage. He learned patience and, in the performance of his brother Robert, saw how not to rule. He could have plotted against Rufus after 1096; he could have sought his fortune elsewhere. He chose loyalty and gained a kingdom. The combination of patience and decisive action, demonstrated in his *coup* of 1100, were characteristic of Henry's later rule. The 1090s also provided Henry with practical lessons in lordship. It is no chance that many of Henry's advisers when king originated in his western Norman lands and neighbouring Brittany including Brian

*Henry I dreaming of threats from peasants,*
*knights, clerics and a storm at sea*
(From the Chronicle of John of Worcester *c*.1140)

FitzCount; Richard de Redvers; Geoffrey de Clinton and Roger
of Salisbury. Such men established and maintained Henry's
power in England. Their support for him and his patronage of
them probably stemmed from the contacts established during his
apprenticeship in Normandy in the 1090s. However, familiarity
and sentiment never swayed Henry's choice of servants: even the
closest and most highly favoured, such as Geoffrey de Clinton,
could be dismissed. Of all his qualities as ruler, one of the most
important was his skill in picking men of ability to serve him.
Young knights flocked to his court to bask in his hospitality,

reputation and employment. For all his many disagreeable traits, Henry had a capacity for affection. Richard de Redvers (d.1107) was a close friend; Henry seems to have been genuinely fond of his nephew Stephen of Blois; and he was an extremely indulgent guardian of the Beaumont twins Waleran and Robert, sons of his chief minister Robert of Meulan (d.1118). Friendship and generosity, the creation of a loyal, privileged *familia* were not simply aspects of a gregarious personality; they were essential tools of government.

The speed with which Henry grabbed the English throne in August 1100 has prompted some historians to suggest there was a conspiracy to kill Rufus. There is no real evidence for this beyond the circumstantial. It was, however, a piece of massive good fortune for Henry, coming as it did just before Robert Curthose had returned to Normandy after the First Crusade. In his exploitation of Rufus's death, Henry displayed the energy, decisiveness, and a precise understanding of where power lay and how to obtain it which subsequently marked his reign. Within hours of the arrow striking Rufus, Henry had secured control of the royal treasury in nearby Winchester; within three days he had been crowned king of the English at Westminster (Sunday, 5 August). Speed was of the essence. Henry acted before a Robertine faction could form. He did not wait until Archbishop Thomas of York could officiate at his coronation, still less for the exiled Archbishop Anselm. Instead he was anointed by his father's former chancellor, Maurice, bishop of London. Control of the royal treasure and hallowing by Holy Oil provided only the basis for Henry's assumption of power. He needed to win over the English baronage and church in anticipation of a challenge from Curthose. He immediately issued a manifesto, later known as his Coronation Charter, in which he promised not to tax vacant churches; to avoid arbitrary alterations to rules governing baronial inheritance and marriages; to exempt lesser royal tenants from the geld and other non-military levies. Such concessions may have depressed royal income by as much as a third; a high but necessary price for political support. However, Henry did not abandon royal rights over the Forests and, in a number of clauses, he significantly instructed his barons to treat their tenants as he treated them and warned that anyone guilty of disseisin during the interregnum (2-5 August) was liable to pay a penalty to the king regardless of whether the land taken was royal or not. Designed to curry favour with those who had suffered from Rufus's rapacity, while at the same time reassuring the royal administration, in its implicit guarantees of the liberties of all royal tenants and sub-tenants it was recalled as a model by the framers of Magna Carta in 1215. In 1100, it was one part of Henry's consolidation of power. Another sop to political opinion was the arrest and detention in the Tower of Rufus's notorious leading adviser, Ranulf Flambard. Others in Rufus's administration were retained, such as the chancellor, William Giffard. Henry was adept at political symbolism.

His marriage, in November 1100, to Edith (also known as Matilda c.1080-1118), daughter of Malcolm III of Scotland, was symbolic and practical. When he became king Henry was unmarried with no legitimate children: he and his adherents needed the security of a clear succession as soon as possible. The choice of Edith was, in English terms, imaginative. Something of a bluestocking, through her mother, Queen Margaret, she was the great-granddaughter of King Edmund Ironsides (d.1016), great-great niece of King Edward the Confessor (d.1066), and niece of Edgar Atheling, who had claimed the throne after Hastings. The marriage served a triple function for Henry. It promised heirs; it united the new dynasty with the old; and it secured the Scottish frontier and thus helped solve the perennial problem of controlling the north, which Henry visited only once, in 1122. It created, therefore, a potential dynastic balance, Anglo-Norman-Scottish, to measure against candidates to the English throne from among William I's other son and grandsons. The association with the Old English kings was celebrated by English writers, including William of Malmesbury whom Queen Edith/Matilda encouraged to write his Gesta Regum Anglorum. Some of the grander Anglo-Norman barons were less impressed, contemptuously referring to the royal couple as 'Godric and Godgifu', no better than English yokels. Whatever else, the marriage was a dynastic success; two surviving children were born, Matilda (1102) and, crucially for Henry's hopes, William (1103). However, marriage did little to make Henry monogamous. In his efforts to excuse Henry's sexual appetite, William of Malmesbury claimed that the king's fornication was driven not by lust but by desire for children. If for nothing else, Henry was notorious for the number of his bastards, at least twenty, nine sons and eleven daughters. Unlike his great-grandson King John, Henry prudently did not prey on the wives and daughters of his barons. Most of his known mistresses came from the lesser nobility, with the exception of the colourful Nest, 'the Helen of Wales', daughter of Rhys ap Tewdwr, prince of South Wales.

The political problems confronting Henry were focussed on establishing his power in England; the annexation and subsequent defence of Normandy; and securing the succession for his son, William, then, after the White Ship disaster in 1120, his daughter, Matilda. At no stage in his reign could Henry rest; although England after 1102 was quiescent, his hold on Normandy was never wholly unchallenged. Henry's achievements came from a shrewd combination of diplomacy and war. Robert Curthose's invasion of England was bought off at the treaty of Alton in 1101. Henry's counter-attack on Normandy was gradually prepared by winning Norman allies (1104-6), before the decisive military victory at Tinchebrai in 1106. His control of the duchy was threatened by Curthose's son, William Clito and his followers (to 1128); by the hostility of Louis VI of France and, until 1128, Fulk, count of Anjou; and by unreconciled Norman barons, notably Robert of Belleme (to 1111) and Amaury de Montfort. There were serious revolts on behalf of Clito 1116-1120 and 1123-4. The Angevin threat only receded through the treaties and marriage alliances of 1120 and 1128, although at the very end of his reign Henry had to resist attacks on the duchy by his impatient son-in-law, Geoffrey of Anjou. The king of France never ceased to fish in the troubled Anglo-Norman waters, even though Henry routed Louis at the pitched battle of Brémule in 1119. Throughout, Henry was forced to react rather than control.

Where Henry could influence events in his favour was with the church. As promised in his Coronation Charter, his fiscal demands fell less heavily on the church than had his brother's. Although he exploited episcopal vacancies without much scruple, he was eager to be cooperative. The church was the greatest single landowner after the king; it provided great scope for aristocratic patronage and for rewarding royal clerks. Henry sought reconciliation with Archbishop Anselm. The issue between them which led to Anselm's renewed exile (1102-7) was lay investiture not as a principle but as a sign of obedience to papal authority. Once agreement had been reached in 1106-7, which preserved royal influence on episcopal elections while honouring clerical scruples about lay interference, Henry worked closely with ecclesiastical leaders, for example over the creation of the see of Ely in 1108. Personally, Henry was a generous benefactor, especially to the Cluniacs and the Austin Canons. His own major foundation was Reading Abbey (1121), a Cluniac house lavishly endowed and richly built, where he was buried. His interest in the Austin Canons was confirmed in the founding of the see of Carlisle (1133). Henry's handling of the church was a model of firm but uncontroversial control, using techniques more pacific than required by his dealings with his secular magnates.

One of Henry's weapons was fear. One story had Henry, in 1090, personally hurling a Norman rebel called Conan to his death from the top of a tower in Rouen. His political violence was little less extreme: in 1106, he had his first cousin William of Mortain blinded; after the 1123-4 rebellion, he ordered three leading rebels to have their eyes put out, including the literary Luke de la Barre, whose main offence had been to mock Henry's appearance and habits in public: apparently Luke preferred to take his own life. Henry's treatment of his daughter Juliana and her children in 1118/9 was reputedly sadistic and barbaric, noted because beyond the normal currency of acceptable political retribution. In 1125, as punishment for debasing the coinage (not entirely their fault) Henry ordered all English moneyers to have their right hands cut off and to be castrated, one of the more extreme examples of a government finding a scapegoat for failed financial policy. Even if physical mutilation were avoided, Henry's opponents risked long imprisonment: Robert Curthose (1106-34) and Robert of Bellême (1111 to after 1130) died as prisoners; the blinded William of Mortain was held incarcerated even longer, from 1106 until after Henry's death, when, in 1140, he was allowed to enter the Cluniac monastery at Bermondsey

instead. Even Waleran of Meulan, once Henry's spoilt and precocious ward, was loaded with chains when imprisoned 1124-9
for his part in the 1123-4 rebellion.

In England, Henry made conspicuous loyalty the test of royal
favour. Those suspected of sympathy for Curthose or other disloyalty were dealt with severely: the great Norman house of
Grandmesnil was ruined in 1101; more spectacularly, Robert of
Bellême and the Montgomeries were destroyed in a crucial trial
of strength in 1102; in 1104, William of Mortain lost his English
fiefs and was banished. The technique employed by Henry
became almost standard: a charge to be answered in the royal
court; a demand for the surrender of castles or other property;
then, if these orders were resisted, the threat or reality of armed
force leading to confiscation, banishment or worse. Henry was
unafraid to use such methods to discipline former allies, such as
Geoffrey de Clinton who was accused of treason in 1130. Such
draconian techniques of political discipline proved highly effective, but they were hardly new. As far back as the laws of Alfred
in the late ninth century, disloyal English magnates had been
liable to confiscation, exile or death.

As the effectiveness of such methods depended upon the king
having sufficient baronial support, Henry had to reward those
who remained faithful, such as the Beaumont brothers Robert of
Meulan and Henry of Warwick. To replace those he ruined and
to balance those who retained favour, Henry promoted newcomers to the higher ranks of the landed nobility, disparagingly and
somewhat misleadingly described by Orderic Vitalis as 'men
raised from the dust'. The result was a baronage, part derived
from older families with provincial power, such as the Bigods in
East Anglia, and part from a newer class of curial magnates who
had risen through service to Henry, all secure only through royal
authority. The currency of this royal power was patronage; its
coin land. In his Coronation Charter Henry promised to abide
by traditional rules of inheritance and marriage, but often
neither were simple: families died out in the male line; there were
more than one potential heir, minorities and wardships; and the
increasing subdivision of fiefs and commercialisation of the land
market gave wide scope for royal intervention in land suits and
the disposal of estates even without political confiscation and

property transfers. Possession of land was complemented by the enjoyment of rights, exemptions and liberties, some of which the king could influence directly. For example, the term of sheriffs' tenure was reduced over Henry's reign, which allowed for greater financial efficiency as well as political control. The almost frenetic insistence on discipline and royal authority signified both Henry's dominance and insecurity.

If his skills in managing the political nation were in most respects traditional Henry's contribution to royal administration and justice were more innovatory. Although good at delegation, Henry presided directly over his government. He heard the most important royal pleas; he confirmed existing charters and issued new ones; he gave orders to his officials in the localities. A flavour of Henry's style is found in a famous writ to his agents in Worcestershire c.1110: 'I order my county and hundred courts to sit where and when they sat in King Edward's time (*i.e.* pre-1066). I forbid my sheriff to make them sit anywhere else to suit some need of his. But I myself, whenever I wish, may have these courts summoned for my lordly needs at my will'. Even more than his administrative direction, Henry's policies determined how England was governed, especially the need for money. His return from France in 1109 seems to have sparked a period of administrative activity. In 1110, to meet the requirements of collecting the massive aid to renew a £500 money fief paid to the count of Flanders and the 10,000 marks dowry on his daughter Matilda's marriage to the German emperor Henry V, the royal accounting office was reorganised as the Exchequer. The king's absences gave unique prominence to his chief minister, Roger of Salisbury, *procurator regni* or justiciar. Roger's task as head of Henry's administration was to run the government on the king's behalf in Henry's frequent absences, represent royal justice and secure income. Whatever administrative reforms occurred in Henry's reign — or, indeed, any other — came about not through any spontaneous combustion of bureaucratic inventiveness but as pragmatic responses to the demands of the ruler. The government of England was the king's in the sense that it served his personal needs, domestic and public: *L'etat c'est lui*. However, in the process of providing for the king's needs there developed institutions of government — the

Exchequer or the Chancery — that operated independent of daily or direct royal scrutiny. In the development of distinct government departments, the reign of Henry I was of considerable significance.

The spur to change came in response to royal needs. However, the government's reaction to the crisis of 1123-4 also shows a continuing intelligent self-appraisal by the king and his advisers. During his regency (1123-6) Roger of Salisbury reduced the sheriffs' terms; established or extended the system of itinerant judges (justices-in-eyre); and punished the moneyers for debasing the coinage. Between 1128 and 1131, a thorough overhaul of the administration was effected. This last exercise may explain the unique survival of the 1130 Pipe Roll. A Pipe Roll recorded the money owed the Exchequer, the amounts paid in, the sums pardoned and any expenses incurred by the sheriffs in their duties. Omitted were money paid directly to the king and royal loans. Given the sophistication and detail of the 1130 Pipe Roll, it must be presumed not to have been the first since the Exchequer was created in c.1110. It may have been preserved because, as part of the administrative reforms, it recorded fully all outstanding arrears as well as current payments. This may explain the huge sums mentioned, larger than on any subsequent Pipe Roll until 1177. The 1130 Pipe Roll confirms the chroniclers' opinion that Henry was massively wealthy: £23,000 had been received; £5,000 were pardoned; expenditure was recorded as £1,500; and £39,000 remained owing. Small wonder that Orderic Vitalis fancifully thought Henry could leave 60,000 marks to Robert of Gloucester.

With his wealth, Henry was particularly remembered for his maintenance of law and order. He was easily identified with the 'Lion of Justice' in Geoffrey of Monmouth's prophecies of Merlin, written at the end of Henry's reign. Significantly, Geoffrey's Lion of Justice fought the French and taxed his subjects heavily. Justice itself was a source of income, through fines for example, as well as a sign and instrument of authority. As his Coronation Charter emphasised, justice was central both to Henry's self-image and his rule. In his reign, there was some attempt to codify and unify both criminal and civil law which, a generation after the Conquest, still divided into the law of the conquerors and the conquered, an untenable position as the two increasingly impinged on each other. By 1135 royal power of confiscation and fines had largely supplanted the older Anglo-Saxon system of compensatory payments. The Crown heard pleas on serious offences; on infringement of royal rights; on the king's role as feudal overlord; and, increasingly, on appeals from tenants and subtenants unable to obtain justice in private, seigneurial courts, usually on matters concerning title to or occupation of land. This last function was to provide the basis for the sweeping reforms of the administration of justice under Henry II. Although it is difficult to talk of the establishment of a recognised Common Law in England much before the end of the thirteenth century, some of the expedients under Henry I certainly presaged it.

The need to define what constituted the law was evident. The 1100 Coronation Charter referred to the laws of Henry's predecessors. To clarify what these may have been, accounts of the laws of Edward the Confessor and William the Conqueror were produced during Henry's reign as well as, c.1110, two collections of the Laws of Cnut. A synthesis of past and current theory and practice was attempted, probably by a royal justice, in the *Leges Henrici Primi* (1114/18) and the *Quadripartitus,* which included Anglo-Saxon laws. Such works show an awareness of the practical, judicial importance of determining agreed laws and an attempt, if only at a rarified literary level, to emphasize the image of kingship, what the *Leges Henrici* described as the *tremendum regie majestatis imperium,* the tremendous power of the royal majesty. Away from the heights of legal theory, however, when king or chronicler thought of law and order they were just as likely to think of the sort of justice meted out by the royal judge Ralph Basset at 'Hundehoge' in 1124 when he sentenced forty-four thieves to be hanged and six more to be blinded and castrated.

If the administrative and judicial institutions survived at least as models for future governments, Henry was only too aware that his own authority would die with him. With the passion of a usurper, Henry spent much of his reign trying to guarantee the succession to his territories for his children. In 1115, the Norman barons did homage to his son William; in 1116 the English tenants-in-chief recognised the prince as heir. In 1120, the marriage between William and the daughter of the count of Anjou was designed to provide diplomatic cover in case the king of France intervened on behalf of William Clito. All Henry's schemes, however, drowned with his son off Barfleur on the evening of 25 November 1120 when the White Ship foundered. Well might Henry now have had nightmares. The only remaining grandson of the Conqueror in the male line was William Clito, the implacably hostile son of Henry's elder brother Robert Curthose who was himself still languishing in prison in Cardiff castle. Other candidates included Henry's other nephews, the sons of his sister Adela of Blois, Stephen and Theobald (whose young son had been chosen to tell Henry the terrible news of the White Ship disaster, a task older and stronger men quailed at). Stephen had, before 1120, received substantial grants of English lands and had married the heiress to the county of Boulogne. But this did not signal that Henry wished to make him his heir. Instead, Henry tried to solve the problem by marrying again within two months Adela of Louvain. When it became evident that there would be no children from this marriage, Henry took the gamble of imposing his daughter Matilda, a widow since 1125, as his successor and marrying her to Geoffrey, son of Count Fulk of Anjou. There never had been a Queen Regnant in England, indeed the prevailing literary topos was distinctly hostile to women wielding political power (e.g. Asser's comments on Queen Eadburh of Wessex which were reproduced by William of Malmesbury). Moreover, the Angevin alliance proved widely unpopular in Normandy and, thus, with the greater Anglo-Norman magnates with estates on both sides of the Channel. Henry's predicament was not unique at the time. Both Alfonso VI of Castile and Baldwin II of Jerusalem designated daughters as their heirs, Urraca (1109) and Melisende (1131) respectively. In 1127, and again in 1131 and 1133, the English barons swore allegiance to Matilda who married Geoffrey in 1128. After the death of Clito in 1128, Henry sought to balance rivalry among potential claimants, Stephen and his eldest illegitimate son Robert of Gloucester, by rehabilitating the Beaumont twins. The pivot of Henry's plan was the birth in 1133 and 1134 of Matilda's sons, Henry (the future Henry II) and Geoffrey. Now Henry, apparently a doting grandfather, could see his dynasty's future: more importantly so could the Anglo-Norman barons on whom the succession in reality depended. In the event, Henry's fears were justified. Masterful in life, in death he was powerless.

The failure of Henry's succession plan which led to a civil war which almost destroyed his achievements may prompt questions about his judgement. Certainly, he was perhaps obstinately determined to retain for his heirs all that he had fought for so long to attain. It is difficult, however, to see that any alternative plan would have been any more assured of success. The succession of every monarch between 1066 and 1272, except Richard I's in 1189, was decided by force of arms. Against that political law of nature, Henry I could do little.

Henry was by no means uniformly successful. His two visits to Wales (in 1114 and 1121), for instance, achieved little. Although he reunited the Anglo-Norman realm of his father, he failed to resolve the tensions within Normandy. But if greatness is measured by the size of difficulties overcome, the complexity of problems solved and the constructive methods employed, then Henry has more than a slight claim to greatness. For contemporary ecclesiastical observers, Henry presented a dilemma. Henry of Huntingdon could not decide whether he was 'a tyrant or a true king'. It is inevitably difficult to know much, if any, of the inner personality of medieval kings. They can only be described through their actions. Like many powerful men, Henry attracted stories. From many of these, he emerges as cruel and selfish, distinctly unpleasant. Apart from his nightmares and fear of assassination, he was known to have worried about his health and retained a large number of doctors, including the Spaniard Pedro Alfonso. He was also an enthusiastic patron of hospitals. Of middle-height, broad-chested, stout, with dark hair, Henry could be cheerful: some nervous subjects feared his jocularity more than his sterner moods. Conventionally pious, his spirituality has been described by J. A. Green as being marked by 'almost morbid awareness of sin and repentence'. His intellect was distinguished by curiosity, in the law, in investigating his rights, even in the natural world; at Woodstock, Henry housed a menagerie of exotic animals. Determined, greedy for treasure, food and women, Henry leaves an abiding impression of energy, even in old age. It was entirely in character that his final illness came on him after a hard day's hunting and that his death was hastened by rejecting his doctor's advice by eating lampreys; according to Henry of Huntingdon, a surfeit.

J. A. Green, *The Government of England under Henry I*, 1986.

**ROBERT OF MEULAN, LORD OF MEULAN and BEAUMONT, EARL OF LEICESTER** (1046-1118), was the leading lay adviser to both William II and Henry I. Although in the course of a long public life he amassed extensive estates in England, Normandy and France, Robert was the nearest thing to a king's minister that contemporary circumstances allowed, the more remarkable as his successors as royal lay advisers — with the exception of his own son Robert of Leicester, justiciar to Henry II — tended to come from less exalted ranks of the nobility, men such as the justiciars Ranulf Glanvill, Geoffrey FitzPeter and Hubert de Burgh. Robert's career made a distinctive impression on contemporaries and affords a rare glimpse into how eleventh century politics worked.

The son of a prominent Norman magnate, Roger of Beaumont, Robert made his name by his deeds at his first battle, Hastings. Thereafter, during his father's lifetime, Robert sought his fortune in England. By 1087, he had become one of William I's active *curiales* and held land in England worth a significant but not spectacular £254. In the early 1080s he had inherited the county of Meulan from his maternal uncle but, despite succeeding to his father's Norman lordships a decade later, his interests and loyalties remained Anglo-Norman. Unusually, he faithfully supported all of the first three post-Conquest kings. After spending much of 1087-93 in France securing his inheritance, from 1093 he emerged as William Rufus's closest counsellor, playing a prominent role in the dispute with Anselm and the king's French campaigns.

On the sudden death of Rufus in August 1100, Robert smoothly transferred his allegiance to Henry I. For the last eighteen years of his life, Robert appears as the most frequent witness to the new king's charters, a reflection of his influence.

By 1107 when, perhaps in reward for his part in Henry's acquisition of Normandy, Robert was given the earldom of Leicester, he had become a major landowner in England as well as northern France, with estates especially extensive in the Midlands. While Roger of Salisbury ran the royal administration, centred upon the Treasury and Exchequer, Robert's influence was in politics, diplomacy and the law. Robert played a crucial role in furthering Henry's cause in Normandy 1103-6 and undermining that of the duke, Robert Curthose, with whom Robert of Meulan had long had strained relations. He continued to be closely involved in the dispute with Archbishop Anselm, his prominence recognised by Pope Paschal II who identified Robert by name for excommuniction in 1105. However, Robert was instrumental in securing a compromise with Anselm, finally concluded at Bec in 1106, and in persuading Henry I to stick to the agreement, to moderate church taxes and restore church lands. In 1109, Robert 'with flattery, coaxing and apology' tried to persuade Archbishop Thomas of York to profess obedience to the see of Canterbury, an attempt repeated with Thomas's successor, Thurstan, in 1116.

As a significant Norman lord, wealthy French count and English earl, with experience of public affairs stretching back to the 1060s, Robert was well placed to further his own interests. He established an elaborate, almost quasi-regal administration for his English and continental lands: in England he had his own exchequer, in imitation of the new royal accounting office. At Leicester, he restored the Anglo-Saxon court of Portmanmote, a tribunal of twenty-four, to replace trial by combat. He insisted that his twin sons, Waleran and Robert, both of whom were to play leading political roles in the next generation, received good educations. He was tenacious of his own rights and lands. In 1111, in revenge for an attack on Meulan, he ravaged the French king's capital at Paris causing so much damage that the Ile de la Cité required extensive rebuilding. Ruthless in manipulating his position and the law to acquire new estates, on his deathbed he characteristically refused to restore any lands he had illegally seized. Robert's private life may not have been untroubled. He had married late (c.1096) Isabel of Vermandois who was alleged to have eloped with William of Warenne, whom she subsequently married, before Robert's death. As in contemporary Romances, so in life, infidelity and chivalry could be close companions.

Robert's interest in public affairs and desire to influence royal business, although personally enriching, was not solely self-seeking. To Robert was attributed Henry I's less aggressive, less ostentatious and more conciliatory tone of government, notably towards the church and in the delicate handling of the prickly Norman baronage. William of Malmesbury wrote of Robert as 'the persuader of peace, the dissuader of strife . . . urging his lord the king rigorously to enforce the law; and himself not only abiding by existing laws but proposing new ones'. Not the least of Robert's achievements may have been to temper Henry's notorious personal brutality. Orderic Vitalis, who may well have met Robert, attributed to him a remarkable political testament delivered to Henry I in 1101. This may stand as a blueprint for effective medieval political management which, even if the chronicler's invention, suggests what policies contemporaries associated with Robert.

'We . . . to whom the common utility is committed by Divine Providence, ought to seek after the safety of the kingdom and of the Church of God. Let our chief care be to triumph peacefully without the shedding of Christian blood, and so that our faithful people may live in the serenity of peace . . . Speak gently to all your knights; caress them all as a father does his children; soothe them with promises; grant whatever they might request and in this manner cleverly draw all to your favour . . . do not hesitate to make magnificent promises, as is fitting to royal munificence. It is better to give away a small portion of the kingdom than to lose both victory and life to a host of enemies. And when . . . we have come to the end of this business (withstanding the threat of Robert Curthose), we will suggest useful measures for recovering the demesnes usurped by rash deserters in time of war'.

It is worth noting that the 'useful measures' mentioned included accusations of treason, deprivation of patrimonies and forced exile. As with all successful medieval politicians, Robert of Meulan knew that violence and the threat of violence was the strongest supporter of conciliation.

S. N. Vaughn, *Anselm of Bec and Robert of Meulan*, 1985.

## ROBERT OF BELLEME, EARL OF SHREWSBURY (1052/6-

*c.*1130) was one of the most powerful Anglo-Norman magnates of the second generation after the Conquest. Son of Roger of Montgomery, first earl of Shrewsbury, he had already acquired large estates in Normandy and Maine before his father's death in 1094 when he received, as the elder surviving son, the patrimonial lands in the duchy. In 1098, on the death of his younger brother Hugh, he received the extensive Marcher earldom of Shrewsbury and the family property in Sussex, to which Robert added the Midland fief of Tickhill by purchase and the county of Ponthieu by marriage. He thus controlled lands stretching from the Somme estuary and northern Maine, through Normandy, southern England to the Midlands and into Wales. He personified a Norman 'Empire' linked rather than divided by the Channel. In Rufus's reign he was notorious for two things: his cruelty and interest in military architecture, both useful attributes for a man in his position. If his power was spectacular, so was his fall. Robert had supported Robert Curthose for the English throne in 1088 and, although he had formally accepted Henry I in 1100, retained this loyalty, possibly calculating that his own power would be the greater under the ineffectual Curthose. In 1102, all his English lands were confiscated after an abortive attempt to resist Henry, who, unable to trust Robert, had determined to destroy him. The rest of Robert's political career was spent in Normandy, his opposition to Henry persisting even after Curthose's defeat in 1106. In 1112 Henry lost patience. Robert was arrested and incarcerated, first in Normandy then, from 1113, at Wareham in Dorset. There he spent the rest of his life, hidden from view except for a reference in the Pipe Roll of 1130 to payments for his maintenance and clothing. The wheel of Fortune had come round. His grandfather had been a minor ducal official in Normandy. Through good marriages, the patronage of William the Conqueror and their own predatory instincts, the family had reached the highest rung of the nobility. Their rise had been spotted with blood, of their opponents and subjects; sometimes their own: Robert's mother, Mabel, had been brutally murdered; his brother Hugh killed by a Viking on a raid to Anglesey. The ascent and destruction of Robert's family provides an object lesson in how Anglo-Norman politics worked away from the sanitized niceties of government book-keeping.

**ROGER OF SALISBURY** (*c*.1065/70-1139; bishop of Salisbury 1102-39) was the dominant figure in English royal administration for a generation. As chief financial and judicial minister of Henry I and Stephen for thirty years, he created lasting institutions of central government, notably the Exchequer, and provided a model for the later Chief Justiciars of the Angevin kings. The shadow of 'Roger the Great', as some called him, lies heavy across all descriptions and discussions of the origins of effective departments of state and national bureaucracy. To his admiring great nephew, Richard FitzNeal, in his *Dialogue of the Exchequer* (1179), Roger was 'the chief mover in great matters'; to his modern biographer, he is 'one of England's greatest statesmen'.

Yet the character, mind and motives of this most powerful of ministers of the crown remain elusive. No minutes of meetings or personal correspondence survive, only a small proportion of the official documents issued or received by him. What exists suggests a man of energy, talent and ruthlessness, but also seriousness and resilience. Like a surprising number of English leaders, he was self-made. In his delight in ostentation and power, he was perhaps more of a Wolsey or a Thatcher than a Thomas Cromwell; in venality more a Lloyd George. As with all these, at his plenitude Roger was both innovative and feared; with them, too, his fall was sudden and complete; but, uniquely in this company, Roger's legacy was incontestably durable.

Roger first came to the notice of the future Henry I as a priest from the Avranchin region in south-west Normandy, probably in 1091. According to legend, Roger recommended himself by the speed with which he said Mass. If this story — written a century later — was designed to cast doubt on Roger's vocation, it may have been wide of the mark. It was unusual for ambitious secular clerks of the time to proceed to full Holy Orders so young. There are signs that Roger's spiritual life, while overlaid with secular employment, was neither assumed nor dormant. The chronicler William of Malmesbury, who knew Roger, mentioned his reluctance to stay in royal service after he became a bishop. Although he amassed an awesome fortune, he was not obviously corrupt and claimed he received no formal salary after becoming a bishop. In 1114, he successfully opposed what he regarded as the king's poor choice of candidate for the archbishopric of Canterbury. A cultured man, with interests in education and the arts, throughout his public career Roger was an active patron of Augustinian canons, a new order with a particular mission to the laity and one popular with some of Roger's contemporaries with unimpeachable spiritual credentials. His most notable benefaction was to St. Frideswide's priory in Oxford. At the end of his life, his contrition for harming the interests of certain religious houses appears focused and genuine. No saint, indeed a notorious sinner with an openly acknowledged mistress, Roger was probably a traditionally committed priest, who saw the separation from secular matters and the imperatives of canon law in a rather more relaxed light than the Gregorian reformers around him. Except to the noisy puritans of his day, this did not make him a hypocrite.

However he caught Henry's eye, by 1100 Roger was a chaplain, possibly steward, in his household in Normandy. After Henry's accession in 1100, as the king's chaplain, he began witnessing charters in England. Early in 1101, Roger became Henry's chancellor, in which capacity he used to dictate charters on the king's behalf. His prominence in the chancery was recognised by his appointment as bishop of Salisbury in 1102 (although consecration by Archbishop Anselm had to await the resolution of the dispute over investiture in 1107). His status within the regime as a whole was clearly signalled by a succession of lucrative grants of castles, estates and benefices beyond those attached to his see. Soon his interests stretched across southern England, from London to Wiltshire. Roger's political prominence was notably confirmed in 1106 by the commital to him of the captive Richard Curthose, the king's elder brother, who remained imprisoned in Roger's castle of Devizes for the next twenty years. The bishop's menage at Devizes was bizarre, the eldest son of the Conqueror rubbing shoulders with the bishop's articulate mistress, Matilda of Ramsbury, and their children. Whether they conversed and, if so, what they had to say to each other, is matter for speculation.

By 1109, Roger had advanced to the forefront of royal administration acting in concert with the regent, Queen Matilda, during the king's absences in France. His activities had become primarily judicial (he had acted as a local justiciar at least since 1106) and financial. Here, at the centre of government, Roger established his authority and wielded power, in the phrase of more than one observer, 'second only to the king'. Here, too, he laid the foundations of a system of central fiscal scrutiny and control that survived for centuries.

The pre-Conquest English kings had apparently kept track of what was owed and paid them by means of tallies, sticks notched according to the amounts received and split into two, so that each party held a record. It seems that this system, operated by 1066 at the main royal treasury at Winchester, was *ad hoc*, there being no regular, central audit to scrutinize revenue. After the Conquest, a larger royal demesne; higher demands on expenditure; the introduction of sheriffs' farms; the perceived necessity for accurate accounts of revenue paid and owing; and even, perhaps, the Domesday Survey, prompted the establishment in the 1090s of regular meetings of royal officials to audit receipts, identify debts and settle disputes. It was this central audit that Bishop Roger reorganised and transformed, almost certainly in response to raising the marriage aid for Princess Matilda in 1110. From that year, at the latest, the office of the household which collected levies, assayed receipts, adjudicated complaints and recorded payments, debts and pleas, was known as the Exchequer.

The Exchequer derived its name from the 5' by 10' cloth marked with white columns of an abacus against a black background (so not actually chequered) which covered the table at which the audit was conducted. The use of this visual computer was, with the various methods of checking the number, weight and content of the coins received, designed to establish the Exchequer calculations beyond doubt. It also speeded up the process of demonstrating to the sheriffs whose accounts were being audited the sums, especially deficits, involved. The unimpeachable accuracy of the Exchequer's accounting was essential as much of its business, and most of its importance, depended on its role as a court, where judgements were delivered on the whole range of the king's fiscal affairs, including fines and profits of justice. In a similar move to secure acceptance of decisions, records of the annual audit held at Winchester each Michaelmas were committed to rolls of parchment and stored. The first mention of these so-called Pipe Rolls was in 1114, although only one survives from Roger's career, that of 1130. As in earlier centuries and across Europe, officials were almost automatically suspect, the distinguished contemporary Arabist and astrologer Adelard of Bath accusing England's chief men of violence, 'the magistrates wine lovers and the judges mercenary'. Given this ritualised suspicion, openness and accuracy were at a political as well as financial premium.

The adoption of the abacus as a tool of bureaucracy was no accident. In and around the English court *c*.1100 there was considerable interest in mathematics and computing. Adelard of Bath himself translated Euclid, studied the abacus and computed horoscopes. The Lorrainer, Robert Losinga, bishop of Hereford (1079-95) may have introduced the abacus into England. One of Henry I's prominent sheriffs, Hugh of Buckland (*d.c.*1115), provided administrative information to the author of a treatise on the abacus, Turchil: either of them may have helped devise the Exchequer itself. Another influence was the school where Adelard had taught at Laon in northern France, with its leading *magister*, Anselm, and his brother, the mathematician Ralph, who also wrote on the abacus. To Laon, Roger sent his nephews, Alexander and Nigel, and employed a Laon graduate, Guy of Etampes as master of the school at Salisbury. Whatever else, the Exchequer was introduced by a circle of clerical administrators well abreast of the most recent developments in scholarship. It needed the practical skills of Roger to translate theory of such as Turchil's into a durable instrument of government.

By the early 1120s, Roger's ascendancy was complete. As early as 1113, his authority was described by a suppliant bishop as 'procuration' (*vestra procuratio*) implying control and management. This Roger particularly displayed in matters fiscal and judicial, but his wider political role steadily grew. The deaths of Queen Matilda (1118) and Prince William (1120) left him the sole viceroy in name as he had been before in action. During Henry's absence 1123-26 Roger ruled England, described by one witness as 'guardian' (*provisor*), by himself as *procurator* of the realm. As viceroy, Roger oversaw all aspects of government and issued writs in his own name authorising expenditure or fiscal pardons. In 1124/5 he organised a major reform of the coinage after Henry's troops had complained of the debased content of the money with which they were being paid. Roger's tactics give an insight into the rougher side of twelfth century administration. Ninety-two minters were summoned to Winchester where most were blinded and castrated. By 1124, Roger had also instituted a system of *ad hoc* itinerant justices to hear royal pleas and supervise the activities of sheriffs. In this period Roger demonstrated the efficacy of a more impersonal rule, a model exploited fully after 1154 when the king of England held more extensive lands and interests overseas. Under the Angevins the Exchequer consolidated its position as the pivotal fiscal and judicial institution of royal control over his subjects and provinces; the tactic of itinerant justices was formalised, after 1168, into regular circuits by justices-in-eyre; and the post of viceroy and king's *alter ego* was vested in the office of Chief Justiciar.

In fact Roger's years of power did not win him total security of royal favour. In 1126, on the king's return, Robert Curthose was transferred into the keeping of Robert, earl of Gloucester, Henry's illegitimate son. In 1128-9, a special audit was held by Robert of Gloucester and Brian FitzCount, which uncovered extensive indebtedness among the sheriffs, many of whom had been appointed by Roger a few years earlier. This audit produced a thorough reorganisation of administration, revealed by the unusually full Pipe Roll of 1130. Not only were some of Roger's associates, such as Geoffrey de Clinton, attacked, but the use of Earl Robert and Brian FitzCount to scrutinize administration as well as their findings implied criticism of Roger's management. Roger never again acted as regent.

One explanation for this apparent decline in royal confidence may have lain in Henry's plan to secure the succession for his daughter Matilda and his son-in-law Geoffrey of Anjou. Although Roger swore to uphold this succession in 1127 and 1131, he may have had misgivings: in 1135 he quickly embraced the claim of Henry's nephew Stephen of Blois. Henry's schemes for the succession had been worked out among intimates outside Roger's circle, two of whom, Earl Robert and Brian FitzCount, both strong Matildine partisans, conducted the 1128-9 investigation. Alternatively, this apparent reining in of his authority may have reflected royal unease at Roger's pre-eminence: in 1129 one royal clerk put Roger's name on a charter instead of the king's.

If Roger's power was restricted, he remained administratively indispensible. Throughout his long tenure of high office, he attracted no whiff of scandal or charges of corruption in his conduct of business. Yet, unafraid to enjoy the fruits of office and the patronage of a grateful monarch, Roger built up a powerful temporal position and, with two nephews installed as councillors and bishops (Alexander at Lincoln 1123 and Nigel at Ely 1133), established a unique dynastic influence. He also found time to be an energetic and effective diocesan. His capacity for work was evidently considerable.

If anything, the death of Henry I in 1135 temporarily restored Roger's position. As guardian of the treasury at Winchester and head of the Exchequer, he played a crucial role in supporting Stephen's successful *coup*. His son, Roger, became chancellor and Adelelm, probably another son, acted as the king's treasurer. Yet the appearance of government as a family firm was deceptive. Roger retained his grip on administration, his style as peremptory as ever, as in a writ of 1138: 'On behalf of the king and myself, I order . . .'. But politically, his star was waning. Roger, now ageing, was unable to control the new king's expenditure, the treasure amassed by Henry I being rapidly and disastrously dissipated. This financial failure, over which Roger presided perhaps helplessly, revealed that the main political decisions were being taken by the king and his own close advisers, notably Waleran of Meulan.

It may have been fears of Roger's entrenched power combined with his possible disapproval of the management of affairs that led to Stephen succumbing to Waleran's determination to destroy Roger and his family. It was rumoured that the bishop harboured sympathy for Matilda, although this is circumstantially unlikely. The fall of Roger was encompassed at Oxford in June 1139, when his men were embroiled in a contrived affray, the bishop then being charged with a breach of the king's peace. Roger was personally treated very badly, at one point being committed to a cowshed. His castle of Devizes, defended by his mistress and nephew, Nigel of Ely, surrendered to the king after Stephen had threatened to execute one of Roger's sons. Although Roger and his episcopal nephews were allowed to retain their sees, their goods and property were confiscated. Such was the gigantic size of Roger's treasure, that this may have been one motive for the bankrupt king's actions. To signal the change of ministry, a new royal seal was made.

The charges against Roger were heard in a church council at Winchester, when the king's breach of clerical privilege was also challenged. In the event Roger was neither convicted nor exonerated; he kept his see but the bulk of his possessions and wealth were lost. Out of office, the ailing bishop spent his last months organising restitution for those he had harmed or neglected, especially in the church. It is said that all political careers end in failure; there are few for whom that failure was seemingly so complete. When Roger died in December 1139, his and his family's fortunes were in ruins; the treasury over which he had presided was empty, except for his own wealth which had been pillaged; his country was embarked on civil war; the administration which he had created was disrupted to the point of extinction. Yet for all that, his method of rule and his institutions of government survived to ensure that Roger's legacy was the most constructive of any single royal official in the early middle ages.

E. J. Kealey, *Roger of Salisbury*, 1972.

**GILBERT CRISPIN** (*c.*1045-1117; abbot of Westminster 1085-1117) was one of the distinguished intellectual Norman clerics who came to dominate the English church in the generation after the Conquest. A fellow graduate of Bec and close colleague, pupil and contemporary of Anselm, he combined administrative skills with academic power. A member of the Norman nobility, he owed his preferment in England to Lanfranc, whom he joined at Canterbury in 1079 before being promoted, on the archbishop's advice, to the politically prominent abbacy of Westminster in 1085. In 1092-3, Anselm took refuge with Gilbert to avoid pressure to accept the archbishopric of Canterbury. Throughout Anselm's episcopate (1093-1109), the abbot was a loyal ally.

At Westminster, showing an awareness of history and the need for indigenous legitimacy, Gilbert nurtured the cult of Edward the Confessor, the ceremonial translation of whose relics he supervised in 1102, to the material advantage of the abbey and monks, whose numbers and buildings he extended. His literary work combined historical interests with a command of the latest developments in Anselmian theology of the proof of the existence and nature of God. His *Vita Herluini* (1109-17) was less of a biography of the founder than a history of the foundation of Bec and Lanfranc's career there. In his theological works, in contrast to the abstract thought of his *magister*, Gilbert applied his arguments to specific problems of dogma, such as the number of places available in Heaven or the identity of Mary Magdalen; the religious life (monasticism as the perfection of Christian life or simony); or the superiority of the claims of Christianity over other religions. Gilbert's *Disputatio Judei et Christiani (Debate between a Jew and a Christian c.*1093) was possibly based upon an actual conversation, although the Jew's remarks were clearly adapted to include the latest Anselmian tags, such as the definition of God as 'that than which nothing greater or more sufficient can be thought' from Anselm's *Proslogion*. The *Disputatio* is, however, a sign of a greater realisation of the existence of the non-Christian world only a few years before the First Crusade. In the 1090s there cannot have been many Jews resident in England, although the community in Normandy was well established. Royal patronage and even Gilbert's building programme itself may have attracted Jewish financiers to Westminster. Gilbert later claimed that a Jew had been converted to Christianity by the debate he recorded and had become a monk at Westminster. The *Disputatio* was immensely popular, twenty manuscripts surviving from the twelfth century alone. For Christians it provided a neat, one-sided confirmation of the truth of their religion, at the expense of another. However, parts were translated for the reverse purpose of refuting Christianity by the Jewish Biblical exegete Jacob ben Reuven in *Sefer Milchamot Ha-Shem (Wars of the Lord)* (1170). Gilbert's attempt to prove the existence of God without recourse to Scripture, his *Disputatio Christiani cum Gentili* (*c*.1093), was not successful.

*Works of Gilbert Crispin, abbot of Westminster* ed. A. S. Abulafia and G. R. Evans, 1986.

**EADMER** (*d.c*.1125), a monk of Canterbury and historian, was Boswell to Archbishop Anselm's Dr Johnson. His reputation rests on two works, the *Life of Anselm* and the *Historia Novorum (History of Recent Events)*. The twin objects of Eadmer's devotion were Christ Church Canterbury and Anselm. From 1093, he was Anselm's constant companion. As a member of the archbishop's household, Eadmer accompanied him in exile (1097-1100 and 1103-6), organised his chapel and looked after his collection of relics. From 1093 to 1100, Eadmer kept extensive notes, which Anselm himself corrected before, in 1100, asking Eadmer to destroy his draft history. Eadmer complied to the extent of destroying one copy and not pursuing his account until after Anselm's death in 1109. However, both the *Life* and *Historia* up to 1100 are based on Eadmer's contemporary observations. After 1109, Eadmer revised and completed the *Life*, but, in response to growing criticism of Anselm particularly at Canterbury, he first added two chapters (before 1114), then a whole book (*c*.1122) on Anselm's miracles. His fellow monks had to be convinced of Anselm's sanctity to deflect their unhappiness at his neglect of their communal interests when he was alive. The *Historia* also suffered a change in emphasis after Anselm's death. Although earlier Eadmer may have exaggerated Anselm's importance, he now added two books justifying the claims of Canterbury to primacy over the English church and, in particular, over York. To support his case, he was unafraid to copy into his work forged papal bulls, concocted between 1121 and 1123 by Eadmer's fellow monks. Eadmer went along with the deception even to the extent of inventing a story of how these documents were 'discovered' in an old Gospel book. The special pleading and polemicism of his later years should not obscure Eadmer's achievement as an historian. In the *Life*, his picture of Anselm is vivid, intimate and convincing. To demonstrate

Anselm's character, Eadmer relies on recounting his conversations and table-talk which at least sound authentic. Eadmer resisted the temptation to reduce his hero to a stereotype, although the insistence that Anselm disliked business, when obviously being very good at it over more than half a lifetime, may be taken as, in some part, a formal disclaimer. The *Historia* was probably intended for a wider circulation than the Canterbury community and it still offers unique insight into how the events of the late eleventh century appeared to one well-informed, self-interested audience. Eadmer's other works included lives of three Anglo-Saxon archbishops and, at the request of the monks there, two bishops of Worcester. In 1120, Eadmer had the chance to put his principles into action when he lost the chance of the see of St. Andrew's by insisting on the primacy of Canterbury over Scottish dioceses. As a historian, Eadmer combined Anglo-Saxon biographical traditions (e.g. Asser's *Life of Alfred* or the eleventh century *Lives* of Queen Emma and Edward the Confessor), with the Bec habit of intimate and immediate biographies of community heroes (e.g. Gilbert Crispin's *Life of Herluin*), bound together by his passionate love of his archbishop and his monastery.

R. W. Southern, *St. Anselm and his Biographer*, 1963.
Eadmer, *The Life of St. Anselm*, ed. & trans. R. W. Southern, 1962.

**STEPHEN HARDING** (*d.*1134; abbot of Cîteaux 1108-1133) was one of the founders of the Cistercian Order of monks which led a spiritual and institutional reform of western monasticism in the twelfth century. Originally simply called Harding, he was born at Sherborne (Dorset) where his parents, who were of middling social rank, presented him as an oblate to the cathedral priory. As a monk, Harding soon found the intellectual and spiritual life at Sherborne stifling and he left to find learning and deeper religious experience. He travelled to Scotland and France, where he received a grounding in the Liberal Arts, and, with a fellow Englishman called Peter, he made a pilgrimage to Rome, during which he adopted the name Stephen. On their return from Rome, the two pilgrims entered the recently founded abbey of Molesme in Burgundy. Stephen's search for a purer, stricter form of religious life, although conducted largely on the continent, may have been inspired by reading the works of Bede of Jarrow preserved in the priory library at Sherborne. On their trip to Rome, Stephen and Peter recited the whole of the Psalms every day, as, according to Bede's *Ecclesiastical History*, had the exiled priest Egbert during his *peregrina vita*, a spiritual and physical journey to God. Some of Stephen's later ideas on monastic organisation perhaps show the influence of Bede's *Lives of the Abbots of Monkwearmouth and Jarrow*.

Molesme had been founded c.1075 as a place of seclusion and monastic simplicity, its monks dedicated to following the literal observance of the Rule of St Benedict which in most Benedictine houses had been severely modified and, in the eyes of some, diluted. Stephen rose to be sub-prior. But in 1098, finding that the original ideals were increasingly compromised at Molesme, he joined the abbot Robert and the prior Alberic and eighteen others in seceding from the abbey and establishing a new haven of ascetic perfection in the nearby forest of Cîteaux. Here Stephen was prior under Alberic's abbacy from 1099 to 1108, when he was elected abbot himself. It was Stephen, through his work as abbot and his writings, who established Cîteaux as a model for a fresh sort of Benedictine monasticism and as the centre of a growing family of monasteries, daughter houses linked together by observance and constitution. Although the survival and expansion of the Cistercian Order was secured primarily by St. Bernard who entered Cîteaux in 1112, it was Stephen who established and preserved the early ideals, traditions and rules of the order in his account of the foundation of Cîteaux, the *Exordium Cisterciensis Coenobii* (c.1115) and the *Carta Caritatis* (1114-1119) which laid down details of how the order was to be governed and decreed uniformity of practice and observance.

Many of the innovations of the White Monks, as the Cistercians became known, were institutional. Each Cistercian abbey had to submit to annual visitations by the abbot of their founding house. Every year a general assembly of Cistercian abbots was held at Cîteaux. Any formal control by laymen was prohibited, all lands being held independent of secular obligations.

Within the monasteries, there were to be no servants, the monks being assisted in their work by lay brothers, *conversi.* To facilitate running the often huge monastic estates, monks were allowed to spend nights away from the monastery in farm houses set at a distance from the abbey known as granges. The literal interpretation of the Rule of Benedict, complete with the injunctions to manual labour, was central. Cistercians, to preserve their ideals, sought remote places to build their monasteries, as far as possible outside existing social, political and economic structures. For an order wedded to strict poverty it was ironic that their organisation proved economically efficient and profitable. Much exploitation of marginal and new lands for cultivation, livestock and settlement was generated across Europe by Cistercians. For all the hopes of Stephen Harding and the other founding fathers, many Cistercian abbeys became large propertied corporations scarcely distinguishable from other Benedictine houses, a sobering fate for an order ostensibly dedicated to living lives of poverty and simplicity, 'the world forgetting, by the world forgot'. Within a dozen years of Stephen's death, a White Monk, Bernardo Pignatelli, sat on the throne of St. Peter as Eugenius III. Nevertheless, in their brief prime, to the mid-twelfth century, the Cistercians set a rigorous tone and example for other monks, such as the Cluniacs, to follow.

To Stephen Harding himself may be credited certain essential features of the new order: the strictness of observance; the emphasis on unity and uniformity; monastic independence from outside influence; the emphasis on trying to establish the best texts of the Scriptures; and the tradition that abbots continue to be part of the monastic community and not, as in other Benedictine houses, set apart. Intriguingly, all have Bedan parallels. However, many are the customary baggage of fundmentalists and, whatever their intellectual origins, owed their adoption in no small measure to the personalities of their proponents. What sustained the early Cistercians was their self-belief. Their discipline they interpreted as *caritas,* a form of love for the souls of others. They were unafraid of self-publicity. An account of the coming of the order to England preserved at Fountains Abbey, the English Cistercian house founded in Skeldale in 1133, describes the Cistercian missionaries as 'men of outstanding holiness and perfect religion' who 'had converse with angels', 'by their virtues glorified the monastic name' and 'whose hearts had been touched by God'. Cistercian pride was the pride of self-abnegation and spiritual rectitude: exciting, strenuous, uneasy, impressive and vulnerable. It is a measure of Stephen Harding's achievement that he lived to see his challenging views accepted across western Christendom. By the time infirmity forced him to resign as abbot of Cîteaux in 1133, the year before his death, he was the titular head of an international order, a far cry from the pilgrim who presented himself at Molesme eager to escape to a purer life. Without Stephen's grasp of management and organisation it is hard to imagine the flight to Cîteaux of 1098 as having led to anything more than an actual wilderness.

H. E. J. Cowdrey, 'The English background of Stephen Harding', *Révue Bénédictine*, ci, 1991.

**GEOFFREY DE CLINTON** (*d.*1130/35) was the first named and most prominent of those advisers of Henry I memorably described by Orderic Vitalis as 'men raised from the dust'. Rather than a sociological fact, Orderic was reflecting the resentment of traditional Anglo-Norman oligarchs at Henry's agents who were challenging their provincial hegemony. Clinton provided a prime example of this. In the 1120s he was raised to the position of a major landowner and sheriff in Warwickshire in order to balance the power of Roger, earl of Warwick, who was suspected of sympathies for William Clito. A prominent curial official, who had been witnessing the king's charters since 1108/9, Clinton was a royal chamberlain and treasurer by the mid-1120s and by 1130 had been appointed to hear royal pleas in eighteen counties. What angered those to whose gossip Orderic Vitalis listened was not his place in the king's household, but the estates and consequent social status with which his services were rewarded, including the marriage of his son to one of the earl of Warwick's daughters and the elevation of his brother, Roger, to the see of Coventry in 1129 (reputedly at a cost to Geoffrey of 3,000 marks). The sudden creation of new provincial dynasts was very unsettling for the old. In fact the charge of obscure origins is inaccurate. Clinton came from small landowning stock in the Cotentin. That his elevation was wholly dependent on royal favour was emphasised in 1128 when, the threat from Clito removed by death, Clinton found himself cut down to size by royal charges of treason. Although he cleared himself and retained very extensive property throughout the Midlands, he was never again quite the local force he had been. Nonetheless the establishment of his dynasty and tenants, many coming from the Cotentin, in Warwickshire demonstrated that a forceful monarch could exert more than passing influence on the localities of his realm. The method, however, was not through novel administrative or legal procedures, but through essentially traditional manipulation of tenurial patronage.

J. A. Green, *The Government of England under Henry I*, 1986.

**RALPH d'ESCURES** (*d*.1122; archbishop of Canterbury 1114-22) is one of the more shadowy occupants of the chair of Augustine. The son of a Norman baron, Siegfried d'Escures, Ralph spent all his early career at the abbey of Séez, a monastery patronised by the Montgomery family. Ralph rose from child oblate to abbot (*c*.1089). There he became friendly with fellow abbot, Anselm of Bec. Having fallen out with the violent and irascible Robert of Bellême, Ralph fled to England where he became a familiar figure at court. In 1104, he played a prominent part in the lavish ceremonies surrounding the translation of the relics of St. Cuthbert at Durham. In 1108, Anselm consecrated him bishop of Rochester, in succession to Gundulf, another of Ralph's friends. Ralph was well-educated and eloquent: a number of his homilies survive. He acquired a reputation for wit which — to some eyes — bordered on the frivolous. He may not have taken his monastic vows as solemnly as others, as he spent eight years outside the cloister before becoming a bishop. He was probably good company. This may have been important when, in 1114, he was the magnates' candidate for Canterbury, instead of the king's doctor, the Italian Fabrizio. A member of the Norman baronage himself, Ralph was seen as congenial: he was one of them. As archbishop, much of Ralph's energies were occupied with an increasingly bitter and tortuous contest with the archbishop-elect of York, Thurstan. In 1120, he suffered a stroke, which left him seriously incapacitated and, apparently, very bad-tempered.

**WILLIAM** (1103-1120), the only legitimate son of Henry I, was more famous in death than in life. Through his mother, Matilda, descended from Ethelred the Unready, on him rested his father's dynastic ambition. To secure acceptance of his son's authority and succession, in 1115 and 1116 Henry made the barons of Normandy and England swear homage and fealty to William. Although designation was not unknown in England, such a formal ceremony was unprecedented, a sign of Henry's own sense of vulnerability. In 1118-19, William acted as regent for his absent father before joining him in Normandy where, the following year, he married Matilda, daughter of the count of Anjou and did homage to Louis VI for Normandy. But Henry's schemes came to nothing when, on the evening of 25 November, the White Ship, carrying William back to England, foundered off Barfleur. The prince had embarked late and so missed high tide; both passengers and crew were reported to have been drunk. As a result, the ship was driven hard into a rock in Barfleur harbour revealed by the ebb tide. In the ensuing panic, William was put into a lifeboat, but, seeing his half-sister still on board the stricken vessel, he ordered the boat to return to her rescue, only for it to be capsized by others desperate for rescue. Few if any on board that or any other Norman ship could swim. William, his sister, another illegitimate brother and many prominent courtiers and barons were drowned. Only Berold, a butcher from Rouen, survived to tell the tale — which he did, frequently. The disaster was so horrific in its political, let alone personal, implications, that none dared tell the king: they left it to a boy. By depriving Henry of a legitimate son, or the prospect of a grandson in the male line, the White Ship disaster changed the course of English history. The last fifteen years of Henry I's reign was spent trying, in the event unsuccessfully, to restore an ordered succession to his dominions. More immediately, the drama of the catastrophe was heightened by its unexpectedness. Between 1066 and 1144 there are no reports of any loss of life or even injuries as a result of a shipping accident in the English Channel, and only one reference to a vessel dragging its anchor in port.

Small wonder contemporary monastic chroniclers had a field day in pointing the moral: man proposes; God disposes.

**ROBERT, EARL OF GLOUCESTER** (c.1090-1147) had all the kingly attributes except one: legitimacy. The eldest of Henry I's twenty or so bastards, literate, intelligent, brave, adept at the factional politics of court and a patron of both the church and the arts, Robert had to stand back to watch others compete for the throne, literally so in 1127 when he lost his claim to precedence over his cousin Stephen of Blois when doing homage to his half-sister the Empress Matilda. It was some measure of an increase in orderliness and legal propriety that William the Bastard could inherit a duchy and win a crown, while his grandson, Robert, whose personal credentials were second to none, had to be content with a supporting role.

Under Henry I, Robert was prominent in a party consistently loyal to the king. In 1119, Robert fought at Brémule against the king of France and in 1123 against the Norman rebels; in 1126, he was given custody of his uncle Robert Curthose. Despite acquiescing in Matilda's succession, he still fought against the Angevins on Henry's behalf in the 1130s. Robert's reward was in lands in South Wales and the West Country and the earldom of Gloucester (1122). After Henry's death in 1135, it was not his loyalty to the Empress which swayed him so much as his own self-interest: arguably, his hesitation in deciding where that lay allowed Stephen to grab the throne.

Admired by William of Malmesbury, Robert has traditionally been seen as a noble, chivalrous defender of the hereditary rights of his half-sister. His actions between 1135 and 1139 suggest more selfish motives. His unusual conditional homage to Stephen in 1136 signalled his importance to the new king but it may also have been forced on him by his isolation among the English baronage and the threat to his lands in South-East Wales posed by a Welsh revolt, the crushing of which, it has recently been suggested, may have prompted Robert's literary protégé, Geoffrey of Monmouth, to write his *History of the Kings of Britain*. Although Robert cooperated with Stephen at the siege of Exeter in 1136, he soon became alienated from the new regime, not least because of the favours granted to the Beaumont twins, Waleran of Meulan and Robert of Leicester, old rivals from the court of Henry I. Opposition to the Beaumonts provide a *leitmotif* in the rest of Robert of Gloucester's career, not least in the fighting at Wareham (1138), Worcester (1139) and Tewkesbury (1140).

It was probably the growing influence of Waleran of Meulan in particular that led to Robert distancing himself from the king in Normandy in 1137 and his fears of assassination by the royalist mercenary, William of Ypres. In 1138, the formal break with Stephen occurred, but after the failure of the Angevins to capture Normandy in 1138-9, Robert, perhaps in desperation lest his English estates would be lost, landed at Arundel with Matilda to dispute the English throne. In England, Robert provided the judicious advice, material support and personal charm that Matilda so conspicuously lacked. That she retained followers at all may in part have been the achievement of her gregarious and generous half-brother with his knack for friendship. Although playing the leading military role on the Empress's side, Robert also managed to use the civil war to build an almost impregnable power-base for himself in South-West England, centred on Bristol, a control that the vicissitudes of the wider dynastic struggle did little to challenge. 1141 saw his greatest triumph in the crushing defeat of the king at Lincoln in February, but his victory exposed the vulnerability of his position. Unless he looked after his own interests, he would have no more guarantee of security at an Angevin than at a Blois court. The former suddenly looked a forlorn prospect after the Rout of Winchester in September, where only Robert's personal courage and chivalry secured Matilda's escape at the price of his own capture.

The subsequent exchange of Robert for Stephen inaugurated stalemate, during which Robert consolidated his hold over the South-West (just as his rival Robert of Leicester extended his grip on the Midlands). To the end, Robert was inflexible, not only over the Angevin claim but, more damaging to prospects of civil peace, in harbouring the factional rivalries and grudges of the 1130s. Robert's death in 1147 allowed English magnates to make private accommodations with each other: Robert's own son, William, even married Robert of Leicester's daughter c.1150. It may be no coincidence that only a few months after her faithful defender died, Matilda left England.

If Robert of Gloucester was a vigorous politician, he was also one of the leading literary patrons of his generation. Apparently something of an intellectual himself, eager at quoting Biblical analogies, Robert was the focus of a group of writers which included the historian William of Malmesbury and the historical romancer Geoffrey of Monmouth, writers of secular narrative histories whose interest in the epic past of Britain was presumably shared by their patron. William of Malmesbury's revised *Gesta Regum* was dedicated to him, as was his *Historia Novella* which extensively eulogises the earl. Not only was Robert one of the dedicatees of Geoffrey of Monmouth's *History*, but he circulated copies of it to his monastic foundations and to his friends, including Walter Espec. Inside the nobility's metal helmets and chain mail were men of cultivation and intellectual curiosity. Robert employed mercenaries such as the bestial psychopath Robert FitzHubert; at the same time he fostered a literary genre that captured the imagination of the civilised world.

D. Crouch, 'Robert, earl of Gloucester and the daughter of Zelopheliad', *Journal of Medieval History*, xi, 1975.

**WILLIAM OF CORBEIL** (*d*.1136; archbishop of Canterbury 1123-1136) was the first post-Conquest archbishop of Canterbury not to have been a monk. A scholar, who had studied under the influential Anselm of Laon; a close friend of Anselm of Canterbury; a clerk of Ranulf Flambard (apparently acting as tutor to Flambard's bastards); and canon of Dover, in mid-career William sought a more rigorous religious life as an Augustinian canon, becoming prior of the new foundation of St. Osyth's in Essex. After the death of Archbishop Ralf d'Escures in 1122, William's past as a well-connected secular clerk and his present as a canon regular (*i.e.* living under a rule) commended him as a candidate for Canterbury to Roger of Salisbury who, with royal backing, was eager to appoint someone who was not a monk. As archbishop William proved himself a vigorous reformer. At three councils at Westminster in 1125, 1127 and 1129, decrees were promulgated extending the definition of simony; limiting the number of fees permitted to be collected by clergy; outlawing clerical marriage and fornication; and prohibiting the inheritance of benefices. As most of these measures challenged traditions and appetites, they were widely ignored. William was more effective in resolving the long running dispute with York in Canterbury's favour, helped by some convenient forged documentary evidence. However, William was most notorious in the twelfth century for crowning King Stephen in 1135, in direct contravention of the oath he and the other bishops had sworn to Matilda in 1128. It was this act of perjury — or policy — which probably lay behind Henry of Huntingdon's damning verdict that William could not be praised 'because there is nothing to praise'. This was harsh, as William, although possibly avaricious, led an austere and blameless life, the priority he gave his spiritual and religious commitment being evinced in his Augustinian vocation. He must also have possessed some distinctive qualities of personality to be friends with both the saintly Anselm and worldly Flambard.

SIMEON OF DURHAM (fl. 1100-1150), precentor and monk of Durham Cathedral in the early twelfth century, has had ascribed to him some important historical works. The *Historia Regum*, a compilation of annals, legends and extracts from other historians covering the period from the seventh century to 1129, contains original material for the years 1119-29. It also preserves much of value from earlier sources, including, it has been argued, material collected in the tenth century of especial interest for the history of Northumbria and the claims of the church of York to ecclesiastical independence from Canterbury. The *Historia* is, therefore, potentially a text of great interest and originality for Anglo-Saxon history. Simeon's attribution as author depends on a reference in a later twelfth century manuscript of the *Historia* by which time, in any case, several modifications had been made. To Simeon has also been ascribed, with no more certainty, the *Historia Dunelmensis Ecclesiae (History of the Church of Durham)*, a history of his diocese down to 1096. Even if the authorship of either book cannot be definitively ascertained, they both point to the growing interest in the past in twelfth century monastic communities. Both try to demonstrate the continuity of the traditions and privileges of the community of St. Cuthbert at Durham, despite the reality that monks were only reintroduced there in the late eleventh century after a gap of three centuries or more. In such works the past was pressed into service of the present. Simeon has also been linked, appropriately perhaps, with an account of the Translation of St. Cuthbert in 1104.

A. Gransden, *Historical Writing in England c.550-c.1307*, 1974.

**THURSTAN (OR THURSTIN) OF YORK** (*c.*1070-1140; archbishop of York 1114-40), royal clerk, combative and independent prelate, patron of new religious orders, protector of hermits, and founder of a new diocese, embodied many of the distinctive features of the twelfth century church, not least the capacity for controversy. His early career was conventional. Like so many Anglo-Norman bishops, he came from Bayeux, the son of a priest, Auger, who later became a canon of St. Paul's. Either at Bayeux or at St. Paul's Thurstan became the protégé of Ranulf Flambard, chief minister of William II and bishop of Durham (1099-1128), joining a tight-knit group which dominated government of church and state. From the 1090s, Thurstan rose through the royal chapel, becoming a clerk of William II, chaplain and almoner of Henry I, and, like his father, a canon of St. Paul's. In 1114, he followed many loyal servants of the crown onto the episcopal bench as archbishop of York. (His brother was made bishop of Evreux at much the same time.) Presumably Henry I thought he had placed a dependable ally in the potentially troublesome northern province. If so, he was wrong. To all appearances one of the old school, Thurstan immediately displayed an obstinate legalism in refusing consecration or ordination from the archbishop of Canterbury. From 1114 to 1121, with the support of Popes Paschal II (1099-1118) and Gelasius II (1118-19) and of Flambard (in exile at Bayeux, but technically his leading suffragan), he defied the king's attempts to force his submission to the primacy of Canterbury, spending much of that period in exile. After formally resigning his see in 1116, he was reconsecrated by Calixtus II (1119-24) in 1119. Weakened by the rebellion of 1118-19 and the death of his son in the White Ship disaster, in 1120 Henry I agreed to Thurstan's return. The archbishop was enthroned at York in 1121 and was soon back in favour, conducting royal business. Compromise with Canterbury was reached in 1125, when Pope Honorius II (1124-30) gave the archbishop of Canterbury legatine authority over the whole English church but did not insist on any formal submission by Thurstan.

Thurstan was notable for his personal piety. He protected and lent support to the hermits Godric of Finchale and Christina of Markyate against institutional jealousy and suspicion from the ecclesiastical hierarchy. A patron of the Augustinian canons who established their mission in the north western counties of England, he was instrumental in the consequent establishment of the see of Carlisle whose first bishop he consecrated in 1133. A year before, Thurstan had sanctioned the exodus of monks from St. Mary's, York to found the Cistercian monastery of Fountains on 200 acres the archbishop gave them in Skeldale, near Ripon. Thurstan, as few others, combined religious enthusiasm, political contacts and administrative efficiency. This ensured him an excellent press from contemporaries, particularly Cistercians. His extended contacts with what could be called the eremitic tendency within the church suggests a religious network of some complexity beyond the formal structures of dioceses, monasteries and parishes. A poweful patron, he seems to have possessed a share of the holiness of Anselm and the dogmatism of Becket, but with an eirenic quality all his own. His reputation was further enhanced by his organisation of northern resistance to the Scottish invasion of 1138 which culminated in the English victory at the battle of the Standard. The chaotic divisions which afflicted the see of York after his death are perhaps the true measure of his skill in reconciling northern interests.

D. Nichols, *Thurstan of York*, 1964.

**ORDERIC VITALIS** (1075-1142/3), author of the *Ecclesiastical History of England and Normandy*, was one of the most important chroniclers of the Anglo-Norman empire, a union he embodied in his own life. He was born at Atcham, near Shrewsbury, but spent the whole of his career as a monk at the Norman

abbey of St. Evroul. Orderic's father, Odelerius, was a French-
man who had come to England to increase his fortune with
Roger de Montgomery between 1066 and 1068. His mother was
English and, as must have been common for children of such
mixed marriages, until he was ten Orderic probably knew no
French. His separation from his family in 1085 left its emotional
scars. Over fifty years later Orderic recalled the moment when
his father 'weeping . . . gave me, a weeping child, into the care of
the monk Reginald, and sent me away into exile for love of God,
and never saw me again. And so, a boy of ten, I crossed the English channel and came into Normandy as an exile, unknown to
all, knowing no one.' The habit of sending children away, tenacious in the English upper classes, had, for Odelerius, a positive
justification: 'he promised me that if I became a monk I should
taste of the joys of Heaven with the Innocents after my death.'
St. Evroul provided Orderic with the surroundings, the books,
the time and the incentive to write history, often in his own hand.
The description of him as 'one of the finest calligraphers of his
day', is borne out by his own holograph manuscript of the *Ecclesiastical History* which survives in the Bibliothèque Nationale in
Paris. Orderic began writing history before 1109. The *Ecclesiastical History*, commissioned by the abbot of St. Evroul, was
begun in 1114/15 and completed in 1141. The original scheme
was to include a history of Normandy and the Normans in England to the reign of Henry I. In 1136, he added two books of universal history and, at about the same time, inserted a digest of
earlier Anglo-French history. He also included, at the request of
the monks of Crowland whom he visited in 1115, Lives of their
patron, St. Guthlac (*d.c.*714), and their benefactor, Waltheof
(*d.*1076). Certain passages were revised in 1141. Initially conceived for the community of St. Evroul, as it grew the *Ecclesiastical History* became a history of the Normans for the Normans.
Orderic's main inspiration was Bede's *Ecclesiastical History*, of
which he made his own copy. His researches were extensive:
documents; over fifty literary sources; and oral evidence. St.
Evroul attracted important visitors and Orderic himself travelled in Normandy, England and France gathering material. Safe
in his cloister, Orderic attacked the lax morals of courtiers and
nobles, writing with some objectivity about the Anglo-Norman

kings. Like Bede, he was careful to establish the provenance of his oral information: for example his information on the White Ship disaster (1120) came from the sole survivor, Berold, a butcher from Rouen, who apparently did the rounds of the duchy relating his ordeal to packed houses. Orderic's attitude to the English was understandably equivocal: he attacked the violence and greed of the Norman conquerors; but condemned the English as degenerate and justified the Conquest as providing necessary church reform. Orderic's vision of the secular world is in the mainstream of Christian historigraphy: the wages of sin are death; there is no help in this world even for the most powerful. Thus, in a typically vivid passage, William the Conqueror's naked, abandoned and rotting corpse testifies to the transience of earthly glory. History was didactic, a series of examples to inspire men to reform their lives. Anglo-Norman society gave Orderic plenty of scope.

*The Ecclesiastical History of Orderic Vitalis*, ed. & trans. M. Chibnall, 1969-80.

**WILLIAM OF MALMESBURY** (*c*.1095-*c*.1143) was one of the most distinguished English historians. The twelfth century witnessed a recrudescence of historical writing, stimulated by a general western European revival of learning and by events. On the continent, polemicists on both sides of the Investiture Contest between Pope and Emperor looked to the past to justify present policies. The First Crusade (1096-99) provoked an avalanche of contemporary narratives seeking to place this remarkable episode in a suitably providential frame as new, incontrovertible evidence of God's immanence. In England, although the unique vernacular tradition of historical narrative of the Anglo-Saxon Chronicle had become attenuated after 1066, the Norman Conquest provided a fresh spur to historical investigation. Monks had to justify their privileges; clerics were forced to reassess the insular Christian tradition in the new circumstances of largely foreign leadership; and scholars felt compelled to explain and judge the cataclysm which had overtaken Anglo-Saxon England. William of Malmesbury did all three.

Born of Anglo-Norman parents, William rose from a child

oblate at Malmesbury to be the abbey's librarian and perhaps, in 1140, an unsuccessful candidate for the abbacy. As a historian he regarded himself as successor to Bede of Jarrow (672-735) whose *Ecclesiastical History of the English People* was the greatest and most influential historical work of early medieval England. Like Bede, William was a polymath whose scholarship found its basis in his monastic library. Through his reading, William mastered scripture, the classics, theology, hagiography, civil and canon law. But he did more. A prominent feature of his writing is his use of topography and buildings as evidence. He appears to have travelled widely in England and his *Gesta Pontificum Anglorum* (1125) (*Deeds of the Bishops of the English*) has been described as an ecclesiastical gazetteer. Elsewhere, he points a wider political and moral argument by contrasting the meanness of Anglo-Saxon dwellings with the magnificence of new building by the Normans.

Such an eclectic approach to source material is parallelled by his extensive use of both past and contemporary literary narratives from Suetonius's *Lives of the Caesars*, Bede, and local historical traditions to eleventh and twelfth century authors such as William of Poitiers, William of Jumièges (for the Norman Conquest) and Fulcher of Chartres (on the First Crusade). Unafraid to flaunt his classical learning, his anthology of texts on Roman history, compiled in 1129, survives in a manuscript now in the Bodleian Library, Oxford. William's range embraced on the one hand archival documents (some, it must be said, forgeries, perhaps in the case of evidence on Malmesbury's antiquity concocted by William himself) and on the other a string of Rabelaisian anecdotes of debauchery and self-indulgence.

Part of William's posthumous reputation has depended on his leaving a substantial corpus of different literary works, the first English historian to do so since Bede. In 1125 he completed the first versions of his *Gesta Regum Anglorum*, a history of England from the arrival of the Saxons in the fifth century down to 1120, and the *Gesta Pontificum Anglorum*, a history of the English church to 1125. Between 1135 and 1143 he revised the *Gesta Regum* twice and the *Gesta Pontificum* once; he wrote a hagiographical Life of St. Dunstan, in which he tried to demonstrate the ancient origins of Glastonbury, with the help of some dubious documentary material from Canterbury; and he completed his *De Antiquitate Glastoniensis Ecclesiae* on the origins of Glastonbury Abbey. In the last three years of his life William, by now an embittered and isolated figure at Malmesbury, compiled a *Historia Novella*, an account of recent events 1128-1142, which was probably cut short by his own death

Apart from local corporate pride, William's historical work was centrally concerned to reconcile the histories of pre- and post-conquest England. His position is unusually ambivalent, which makes it more interesting. He wished to preserve the reputations of Anglo-Saxon saints; he called 14 October 1066 'a fatal day'; he stressed the continuity of English history. Yet he also sought to justify the Norman Conquest by condemning the English for sins of the flesh and casual religious observance. Harold II may have been personally brave, but his people were sinful and effeminate: William was always hot in disapproval of long hair and fancy clothes.

Of particular technical interest was William's development of a critical method in handling his sources. For example, he had little time for stories of Arthur, although this may have had as much to do with his dislike of the Welsh as his distrust of Geoffrey of Monmouth's fables. William laid claim to objectivity, although much of his account of 1066 is derived from Norman propaganda and his treatment of the early years of the civil war under Stephen is clearly that of a Matilda partisan. What is notable is that he admitted as much. Although happier in relating past events, his description of his own times in the *Historia Novella* is possibly the more intellectually remarkable, as he had no sources to guide him. Here his central interest in human affairs comes to the fore. More strongly than many medieval historians, William is prepared to speculate on human motive not just Divine judgement. For example, he attributes Urban II's launching of the First Crusade to the pope's 'little known' desire to exploit any political disruption caused by the crusade to win back papal lands in central Italy. Among western writers, this secular analysis of the supreme sacred political event of the age is unique.

But there was another side to William of Malmesbury. Like many another apparently humane Benedictine scholar, he was snobbish; anti-Semitic; a toady to patrons such as Robert of Gloucester, Matilda's chief supporter; a political time-server, as in his mealy-mouthed description of the distinctly unlikeable Henry I; and, for instance in his account of William Rufus, priggish to the point of prurience. But his achievement in restoring an English past to the Anglo-French elite of his day and subsequent generations remains one of the most impressive academic and intellectual feats in twelfth century England.

R. Thomson, *William of Malmesbury*, 1987.
A. Gransden, *Historical Writing in England c.550-c.1307*, 1974.

**WALTER ESPEC** (*d.*1153/58) was a second generation Anglo-Norman landowner who did well out of the reign of Henry I. Probably the son of William Spech (*fl.*1086) from western Normandy, Walter first witnessed royal charters in 1122. Inheriting lands in Bedfordshire, he acquired, possibly from the king, substantial property in Yorkshire, centred upon the castles of Wark and Helmsley. These grants made Walter a leading figure in the north as one of the king's most loyal agents in a potentially troublesome region. By 1130 he was a royal justice in Yorkshire, Northumberland, Carlisle and Westmorland and was responsible for receiving royal income from Yorkshire and the vacant see of Durham. He played a central role during the Scottish invasion of 1138 when his castle at Wark had to withstand a vigorous siege. Although already an old man, he organised and led the northern barons in the victory over the Scots at the Battle of the Standard. His friend Ailred of Rievaulx described Walter as the *dux et pater* of northern barons. Walter was supposed to have delivered a rousing speech before the battle summoning up the fame and traditions of the Normans as a spur to valour. Yet, for all his pride in his Norman ancestry, he was also regarded as a protector by influential English northerners such as Ailred. But Walter was more than soldier and administrator. His most lasting contribution to the north was as a patron of new religious orders. Without surviving children of his own, he used his wealth to found an Augustinian priory at Kirkham (1121), the Savignac monastery at Byland (1138) and the Cistercian house at Rievaulx (1132), as well as another

Cistercian house at Wardon in Bedfordshire (1136). He is most identified with Rievaulx, close to his castle at Helmsley. Rievaulx was the most successful of his foundations, one in which he kept a firm interest, and to which he directed its most famous abbot, Ailred in 1134. Ailred, in return, praised his patron in his account of the battle of the Standard. In the *Relatio*, Walter is described as being tall, with black hair, a full beard, broad features and a loud voice. Whether literate or not (and his official duties make it a possibility), Walter had a genuine enthusiasm for history and its imaginative counterpart the *chansons de geste*. From Robert of Gloucester, he borrowed an early copy of Geoffrey of Monmouth's *History of the Kings of Britain*, perhaps the greatest work of fiction masquerading as history of the middle ages. This Walter almost certainly showed to his neighbour, Ailred of Rievaulx, sometime before 1143. Walter's career touches many important themes of the early twelfth century: the skilful use of patronage to impose royal control across the kingdom; the development of a system of itinerant justices with local ties and central loyalties; and the establishment of the new continental orders of monks in English society. Walter may appear typical, but no cypher. He was, it seems, rather more than a pious thug.

For his role as literary patron,
A. Gransden, *Historical Writing in England c.550-c.1307*, 1974.


**GILBERT OF SEMPRINGHAM** (1083/89-1189), apart from being one of the few probably authentic centenarians of the Middle Ages, was the founder of one of the more unusual new orders of the twelfth century. Of Anglo-Norman parentage, after education in France, Gilbert was presented by his father with the living of Sempringham in Lincolnshire, although he spent most of his time, perhaps as a teacher, in the households of successive bishops of Lincoln, Robert Bloet(1094-1123) and Alexander (1123-48). The latter ordained him. In 1131, he withdrew to Sempringham and built an enclosure next to the parish church to house a group of seven devout women. On the advice of Abbot William of Rievaulx (1132-45), Gilbert added lay

sisters to his embryonic order of nuns. To support this community with agricultural labour and the collection of rents and
dues, Gilbert provided for lay brethren on the Cistercian model.
In 1147, after being refused incorporation by the Cistercians,
Gilbert was authorised by Pope Eugenius III to rule the order
himself and he established a fourth branch of his order, that of
Canons, to act as chaplains. Thus the final constitution of the
order, which Gilbert himself only joined in the 1170s, comprised
nuns, under a Cistercian rule; lay sisters; canons, under the
Augustinian rule, and lay brothers. For lay members, there were
initially very strict rules regarding food and clothing, which
Gilbert had to modify c.1186. The community lived in double
monasteries, divided architecturally. The Gilbertine joint houses
were the first such since the great early Anglo-Saxon monasteries of the seventh century, such as Whitby or Hartlepool.
Gilbert's highly eclectic, not to say eccentric system proved
locally popular. By 1150, three other houses had joined the
order, and it has been estimated that by 1200 there were over
nine hundred nuns and lay sisters and more than five hundred
canons and lay brothers in the order as a whole. Some of the
problems the order encountered were predictable. The different
branches complained of the behaviour of others, the lay brothers being particularly resentful of the canons. With the proximity of the sexes, scandal and rumour were never far away,
although nothing compared to the real life horror of the nun of
Watton (see NUN OF WATTON). Other problems were self-
inflicted, such as the admission of girls to be nuns from the age
of four. Despite the difficulties, the order survived and prospered, playing its part in the economic expansion of England
through the drainage and cultivation of the fens, and in the religious life of the country by the acceptance of the vocation of
pious women. Gilbert's own reputation was unsullied. Despite
his support for Becket, Gilbert was protected by Henry II. Blind
and infirm, he gave up administration of the order in 1178,
although he retained ultimate authority until his death in 1189.
Never an international order, the Gilbertines nonetheless were
evidence of the variety of entrepreneurial opportunities in the
religious as well as secular life provided by an expanding society
and economy.

*The Book of St. Gilbert*, ed. R. Foreville & G. Keir, 1987.

RICHARD OF FOUNTAINS (*d*.1139), the first abbot of the great Cistercian Abbey of Fountains in Yorkshire, presents a revealing example of how the new wave of spirituality associated with the Order of Cîteaux became established; how it differed from existing practices; and how, equally, it grew from traditional monasticism. Richard was prior of St. Mary's, York, a wealthy Benedictine house, under an aged, easy-going abbot, Geoffrey. In 1132, with the help of his friend the ascetic Archbishop Thurstan, patron of hermits and sponsor of the first Cistercian house in the north at Rievaulx, Richard led a schism, not unlike that from Molesme to Cîteaux in 1098. With the example of the white monks recently settled at Rievaulx, and the encouragement of Bernard of Clairvaux, Richard and a few of his fellow monks established a new monastery in Skeldale on land given them by Thurstan. Soon known as Fountains Abbey, this became the leading Cistercian house in Yorkshire and exerted a profound influence throughout the northern province. Richard's departure from St. Mary's was caused by his impatience at the failure there to follow the pristine Rule of St. Benedict, in particular over time for prayer, study and work; silence; and diet. He sought a more eremitic existence. Initially he had hoped to find it in reforming St. Mary's. Only when this was rejected did the archbishop effectively allow him to break his vow of obedience in order to follow a new vocation. Yet in spite of the inter-order polemic that characterised much of the monastic debate in the twelfth century, relations and exchange between Benedictines and Cistercians continued close and frequent, in both directions. It was the logic of institutional inertia; the ties of custom; the responsibilities of possessions; and the wishes of the majority that prevented reform within established houses as much as any burning radical desire by reformers to secede. Richard and his abbey quickly found that they too became part of a not entirely other-worldly organisation. Richard himself died not in Skeldale, but in Rome in 1139 on Archbishop Thurstan's business. His career suggests that the Cistercian démarche was far less a rejection of traditional forms of regular religious life than either the hermit movement of the twelfth century or the friars in the thirteenth.

**ADELARD OF BATH** (*b.c.*1080-after 1151) was one of the most versatile intellectuals of his generation whose interests stretched from falconry to astronomy, from Euclid to magic, from Arabic science to playing the harp. His father was a tenant of the bishop of Bath and Wells and Adelard himself witnessed charters of Bath priory in the early twelfth century. Educated at Tours and familiar with the schools of northern France, by the 1130s he had established contacts at court, perhaps as an astrologer. In the 1140s he wrote a book explaining the use of the astrolabe in predicting the movements of stars and hence the future for the young Henry FitzEmpress. About 1110, Adelard visited southern Italy and Salerno in Sicily and it was probably there that he came into contact with Arabic and Greek learning. Although there is no direct evidence that he could read either language, he is credited with supervising the translation, perhaps by commissioning local scribes, of numerous Arabic works on astronomy and astrology, in particular the astronomical tables of al-Khwarizami (1126). Adelard was also responsible for a Latin version of Euclid's Elements of geometry, a textbook on the abacus, glosses on Boethius's *De Musica* and a book on magic. His book on falconry marks Adelard's social status, a scholar with the background of a country gentleman. His fascination with astronomy, which formed part of the formal academic curriculum of the period, was shared by many of his contemporaries, for example Walcher, prior of Malvern who produced an astronomical treatise *c.*1120 with the help of one of Henry I's many doctors, the converted Spanish Jew Pedro Alfonsi. The abacus was also of wide interest. Introduced into England probably by another learned cleric, Robert Losinga, bishop of Hereford, the abacus was not only of use to mathematicians, but also provided the essential method of computing royal accounts in the newly organised Exchequer at Westminster. In his travels and his translations, Adelard exemplifies the opening up of Europe and the increasingly cosmopolitan nature of academic life in the twelfth century, the precursor to the age of the great international universities. In presenting Arabic and

Greek knowledge to a western audience, Adelard, and others of his and the next generation, enriched and extended traditional classical and christian philosophical and scientific learning. Adelard himself, however, presents a series of contrasts which warn against any facile perception of a new rationality or modernity in his or his contemporaries' thought. On the one hand he had a genuine interest in the natural sciences for their own sake, producing at least two substantial works on the subject, *De eodem et diverso* and *Questiones naturales* based on his acquaintance with Arabic texts. He could write in the spirit of empirical observation: 'Of course God rules the universe, but we may and should enquire into the natural world. The Arabs teach us that'. On the other hand he cast horoscopes, wearing for the purpose a special green cloak and ring. The horoscope he cast for Henry FitzEmpress in 1151 at Bristol still survives in Adelard's own hand in the British Library. This apparent paradox of the scientist magician, the philosopher and mathematician who predicted the future by reading the stars exposes the very distinctive, inclusive approach to knowledge typical of a period before specialis–ation, when knowledge scholars sought to embrace was universal. Reason and divination were thus two aspects of the systematic and comprehensive attempt to understand God's creation and Man's place in it.

C. Burnett (ed.), *Adelard of Bath*, 1987.

**HENRY OF HUNTINGDON**, (?1080s-*c*.1155), archdeacon of Huntingdon wrote the most extensive work of history composed in the reign of King Stephen, the *Historia Anglorum*. Born in Huntingdonshire or Cambridgeshire, Henry spent his career attached to the households of successive bishops of Lincoln, Robert Bloet (1093-1123), who appointed him archdeacon of Huntingdon in 1109, and Alexander (1123-48), nephew of Roger of Salisbury, whose lifestyle was notoriously lavish, and whose contacts with court may have proved valuable to Henry who wrote his history at Alexander's commission. Henry also wrote a number of formal letters, designed for publication, and a collection of miracle stories, both of which he incorporated into the *Historia*. Henry wrote the *Historia* between 1129 and 1154 in a number of volumes and editions which he constantly expanded and revised. From 1130 onwards he was describing contemporary events, different instalments being issued throughout the 1130s and 1140s. His models, however, were Bede and the *Anglo-Saxon Chronicle*. By 1150, a number of copies of the *Historia* were in circulation, at least one in northern England, others at Bec and Mont-Saint-Michel in Normandy. Henry had good contacts. On his visit to Rome with Archbishop Theobald in 1139, he may have taken the opportunity to publicise his own work, for example when he met the Norman historian Robert of Torigni at Bec. The *Historia* was popular and widely used by later historians of the twelfth and thirteenth centuries. This must partly have been due to Henry's good stories and dramatic accounts of fighting, which appealed alike to writers of vernacular historical romance and fiction, such as Geoffrey of Monmouth and Geoffrey Gaimar, and conventional historians, such as William of Newburgh or Roger of Wendover. But Henry was scrupulous in his work, ranging widely for his sources, and copying documents into his text. It is for his stories that he is best remembered: Cnut and the waves and Henry I dying of a surfeit of lampreys first appeared in Henry's *Historia*.

A. Gransden, *Historical Writing in England c.550-c.1307*, 1974.

**ROBERT PULLEN** (*d.*1146) was one of the very few English cardinals in the twelfth century, but his domestic fame rests more with the assertion that he was one of the earliest Masters at the embryonic University of Oxford. The truth is more prosaic. Born in Dorset, he studied theology in northern France before returning to England as an itinerant scholar. By 1133, he was teaching in Exeter, presumably at the cathedral school at which Baldwin of Ford (archbishop of Canterbury 1184-90) was educated, almost certainly after Pullen's time. Between 1133 and 1138/9, Pullen taught Scriptural theology at Oxford and acquired the archdeaconry of Rochester before moving to Paris, where he taught 1139-44. Among his pupils there was John of Salisbury. In 1144, he was summoned to Rome to become papal chancellor. In this position he probably attracted a number of Englishmen to the Papal Curia, including, perhaps, the future

pope, Nicholas Brakespeare. Although highly spoken of by
Bernard of Clairvaux, Pullen remains a shadowy figure. He is
said to have refused a bishopric offered by Henry I: but such
claimed refusals, in all ages, tend to indicate ambition or reputation rather than actual fact. As a scholar, his theological works
follow the critical methods of Abelard, although his own *Sentences of Theology* were soon overtaken by those of Peter Lombard. He evidently gained renown as a teacher, as the Parisian
schools of the early 1140s were not for the second-rate, although
they were, in the aftermath of the recent condemnation of
Abelard, a place for the orthodox. Pullen must have had a reputation for administrative as well as intellectual skills to become
papal chancellor: we know from Bernard of Clairvaux's correspondence that he had influential friends. The significance of his
time in Oxford is clearer. The only previous known Master to
teach in Oxford had been Theobald of Etampes, who seems to
have lectured on the liberal arts from before 1100 to the early
1120s. There was no continuous school at Oxford. Pullen had no
successor until late in the century, the university being a creation
of the early thirteenth not early twelfth century. Many English
towns boasted academic Masters: Northampton, for example,
gaining an earlier reputation for its schools than Oxford. But
Pullen's presence in Oxford coincided with the residence there of
men such as Geoffrey of Monmouth and suggests that the town,
with its many religious foundations, castle and royal palace, was
beginning to be attractive to scholars and their clients.

J. Catto (ed.), *History of the University of Oxford*, vol i, 1984.

STEPHEN OF BLOIS (*c*.1096-1154; king of England 1135-54)
is chiefly remembered as an unsuccessful king whose reign
formed a chaotic interlude between the masterful rule of Henry
I and Henry II. The damning verdict of the Peterborough version
of the *Anglo-Saxon Chronicle* has stuck: 'People said openly
that Christ and his saints slept'. English historians and their
audience prefer strong kings, whatever their cost in terms of misery. For eight and a half centuries Stephen, who eminently failed
to control events, has received short shrift. Yet it is not entirely
obvious that conditions in England, when viewed from a

*Stephen*
(From the obverse of his seal: the king in majesty)

perspective other than that of royal government or hostile and judgemental monastic chroniclers, were markedly worse than under more effective monarchs. Devastation was local, confined to areas most affected by civil war, such as parts of the West Country, or temporary, as in East Anglia during Geoffrey de Mandeville's ravaging of 1144 or the areas affected by Henry FitzEmpress's destructive campaign of 1153. When compared to other parts of Europe, for example Stephen's native northern France where baronial banditry and terrorism were endemic in the early twelfth century, the contrast is less apparent. Stephen was faced with identical problems to those which confronted all new kings in this period: how to secure his position and to manage his kingdom and magnates. His lack of success speaks loudly of the scale of his difficulties and his personal and political incapacity to deal with them. It is less clear that his reign witnessed particular social or political disintegration. What his accession did reinforce was the tradition that the kingdom of the English was reigned over by foreigners: Danes and Norman French in the eleventh century; French in the twelfth and thirteenth; Welsh (of a sort) in the late fifteenth and early sixteenth; Scots in the seventeenth; and varying sorts of Germans ever since. England's place in Europe was never more underlined than in its rule by King Stephen whose previous interest in the realm had been purely tenurial. That he became king at all demonstrates that modern concepts of nationalism, so intrinsic to the medievalists of three and four generations ago, cannot be applied to English politics of the twelfth century.

Stephen was the third son of Stephen, count of Blois and Adela, daughter of William the Conqueror. His forceful mother, widowed in 1102, sent him to be educated at the court of her brother, Henry I of England. Stephen soon became the recipient of regular and lavish grants of titles and lands from his uncle in Normandy and England. By 1113, he was count of Mortain and received the extensive honour of Eye in Suffolk. The following decade saw his holdings extend into at least twenty-one counties. In 1125, he was given the valuable and strategically important county of Boulogne on marrying its heiress. By 1130, his demesne property in England alone amounted to at least 1,339 hides making him one of the richest magnates in the realm.

Although, with the other barons, Stephen had sworn to uphold the rights to Normandy and England of Henry I's sole surviving legitimate child, the Empress Matilda, as the king's nephew and favourite, and supported by an influential faction of barons, he retained a keen interest in the succession. Henry I died on 1 December 1135 at Lyon-la-Forêt in Normandy. Immediately on hearing the news, Stephen crossed from Boulogne to England and, within three weeks, had secured the support of London, Henry's government officials and the church. Recognition by the royal administration based at Winchester under Roger, bishop of Salisbury was crucial as it gave Stephen access to the royal treasure. Stephen was crowned by the archbishop of Canterbury, William of Corbeil, on 22 December 1135.

The speed of Stephen's *coup* took his rivals — Matilda and her husband, Geoffrey of Anjou; Stephen's elder brother, Theobald; and Henry's illegitmate son Robert of Gloucester — off-guard. News of Stephen's coronation ended plans of the Norman barons to offer the duchy to Theobald. Stephen's quick action was reminiscent of Henry I's seizure of the throne in 1100: once the king was crowned the only alternative to acceptance was rebellion and civil war. By May 1136, all the English barons, including Robert of Gloucester, had recognised the *fait accompli*; the Church had been granted a Charter of Liberties as the price for its support; and the hostile King David of Scotland, who himself could have constructed a claim from his direct descent from Ethelred the Unready, had been bought off. But Stephen's success had not been achieved without cost. Whatever he and his ally Hugh Bigod implausibly claimed, he had not been designated king by his uncle, and he did not have the best hereditary right. Internally, his position depended on the forbearance and cooperation of those who had acquiesced in his 'election', even though, as the contemporary chronicler Henry of Huntingdon gloatingly pointed out, such approval meant breaking their oaths to Matilda. Externally, he could hardly expect his cousin and the Angevins to surrender their expectations without a fight. To combat possible disaffection, Stephen was precariously dependent on the support of a few powerful individuals, such as Robert of Gloucester or Stephen's brother, Henry, bishop of Winchester, who had been energetic on his behalf in December 1135.

The new king's vulnerability was emphasised by his inability to prosecute the siege of Exeter (1136) against Baldwin de Redvers because of his troops' lukewarm support and the fiasco of his campaign against Geoffrey of Anjou in Normandy (1137), when his army disintegrated into rival fighting groups of Normans and Flemish mercenaries. The massive treasure left by Henry I was dissipated for little tangible gain. Stephen tried to build a faction of his own to control government centred on the glamorous but feckless Waleran, count of Meulan. Experienced sheriffs were replaced and, in 1139, Roger of Salisbury and his nephews, who had run the royal financial administration for a generation, were crudely ousted from power, and their castles seized. Henry of Winchester, who, as papal legate (1139-43), was effectively head of the English church, was alienated by the appointment of Theobald of Bec as archbishop of Canterbury in 1138. Disenchantment and self-interest in the face of a king who seemed alternately aggressive and inept, led to defections, notably Robert of Gloucester's in 1138. In an attempt to exploit this dissatisfaction, in 1139 Matilda landed at Arundel opening the way to civil war.

Matilda's support came less from those wedded to her hereditary claim than from those who had felt cheated of lands by Henry I or preferment under Stephen, and those whose allegiances were determined by local rivalries or the need to protect their lands. Although enjoying military superiority, Stephen appeared to lack adequate resources or resolve to crush his opponents, whose strength was based around Robert of Gloucester's estates in the West Country. Increasingly the conflict turned on the control of strategic towns and castles, such as Wallingford, Cricklade and Oxford in the Thames valley. The only prospect of a decisive end to the struggle came in 1141. On 2 February, Stephen himself was captured at the battle of Lincoln and imprisoned at Bristol. For a brief moment, the accession of Matilda looked possible, especially when both Henry of Winchester and Waleran of Meulan came over to her side, although the latter only did so to protect his continental possessions from Angevin attack and the former was soon alienated. Matilda's victory was clouded by her boorishness, especially her off-hand treatment of the Londoners which prevented her consecration. Her support remained tentative, and crumbled in the face of a vigorous offensive by Stephen's wife (also called Matilda) and his mercenary commander William of Ypres. In September 1141, Robert of Gloucester was captured at the so-called Rout of Winchester, from which the Empress only narrowly escaped, and was promptly exchanged for Stephen. To signal his rehabilitation (and emphasize a crucial distinction with Matilda), the king attended a legatine council at Westminster in December 1141 at which the legate, Henry of Winchester, and the clergy reaffirmed support for Stephen as the anointed king. Thereafter, neither side established a clear military advantage in England. Matilda's partisans held important castles in the South West and East Anglia, but Stephen secured London, Winchester and the Midlands, improving his position in 1142 by capturing Oxford whence Matilda had to flee by night through the enemy lines across the snow and frozen Thames camouflaged in a white cloak. On the continent, however, Stephen lost ground decisively between 1141 and 1145 as Geoffrey of Anjou completed the conquest of Normandy. This further strained loyalty to Stephen as some, like Waleran of Meulan, were forced to submit to the Angevins to protect their Norman patrimonies.

Relations with the Church, since the arrest of the bishops in 1139, were soured. Personally conventional in his patronage of religious orders such as those of Savigny and Cluny, Stephen was the first English king for centuries to lose control over some major ecclesiastical appointments, such as the election to the archbishopric of York after 1140. He was further undermined by the consistent opposition of Bernard of Clairvaux, the self-appointed and widely acknowledged keeper of the public conscience of Christendom, and his pupil, Pope Eugenius III (1145-1153), both members of the increasingly influential Cistercian order which in 1147 swallowed up the Savigny order. Archbishop Theobald's flight to the council of Rheims (1148), in defiance of a royal prohibition, and his later sympathy for the Angevins confirmed Stephen's weakness. After failing to retain his legateship, Henry of Winchester's authority and ability to deliver ecclesiastical support faded. One damaging political result of the coolness between king and Church was the latter's refusal to crown Stephen's eldest son, Eustace, in his father's lifetime. Stephen and James II are the only post-Conquest monarchs of England to fail to secure the succession of living legitimate sons. Perhaps that is the true measure of Stephen's failure. Even King John did better.

In England, Stephen pursued an erratic course. Anxiously eager to win quick advantage, he cast an essential prerequisite of good lordship, trustworthiness, into doubt. He spectacularly broke his own safe-conducts when he arrested at court the powerful and potentially dangerous magnates Geoffrey de

Mandeville (1143) and Ranulf of Chester (1146) at times when they were professing loyalty to him. Hardly surprisingly they both rebelled as soon as they were released. If Stephen could not be trusted, neither could he be feared as his uncle had been. Although a vigorous campaigner, Stephen lacked ruthlessness; withdrawing from Bristol in 1138; allowing Matilda safe-passage from Arundel to Bristol in 1139; releasing Geoffrey and Ranulf; paying for Matilda's son, Henry's withdrawal from England in 1149. A typical incident occurred in 1152 when Stephen was besieging John Marshal's castle at Newbury. To allow time for a parley, John sent his son William to Stephen's camp as a hostage promising that, during the lull in hostilities, the garrison would not be reinforced. John broke the conditions, but Stephen failed to execute the five-year old William, who thought the whole thing a game, especially as he and the king had played 'knights' (a tournament game played with straw figures) in the royal pavilion. The future regent of England was unlikely to have learnt much statecraft from this encounter, but he later recalled the old king with some affection. Yet in the twelfth as in other centuries, nice people rarely make effective rulers.

By the late 1140s, the civil war had reached stalemate. Despite the death of Robert of Gloucester (1147), the final withdrawal to Normandy of Matilda (1148) and the failure of Henry FitzEmpress's invasion of 1149, final military victory eluded Stephen. However, his grip on most of England seemed secure. Central government continued to work. The chancery seems to have been little affected by the troubles although, with a number of counties outside royal authority, the exchequer operated on a reduced scale. To combat local insecurity and to try to prevent a collapse of law and order, Stephen appointed earls in many counties whose office supplemented existing royal agents, such as the sheriff. However, the weakness of royal power was obvious. Between 1149 and 1153 a series of private treaties were agreed between magnates on opposing sides designed to limit mutual hostility in case of a renewal of the civil war, the most famous being the 'final peace and concord' arranged by Robert of Leicester and Ranulf of Chester. Although these treaties were not, in fact, very effective in keeping the peace, they signal the king's inability to provide justice and a common desire among the barons to protect themselves from unnecessary or excessive damage in the protracted struggle for the throne.

Increasingly this struggle was one Stephen could not win. After 1150, the rival candidate was Matilda's son, Henry, who held unchallenged control of Normandy and, after his father's death in 1151, Anjou and enjoyed the tacit approval of the papacy. In 1153, Henry invaded again and after a deliberately violent campaign in the south and Midlands, the magnates, fearful of the destruction promised by the Angevin's scorched earth tactics, forced each side to negotiate for peace at Wallingford. During the subsequent negotiations, Stephen's son Eustace conveniently died. The final treaty of 1153, accepted in principle at Winchester (in November) and promulgated at Westminster (in December) provided for Stephen to remain king for his lifetime then for Henry to succeed as the hereditary heir of Henry I. Stephen remained active, but king only on sufferance of his successor. He died on 25 October 1154.

The events of Stephen's reign have proved fertile for historical debate and have been interpreted variously as 'feudal' anarchy; a war of succession; and a struggle by the baronage to establish recognised hereditary succession to their fiefs. The causes of the collapse of royal control have been attributed to Stephen's lack of financial resources by 1138; to a baronial desire to maintain or recreate Anglo-Norman unity; to a noble reaction against weak kingship; and to accident. The circumstances of 1135 made civil war almost inevitable and Stephen, his *coup* achieved, failed to master the problems of faction and local baronial disputes. So soft-spoken that, it was alleged, he had a spokesman to address his troops before battle; chivalrous; energetic; by turns foolhardy and indecisive, Stephen, for all his lineage, opportunities and position, appears as rather colourless, unimpressive in an age when personal impressions counted for much. He was no match for the forces which, in order to succeed, he needed to dominate.

R. H. C. Davis, *King Stephen*, 1967.

**MATILDA** (1102-1167), for a few months in 1141, seemed about to become the first queen regnant in English history. Her failure to do so rested as much on her own mistakes as on the deep-seated mysogyny of twelfth century public life. Two of her contemporaries, Urraca of Castile (in 1109) and Melisende of Jerusalem (in 1131) inherited their fathers' crowns, although not without controversy. Matilda's inability to make good her claim may have been predictable, but not inevitable. Her career falls into three periods: marriage to the Holy Roman Emperor (1109-25); heiress and claimant to the Anglo-Norman realm (1127-42); patroness of the inheritance of her son, Henry, in England (1142-48) and Normandy (1148-53). Like all noble heiresses outside the cloister, Matilda's life and actions were defined by men: her father, husbands, rivals, allies and son. Unlike many, however, Matilda played an active role in her own destiny, provoking one contemporary to call her 'a woman of the stock of tyrants'.

The eldest child of Henry I, Matilda received a blue-stocking education, first in England at the cultivated court of her mother, Queen Matilda, then, after 1110 and her betrothal, in Germany by Archbishop Bruno of Trier. This training for a politically influential life was hard, Matilda later recalling being beaten regularly by a terrifying aunt. The marriage alliance with Germany, concluded in 1109, was of considerable diplomatic importance for Henry I, witnessed by the dowry of 10,000 silver marks he offered. Henry stood to gain an ally against the king of France and, equally important to a monarch whose authority rested on *coup d'etat* and military conquest, enhanced status as the emperor's father-in-law. For Matilda, her marriage to Henry V, solemnised in 1114, was a defining moment. Although she survived Henry by over forty years, took another husband, and identified herself with Normandy and England, she retained the title of Empress: her son by her second marriage was known as Henry FitzEmpress. Matilda was no passive consort; she witnessed royal *acta*; channelled petitions to the king; performed as titular regent in Italy (1118-9); corresponded with her father; and, on her husband's death from cancer in 1125, was entrusted with the imperial insignia. On the election of Lothar of Supplinberg as the new king of Germany, Matilda returned to her father, laden with jewels and relics, ready to be groomed for a new, no less exalted position than the one she left behind.

In 1120, Matilda's brother, William, drowned in the White

Ship, leaving her Henry I's sole surviving legitimate child. Although he remarried in 1121 (Matilda's mother having died in 1118), Henry had no more legitimate children, nor, by 1126, as he neared sixty, was he likely to after five years of childless marriage. Henry's choices were limited. His elder brother, Robert, was still in one of his prisons and, unsurprisingly, the king rejected Robert's son, William Clito. Of his own bastards, the eldest, Robert of Gloucester, was suitable in all things except his unacceptability to the church and, increasingly, to a lay baronage whose titles to land rested on legitimacy. Henry had showered lands and honours on his nephew, Stephen of Blois, son of his sister Adela, but more as a means of building up a loyal family block of support for his designated heir rather than as a signal of preference for the inheritance itself. His choice was eased by what he may have seen as his daughter's aptitude for public business. Her training had ensured she had a mind of her own and sufficient, perhaps excessive, self-confidence to act independently. Whatever his emotional attachment (hardly strong in practice as he had scarcely seen her between her ninth and twenty-fourth year), Henry decided that his dynasty was to hold the throne, not those of his siblings.

His decision is explicable in the context of his rise, against expectations, to power through his own initiative and skill. It was also not unique. At precisely the same time, another self-made monarch, Baldwin II of Jerusalem, was facing death with no sons. Like Henry, he settled the succession on a daughter, Melisende. The parallel was hardly coincidental, as the Jerusalem and the Anglo-Norman arrangements were closely linked. To secure Matilda's succession, two things were necessary: her formal acceptance by the magnates and a husband, to provide heirs and military leadership. Henry extracted oaths of allegiance to Matilda in 1127, 1131 and 1133 (and possibly 1128); and in 1128, she was married to Geoffrey of Anjou whose father, Count Fulk, departed immediately after the ceremony to become the consort of Melisende of Jerusalem, leaving Geoffrey as count of Anjou and, thus, a suitable match for Henry I's heir. There was, however, a difference in Baldwin's and Henry's succession settlements: under the former, Fulk became king of Jerusalem on Baldwin's death alongside his wife; Geoffrey was designated no such status, the allegiance sworn to Matilda in 1131 being to her alone. She was to be more than the vessel of the dynasty's continuity.

In fact that continuity was by no means easily secured. Matilda had been reluctant to marry Geoffrey, a decade her junior. The match made good diplomatic sense, protecting Normandy's southern flank and balancing the perennial hostility of Capetian France and the prospective antagonism of Blois. But the Angevins were traditionally suspect to the Norman baronage, with whom, especially with loyalists such as her half-brother Robert and Brian FitzCount, Matilda had forged close political links. Matilda possibly contrasted the status and surroundings of her two husbands. Equally, she had a notoriously sour nature and he a famously shallow one. Despite the urgency to provide Henry I with a grandson, they lived apart between 1129 and 1131 and perhaps only the prospect of the succession to Anjou going to his Jerusalem half-brothers in Palestine (the first of whom was born in 1131) persuaded Geoffrey to a reconciliation. More certain was Henry I's hostility towards Geoffrey which could only be assuaged (and then only partially) by producing the desired heir. Thus a combination of duty and greed led to the births of Henry (1133); Geoffrey (1134) and William (1136).

While Henry I denied his son-in-law any influence in Normandy, still less England, Matilda spent much time at Rouen where her father and his ministers could introduce her to government administration. But Henry's preparations came to nothing after his death in December 1135, his failure to admit Geoffrey into favour being perhaps crucial, as it left the field free for Stephen of Blois's *coup d'etat*. By Easter 1136, only one English tenant-in-chief had not acknowledged Stephen as king, including those most closely associated with Matilda. Her attempts to reverse the decision of 1135-6 were hampered by the fact of Stephen's coronation and anointing; the near-unanimity of secular and ecclesiastical acceptance of his title once he had been crowned; and Geoffrey's lack of interest in England: throughout his marriage his main concern was to further Angevin interests by annexing Normandy.

If Stephen had proved a successful ruler, Matilda's claim

would have languished and lapsed. But a series of mistakes, blunders and defeats, most notably the failure to gain firm control of Normandy in 1137, opened a path for Matilda to contest the throne. Although the Welsh and Scots, whose king, David, was Matilda's maternal uncle, failed to dent Stephen's regime in 1138, dissaffection grew in 1139, encouraging Matilda to assert her rights. Landing in Bristol in September 1139, she attracted the support of former allies, officials and favourites of Henry I, including her half-brothers, Robert of Gloucester and Reginald of Cornwall; Baldwin de Redvers; Miles of Gloucester; Bishop Nigel of Ely and Brian FitzCount. Her followers shared no obvious guiding principle (although political disappointment and the desire for recognised tenurial legitimacy have been suggested) other than loyalty to Henry I's wishes — and self-interest. Matilda's power was confined largely to the west country and her supporters' estates. For most of the next decade, victory or defeat were impractical, as neither Matilda nor Stephen attracted overwhelming baronial backing. The king usually enjoyed majority allegiance, but Matilda's adherents were a powerful, loyal and tight-knit group that could not be destroyed by the royalists. In addition, after 1137 Stephen could not rely on Normandy, which was finally lost to Geoffrey in 1144. Military equilibrium was matched by political *impasse*. There were no grounds for compromise. Either Stephen was king or not: only death or decision of war could alter that.

The stalemate was briefly broken in 1141 after the defeat and capture of Stephen at the battle of Lincoln (February). From his prison at Bristol Stephen released his vassals from their allegiance; his brother, the papal legate Bishop Henry of Winchester, accepted Matilda as 'Lady of the English' in March; Stephen's party began to collapse; Normandy rapidly gave way to Count Geoffrey, who overran the duchy except for some pockets of resistance only finally overcome in 1144. But Matilda's support was fragile. There was a disappointing attendance at an assembly at Winchester intended to confirm her authority (April) which was disrupted by royal partisans who were being rallied by Stephen's wife. More serious was Matilda's failure to secure the surrender of significant garrisons between her and London, notably Wallingford and Windsor. With Kent and

London itself in the hands of royalist sympathisers, Matilda's hopes of coronation at Westminster depended on further appeasement. In June, she bought the adherence of Geoffrey de Mandeville, castellan of the Tower. This allowed her in June to establish herself temporarily at Westminster. Here her high-handedness, arrogance and lack of tact alienated baronial support and infuriated the Londoners. She even managed to fall out with Henry of Blois, on whose continued support she depended for her chance of success. When she haughtily threatened the Londoners with a heavy tax, they attacked Westminster, forcing her to flee unceremoniously to Oxford. A few weeks later, the Rout of Winchester (August), from which Matilda herself barely escaped, reversed the verdict of Lincoln with the capture of Robert of Gloucester. By the end of 1141, after the exchange of prisoners, Stephen was restored and, if anything, Matilda's position was worse than it had been twelve months earlier. Her behaviour, domineering towards allies and vindictive towards opponents, exacerbated doubts as to the suitability of a woman as monarch.

Although remaining the focal point of resistance to Stephen until 1148, Matilda's chance of the throne had gone. A new pattern emerged. After her dramatic escape through enemy lines from Oxford on a snowy winter night in December 1142, Matilda maintained her base at Devizes. The beneficiary of Stephen's political mistakes, such as his ill-judged mistreatment of Ranulf of Chester (1146), she was unable to make headway against secure royalist domination to the east and north. Her pleas for assistance to her husband, who completed the conquest of Normandy in 1144, were ignored. From the moment of his perilous landing in England in November 1142, Matilda's hopes were concentrated on her son, Henry. Increasingly irrelevant to the future of English politics, in 1148, a year after the death of Robert of Gloucester, Matilda settled in Normandy leaving her son to make good his own claim in England. It might have been more prudent for Henry I to have designated his grandson heir in the first place: perhaps his daughter refused to countenance being by-passed; it would have been in character.

The rest of Matilda's life was spent nurturing her son's interests, as viceregent in Normandy and in diplomatic dealings with

Germany and France. To the end of her life, when she attempted to mediate between Henry II and Louis VII of France, she refused to embrace dignified inaction. Perhaps that was one of her problems: against the logic of the times she had insisted on an effective political role as the head of her own party. By doing so, in some eyes she compromised her cause. Her qualities of energy, arrogance, bravery, commendable in a man, were condemned in a woman. In all senses she could not win. Described by contemporary writers as a striking, forceful and unbending woman, her attempts to rule were seen as unfeminine. On the other hand, she successfully retained the loyalty of important English magnates and displayed considerable tenacity in adversity. It was her failure to match this with charm and magnanimity that sealed her fate. Constitutionally, it is hard to see that Matilda represented anything except herself and her family interest. Her eagerness to disinherit Stephen and his heirs of the Honour of Boulogne in 1141 demonstrated she stood for no principle of inheritance or legitimacy. Her career emphasised that, in spite of largely clerically-inspired theories of election and consecration, and the secular lip-service paid to inheritance and designation, royal power depended chiefly on occupancy. This Stephen achieved in 1135-6 and Matilda failed to grasp in 1141. Yet her career was not entirely unsuccessful: all subsequent monarchs of England have been her descendants, not Stephen's.

M. Chibnall, *The Empress Matilda*, 1991.

**DAVID I, KING OF SCOTS** (*c*.1085-1153; king 1124-53) was the sixth son of Malcolm III and his second wife, Margaret, great-grand-daughter of Ethelred the Unready (king of England 978-1016), and sister of Edgar Aetheling who the English legitimists had briefly tried to make king of England in 1066. David's English connections were reinforced by education at Ramsey Abbey and at the court of his brother-in-law, Henry I who had married David's sister Matilda (also known as Edith). In 1113, he further tied himself to English affairs by marrying Matilda, daughter and heiress of Earl Waltheof, in whose right David, already since 1107 earl of Cumbria, became earl of Huntingdon. After his accession in 1124, his English connections had two main repercussions, one on English politics, the other on Scottish. In Scotland, his reign saw an influx of Anglo-Norman lords being granted fiefs, especially in the Lowlands. Royal relations with the nobility were increasingly articulated in vassalic terms familiar to the southerners. At court and in local administration, David's government was penetrated by Anglo-Norman procedures, offices and methods. David's impact on England was twofold, as a prominent baron and as the representative of one branch of English royalty. In 1127 David had sworn to uphold the rights of his niece, Matilda, on whose ostensible behalf he invaded England in 1136, although his more likely object was to secure the earldom of Huntingdon for his eldest son, Henry. His second invasion in 1138 ended in a military catastrophe at the battle of the Standard to rank beside the famous Scottish defeats at Alnwick (1093), Neville's Cross (1346) and Flodden (1513). Despite military failure and the barbarity of his Galloway troops, David managed to extract favourable terms from the weak King Stephen at the Treaty of Carlisle which confirmed David's son Henry as earl of Northumberland. In 1141, David hurried to join Matilda's triumph after the battle of Lincoln, withdrawing hurriedly after her rout at Winchester. During this period, it cannot have been beyond imagination that if the new Anglo-Norman dynasty failed (and between 1128 and 1133 its survival after Henry I hung on his daughter alone), David's claim could have been asserted. It was surely of some significance that Henry FitzEmpress, the future Henry II, chose to be knighted by his Scottish uncle in 1149 as being, in one sense, the senior male of the royal family. It also signalled the end of any lingering dynastic ambitions for David. Away from politics, David was apparently a keen gardener, in particular a fruit-grower who took an interest in improving fruit cultivation by grafting cuttings from one plant onto the stems of others.

**MATILDA OF BOULOGNE** (?1103-1152; queen of England 1135-52; wife of King Stephen) was the daughter of Eustace III, count of Boulogne. Matilda proved herself a vigorous and effective politician in her own right, one of a number of such tough twelfth century bluestockings such as her namesake and rival the Empress Matilda; Eleanor of Aquitaine; or the two Languedoc

Ermengards, of Narbonne and Béziers. As well as being heiress
to one of the more strategic counties of north west Europe and
a large fief centred on Essex, Matilda was closely related to the
kings of Jerusalem, the counts of Flanders, and the kings of
Scotland (Malcolm III was her maternal grandfather). Through
her mother she was a direct descendent of Ethelred the Unready:
through her father, of Charlemagne. Married to Stephen of Blois
in 1125, Matilda brought to her husband spectacular lineage,
significant wealth and a determination and energy which he
often lacked. It was from her county that Stephen launched his
successful coup in 1135. In 1138, Matilda supervised the capture
of Dover castle from the Empress's partisans. The following
year, she negotiated a treaty with her uncle, David I of Scotland.
In 1140, she arranged a marriage alliance with France and discussed the prospects of peace with Robert of Gloucester at a
conference at Bath. In 1141 Matilda's role was crucial for the
survival of Stephen's cause. She rallied his supporters after the
king's defeat and capture at Lincoln; harried diplomatically the
turncoat bishop of Winchester, finally winning him back to
Stephen's side; manipulated the favours of the Londoners
against the Empress; and played an important role in the rout of
the king's enemies at Winchester. The royalist *Gesta Stephani*
admiringly described Matilda as 'a woman of subtlety and a
man's resolution' who 'bore herself with the valour of a man'.
In later years she seems to have concentrated on the prospects of
her children, in particular her son and heir, Eustace. In her vigorous pursuit of her family's interests and her ability to replace
her husband when required, Matilda conformed to a type of
medieval heiress far removed from the blushing, playful, politically neutered objects of contemporary romancers' imagined
devotions.

R. H. C. Davis, *King Stephen*, 1967.

## WALERAN, LORD OF MEULAN, EARL OF WORCESTER

(1104-1166), for a few years at the beginning of Stephen's reign
was possibly the most important man in England after the king.
A descendant of Charlemagne, vain, rash, ambitious and proud,
Waleran's career was one of brilliant failure. The elder of the

twin sons of Robert of Meulan (d.1118), Henry I's chief adviser, Waleran and his brother Robert, later earl of Leicester, were well educated, precocious and spoilt, not least by Henry I. After achieving majority in 1120, Waleran, having received the family lands in Normandy and France, experienced sharp changes of fortune. Eager for martial glory, Waleran rebelled against Henry I in 1123-4 on behalf of William Clito only to be crushingly defeated at the battle of Bourgtheroulde (March 1124). Imprisoned for five years, some of the time in chains, he was suddenly released and restored to high favour in 1129. One reason for this royal *volte face* may have been Henry's desire to balance the court factions as part of his plans for the succession of his daughter Matilda. Another may have been the king's seduction of Waleran's sister, Elizabeth, who subsequently bore one of Henry's twenty or so illegitimate children. Whatever the cause, Waleran's restoration was complete. For the rest of Henry's reign, he and his brother was regularly at court and enjoyed extensive royal patronage. On Henry I's death in 1135, the twins, in return for large grants of land, supported Stephen. With his wide estates and political contacts in northern France, between 1136 and 1139 Waleran played a central role in trying to secure Norman allegiance to Stephen and repelling invasions by the rival Angevin claimants. Created earl of Worcester late in 1138, between 1139 and 1141 Waleran was the leading adherent of the king's party in England, especially after he had engineered the fall of the Justiciar, Roger of Salisbury (in the words of one royal sympathizer, because of 'a furious blaze of envy') and Robert of Gloucester had defected to Matilda. It was probably Waleran who obtained the unexpected appointment of Theobald of Bec as archbishop of Canterbury. In the early years of the civil war, Waleran was vigorous in the king's cause, especially in Worcestershire and Gloucestershire where the fighting was fiercest. 1141 brought disaster. Although fleeing in panic from the royalist defeat at Lincoln in February, Waleran remained loyal to Stephen and stood by Queen Matilda. However, the Angevin advances in Normandy put his French lands in jeopardy. In order to save them, in September 1141, under a truce negotiated by his brother, Waleran changed sides, accepted the claims of the Empress Matilda and left England, never to return. By virtue of his wealth and lineage, Waleran was welcomed by the Angevins, but as Henry FitzEmpress grew to maturity, his influence waned. Absent from France on pilgrimage (1144/5) and crusade (1146-9), after 1150 Waleran was gradually excluded from power in Normandy. His Worcester lands were confiscated in 1153 and, unlike his brother, there was no place for him at Henry II's court after 1154. Thereafter, his sympathies lay increasingly with French rather than Angevin interests. Waleran, an impulsive politician and notable intriguer, was unwilling to compromise self-interest to achieve power. He proved a destructive friend to Stephen by alienating other royal support and, ultimately, ruined himself, brought down by the circumstances of a divided Anglo-Norman state and his own pride. It is revealing that on at least three occasions he described himself as 'by Grace of God count of Meulan', a typical insistence on his own importance and independence that proved fatal to his ambitions. There was another side. Waleran inspired personal devotion; he was loyal and generous; a patron of learning who himself dabbled in Latin verse. On the contemporary scale of values, such attributes commended respect and gained applause.

D. Crouch, *The Beaumont Twins*, 1985.

**ROBERT, EARL OF LEICESTER** (1104-1168) was the younger of the twin sons of Robert of Meulan (*d*.1118), Henry I's chief adviser. While his brother, Waleran, was mercurial, even flashy, Robert was renowned for patience and circumspection. Until the 1140s very much under Waleran's shadow, Robert slowly built up one of the largest baronies in England and a major political position through alliances with other magnates and a growing network of vassals whose loyalty was secured by firm discipline. By 1154, Robert was perhaps the most powerful baron in England as well as being a political veteran whose experience embraced over thirty years. He had also gained a reputation as an administrator, negotiator and lawyer, (in the words of Richard FitzNeal who knew him 'a man of sound judgement, well educated and practised in legal affairs'). Something of an intellectual, his views on royal authority and treason were quoted by John of Salisbury in his *Policraticus* and he himself

wrote on philosophy and astronomy. In 1155, Henry II har-
nassed both Robert's territorial power and his personal talents to
the new regime by appointing him Justiciar, an office which he
held, as the senior partner to Richard de Lucy, until his death.

Under his father's will, Robert received the family lands in
England, including the earldom of Leicester, but in 1121 his marriage to Amice, heiress of Breteuil brought him a strategically
important fief in Normandy. Brought up at Henry I's court, by
the early 1130s, Robert shared in the high favour bestowed on his
family and their connections; he also witnessed fifteen royal
charters between 1130 and 1135, a sign of things to come. With
the death of Henry I and the accession of Stephen, Robert
shared in the heyday of Beaumont power, taking the opportunity
to settle old scores with territorial rivals, such as the Tosnis in
Normandy. In 1139 he helped his brother destroy Roger of Salisbury, receiving from Stephen the city and earldom of Hereford
the following year. Robert's diplomatic skills were exercised in
1141 when he negotiated the division of the family lands so that
he could retain his English estates as a supporter of Stephen and
his brother Waleran his French lands as an adherent of the
Angevins. Although remaining a close associate of King
Stephen, Robert spent much of the rest of the reign securing his
own position. Independent of the king, he formed treaties with
Angevin magnates, such as Ranulf of Chester, in order to reduce
the prospects of damage to his landed interests, especially in the
Midlands. He was notorious for controlling his tenants over
whom he lay the constant threat of disseisin. In 1153, he changed
sides, soon becoming one of Henry FitzEmpress's chief counsellors and having his Norman estates restored.

As Justiciar, he acted as Henry's main adviser at court and his
representative when the king was abroad. Although prominent
in the Becket controversy, he avoided the excommunications of
1166, perhaps because the archbishop saw him as of independent mind, a possible mediator. His duties as Justiciar included
presiding at the Exchequer; carrying out royal writs; overseeing
local royal officials; acting as a judge in hearing major pleas of
the crown; provisioning royal castles and palaces; paying troops
and transporting treasure. Robert was a dominant figure in government and aristocracy, with unrivalled royal confidence and

*Robert of Leicester*
(From his seal)

estates to match, stretching from Wales to East Anglia. Much of the later prestige attached to the Justiciarship derived from Robert's own reputation as a politician of unequalled experience; a royal servant of expertise and a baron of the highest lineage and unsurpassed wealth. Yet sometimes his dual role found him out. In *c.*1167, he had obtained a special writ of exemption from demands on his lands under the Forest Laws. This caused outrage among the old Exchequer hands led by Nigel of Ely who insisted that anyone who sat at the Exchequer possessed *ex-officio* exemption which did not require specific royal approval.

It is one case of many where Earl Robert's first thought was to promote and protect his own property and interests while at the same time serving the king. FitzNeal described Robert as strong-minded and diligent. Henry II recognised his quality and, again in FitzNeal's words, made him 'head not only of the Exchequer, but of the whole kingdom'.

Born to greatness, Robert acquired further greatness by doing well out of the civil war of Stephen's reign and was thus in an unrivalled position to exploit his opportunities when high office was thrust upon him. Robert has been called 'the model of the curial magnate' and his career, taken with those of his father and brother, expose how unrealistic is the historical cliché which pits kings against barons. Medieval realms only operated through intimate cooperation between ruler and the most powerful of the ruled. Such relationships were inevitably at times tense and could degenerate into acrimony and violent confrontation especially if, as under Stephen, the king was a poor manager of men. But such dislocation was the product of mutual dependency not separation of interests. Robert did well out of kings and did well for kings: in him and those like him, we can see how effective medieval government operated to the desired benefit of all involved. Sectional interests as often as not united monarch and magnate as divided them. Twelfth century kings had no option or desire to base their rule on others than the natural leaders of society of whom few were more effective than Robert of Leicester who combined self-interest and loyalty to the material advantage of master and minister alike.

D. Crouch, *The Beaumont Twins,* 1985.
F. J. West, *The Justiciarship in England,* 1966.

**HENRY OF BLOIS** (*c.*1100-1171; abbot of Glastonbury 1126-71; bishop of Winchester 1129-71) was a prince-bishop of a kind familiar in continental Europe, but uncommon in England. Henry was a grandson of William the Conqueror, fourth son of Adela and Count Stephen of Blois. He became a monk at the grand and influential Burgundian monastery of Cluny. In 1126, his uncle, Henry I, secured for him the abbacy of Glastonbury, to which he added the wealthy see of Winchester in 1129, the younger Henry holding the two in plurality for the rest of his life, to the disgust of monastic purists such as the Cistercians. Whatever spiritual lead he gave, Henry was an energetic administrator, his abbey's and see's profits being channelled into lavish building programmes as well as his own capacious pocket. Henry possessed a taste for the finer things of life, but he was also a serious churchman in the Cluniac mould. His political ideal was of an independent church, run by monk-bishops, basking in the protection and cooperation of pious kings and noble patrons who deferred to their spiritual advisers. Heavily criticised by many for his political involvement and worldly machinations, it was nonetheless in keeping with his principles that he was one of the most sympathetic English bishops towards the hounded Becket in the 1160s, earning for himself the saint's praise as 'a wall of Israel'.

Henry was ambitious, for himself, his family and, after his own fashion, the church. In 1135, he was instrumental in securing the English throne for his brother, Stephen, from whom he extracted formal guarantees of the freedoms of the Church (in the so-called Oxford Charter of Liberties 1136). Hopes of a dominant political role were undermined by Stephen's reliance on others, notably the Beaumonts, whose influence ensured the elevation of Abbot Theobald of Bec to the archbishopric of Canterbury in 1138, instead of Henry, who had expected the job. But Henry's good contacts at the papal curia led to his appointment as papal legate in England (1139-43) with jurisdiction even over the archbishop. Henry used his power to effect. After Stephen's brusque arrest of Bishop Roger of Salisbury and his clan, the king was summoned to appear before Henry's legatine court to answer for his actions. Although Henry failed to make any charges stick, the king's recognition of the court's jurisdiction was a significant concession to church authority. The legateship allowed Henry to pursue an independent policy in the civil war, but only to 1143. In his attempt to retain effective control over the English church, he failed; in his political trimming, he attracted opprobrium from the papacy and diehards on both sides of the succession dispute. Throughout the 1140s, his position was precarious, between pope, king and claimant, to each of whom he had been alternately lieutenant and enemy.

*Henry of Blois*
(From an enamel plaque commissioned by the bishop during his lifetime)

In 1140, his attempts at mediation between Stephen and Matilda failed; in 1141, Stephen's defeat at Lincoln forced him to come to terms with Matilda, but her refusal to compromise soon led him back into Stephen's camp, a translation sealed by the royalist victory at the Rout of Winchester. Subsequent loyalty to Stephen was offset by the loss of his legatine commission in 1143 on the death of Innocent II; his ultimate defeat at the hands of the new pope, the Cistercian Eugenius III over his attempt to maintain his protégé and relative William FitzHerbert as archbishop of York; and by the collapse of his plan to elevate

Winchester into an archdiocese to compete with Canterbury. In 1148, he was suspended for failing to attend the papal council at Rheims; yet in 1150, he was attacked at a council in London by Archbishop Theobald for his ultramontane behaviour as legate. As a consequence, Henry had to plead his case personally at the papal curia. However, Henry was nothing if not resilient. In 1153, he played a significant role in arranging acceptable peace terms, finally agreed at Winchester and Westminster.

Despite his part in the Angevin succession, after Henry II confiscated his castles in 1155, Henry withdrew to Cluny for a few years. In Stephen's reign, he had been a considerable secular political force: apart from the castles he built (*e.g.* at Winchester, Farnham and Taunton), he was *de facto* earl of Hampshire. The new reign was characterised by the king's refusal to tolerate any autonomous focus of power. Furthermore, Henry was too compromised by his relationship with Stephen and his prominent place in royal councils in the years Henry FitzEmpress was trying to make good his claim (1142-53). On his return to England (*c.*1158), Henry adopted the role of senior statesman. He continued to attend court. In 1162, he presided over the election of Becket as archbishop; in 1166, he acted as a papal judge delegate in a case of mutinous Gilbertine lay brothers. But his days of power were gone.

His behaviour during the Becket controversy showed that he retained an independent spirit. His contact with Becket may have been of long standing: one source suggests he was party to Becket becoming chancellor in 1155. Henry ordained the new archbishop at his consecration in 1162 and earned Henry II's displeasure by his support for the beleaguered primate at Northampton in 1164. Although he probably disapproved of Becket's extremism, and went along with royal attempts at papal arbitration in 1166-7, he kept in touch with the exile, keeping him informed and financially solvent. On his deathbed in 1171, he rebuked Henry II for his handling of the Becket affair. It is hard to conceive a greater contrast between the suave, urbane and worldly Henry and the intense, dogmatic and tactless martyr. Yet the proud prelate was also a monk. Throughout his career, he had taken sabbaticals at Cluny: his appears to have been more than a vocation of convenience.

But as a Cluniac, he saw it as his duty to influence secular events. Henry's abilities were only little less than his ambitions. It is hard not to think that his mother had chosen the wrong younger son to go into the church: Henry could have made a more formidable monarch than Stephen. As it was, there have been few English bishops to match the elevation and extent of his contacts, the boldness of his political and ecclesiastical aspirations, or the opulent magnificence with which he surrounded himself. His interests were as expansive as his style of living. He collected birds and animals; he may have commissioned some of the finest manuscripts of the so-called Winchester school; he brought international motifs as well as money to the elaborate rebuilding schemes at Glastonbury as well as to his palace at Wolvesey, near Winchester. If he ordered the commemorative enamels which bear his portrait, his taste was as good as it was expensive. He liked large jewels and rings. Contemporaries found it hard to make him out. John of Salisbury preserves a vivid picture of him on a visit to Rome: a quiet, solemn figure, with an unfashionably large beard who, between exchanges of barbed wit with the pope and pleading his case against his ecclesiastical enemies, took the opportunity to purchase a large collection of classical statues.

R. H. C. Davis, *King Stephen,* 1967.
John of Salisbury, *Historia Pontificalis,* ed. M. Chibnall, 1956.

**HERVEY DE GLANVILL** (*fl.*1140-50) was a member of an Anglo-Norman family which had, by 1086, already established itself among the significant landholders in East Anglia, especially Suffolk. Except for two moments in his career, almost nothing is known of Hervey's life. His son, Ranulf, rose to become Henry II's justiciar 1180-89, and a number of other family members achieved royal office. In 1147, he appears as leader of a group of East Anglian crusaders who combined with others from England, Normandy, Flanders and the Rhineland to travel by sea to the Holy Land. At Dartmouth, where the fleet mustered, the leaders of the separate contingents formed a sworn commune, under which they agreed to be ruled in matters of discipline, justice and policy. During their passage along the

Atlantic seaboard, the crusaders were asked to help the king of Portugal capture Lisbon from the Moslems. In the debate over the proposal Hervey's strong appeal to martial honour and the unity of the commune apparently secured agreement. There survives a vivid, eye-witness account of this and the Lisbon campaign, the *De Expugnatione Lyxbonensi,* probably written by a member of Hervey's own entourage. Whether or not Hervey subsequently proceeded to Palestine is unclear, although many of his colleagues did. In 1150, Hervey appears again, at a joint meeting of the shire moots of Norfolk and Suffolk, held at Norwich in the bishop's garden, attended by the king's steward, the bishop of Ely and other East Anglian barons. The case hinged on the rights and immunities of the abbey of Bury St Edmund's which the royal advocates were attempting to set aside in order to prosecute one Hubert and his accomplices. Once again, Hervey's eloquence swayed the meeting, this time, as far as can be ascertained, according to a neutral witness. Hervey pleaded for the traditional jurisdictional independence of the abbey to be upheld against royal encroachment, citing in support of his testimony fifty years' experience of shire court business. As in Portugal a few years before, Hervey stood his ground on precedent and established legal agreements. It has been assumed that the two Herveys, crusader and shire court veteran, are the same man. The eloquence and conservatism of both support this. Furthermore, Hervey's legal interests and skills were inherited by his son Ranulf. However, Hervey's age presents a problem, especially if, as is possible, he was still alive in 1166. Could the crusader have been, as the 1150 evidence requires, about seventy at the youngest? Was he in his fifties when his son Ranulf was born? Hervey, as is the way of public speakers, may have exaggerated his seniority for effect at the shire moot. Alternatively, there were two Hervey de Glanvills, although there is no proof of that either. The sharp focus of the two incidents and the obscurity surrounding them demonstrate the pitfalls awaiting medieval historians. Whether one or two, Hervey de Glanvill nevertheless indicates the complexity of experience in the ranks of the second-rate provincial nobility: military adventure; idealism; horizons at once local and limitless; practical expertise in law as in the management of men or estates.

C. W. David (ed), *De Expugnatione Lyxbonensi*, 1975.
H. M. Cam, 'An East Anglian Shire Moot of Stephen's Reign', *English Historical Review*, xxxix (1924).

**RANULF II EARL OF CHESTER** (before 1100-1153), nicknamed *aux Gernons* (*i.e.* moustaches), played a prominent and vacillating part in the civil war of Stephen's reign, his actions, in common with most of his peers, springing from personal grievance rather than dynastic loyalty or principle. Ranulf's father, Ranulf I, had been granted the earldom of Chester in 1121 after his maternal uncle had drowned in the White Ship disaster (1120) but, in return, had been compelled to surrender Cumberland and his patrimony of Carlisle. The restoration of these lost estates was the mainspring of much of Ranulf II's political life. Inheriting the Chester earldom in 1129, he initially supported Stephen as king after 1135. However, successive treaties between Stephen and King David of Scotland in 1136 and 1139 gave the Scots large tracts of lands in Cumberland coveted by Ranulf who reacted by seizing the town and royal castle at Lincoln in 1140. Stephen retaliated early the following year by driving Ranulf from the town and beseiging the castle. Ranulf now allied with the Empress Matilda in defeating the king at Lincoln in February 1141. Ranulf's association with the Angevin party was cemented by his marriage in 1141 to the daughter of Robert of Gloucester. However, his territorial ambitions were no closer realisation as the king of Scots was also a close ally of Matilda. In 1145, Ranulf was reconciled to Stephen. However, there was no love lost between Ranulf and the king's entourage, many of whom had suffered at his hands. In August 1146, at Northampton, Ranulf was suddenly arrested and put in chains when he refused the king's demand to restore all lands he had taken. He was only released when he surrendered all former royal property, including Lincoln. Stephen's arrest of Ranulf was a public relations disaster. He had broken his oath of reconciliation of 1145 and his own promise of protection, thus detering any more defections from the Angevin faction. Stephen had breached a central tenet of effective medieval rule, that of being a good — *i.e.* fair — lord. In 1149, Ranulf joined Henry FitzEmpress and was reconciled with David of Scotland who, in return for the lavish grant to Ranulf of most of Lancashire, retained Carlisle. But Ranulf was never a party man. His priorities remained centred on his own territorial and dynastic advantage, as shown by his *conventio* with a leading royalist baron Robert of Leicester (1149/53). Under this treaty, the two magnates, independently of their rival liege-lords Stephen and Henry FitzEmpress, agreed to limit any hostilities forced between them by their masters and to protect their respective tenurial positions. Ranulf's career, notorious for his arrest in 1146, is more significant as evidence that the drama of high politics was played against a dense background of baronial competition for rights, lands and inheritances which took precedence over any claims of royalty.

R. H. C. Davis, *King Stephen*, 1967.

**BRIAN FITZCOUNT** (*d*.1147/49) was the son, possibly illegitimate, of Alan Fergant, count of Brittany. Brian, with a number of other Bretons, found favour at the court of Henry I, who knighted him. By 1114, Brian appears as a witness to royal charters and rose to become one of the king's constables. By 1119, marriage had brought him the rich and strategically vital honour of Wallingford and royal grant the no less important Marcher lordship of Abergavenny. One of Henry's intimate circle, in 1127 he played a leading role in securing Matilda's marriage to Geoffry of Anjou. At about the same time, he and the king's bastard son, Robert of Gloucester, conducted a special audit of the exchequer. Although he recognised Stephen in 1136, he declared for Matilda as soon as she had landed to stake her claim to the throne in 1139. Thereafter, his loyalty never wavered, even though, as castellan of a stronghold surrounded by enemies, his estates were ravaged and he lost the fortune he had amassed as a protégé of Henry I. He was an unusually articulate supporter of Matilda's cause. Around 1143, he wrote or dictated a stinging rebuke to the vascillating bishop of Winchester on the virtues of consistency. From this letter something of the authentic voice of a twelfth century nobleman may be caught, in his concern for the destruction of his crops; in his respect of the First Crusaders as models not of piety but of honour; and in his robust impatience with clerical casuistry. In response to the bishop's injunction to remember the fate of Lot's wife and not look back to the past and the oath to Matilda, Brian's letter spat: 'as for Lot and his wife, I never saw them not knew them or their city, nor were they alive at the same time (as me)'. Whatever this may reveal of laymen's grasp of Scripture, it certainly suggests irritation with donnish pretentiousness. Brian was also the author, probably by dictation, of a book or pamphlet in which he set out the validity of Matilda's claim. Brian's career, royal poodle to principled rebel, suggests the image of the barons of Stephen's reign as self-seeking boors is flawed. In common with contemporaries such as Robert of Gloucester and Walter Espec, Brian was intelligent and thoughtful, as capable of expressing ideas as of leading a charge or counting profits.

H. W. C. Davis, 'Henry of Blois and Brian FitzCount', *English Historical Review*, xxv, 1910.

**MILES OF GLOUCESTER** (*c*.1100-1143) was a leading protagonist in Matilda's attempt to win the English throne. Sometimes regarded as one of Henry I's 'new men', Miles was the hereditary sheriff of Gloucestershire and castellan of Gloucester, position first acquired by his grandfather, Roger of Pitres, in the reign of William the Conqueror. Miles succeeded his father, Walter, sometime before 1126. By marriage, he secured the Welsh lordship of Brecknock and from Matilda in 1141-2 the sub-tenancy of Abergavenny. His power in the west was consolidated by his acting as local justiciar. Loyal to Henry I, he nevertheless soon recognised Stephen and by Easter 1136 was acting as his constable. Miles remained close to Stephen in the early years of the reign, playing an important role in the supression of the Welsh rising of 1136.

In 1139, however, he joined Matilda almost as soon as she landed. Given the adherence to Matilda of Miles's more powerful neighbour, Robert of Gloucester, this change of allegiance may have been prompted by self-preservation as much as legitimist devotion. Whatever his motives, Miles proved one of Matilda's most effective commanders: in 1139 alone he secured Gloucester and Hereford; relieved Wallingford and sacked Worcester. In 1141, however, he only managed to flee the Rout of

Winchester by abandoning his weapons and stripping off all his armour so that he arrived at Gloucester 'weary, half-naked and alone'. Earlier that year, at the height of her power, Matilda had created Miles earl of Hereford, confirming his position as a sort of military viceroy in the southern Marches. One of his duties was to raise finance for Matilda's campaigns, but he encountered stern opposition when he attempted to tax the church. Even though supported by Gilbert Foliot, then abbot of Gloucester and his protégé, Miles was placed under an interdict by Robert of Béthune, bishop of Hereford. Such fiscal expedients, common to both sides in a civil war, no doubt played a part in colouring the gloomy and hostile tone of ecclesiastical commentators on the conflict. Few issues aroused the moral indignation of medieval established clergy more certainly than heavy financial exactions levied on their institutions. Miles himself came to an unfortunate end, accidentally shot dead by one of his companions when out hunting in the Forest of Dean, an accident eerily reminiscent of the death of William II.

Despite his apparent fickelness, Miles was far from being a representative of any so-called 'feudal anarchy'. His local authority depended on his maintenance of a combination of public justice, royal favour and private acquisition of land; thus did he calculate his political advantage. Once decided, he seems to have acted with conspicuous loyalty. Nearly the last thing he, or his fellow magnates, wanted was a baronial free-for-all with its promise of the last thing they wanted: loss of estates and titles.

D. Walker, 'Miles of Gloucester', *Bristol and Gloucester Archeological Society,* 1958-9.

**GEOFFREY DE MANDEVILLE** (*d.*1141) has been regarded as the archtype of the violent, factious, self-interested and venal magnate, the overmighty subject who took advantage of a weak monarchy to indulge his private ambitions, sell his loyalty to the highest bidder and provoke 'feudal' anarchy. To generations of historians wedded to the idea that firm central authority was 'good' and baronial autonomy was 'bad', Geoffrey represented all that was reactionary and regressive in medieval England, a warning of the disintegration of the realm which might have occurred but for the stern yet beneficent rule of Henry I, Henry II and Edward I. More recently the disapproval of J. H. Round has given way to a more sympathetic and realistic view, championed by R. H. C. Davis, of a baron whose family tradition of royal favour and service was compromised by the strains and contradictory pressures of civil war; whose especial difficulties were the result less of inherent anarchic tendencies than of the uniquely important strategic position of his lands and castles.

Before Stephen created him earl of Essex in 1140, Geoffrey, like his father before him, had been sheriff of Essex and castellan of the Tower of London. He also possessed castles at Saffron Walden and Pleshey (both in Essex) as well as extensive lands strung across the Home Counties north of London. Inevitably, in the crisis of 1141 and the struggle for London, Geoffrey was pivotal. Far from the cynical, ruthless turncoat of tradition, Geoffrey, while exploiting the situation for advantage, leant towards loyalty to Stephen, only reluctantly and briefly entering into Matilda's allegiance after the king's capture at Lincoln. Despite his public support, and Matilda's confirmation of his possessions, the Empress failed to secure control of London. By September 1141, before the Rout of Winchester restored the royalist cause, Geoffrey was back on the king's side. With Stephen in prison, accommodation with Matilda had been prudent and inevitable, but, in common with others, Geoffrey found Matilda less than congenial and reverted to his original loyalty: hardly the actions of a mercenary thug with eyes only for his main chance.

Geoffrey was able to extract a very high price, Stephen confirming him as keeper of the Tower of London and justicar and sheriff of London, Middlesex, Essex and Hertfordshire in hereditary right ('and his heirs after him' the charter reads). In effect, Stephen was contemplating granting away from the crown, apparently permanently, the most important castle in the kingdom and authority over four shires closest to the seat of government. Such a hereditary grant was a measure of the precarious or naive nature of Stephen's regime as it implied, in the words of M. T. Clanchy, that 'the English monarchy . . . would have ceased to exist as an effective government'. Perhaps Stephen, understandably, had no great faith in the durability of political alliances or the agreements made to secure them. In 1143 Geoffrey was suddenly arrested by the king and forced to hand over all his castles. A pro-Stephen chronicle, the *Gesta Stephani*, hints that he was contemplating going over to the Empress, but this is unlikely. A more probable explanation is Stephen's lingering outrage at Geoffrey's detention in the Tower in 1141 of his daughter-in-law, Constance of France and his unease at Geoffrey's power.

In response, Geoffrey rebelled, launching a vicious campaign of ravaging in the Fens and East Anglia, attracting excommunication for his seizure of Ramsey Abbey, which he used as a base. Geoffrey now fought for himself, with ferocity born of betrayal and isolation. Noted for his shrewdness, courage, firmness of purpose, skill in war, as well as savagery, Geoffrey was as much a victim of the collapse of political order as its instigator. He was mortally wounded in the siege of Burwell, dying on 16 September 1144. His final mistake, apart from taking off his helmet and being wounded in the head by an arrow, was to be perceived as a persecutor of the church. His reputation paid dear for his attack on Ramsey. More widely, the last phase of his career helped establish the conventional view of the misery and chaos of Stephen's reign. It was at Peterborough Abbey, near to Ramsey and the scenes of Geoffrey's final mayhem, that the most famous and lurid account of these years was written, words which condemned a whole reign as a time when 'men said openly that Christ and his saints slept'. If true, Geoffrey, for all his grasping nature, suffered in their neglect as much as any.

R. H. C. Davis, 'What Happened in Stephen's Reign', *English Historical Review,* lxxix, 1964.

**GEOFFREY OF MONMOUTH** (*d.*1154/5) was the author of the *Historia Regum Britanniae (History of the Kings of Britain)*, one of the most popular and influential secular works of the Middle Ages. Purporting to recount the history of the British from pre-Roman to Saxon times, the *Historia* invented a Celtic past which exerted a tenacious hold on subsequent generations with stories of Cymbeline, Gorboduc, Old King Cole, Lear,

Merlin and, most famously, King Arthur. Geoffrey's *Historia* inspired a new genre of vernacular romantic fiction, in verse and prose, the so-called 'Matter of Britain', adding a new dimension to the collective imagination of western Europe.

Geoffrey came from the Monmouth area, possibly of Breton origin. By 1129, he was in Oxford where, until 1149, he was a secular canon of St George-in-the-Castle, which was then absorbed by Osney Abbey. He may have done some teaching, as he is occasionally referred to at this time as *magister*. In 1151 he was elected bishop of St Asaph's, being consecrated the following year, although he never visited his diocese. He witnessed the peace treaty of Winchester between Stephen and Henry FitzEmpress in 1153, the only Welsh bishop to do so, recognition, perhaps, of his contacts with leaders of the Angevin party. He died soon after.

Geoffrey's literary works date from his time in Oxford. The *Prophetie Merlini* (before 1135), dedicated to Bishop Alexander of Lincoln (in whose diocese Oxford lay), was a collection of prophecies, allusive to the point of obscurity, of a sort popular throughout the Middle Ages. Geoffrey claimed the *Prophetie* were copied from a British verse version of prophecies delivered by Merlin to King Vortigern in the fifth century. Spurious authenticity and provenance was a hallmark of Geoffrey's work and not only followed medieval convention (often fully justified) to disclaim originality, but also supported the fiction. Merlin was again pressed into service after 1148 in a verse *Vita Merlini*, a collation of legend, false history, philosophy and astrology, probably aimed at an educated audience.

The *Historia Regum Britanniae* was begun before 1135 and finished in 1138. Geoffrey insisted it was based on an ancient Breton book shown him by an Oxford colleague, Archdeacon Walter of Coutances. There is no evidence this was true. There are two Latin Breton texts with narratives similar to parts of the *Historia* which may pre-date it, but probably do not. In fact, Geoffrey used Gildas, Bede, Nennius's *Historia Brittonum*, classical Latin literature, genealogies, possibly Welsh and Breton legends, and folklore on the origins of places. Above all, Geoffrey used his own imagination. The achievement was remarkable, from the sustained narrative of events in a legendary history of many centuries, through the weaving of the fiction into existing knowledge, to the ingenious use of phoney etymology to support his inventions (thus King Lud, founder of London; king Cole, founder of Colchester). Geoffrey's fame is that of a creative artist not a historian. As history, the *Historia* is worthless. From Russia to Italy, the twelfth century saw histories written or invented to legitimise present political circumstances or aspirations. None had the literary and cultural impact of the *Historia*, nor were as creative or original.

Circulation was rapid; its impact immediate. Geoffrey wrote three separate dedications: to Robert, earl of Gloucester; Robert and Waleran, count of Meulan; and Robert and King Stephen, *i.e.* the three most powerful men in the kingdom. This cultivation of the great helped circulation. One copy was borrowed from Robert of Gloucester by Walter Espec. He showed it to Ailred of Rievaulx, and then passed it on to Ralph FitzGilbert, the patron of the vernacular poet Geoffrey Gaimar who, by 1140, had incorporated Geoffrey's work into his popular *L'Estoire des Engleis*. Another copy found its way to the Norman abbey of Bec by the beginning of 1139, where it was seen by the English historian Henry of Huntingdon, who was asked why his *Historia Anglorum* ignored the British past revealed by Geoffrey. Few books have changed received perceptions of the past so quickly and radically.

Why did Geoffrey write such an elaborate pseudo-history? There is an element of parody of established contemporary historians of England's past, William of Malmesbury and Henry of Huntingdon. There was, too, a positive purpose, to provide Britain with a heroic and distinguished past. It is unclear, however, whether this was a backhanded compliment to the Normans as conquerors of most of Britain, including parts of Wales or, as some have argued, a reaction to the French habit of denigrating the Welsh in general and to the unsuccessful Welsh revolt of 1136/7 in particular. Was Geoffrey, the well-connected Oxford *littérateur*, indulging in covert sedition at the expense of his patrons? Were his creations, Merlin and Arthur, the first heroes of Welsh nationalism? If so, they were soon transmuted into central figures in the chivalric traditions of north-west Europe: Celtic warriors into French knights.

Whatever his intentions, Geoffrey of Monmouth invented, in Arthur, a figure to match the greatest epic heroes. His alternative fantasy history gained almost universal acceptance. It troubled Henry of Huntingdon, aroused the disapproval of Ailred of Rievaulx. Some, like William of Newburgh dismissed it as impudent lies. Significantly, Geoffrey's fellow countryman, Gerald of Wales, was also sceptical. They were isolated voices. Within a generation, Arthurian romances by poets such as Chrétien de Troyes had become all the rage. It is even possible that a passage from the *Historia* indirectly influenced one of the most renowned clauses in *Magna Carta,* no 12 on the levying of scutages or aids, by providing the inspiration for the phrase 'unless by the common counsel of our kingdom'. In 1301, Edward I even cited Geoffrey in refutation of papal claims to jurisdiction over Scotland. Geoffrey's protean creation pervaded the mentality of the west. He remains particularly what he called himself: 'Galfridus Arturus'; Geoffrey the Arthur man.

*Historia Regum Britanniae,* vol i, ed. N. Wright, 1985.

**WILLIAM OF NORWICH** (1132/3-1144) was an apprentice leather worker in Norwich whose unexplained murder provoked the first accusations of ritual killing of Christians by Jews and was the excuse for the creation of a cult which lasted until the Reformation. The charges against the Jews were not immediate on the discovery of William's body in a wood on the outskirts of Norwich, but his family, especially his uncle, a priest called Godwin, soon concocted a case for the Cathedral authorities. Unnamed Jews were accused of kidnapping William and torturing him before crucifying the boy on Good Friday. The elements of blasphemy and ritual slaying, long part of medieval Christendom's myths about Judaism, were a potent mixture. There is not a shred of evidence to support the family's claims. The Jewish community in Norwich, there under the protection of the French authorities, was of very recent import. The growing prosperity of the third wealthiest town in England may have increased their business in providing financial services. Resentment, and the initial popularity of the cult, seems to have come from those with modest means, urban artisans who, perhaps for the first time, were sufficiently well-off to get into debt. Whatever social or economic tensions the slanders concealed, the cult itself was manufactured by three people: Godwin; William Turbe, prior of Norwich, then bishop 1146-74; and Thomas of Monmouth, who took over from Godwin as the cult's manager in 1150. Thomas supervised numerous translations of the pathetic corpse which, on one occasion, he relieved of some teeth for his private relic collection. In 1173, he composed the *Life and Miracles of St William*. The desire of the Norwich monks for an attractive cult of their own was as powerful as their anti-semitism. In the early years the pilgrims who received the saint's cures were very local, although by the time Thomas wrote the *Life*, the novelty had worn off in the immediate neighbourhood. The cult survived until the 1530s. The story of young William's killing was copied repeatedly, most famously in the events leading to the grisly pogrom surrounding the supposed martyrdom of nine-year-old Hugh of Lincoln in 1255. Chaucer's Prioress's Tale is very similar. The corruption of innocence made it an attractive literary device. More sinisterly, the cynical exploitation of an obscure tragedy set a pattern for self-righteous prejudice which increased as Jewish communities spread across Angevin England. The intolerance towards the Jews may have been fed by ignorance and a fear born of the endless repetition in words and images of the Passion and Crucifixion. But the outbreaks of anti-semitic violence, notably the massacres of Lent 1190 in Stamford, King's Lynn and York, were rarely spontaneous. Like the cult of St William, they were concerted expressions less of religious zeal than of secular antagonism for which horror stories such as the one invented by Godwin and his relations in Norwich in 1144 provided convenient fuel.

R. Finucane, *Miracles and Pilgrims,* 1977.

**WULFRIC OF HASELBURY** (*c.*1090-1155), a parish priest in Wiltshire turned anchorite, lived in a small cell attached to the parish church of Haselbury Plucknett (Wiltshire) for thirty years from 1125 until his death. In the 1180s Prior John of the Cistercian house at Ford wrote an admiring biography which allows sharp insights into the function of a holy man in twelfth century society. The central feature was the most obvious. By virtue of being restricted to his cell or the adjacent parish church and his extreme religious exercises, such as praying all night in the church or even in a tub of cold water, Wulfric was dissociated from the world. He was thought of as neutral in the social tensions of an economically prosperous and expanding locality, but powerful through his personal relationship with God. In fact, Wulfric had an unrivalled network of local information and gossip and a keen self-interest which showed itself in his lethal habit of cursing his enemies — from mice to men — who tended to drop dead on demand. A combination of a one-man Citizen's Advice Bureau, consultant psychologist and local ombudsman, Wulfric established his credentials as social arbitor, prophet and healer by results, for which he was financially rewarded by grateful clients. He amassed wealth, which he used to distribute alms and endow monasteries. Although his food came from the Cluniac house of Montacute, Wulfric was particularly close to the Cistercians for whom he conducted recruitment interviews. It was this connection which probably explains John of Ford's enthusiasm. Wulfric's education and knowledge of French allowed him to upstage the parish priest in dealings with the aristocracy, and thus provided an important and seemingly dispassionate link between social groups. Having apparently opted out of the secular and ecclesiastical rat race, Wulfric acquired considerable power, certainly more than if he had remained a parish priest. With his wide contacts, energetic servant, full-time scribe and full treasure chest, Wulfric was running a profitable business under the guise — genuine or not — of simplicity and self-abnegation. His wealth included livestock, gold, silver and expensive textiles. His advice, especially medical, was often common sense, but it was authoritative and acceptable from a man uniquely placed to resolve local disputes and negotiate with external forces such as landlords, other villages and God. Wulfric's curses and manipulation of gossip reveal a nastily vindictive, neurotic personality for whom less restricted or contrived contact with the outside world might have proved disastrous. His proclaimed purpose was moral improvement of his fellow men. To this end he acted as a relief agency. An unusual entrepreneur in an age of opportunism, his career demonstrates that holiness can be materially significant but that holy men are not necessarily nice people.

H. Mayr-Harting, 'The Functions of a Twelfth-Century Recluse', *History* lx, 1975.

**HADRIAN IV** (*c.*1100-1159; pope 1154-59) to date is the only Englishman to become pope. His career was almost entirely outside England, evidence of the opening of twelfth century Europe to an international clerisy of ambitious, mobile and educated ecclesiastics whose careers could be as cosmopolitan and opportunist as any freebooting Viking of earlier centuries. Born Nicholas Breakspear(e) at Abbot's Langley, near St Alban's, his father was a minor royal official who entered St Alban's as a monk. This suggests that there was money in the family. Sometime after 1120, Nicholas left England, studied in France, and entered the community of canons regular at St Rufus, near Avignon. He rose through the ranks to become abbot *c.*1137/40. He was not popular, the canons complaining to Rome of his strictness. This quality of determination (or alternatively tactlessness) was to make him a brilliant papal legate and a maladroit pope. Sometime in the late 1140s he visited Rome, perhaps making contact with Englishmen at the Curia, such as Robert Pullen. What prompted Eugenius III to create him Cardinal Bishop of Albano in 1149 is obscure. Nicholas made his name as papal legate to Scandinavia (1150-53) when he brought the Norwegian and Swedish churches decisively into the orbit of the Roman church. He established Trondheim as the metropolitan see for Norway; laid the foundation for the archbishopric of Uppsala; and gained local agreement to the payment of Peter's Pence. The Danish historian Saxo Grammaticus thought him a skilled administrator and diplomat. His unanimous election as pope in December 1154 after his return to Rome is, nevertheless, hard to understand. He had no obvious patrons or curial pedigree. His time as cardinal had been spent mainly abroad. Perhaps, as in other leadership elections, he had an indefinable aura of success which attracted the jaded power brokers in Rome. Since the reign of Paschal II (1099-1118), popes had become victims rather than directors of events. Perhaps his colleagues hoped Nicholas, the

Apostle of the North, would break the mould of compromise, stagnation and failure which had so recently been confirmed in the fiasco of Eugenius III and the Second Crusade. If so, they were to be disappointed. Nicholas took the unusual papal name of Hadrian, the first for two hundred and seventy years, perhaps in honour of Hadrian I (772-95) who, it was claimed, had given the first papal privileges to the abbey of St Albans's. Certainly, the new pope extended papal protection to St Alban's (1156). Hadrian's main challenge was his political weakness in Italy, especially in Rome. Initially he relied on an alliance with the German experor, Frederick Barbarossa, but when it became apparnt that papal and imperial interests in Italy were incompatible, Hadrian performed a diplomatic somersault at the Treaty of Benevento (1156) by allying with the papacy's adversary, the king of Sicily. This *démarche* in fact did little to secure Hadrian's permanent hold on Rome. Relations with the emperor deteriorated further in 1157 when Hadrian's envoys at Besançon implied that Frederick was the pope's vassal. Despite attempts to mollify the emperor, Frederick pressed ahead with his territorial claims in Italy. By the time of his death, Hadrian had confirmed the papacy's political vulnerability. At the Curia, Hadrian gathered around him Englishmen such as John of Salisbury and his nephew Boso, whom he placed in charge of papal finances. Through John of Salisbury and his own letters, Hadrian tried to encourage Archbishop Theobald to adopt a more robust stance over papal jurisdiction in England, to little immediate effect. As in Scandinavia, Hadrian wished to reassert, under papal control, episcopal authority over the church after a generation when the lead in reform and church government had been increasingly in the hands of monks and abbots, especially Cistercians: during his reign the papal title of Vicar of Christ became current. It was in this context that Hadrian, probably at the request of John of Salisbury and Archbishop Theobald, issued the bull *Laudabiliter* (*c*.1155/6) which ostensibly encouraged Henry II to incorporate Ireland in his empire. One consequence of any such conquest, the clerics hoped, would be the extension over the Irish church of the jurisdiction of Canterbury and, ultimately, Rome, an arrangement which Hadrian had perfected in Scandinavia. Personally, Hadrian, like so many successful clerics, was said to have had a good singing voice. According to Boso and John of Salisbury, he was a generous host and a good companion. Such was local pride in Hadrian's pontificate that Walkelin, archdeacon of Suffolk, named one of his bastards Adrian and proposed to call the next, if a girl, Adriana.

R. W. Southern. 'Adrian IV', in *Medieval Humanism*, 1970.

**WILLIAM OF YPRES** (*d.*?1165), one of the leading mercenary captains of the mid-twelfth century, played a prominent role in support of King Stephen in the late 1130s and early 1140s. The illegitimate son of Philip of Loo and a wool-carder of Ypres, and a grandson of Count Robert I of Flanders (1071-93), he may have been involved in the plot to assassinate Count Charles the Good in 1127 and certainly was one of the competitors for the county in 1127-8. Expelled from Flanders in 1133, William found refuge in England. For a decade after 1135 he led Stephen's Flemish mercenaries, proving himself the king's most loyal and effective commander. In the process he acquired an evil reputation for ruthlessness and violence, beginning in Normandy on Stephen's ill-fated visit in 1137, when he and his troops antagonised and frightened the Norman aristocracy in equal measure. In 1141, he apparently abandoned Stephen to capture at the battle of Lincoln (February). But at least he and his soldiers lived to fight another day and in the following months when Stephen's cause hung in the balance he showed unswerving loyalty. It was William's tactical skill which led to the capture of Robert of Gloucester and the Rout of Winchester (September 1141) which restored the king's fortunes.

Later in the 1140s, as the general fighting died down, William appears to have mellowed, perhaps because he went blind. He turned his energies to ecclesiastical patronage, founding Boxley Abbey (1144-6), and political mediation, as in 1148 between Stephen and Archbishop Theobald. Stephen rewarded William with large estates and revenues in Kent which Henry II allowed him to keep, at least until 1156/7. As did many violent men of the time, William ended his days in the cloister, at St Peter's, Loo, in his native Flanders

Although the civil war highlighted his importance, it should be remembered that he was engaged by Stephen at the height of the king's power early in the reign. Mercenaries, *i.e.* paid soldiers, were not emergency expedients in the armies of the central middle ages, but a permanent and necessary presence. For instance, William II's reputation as a powerful warlord depended, according to Abbot Suger, on his being a 'brilliant recruiter and paymaster of knights'. William of Ypres's career presents a striking contradiction to the supposed norms of chivalric society. Against the topos of devoted martial valour of men serving their lords out of 'feudal' loyalty so carefully nurtured by predominantly clerical writers at least since the eighth century, William, who openly served for material profit, proved both more skilful and more loyal than his baronial colleagues. He, William Marshal and Richard I's mercenary commander Mercadier give the lie to the politically and socially comfortable conceit that trust could not be bought. Indeed, their activities suggest that it was not profit but the traditional bonds of aristocratic society that bred untrustworthiness. The barons who forced King John to sign *Magna Carta* in 1215 tacitly accepted this in their condemnation, by name, of the king's mercenary leaders in Clause 50. Gerard d'Athée, Engelard de Cigogné and the rest were dangerous precisely for the firmness of their devotion to the king: a marked contrast to their noble critics.

R. H. C. Davis, *King Stephen,* 1967.

**WILLIAM FITZHERBERT** (*d.*1154; archbishop of York 1141-7 and 1153-4; canonised 1226) was one of the more unlikely saints of medieval England. The son of the half-sister of King Stephen and his brother, Henry of Blois, bishop of Winchester, by 1138 he had risen to be Treasurer of York. In January 1141, on the orders of the king, he was elected archbishop of York. Although no enemy to the monastic reformers in the North, William had defeated a Cistercian candidate. That alone was enough to excite the fury and vindictiveness of Bernard of Clairvaux. Worse still was the obvious interference by the king and his brother Henry, then papal-legate in England. Both parties appealed to Rome. Initially, Henry of Blois held the advantage and, with the approval of Innocent II (1130-43), consecrated

William archbishop in 1143. Henry drew the full force of St Bernard's invective ('here I say is the enemy, . . . the man who walks before Satan, the son of perdition, the man who disrupts all rights and laws'). The deaths of Innocent (1143), Celestine II (1143-44) and Lucius II (1144-45) delayed the granting of the *pallium* to William. The accession in 1145 of St Bernard's pupil Eugenius III (1145-53) put it out of reach. At Rome, Eugenius upheld his Order's interests by deposing William in 1147, rejecting another royal candidate and instead consecrating the Cistercian Henry Murdac, abbot of Fountains. The struggle symbolised the political weakness of King Stephen, who could not even get his candidates into the second see of the realm, and the new power in the North of the Cistercians. Self-righteousness allied to landed wealth made them confident and aggressive, and provoked conflict. After 1147, William retired to the protection of Bishop Henry at Winchester. That his fate had been largely a matter of politics not principle, despite St Bernard's fulminations, was tacitly recognised after the deaths of Murdac, Eugenius and Bernard when Anastasius IV (1153-54) restored William to his diocese in 1153. William died in 1154, it was rumoured from a chalice poisoned by the archdeacon. To the end, William aroused controversy. According to his enemies, a lazy man of lax morals, William was caught between the traditional structures of ecclesiastical patronage and the demands for recognition by the newly endowed purists of the Cistercians who, far from being content to 'forget the world, and be forgotten by it' as their founders claimed, wished to capture the strategic heights of ecclesiastical power in a region they had come to dominate. William's canonisation owed nothing to either position, but to the desire of the clergy of York Minster for a saint of their own to compete with the local cults at Ripon and Beverley. Honorius III obliged in 1226.

**HENRY MURDAC** (*d*.1153; abbot of Fountains 1144; archbishop of York 1147-53) took full advantage of the brief period when the Cistercian order combined political power and moral authority to achieve high ecclesiastical office in the face of royal hostility and local opposition. A Yorkshireman who held lucrative preferments under Archbishop Thurstan, he abandoned teaching as a secular clerk to enter Clairvaux under its charismatic and forceful abbot, St Bernard. Murdac, a man of intellect, asceticism and conviction, became one of Bernard's favoured disciples, being appointed successively abbot of Vauclair and then Fountains, in his native Yorkshire. At Fountains, Murdac proved himself combative, rigid in imposition of strict Clairvaux rules and entrepreneurial. Daughter houses were sponsored, even as far away as Norway. Locally, he began to assert Cistercian influence beyond the cloister in opposing the election as archbishop of York of William FitzHerbert, a secular clerk and close relative of King Stephen. In his campaign Murdac was able to recruit his patron Bernard, seen by many — himself included — as the conscience of Christendom, and, crucially, Bernard's pupil, Pope Eugenius III (1145-53). At one point in the conflict, William's men sacked Fountains itself: they knew who their enemy was. Murdac's motives may or may not have been selfless. What is certain is that after William's desposition by Eugenius in 1147, Murdac attracted enough support in a divided election for the same pope and fellow Cistercian to appoint him archbishop in William's stead.

As archbishop, as when abbot, Murdac scarcely conformed to the often proclaimed Cistercian model of the retiring eremite, shunning the world, finding spiritual fulfilment only in the cloister. Despite the refusal of the king and the York clergy to accept him, Murdac pursued a vigorous policy of asserting archiepiscopal rights often in the direct interests of the Cistercian order. He also maintained close control over the affairs of Fountains, using his archiepiscopal authority as a cover for hiring and firing a series of abbatial stooges. Recognised by the King in 1151 in return for his help in persuading Pope Eugenius to consecrate Stephen's son king, Murdac remained energetic in imposing what he saw as the highest ecclesiastical standards throughout the church, but his effectiveness was limited and transitory. After his death, a non-Cistercian pope, Anastasius IV, restored Archbishop William. Murdac, for all his personal qualities, exposed flaws in Cistercian policy eagerly siezed upon by opponents. His rectitude appeared self-righteous; his probity smug; his conviction arrogance; his actions no better than those of any other self-interested ecclesiastical faction. Such were the contradictions of success. To them Murdac added his own abundant taste for acrid controversy. York never again had a Cistercian archbishop.

F. Barlow, *The English Church 1066-1154*, 1979.
D. Knowles, *The Monastic Order in England*, 1949.

**AILRED OF RIEVAULX** (1110-1167) was one of the most influential twelfth century leaders of the Cistercians in England whose widely acknowledged spiritual standing was reinforced by an unsurpassed network of contacts with the secular great as well as the religiously good. His family history embodied much of the reality of church and monastic reform. Ailred came from a long line of prosperous married clergy. His great-grandfather, Alured, sacrist of St Cuthbert (*c.*1020), spent his time stealing relics of Northumbrian saints to add to his community's collection. Thus did Bede's bones find their way to the shrine of Cuthbert. Ailred's father, Eilaf, was a priest at Hexham. In 1113, Archbishop Thurstan of York imposed Augustinian canons at Hexham, although Eilaf retained a life-interest in his benefice, a compromise perhaps more common than purist zealots would have liked and one which allowed institutional change without the friction of dispossession. In 1138, Eilaf joined the monastic community at Durham.

Ailred's roots were, therefore, in the English clerical aristocracy of north-east England, a background which influenced his preferment but also instilled an affection for the English past, its saints, such as Cuthbert and Edward the Confessor, and language, which he spoke even on his deathbed. Probably educated initially at Hexham, Ailred was subsequently attached to the court of King David of Scotland, where he made friends with the king's son, Henry, and stepson, Waldef. The easy contacts between the Scottish court and the nobility of northern England were those to be expected in what was still a disputed frontier area. Perhaps, additionally, David, a direct descendent of Ethelred the Unready, attracted ambitious Englishmen when most power in England remained firmly in the hands of the Anglo-French. Ailred rose to be *dispensator* (steward) of the king's household, as well as following his family tradition in becoming a canon of Kirkham. Although in his later incarnation as a monk, Ailred tended to depict his time at court as one of spiritual anguish, the education, personal contacts, and experience of court politics and administration served him well in his future life; they could, despite his own testimony, be said to have been the making of him.

In 1134, Ailred abandoned life in the secular world by joining the newly founded (1132) Cistercian abbey of Rievaulx, near Helmsley in north Yorkshire. Although described as a profound spiritual conversion, his entry into the Order of White Monks proclaimed Ailred as no ordinary recruit. He had been on an embassy from King David to Archbishop Thurstan of York, both of whom were early supporters of the new order. He had heard of Rievaulx from a friend, probably Waldef (who had entered Rievaulx a couple of years before) and was introduced to the abbey itself by its founder, patron and protector, Walter Espec, lord of Helmsley, with whom Ailred was staying. Far from diminishing his vocation, such elevated social contacts were not untypical of those who joined the Cistercians, an order which insisted on the ascetic dimension of a purer, pristine exercise of the Rule of St Benedict. Ascetism flourished in the midst of affluence, particularly amongst the affluent. Institutionally, too, the Cistercians, as befitted a self-conscious elite corps of spiritual warriors, tended to be lead by men of noble or well-to-do origins. The poor layman wishing access to the order were usually confined to the role of lay brother (*conversus*). Cistercian monks were no more socially egalitarian than any other established twelfth century community.

At Rievaulx, Ailred thrived, as a writer, teacher and administrator. According to his biographer, and from his own works, he emerges as handsome, charming, undomineering, well-educated with an almost nineteenth century public school passion for close friendship. Ailred soon rose in the hierarchy. In 1142, while on a visit to Rome to protest against the election of a non-Cistercian archbishop of York, William FitzHerbert, he visited Bernard of Clairvaux, the dominant figure in the order. Apparently, Bernard was impressed, urging Ailred to write his first book, *Speculum Caritatis (The Mirror of Charity)*. Returning to Rievaulx, Ailred became novice-master (1142-3) and abbot of Rievaulx's daughter house of St Laurance at Revesby in

Lincolnshire (1143-7) before being elected abbot of Rievaulx in 1147.

As abbot (1147-67), Ailred's impact was threefold, through his administration of the abbey; his contacts with the secular world; and his writing. In fact the three were inextricably entwined. As with all successful twelfth century abbots, Ailred's main achievement at Rievaulx was to increase its numbers and wealth. He was notorious for encouraging all comers, a *laissez-faire*, open house attitude which swelled the community at Rievaulx from three hundred in 1142 to six hundred and fifty in 1165. By ignoring the suitability of recruits, Ailred was storing up trouble for his successors and was placing a strain on the operation of the strict Cistercian Rule. It was only Ailred's forceful personality that saved the monastery from division and laxity. Popularity brought its own rewards in the form of attention and donations. Just as, in Ailred's words, 'the strong and the weak alike' found the gates of Rievaulx open, so did their lay relatives and acquaintances. During the civil war of Stephen's reign, Ailred encouraged gifts of land 'because he realised that in this unsettled time such gifts profited knights and monks alike . . . the possessors of goods were helped to salvation'. The benefit to the monks was more material. The close embrace between monastery and nobility was crucial to the very nature and achievement of twelfth century monasticism.

Ailred had a more individual role in secular affairs. His friends included the English justiciar Robert, earl of Leicester and Gilbert Foliot, bishop of London. Even before 1154, he had ingratiated himself with Henry of Anjou by dedicating to him a *Geneaology of the Kings of England* (1152-3), which emphasised to the future king the union of English and Norman lines: Henry II was the first post-Conquest king to be descended from both Alfred the Great and Rollo of Normandy. Ailred's political and personal loyalties could be divided, as when, c.1155-7, he wrote his account, *Relatio de Standardo (Story of the Battle of the Standard)*, of David of Scotland's invasion of 1138 which was defeated by Walter Espec. Characteristically, perhaps, Ailred solved the problems by praising both his patrons. His audience was probably confined to his monastery.

Away from Rievaulx, Ailred frequently acted as an arbitor or judge in ecclesiastical disputes, including anything from the precedence of the prior of Durham to a lurid sex scandal at the nunnery at Watton. He was a patron of the hermit, Godric of Finchale, whose biography he commissioned from Reginald of Coldingham. He was a sought-after preacher. Alone, however, such activity would not explain his reputation. To a large extent, this depends on the affectionate biography of him by one of his own monks, Walter Daniel, and on his own writings.

Modern historians have been convinced that they know something of Ailred's personality because his surviving works not only reflect his interests and career but are often composed in a manner which invited sympathy and in a tone which suggests intimate revelation. This is especially true of Ailred's most famous work, *De Spirituali Amicitia (Spiritual Friendship)*, written between 1150 and 1165. Based on Cicero's *De Amicitia*, Ailred's book purports to use his own emotional experience to assert the spiritual importance of friendship: 'it is easy to pass from man's friendship to God's by reason of their similarity'; 'suddenly and unawares love changes its object and being so near touches the sweetness of Christ . . . thus rising from that holy love which reaches the friend to that which reaches Christ, he will joyfully pluck the rich fruit of friendship'. It is, in fact, difficult to know whether to take apparent confessions of emotion at face value, especially as the object of the work was to confirm and enhance the faith of monks living in a community within which a cult of spiritual friendship was of evident value. Walter Daniel's account of Ailred was designed to serve a similar purpose.

Firmer evidence of Ailred's interests are found in his other works. His sermons and theological works, for example on the Soul or the Book of Isaiah, show him as a teacher. Rievaulx possessed a tradition of scholarship before Ailred's abbacy, in particular local hagiography. Ailred's contribution was typical. His *De Sanctis Ecclesiae Haugustaldensis* (1154/55) is a tract on the relics preserved at Hexham. Hexham was Ailred's family church and he took the opportunity to emphasise, and probably exaggerate the role that successive generations of his ancestors had played in the history of Hexham and its relics. Perhaps Ailred was the more conscious of family pride as he had chosen celibacy (as had his sister). His admiration of Northumbrian saints was matched by his affection for Edward the Confessor, canonised in 1161, at whose translation at Westminster in 1163 Ailred preached. He followed this with a *Life of Edward the Confessor* (later translated into French by Matthew Paris for Henry III's queen). Whatever national or local political or ecclesiastical points he wished to make, such diverse literary output places him in the forefront of the intellectual monastic world in England. More learned than many efficient abbots, he was also less credulous: he dismissed Geoffrey of Monmouth's Arthurian stories as fiction as early as 1142-3.

However much his vocation was particularly novel or Cistercian, the chief impression Ailred has left is that of a traditionally scholarly ecclesiastical administrator, whose provincial connections and pride in local saints place him firmly within the expectations of his own ancestors as much as those of his new, more abrasive colleagues in the Order of Cîteaux.

Walter Daniel, *Vita Ailredi*, ed & trans F. M. Powicke, 1950.

**THE NUN OF WATTON** (*fl.* late 1150s or 1160) was one of the victims of a monastic system which is more often remembered for its heroes. Although her name is unknown her story was recounted by Ailred of Rievaulx who was consulted over the case. Watton was a Gilbertine house in which nuns, canons, lay sisters and lay brothers lived, although rigidly segregated. The story reveals a darker side of the religious life, a world of tense closed communities in which a breakdown in discipline caused dislocation when spiritual harmony could be replaced by vengeance, cruelty, and barbarous violence; in which a social crisis released pent up forces of sexual jealousy or anxiety which, in turn, demanded harsh repression before an ordered norm could be recovered. There are elements of social ritual as well as religious extenuation in Ailred's account. The nun was caught in an affair with a lay brother. After she confessed, her fellow nuns beat her up; the younger nuns even wanted her burnt, flayed and branded. Although she avoided that, the nun was incarcerated in solitary confinement, her legs in chains, and fed on bread and water. When she was found to be pregnant, she was prevailed upon to disclose where her lover, who had fled the monastery, was living. By this time, the business had reached the ears of the founder of the order, Gilbert of Sempringham. On his orders, some other lay brothers caught and mugged the miscreant who was then handed over to the nuns. What happened next almost defies belief. The nuns 'wished to avenge the injury to their virginity'. While the man was held down by the other nuns, his mistress was forced to cut off his testicles, which were then thrust into her mouth 'just as they were, befouled with blood'. The man was returned to the lay brothers, and the nun to her prison. There, although this is concealed by a story of heavenly visitations, her baby was either aborted, still-born or disposed of, killed most likely, at birth. At this, the nun appeared 'virginal' again, and was released. God, as Ailred commented, had protected the nuns whose prayers throughout had been that He should be 'mindful of their virginal shame' and 'counteract the infamy and ward off danger'. As to the scenes of sadistic violence and sexual humiliation, Ailred expressed himself unhappy at the shedding of blood, although he commended the nuns' zeal in exacting revenge for what he, as they, saw as an insult to Christ. For Gilbert and Ailred, the matter was of discipline and upholding the sacred vows of the nuns, particularly in a new order which was bound to run risks of such liaisons. What they ignored were the dangers of admitting oblate nuns as young as four years old. The honour of the community is throughout seen as paramount over the individual: that, after all, was a central theme of rigorous monasticism. However, the problems of communal celibacy were heightened by an official imagery shot through with sublimated sexuality: Christ the bridegroom; the Church his Bride; the nun 'marrying' Christ etc. Even Ailred talks of nuns' 'ineffable raptures' at Mass. Above all, whatever the emotions and feelings of the actors in the drama, the events were seen, perhaps even by the participants, through a prism of absolute belief in a determining Divine Providence which stripped actions of temporal meaning by endowing them with spiritual significance. Ailred, making an edifying story out of the sordid scandal, was eager to avoid criticism of the community and, by implication, the monastic vocation. What is intriguing is that most educated contemporaries may have agreed with him.

G. Constable, 'Ailred of Rievaulx and the Nun of Watton',
*Mediaeval Women*, ed D. Baker, 1978.

**GODRIC OF FINCHALE** (*d*.1170) was a merchant-turned-
holy man who settled at Finchale, on the River Wear near
Durham, who received wide attention during his life and around
whom there developed a strong local cult which lasted to the end
of the Middle Ages. As with other twelfth century ascetics,
Godric's reputation depended not on his poverty or isolation (he
had neither) but on his simplicity, his contact with nature, and
his openness to rich and poor alike. His cult was unusual in the
very high proportion of women it attracted.

Much of the information of Godric's life comes from a biography written by Reginald of Coldingham, one of three Durham
monks who wrote contemporary *Lives* of the hermit, evidently
in the hope of annexing his fame to their priory. Reginald's *Life*,
commissoned by the prior of Durham and Ailred of Rievaulx,
was reluctantly authorised by Godric himself who supplied
details of his early career and lived to receive a finished copy.
Whether the subject's cooperation makes the *Life* more or
less accurate is a moot point. Certainly, Reginald frequently
introduces Godric's apparent devotion to Durham's own patron
saint Cuthbert. However, the *Life* reveals much about the
nature of the eremitic vocation and its uses in twelfth century
England.

A Norfolk man of English parentage, Godric began his career
as a merchant. From modest beginnings as a local pedlar, as his
business grew he took to the sea, trading throughout the North
Sea and beyond. His travels took him to the major pilgrimage
centres of Compostella in Spain, Rome, and St Gilles in Southern France, as well as British shrines at St Andrew's and the
Farne Islands. Godric twice visited Jerusalem, although whether
in the course of his international trading or, as the *Life* implies,
as part of his renunciation of Mammon, is unclear. Godric's
business interests also included acting as steward to rich
landowners in Norfolk. Godric evidently took full advantage of
the varied entrepreneurial opportunities offered by the growing
economy of the early twelfth century.

Retiring from commerce, Godric wandered around northern

England until, under the patronage of Ranulf Flambard, bishop of Durham, he settled (c.1112) at Finchale where he built a chapel and was joined by a substantial entourage, including his own priest. His holiness had practical application. A French speaker, he could mediate between the English locals and their masters, lay or clerical. Credited with the useful powers of prophecy and healing, he also acted as a banker, amassing a large treasure: 'the wealth of many had been . . . entrusted to him'. The hoard was a target for thieves and, in 1137/8, Scottish invaders who, frustrated in their search for it, slaughtered his livestock. Adjacent to the major centre of ecclesiastical and secular authority in the north-east, Godric was ideally placed to give spiritual, medical or financial advice unencumbered by the constraints of the established social or clerical hierarchies. In a sense, he remained an entrepreneur, a trader in conspicuous holiness with which he eased or solved his clients' problems. His services encouraged donations. Apart from guardianship of the riches of others, he kept livestock; had the materials to paint and sculpt; and could afford to rebuild his original wooden chapel in stone.

Of course his effectiveness, as financial consultant or thaumaturge, was attributed to his being a 'man of God'. As such, he came to the notice of Becket, Ailred of Rievaulx, King Malcolm of Scotland, even Pope Alexander III. But his appeal was essentially to a smaller, humbler audience. After he died, apparently in extreme old age, in 1170, the monks of Durham began to nurture a cult. From 1172, Godric's relics performed miracles of healing which drew a regular stream of pilgrims over the next few centuries. The cult was strictly local: almost all known pilgrims came from a forty-mile radius of the shrine which, in the thirteenth century, was extended as part of a new priory built on the site of Godric's hermitage. Godric's cures appealed especially to women (comprising ⅔ of the 244 recorded miracles) and those without social pretentions. This may say something about the expense and misogyny of the more famous, elite shrines run by monks, not least that of neighbouring St Cuthbert.

*Libellus de Vita et Miraculis S. Godrici Heremitae de Finchale,* ed. J. Stevenson (Surtees Society), 1847.

**CHRISTINA OF MARKYATE** (*c*.1096/98-*c*.1155/66) was a recluse under the patronage of the monastery of St. Alban's. Her contemporary importance is witnessed by her possession of an elabrate luxury Psalter (now at Hildesheim) and the elevation of her hermit's cell into a nunnery in 1145. Her posthumous reputation rests on a surviving *Life*, written at St. Alban's in the twelfth century, probably by a close acquaintance.

Christina came from a family of wealthy English landowners in Huntingdon. Her reaction to puberty was to take a vow of virginity on a visit to St. Alban's. The crisis of her life came around the year 1114 when her aunt's former lover, Ranulf Flambard, bishop of Durham, tried to seduce her. Although fearful of rape, Christina successfully resisted. In revenge, Flambard helped arrange a forced marriage for Christina to a local man, Burhred. Even then, Christina defended her chastity. In the end, released from her marriage and cut off by her parents, Christina fled from home and was placed under the care of a group of hermits near Dunstable, first Alfwen of Flamstead and then Roger of Markyate, a former monk of St. Alban's. On Roger's death, *c*.1122, she attracted the protection of Archbishop Thurstan of York before finally establishing herself at Markyate *c*.1123. From then on, with the patronage and friendship of Abbot Geoffrey of St. Alban's, Christina became an established and respected figure in influential religious circles. She resisted offers of preferment to nunneries in York, Marcigny-les-Nonnains and Fontevrault. In 1155/6, Henry II himself made her a grant of fifty shillings. Although her influence was largely personal, on her important friends, such as Abbot Geoffrey or by the example of her eremtic privations, a nunnery was established at Markyate by 1145. It is clear from the richness of the Psalter prepared for her use and the *Life* that her vocation had a practical dimension. One charge of her detractors was that she was 'just a worldly-wise business woman'. The were right although her admirers attributed her material as well as spiritual success not to 'earthly prudence' but to 'a gift of God': a distinction without a difference, perhaps.

Many of Christina's contemporaries affected to flee the world and, like Wulfric of Haselbury or Godric of Finchdale, set themselves up profitably as mediators between God and man, man and nature and, most importantly, man and man, across class or race. There was, in a changing and increasingly affluent society, a clear place for the professional outsider whose escape from the world was more apparent than real. In England, the complexity of social and economic relations was compounded by the barriers of French and English. It is no coincidence that most of the twelfth century recluses were *bien pensant* English (Wulfric; Godric; Christina herself and her companions, such as Alfwen of Flamstead) who could converse in French. They were of a social or economic status to compete with the French-speaking elite, symbols not so much of any Ivanhoe-like Anglo-Saxon nationalism as of social contact, protection, even power; aloof and therefore useful; social as well as spiritual interpreters.

Christina, in her cell almost on Watling Street (the present A5), one of the main highways of medieval England, close to, and protected by the neighbouring abbey of St. Alban's, one of the leading Benedictine houses, fitted this pattern. Well connected, patronised by the great of the church, her seclusion was relative, and operated within semi-formal constraints which became official when, after sixteen years as a freelance, she took the veil at St. Alban's in 1131. Hermits were organised, as witnessed by the group under Roger of Markyate, and, in a sense, licensed by more orthodox or regular clergy, very different from the eccentric liminal figures of contemporary Arthurian romances. Two features, according to the *Life,* distinguished Christina from other hermits. Her miracles seem to be confined to prophecy (a useful commodity in any age), and restricted to her own circle with only a few externally useful acts; indeed only one cure is mentioned. This may suggest that the *Life* had a limited purpose of praise of an example for the inspiration of Markyate priory, which lasted until the Reformation. The other eccentricity was her recorded obsession with sex, or rather, the lack of it.

Christina's sexual status, as a virgin, is the *leitmotif* of her biography. It is littered with thwarted seducers, frustrated husbands, lecherous hosts and guilt-ridden clerical associates. Temptation is everywhere, and recognised by Christina herself who worries about her feelings towards her friend, the abbot of St. Alban's. It could be that the reader is supposed to take these stories allegorically; Christina's embattled virginity representing the difficulties of spiritual purity, a metaphor of the religious life, or even the Church itself. The vivid circumstantial details, however, suggest actuality. The dramatic scene in Bishop Flambard's bedroom is a classic:

> Satan put it into his heart to desire her. Busily, therefore, seeking some trick of getting her into his power, he had the unsuspecting girl brought into his chamber where he himself slept, which was hung with beautiful tapestries, the only others present with the innocent child being members of his retinue. Her father and mother and the others with whom she had come were in the hall apart giving themselves up to drunkenness. When it was getting dark the bishop gave a secret sign to his servants and they left the room, leaving their master and Christina, that is to say, the wolf and the lamb, together in the same room. For shame! The shameless bishop took hold of Christina by one of the sleeves of her tunic and with that mouth which he used to consecrate the sacred species, he solicited her to commit a wicked deed. What was the poor girl to do in such straits? Should she call her parents? They had already gone to bed. To consent was out of the question: but openly resist she dared not because if she openly resisted him, she would certainly be overcome by force.
>
> Hear, then, how prudently she acted. She glanced towards the door and saw that, though it was closed, it was not bolted. And she said to him: 'Allow me to bolt the door: for even if we have no fear of God, at least we should take precautions that no man should catch us in this act.' He demanded an oath from her that she would not deceive him, but that she would, as she said, bolt the door. And she swore to him. And so, being released, she darted out of the room and bolting the door firmly from the outside, hurried quickly home. This was the beginning of all the frightful troubles that followed afterwards. Then that wretch, seeing that he had been made a fool of by a young girl, was eaten up with resentment and counted all his power as nothing until he could avenge the insult he had suffered. But the only way in which he could conceivably gain his revenge was by depriving Christina of her virginity, either by himself or by someone else, for the preservation of which she did not hesitate to repulse even a bishop.

*The Life of Christina of Markyate*, ed. C. H. Talbot, 1959.

C. Holdsworth, 'Christina of Markyate' in *Mediaeval Women*, ed. D. Baker, 1978.

THEOBALD (*d*.1161; archbishop of Canterbury 1138-61) was one of the most effective medieval archbishops of Canterbury, although by no means one of the most colourful. He came to Canterbury with the classic credentials of an abbot of Bec, but, unlike his illustrious predecessors Lanfranc and Anselm, his elevation was unexpected and controversial. In 1138, Theobald, a native of Lower Normandy, was unknown in England, a political nonentity who had only become an abbot two years previously. Perhaps his inexperience and lack of involvement in the factional manoeuvring of the early years of Stephen's reign actually commended Theobald in preference to the obvious candidate, Stephen's brother, Henry, bishop of Winchester. In the event, his abbacy proved of less importance than the influence of Bec's lay patron, and Stephen's closest lay advisor, Waleran, count of Meulan. However, as with so many of Stephen's political calculations, the appointment of Theobald, rushed through on 24 December 1138, failed to bring the expected benefits. The king had alienated his powerful brother, while, initially, the *ingénu* archbishop was unable to provide any balancing weighty support. Once Theobald did establish his political bearings, although whenever possible observing public loyalty to Stephen, he proved a closet Angevin, resistant to royal control and the king's increasingly urgent demands for the coronation of his son.

Overshadowed between 1139 and 1143 by Henry of Winchester's appointment as Papal Legate in England, Theobald was content to follow events. In December 1141 he recrowned Stephen and his queen in Canterbury, but after the Angevin conquest of Normandy (1141-44) Theobald pursued an increasingly independent role. In this he was aided by the Angevin sympathies of Popes Celestine II (1143-44) and Eugenius III (1145-53) and Stephen's enfeebled control over the English Church. Henry of Winchester's legateship expired with Innocent II in 1143 and Stephen's failure to impose his candidate as archbishop of York led to a schism in the northern province which left Theobald unchallenged in leadership of the Church, a dominance confirmed in 1149/50 by his own appointment as papal legate.

In 1147 he visited Paris at the same time as Geoffrey of Anjou. The following year he defied a royal ban and travelled, at some personal risk, to the papal Council of Rheims. Once there, he characteristically interceded to prevent Pope Eugenius from excommunicating King Stephen. During this exile, he and the young Henry FitzEmpress persuaded the pope to create Gilbert Foliot bishop of Hereford: securing jobs for people was one of Theobald's chief attainments. Theobald wished to establish the firm authority of both church and state. A weak king meant a threatened church. For the remainder of Stephen's reign, Theobald sought political compromise with his ultimate objective being an Angevin succession. Thus he attempted mediation in 1148 and played a central role in the final agreement of 1153 between Stephen and Henry FitzEmpress, but he refused point blank to crown Stephen's son Eustace in 1152, preferring another brief exile. Seeing royal and ecclesiastical authority as complementary, Theobald was nevertheless concerned to assert his rights as archbishop of Canterbury, not least against unnecessary papal interference. He regarded Henry of Blois's legateship as doubly threatening in its reliance on papal power and usurpation of Canterbury's primacy. Even the crisis of 1148 can be seen not so much as an assertion of papal authority, more a vindication of Canterbury's right to represent the English church at the Council. This view may have rubbed off on one of Theobald's companions in the open boat which took the archbishop across the perilous Channel on the way to Rheims: Thomas Becket.

Under Henry II, Theobald continued to promote ecclesiastical authority, particularly his own in harmony with the king. It must be uncertain how Theobald would have reacted if Henry had insisted on defining the jurisdictional parameters of Church and State as he was to do at Clarendon in 1164. He certainly desired a demarcation of the spiritual and temporal spheres in justice as elsewhere. But his response to the Papal Schism of 1159 is perhaps typical. Two popes had been elected, Alexander III and Victor IV. Theobald adhered to the former, but he wrote to Henry: 'while the matter is in suspense we think that it is unlawful in your realm to accept either of them without your approval', although he urged the king to take the advice of the clergy, which the king did.

As archbishop, Theobald maintained the traditional hostility towards the monks of Canterbury, particularly over their administration of estates and revenues. Although a Benedictine monk himself, Theobald preferred the company of secular clerks, men of intellect rather than conspicuous piety. There can have been few more distinguished clerical households in the Middle Ages to compare with the men assembled by Theobald, and fewer still on whom the golden rewards of patronage and preferment were showered more lavishly. Roger of Pont l'Eveque became archbishop of York (1154-81); John of Pagham, bishop of Worcester (1151-7); John of Canterbury, bishop of Poitiers (1162), archbishop of Narbonne and finally archbishop of Lyons (1182-93); Bartholomew, bishop of Exeter (1161-84); Theobald's brother Walter, bishop of Rochester (1148-82). Also attracted to Theobald's househod were John of Salisbury, one of the leading European intellectuals of his generation, who wrote many of Theobald's official letters; Master Vacarius, a canon lawyer of international repute from Bologna; Jordan Fantosme, later master of the cathedral school at Winchester and author of a French verse account of the great rebellion of 1173-4; and Thomas Becket, the drama of whose career has tended to cast his old mentor in the shade. Yet it was Theobald who chose these men and, in many cases, provided their opportunity for public prominence.

Personally, Theobald presented an apparent contradiction. In private he was sharp tongued, garrulous and short tempered, but, according to Robert of Cricklade, trimmed his conversation when talking to powerful men. Patient, occasionally obsequious to superiors, Theobald could be aggressive, overbearing even violent towards inferiors. But, unlike his archdeacon and successor, Becket, he did not over-react to people or events. Publicly cautious and patient, he calculated his advantage with care, as when he arranged for Becket to become Henry II's chancellor in 1155 as the young, untried, foreign king's minder. Unglamorous; by no means a saint, even posthumously; a nepotist and a far from passionate monk, Theobald achieved much. He saw off the challenge of Henry of Blois to ecclesiastical dominance; he checked the business incompetence of the Canterbury monks; he firmly established the de facto primacy of Canterbury over York; he secured a reasonably smooth Angevin succession after a generation of civil war; he successfully promoted his protégés; he defined a semi-detached working relationship between the English church and the increasingly intrusive legalism of the papacy; he maintained the independence of the church without challenging its interdependence with the state. The measure of his achievement is perhaps to be found in the explosive chaos which followed his death: even that can be attributed in part to his success as a patron.

A. Saltman, *Theobald, Archbishop of Canterbury*, 1956.

**NIGEL OF ELY** (*d*.1169; bishop of Ely 1133-69) was a member of the remarkable family of royal administrators established by his uncle, Roger, bishop of Salisbury, Henry I's justiciar. This included his brother, Alexander, bishop of Lincoln; his cousins, Roger and Adelelm, respectively chancellor and treasurer in the early years of Stephen's reign; and his own illegitimate son, Richard FitzNeal, treasurer to Henry II and Richard I. Educated at Laon under the renowned *magister* Anselm and his brother, the mathematician Ralph, Nigel became treasurer to Henry I in the mid-1120s, the post probably being created for him by his uncle Roger when (1123-6) viceroy of England. As treasurer, Nigel, who may have picked up the latest computing techniques at Laon, coordinated the financial operations of the king's chamber and the treasury. He remained at the heart of government after his appointment as bishop of Ely in 1133 until he shared in his uncle's ruin in 1139. Nigel's response to Bishop Roger's arrest was characteristic. Used to a substantial military entourage, Nigel withdrew to Devizes castle prepared to fight, only surrendering when the king threatened to hang his cousin Roger. Excluded from court and stripped of office, Nigel retained his see and from there continued to resist Stephen, hiring troops and fortifying the Isle of Ely. Driven out by royalist forces, Nigel joined Matilda in the west country, being at her side throughout the triumphant months of 1141. When the pendulum swung against the Empress, Nigel became an especial target of the king, fearful lest the bishop combine with other East Anglian rebels. In 1143, Nigel was forced to appeal to Rome against charges brought by the papal legate, Stephen's brother, Henry of Winchester. On his return in 1145, he made peace with the king, giving his teenage son Richard as hostage.

In 1154, at the repeated and urgent requests of the new king Henry II, he came out of retirement to help reconstruct administration at the exchequer which had been severely run down during the civil war. Nigel's reluctance was understandable. Most of his new colleagues, including the two justiciars, had served Stephen, one of them, Robert of Leicester, being implicated in the coup of 1139. The urgent problems at the exchequer were re-establishing control over sheriffs; restoring procedures of effective audit; and the revival of clear, comprehensive and coherent records on the Pipe Rolls. All these, by the time Nigel retired through ill-health in 1164-5, had, to a great extent, been achieved.

For Henry II, Nigel represented expertise and experience. In the flattering account by his son in the *Dialogue of the Exchequer*, he appears as a master of procedure and exchequer business. Although his position was informal, Nigel was influential enough to be able to give the justiciar, his old enemy Robert of Leicester, a severe dressing down when he breached precedent over exchequer privileges: the exchange must have given the aged bishop some pleasure. The impression given in the *Dialogue* that Nigel recreated the exchequer is probably untrue, but he did restore it on the same lines as it had operated under his uncle, providing Henry II with effective means to implement his wishes. To his son, Nigel was a heroic bureaucrat. He certainly was industrious. At Ely, he instituted inquests into the see's lands; established a diocesan exchequer; and vigorously pursued resumption of estates lost in the severe depredations of the civil war. Combined with his actions under Stephen and his charters, the evidence shows Nigel to have been, as his enemies portrayed him, a man more adept at secular lordship than spiritual leadership.

**JOHN OF SALISBURY** (*c*.1115/20-1180) had an international career typical of the well-connected and highly-educated twelfth century ecclesiastic. Although in the second rank of academics, lawyers and administrators, John was a prominent member of the closely interlaced clerisy of clever secular clerks who glided seemingly effortlessly between the courts of kings, popes and prelates. John's contacts are a roll-call of the intellectual and spiritual leaders of western Christendom in the mid-twelfth century: Abelard, Pullen, Becket, St. Bernard, Eugenius III, Hadrian IV, Alexander III, Archbishop Theobald. John's contribution to this circle was literary and secretarial. Education at Exeter and Paris was followed by travel and employment across Europe. Although no lawyer, he spent much of his career advising on legal matters, for example on appeals from the English church to Rome. An ability to get on with people secured him an ill-defined administrative post at the papal curia in the late 1140s, followed in the 1150s by employment as secretary to Theobald of Canterbury. In England he became a friend of Thomas Becket, whom he preceded into exile in 1164, only returning in 1170. Apart from the letters he composed for his masters, John's main literary works were the *Metalogion*, a defence of the study of the liberal arts; the *Historia Pontificalis* a gossipy account of the papal curia between 1148 and 1152, written in exile during the 1160s; lives of Anselm and Becket; and the *Policraticus*, written in the 1150s, which combines a critique of contemporary rulers with a treatise on political thought. The *Policraticus* presents a moral view of rule. There is a single principle of government derived from the teaching of the Church. However, although God's law is sovereign, in the secular sphere the monarch possesses unassailable authority. John describes a republic (*i.e.* secular state) as a living organism whose head governs the other members. Only where the monarch is illegitimate, and, in John's terms, therefore tyrannical, was there a right to depose or kill him to restore the moral order. The very unoriginal practicality of the *Policraticus* commended it to later humanist lawyers of the fourteenth century and after who were attempting to construct a theory of authority not dependent upon the self-validating minutiae of lawyers and theologians. John's writing was characterised by a lack of dogmatism and a sense of irony, even objectivity in assessing men and events. John's eye for detail, imagery and allusion made up for his lack of intellectual depth, a fact of which he may have been conscious, as a number of his classical references and quotations are entirely bogus. But they look impressive. There is a refreshing humanity in John. An observer more than an actor, when caught up in the century's most famous act of violence, the murder of Becket, he made his position clear to the archbishop: 'We are sinners and not yet prepared to die: I see no-one here except you who is anxious to die for dying's sake'. At the entry of the knights into the cathedral, John quickly hid. Yet his association with the martyr did him no harm, perhaps even identifying him as a candidate for the high office he attained at the very end of his career as bishop of Chartres. John confessed to another human weakness: drink. He regarded himself as something of a connoisseur of wine, being particularly harsh on Sicilian, Greek and Cypriot wines which he thought lethal. But he was no wine snob. In 1157, he wrote to a friend: 'I am fond of both wine and beer, and do not abhor any liquor that can make me drunk'. As has recently been written, 'John's fame is as a mirror of his age'.

M. Wilks, ed., *The World of John of Salisbury*, 1984.

**HENRY II** (1133-1189; king of England 1154-89) has been seen as one of the most important English monarchs. To nineteenth century constitutional historians, he was the 'gravedigger of feudalism', the 'father of the common law', a king whose sagacity and insight put England and Englishmen on a path to equality under the law. In the twentieth century, what has impressed is the scale of Henry's activities and his energy, the man who pacified England; held together a French empire that stretched from the Channel to the Pyrenees; had designs on hegemony in the British Isles; whose itinerary embraced Dublin and Toulouse; and whose policies set the political agenda for half a continent. Where his regime has been criticised for harshness it has been praised for efficiency and effectiveness. Although there are many other candidates, Henry II is possibly the most overpraised monarch in English history.

In fact, Henry II had no grand design of rule, no lucid strategy for law or government, and no especial interest in England. His accession to the throne honoured a dynastic obligation but returned England to the status of a province of a continental ruler. Henry, born at Le Mans, dying at Chinon, buried at Fontevrault, saw the world from the patrimony of his ancestors, counts of Anjou and dukes of Normandy. Henry spent two thirds of his long reign out of England; his main concern with his kingdom was the exploitation of his rights and collection of revenue. Many previous views of Henry have been distorted by an anachronistic or insular perception of what constituted government in the twelfth century and, specifically, what role in government was played by the monarch. The king may have been the soul of the polity, but the workings of administration and society possessed free will. Henry's achievement was not as a builder of political structures, legal systems or administrative coherence, rather that he survived, almost to the end, as undisputed ruler of his dominions, whose lordship validated the power of his magnates and who maintained the inheritance of his predecessors, counts of Anjou, dukes of Normandy and kings of England. With only a consort's interest in Aquitaine, there he was content to allow his son, Richard of Poitou, autonomous control provided it did not clash with his own concerns. Although owing more to hostile imagination than truth, Henry's deathbed words

*Henry II*
(From his effigy at Fontevrault Abbey in Anjou)

invented by the splenetic Gerald of Wales have a ring if not of authenticity then of empathy: 'Shame! Shame! on a vanquished king'; less a lament on traduced regality, more an apostrophe of self-pitying failure. From the moment of his birth, Henry had great expectations. As eldest son of Matilda, heiress of England and Geoffrey, count of Anjou, one of his grandfathers was Henry I, duke of Normandy, also king of England; the other Fulk, formerly count of Anjou, then king of Jerusalem. Henry's potential inheritance included England, Normandy, Maine, Touraine and Anjou. The aura of destiny which clung to the young prince was explicit in the name by which contemporaries knew him: Henry Fitz-Empress (his mother's first husband had been Holy Roman Emperor). Throughout his adult life, Henry displayed the insouciant disregard and dislike for the trappings of power and lineage in which only those totally secure in both can afford to indulge.

However magnificent, every piece of Henry's inheritance had to be won: England and Normandy from King Stephen and the house of Blois; and the Angevin patrimony against the claims of Henry's younger brother, Geoffrey, to whom they had been promised by family agreement in 1151. Duke of Normandy in 1150; count of Anjou on his father's death in 1151; duke of Aquitaine and count of Poitou by virtue of his marriage with Eleanor of Aquitaine in 1152, Henry's accession to the throne of England in 1154 marked a personal fulfilment rather than an inevitable progress or political epoch. His accumulation was literally unique, fortuitous and apparently transient. That it came to be seen as something rather more than that owes much to Henry himself.

Henry received an excellent education, academically from some of the best scholars in England and northern France; politically and militarily from his own experiences in the struggle for his English inheritance. Henry posed as something of an intellectual and scholar; he was a good linguist, fluent in French and Latin; he was reputed to have helped compile his own legislation. He was renowned for his political deviousness (or skill depending on the point of view) and has also been credited with contributing to a military revolution in his concentration on castles as the key elements in warfare. Whatever Master Matthew at Bristol or Adelard of Bath taught him, Henry, figurehead of his dynasty's cause since his first visit to England in 1142, learnt most about ruling and statecraft from his English campaigns of 1147, 1149 and 1153. He was knighted in 1149 by David I of Scotland, who, as a great-grandson of King Edmund Ironsides (*d*.1016), had a claim to the English throne which he effectively renounced. In 1153, Henry determined the issue of the succession by force. Agreements at Winchester and Westminster were brokered by a baronage whose security had been undermined by constant shifts in political prospects and alliances. With a scorched-earth campaign reminding them of the possibility of a continued struggle and his refusal to abandon his hereditary rights, Henry secured approval for his succession, his path eased by the death of Stephen's eldest son, Eustace.

The key to the 1153 compromise, hereditary right, was a theme to which Henry repeatedly returned in official pronouncement for the rest of his reign. But it also posed a problem. If his succession guaranteed the rules of legitimate inheritance, where did those rules end? Were all holdings, titles, lands, offices, castellanies etc., to be included, as in France? One of the features of Henry's rule was the distinction drawn between what was considered a royal office — a sheriff or local justiciar — and what was allowed as a heritable title — earldoms, baronies *etc.* There was little logic to this: an earl was originally just as much a royal officer as a sheriff. Equally, both Stephen and Matilda had created hereditary sheriffs. Yet Henry tenaciously sought to restrict, limit and supervise the rights of all freemen, culminating in the so-called Inquest of Sheriffs of 1170 which investigated, as the commission had it, 'archbishops, bishops, abbots, earls, barons, sub-tenants, knights, citizens and burgesses, and their stewards and officers'. However, Henry was not trying to establish a coherent framework of property law or a new system of public jurisdiction taking precedence over private franchises, although this ultimately was the effect. His motives were primarily political not legal. To secure his new dynasty in England — his policies in his continental lands were subject to other constraints — Henry wished to eradicate autonomous franchises prejudicial to royal authority. Hence his consistent vigilance over the custody of castles, which had played such a crucial role in the civil war of Stephen's reign and were to prove pivotal in the Great Rebellion of 1173-4. In terms of law, England was similar to northern and western France. Differences lay in the political ramifications. Whereas in France the count or seigneur held his castles free from royal interference, this was not the case in England under Henry II.

But even here, Henry was supported by tradition not invention. Unlike in France, from the tenth century English kings retained formal control of public jurisdiction. All freemen were liable to swear a general oath of obedience to the king; there was no tradition or right of private war; earls were regularly disciplined, their lands confiscated or restored according to political circumstance and royal will; there existed a working central administration. After the Conquest royal powers were confirmed or reinforced. William I and Henry I were among the most powerful and assertive monarchs of their time. It was to this legacy that Henry II appealed, explicitly. Again and again he insisted that he was intent on restoring the rights held by his grandfather alienated by Stephen. However, Henry's main concern was the pursuit of his rights, unfettered by tradition. It was this constant manipulation and extension of his prerogatives that earned Henry the reputation simultaneously as a creator of new laws and a ruler who governed by selfish caprice, in the phrases of the time *ira et malevolentia* and *vis et voluntas*: anger, malice, force and wilfulness.

Henry's power was personal. His conception of rule, for all his and his courtiers' scholarly idealising, was practical, the advice and support of his magnates counting for more than any philosophical statement of monarchical authority. The lack of coherent ideology is most obvious in the contrast between his treatment of his subjects in England and his king in France. His theory of good government comprised what was good for him. Henry, like any other contemporary ruler, wished to secure his rights for his own advantage and his possessions for his dynasty. Thus his rule tended to the piecemeal and *ad hoc* rather than the ordered or systematic. To take a famous example, Henry's dispute with Becket (1163-70) was conducted by the king both as a pesonal vendetta and an intellectually incoherent attempt to safeguard royal rights to justice and ecclesiastical patronage. Against Becket's protestations of universal laws and definitions of authority, Henry proposed an empirical appeal to tradition and expediency. Ironically, although Henry lost the academic debate and the propaganda war so disastrously, his pragmatism was vindicated in church/state relations in the years after Becket's murder. What was true for the church was also true for the state. Henry wanted what he thought was owed him from England, chiefly wealth. To secure this he was unafraid to regulate and codify legal procedures and practice or to discipline his subjects, where necessary and possible. He was no philosopher king; no legal genius in huntsman's disguise.

The impression of farsighted creativity in part derives from the sources for Henry's reign, particularly the increasing use of writing in law and administration. Legal procedures long determined orally in courts that kept records in the memories of the wise appeared more orderly when committed to writing and, indeed, became more standardised — or fossilized as Michael Clanchy has it — as a result. The chroniclers of Henry's reign were either Angevin apologists who lauded the advent of 'the peacemaker' after 1154; or were courtiers and officials, often directed by hindsight to compare Henry's reign with the uncertainties of Richard's and the disasters of John's. Thus, a king almost universally disliked and mistrusted in life, in retrospect became a by-word for good government.

The essence of twelfth century government was the king, his personality and desires. Despite the Exchequer's role in administering his will, royal influence was controlled from the king's chamber. Despite itinerant justices after 1168 and the beginnings of a central bench of judges at Westminster (1178), justice followed the household of the king. Henry was literally mobbed and jostled by petitioners wherever he went. The king personally presided over important cases involving lay or clerical tenants-in-chief. In such circumstances, Henry's character and habits determined the nature of his rule far more certainly than developments in fiscal or judicial bureaucracy. Belying his posthumous reputation as a lion of justice, Henry was a dilatory judge and his officials notoriously venal and corrupt. Some suitors died before their cases came to judgement. He left the Bigod inheritance unresolved for the last twelve years of his reign. Richard of Anstey was luckier, but he had to chase Henry across England and France for over five years, at great personal cost, before he finally secured a decision in 1163. Royal caprice, inattention, absence and indifference may all have contributed; but there was also method. According to one of his courtiers, Henry's forceful mother — not known as a paragon of patience herself, it must be said — had advised him to 'spin out all the affairs of everyone'. She was thinking primarily of patronage, the allocation of offices, but legal judgements were a comparable aspect of royal largesse. Complaints about access, delay and corruption in the judicial process feature prominently in Magna Carta (*cc*.17-19 and 40).

During Henry's reign there were numerous codifications and clarifications of customary law: the Constitutions of Clarendon (1164); the Assizes of Clarendon (1166), Northampton (1176), of Arms (1181) and Woodstock (1184). The feudal obligations of tenants-in-chief was investigated in the *Cartae Baronum* of 1166 and the administrative duties of his subjects and officials in the great Inquest of 1170. From official documents and the memoirs of courtiers there emerges a picture of an intellectual court, intent on using the fashionable techniques, or at least vocabulary, of inquiry to reveal the truth and of employing the technology of writing to facilitate the running of government. From 1168, justices-in-eyre, itinerant judges, were sent out on regular circuits of counties, to hear royal pleas, including the imposition of fiscal rights as well as criminal and civil cases. Legal historians see the justices as harbingers of effective, rational government: contemporaries saw them as extortioners.

Central to Henry's image as a legal innovator are the so-called possessary assizes. Between 1166 and 1176, Henry and his advisers perfected new procedures in minor pleas over the occupation or inheritance of property (respectively novel disseisin and mort d'ancestor) and, for major pleas of right, replaced trial by battle. The new system depended on plaintiffs initiating a writ from the king to his sheriff to investigate and settle cases. Juries, of knights for 'grand' assizes and freemen for 'petty' assizes, were sworn in to testify to the evidence. Increasingly, itinerant justices delivered the final judgements. These procedures give the impression of a legal revolution mainly because of the survival of writs and records of the judicial eyres. The reality was less novel. The suits were the same; the law was the same as before; the traditional weight of local opinion continued to be felt through the jurors. Justice was not blind, even if now its operation was more transparent. No new law was made, although the increasing bulk of recorded cases exerted a profound influence in establishing a coherent or, at least, standard common law in the thirteenth century. There was no greater guarantee of equity under the new system than previously. There was considerably greater potential for royal exploitation of both plaintiffs and defendants. Above all, there was no strategy of reform on Henry's part beyond attempting more efficiently to pursue his rights and exercise his responsibilities.

It is away from those areas traditionally associated with Henry's supposed genius that his character and intentions must be sought. The events of his reign reveal no especial control over events. Throughout, Henry's course seems to have been determined by a vigorous pursuit of his rights and a tenacious insistence on the establishment of his dynasty through the preferment of his four adult sons. It was not entirely fortuitous that Henry bequeated his lands essentially intact in 1189. Although he had settled his wife's lands of Poitou and Aquitaine on Richard, Brittany on Geoffrey and Ireland on John, there was the presumption that the eldest son, Henry, to whom was allocated the patrimony of England, Normandy and Anjou, was to be the head of the family firm, to whom the others were to pay homage and whose precedence was recognised by his designation and coronation as king of England in 1170. Although there was no strategic aim or intellectual concept of an Angevin 'empire', the association in the Young Henry's inheritance of Anjou with England and Normandy was novel. With the death of the Young King in 1183 and the succession of Richard of Poitou in 1189, to this patrimony was added that of Aquitaine, all of which consisted of John's inheritance in 1199. By 1216, Henry III could lay claim to all Henry II's lands except Brittany as his patrimony, even though he was incapable of making good that claim.

Henry's reign falls into distinct periods. In the 1150s came the re-establishment of royal authority: the seizure of castles; the reconstitution of the Exchequer; the reconciling of factions by the appointment of two former Stephen partisans as justiciars, Richard de Lucy and Robert of Leicester; and the elevation of a protégé of Archbishop Theobald to chancellor and confidential adviser, Thomas Becket. Henry felt sufficiently secure that, from 1158 to 1163, he could leave the administration of England to proxies. The 1160s became dominated by the Becket dispute and Henry's plans for his dynastic settlement. Whereas the latter required defining his relations with magnates and his French overlord, the former imposed a definition of his rights over his subjects, clerical (Constitutions of Clarendon 1164) and lay (Assize of Clarendon; *Cartae Baronum*; justices-in-eyre; Inquest of Sheriffs). The two strands came together in 1170 with the coronation of the Young Henry, the Inquest into ecclesiastical as well as lay officials, Becket's excommunication of those who crowned the Young King and Becket's murder. That Henry had risked the fragile accommodation with Becket for the coronation was a sign of his eagerness to avoid the fate of his predecessor who had consistently failed to engineer the coronation of his son during his lifetime. This sense of insecurity was genuine, almost usual. Every English monarch from 978 to 1189 either possessed a disputed title or was establishing a recent claim.

However, Becket's murder threw Henry's rule into the hazard, not least because of the personal venom which had infected the dispute and the king's alleged encouragement of the murderers. The early 1170s witnessed a crisis in Henry's affairs. In 1171, he attempted to portray himself as a loyal sword-arm of the church by invading Ireland, ostensibly to effect the wishes of the papacy expressed in the bull *Laudabiliter* (1155). The expedition also had the advantage of asserting Henry's power over potentially unruly Marcher vassals who had already begun to dabble in Irish politics and expanding the scope for Angevin dynastic aggrandizement: in 1177, John, Henry's youngest son, was designated lord of Ireland. However, the brief foray into Ireland was hardly an attempt to create a sovereignty over the British Isles. With Scotland, Henry was content to restore English control of Northumberland (1157) and impose English garrisons in some strategic Scottish castles (at the Treaty of Falaise 1174). In

Wales, Henry shared the fate of his predecessors. The failure of a large-scale invasion in 1165 led to accommodation with the Welsh princes in 1170.

The breach with the church and his dynastic plans continued to undermine Henry. Only at the Compromise of Avranches of 1172 did Henry obtain absolution for his part in Becket's murder. Only in 1174 did he perform personal penance at Canterbury, driven, it must be suspected, as much by his parlous political situation as by acute remorse. In 1173, a dangerous coalition of Henry's elder sons, Henry, Richard and Geoffrey, egged on by his wife, Eleanor, allied with the king of France, Louis VII, William, king of Scots and Philip, count of Flanders, and supported by a jumbled assortment of ambitious and disaffected magnates in England and Normandy, launched a series of invasions and revolts. The loyalty of key barons and officials, led by the justiciar Richard de Lucy; lack of coordination among his opponents; and his own unflappability enabled Henry to survive and to trounce his enemies. The aftermath of the Great Rebellion showed Henry in characteristic light. Although lenient towards his chief opponents, he set about reinforcing the exercise and exploitation of royal rights. The writ of mort d'ancestor was devised to ease access to royal courts of plaintiffs who had lost out in the quickening land market: what went to royal courts avoided or superseded baronial ones. Castles, such as those of the rebel Hugh Bigod in East Anglia, were destroyed. The itinerant justices system was overhauled with new orders for criminal justice decreed giving them greater authority (Assize of Northampton 1176). Forest Laws were resumed in their full severity. To emphasise how much Henry depended upon his standing administration in England, Richard de Lucy was allowed, as Roger of Salisbury had been under Henry I, to issue writs in his own name, a royal *alter ego* indeed. Although all these measures have come to be seen as typical of Henry's robust and intelligent governmental style, none of them was inevitable, all were the children of expediency rather than ideology.

What made Henry's rule work was not administrative genius but physical energy. Henry was almost pathologically restless; his household and court were always on the road, sometimes at very short notice. If his courtiers were exhausted, their master never was. The speed with which Henry travelled from Ireland to Normandy via Wales and England in the Spring of 1172 — Wexford to Savigny in a calendar month — prompted the rather sour comment of Louis VII: 'the king of England seems rather to fly than to travel by horse or ship'. One courtier, Walter Map, declared that Henry 'covered distances like a courier', adding bitterly 'showing no mercy to his household'. Constantly on the move, Henry was able more easily to impose his personality on his subjects and his will on events. Where he was absent, his interests were pursued by agents acting in his name and, crucially, answerable to him for their conduct. This habit of scrutinizing his officials provided the incentive to efficiency. Another acute observer, Peter of Blois, described Henry as 'hunting through the provinces inquiring into everyone's doing, and especially judges those whom he has made judge of others'. Henry did not govern his people; he governed his interests.

The effectiveness of Henry's authority depended on local acquiescence obtained by identifying mutual self-interest or coercion. It was as a politican that Henry earned respect, because he rarely chose outright military action if it could be avoided. Indeed, as king he led only three major military expeditions — to Toulouse in 1159; Wales in 1165 and Ireland in 1171 — none of which were unqualified triumphs. Henry's tactic was the siege, the threat of ravaging, the pressure of gaining local loyalties, the agreed settlement. Although from youth he campaigned almost every summer of his life Henry never fought a pitched battle. It was as a negotiator, a man who understood the political as much as military weaknesses and anxieties of his enemies, that Henry got his way. Where he resorted to brute force — at Toulouse or with Thomas Becket — he failed. There was something of the showman in Henry. One of his favourite roles was that of humble penitent. The very public penance at Canterbury was only one of a number of convenient displays. In 1187, in trying to reach a truce with the French, he appeared before their negotiators in floods of tears, confessing his sins and protesting that he would reform his ways as signal of which he intended to go on crusade. The performance had some effect, although the king of France, Philip II, justly twitted his negotiators: 'You believed all that?'.

W. L. Warren argued that when Henry made a will in February 1182, he was at the peak of his career. He had imposed his will on his dominions; England in particular was peaceful, which is not the same as being content. Henry's victory in 1174 led to an extended period of internal peace: no royal army had to tackle a concerted rebellion in England until 1215. In that, if in nothing else, Henry II had emulated his grandfather. The church was now an ally, under his protection and subject to his patronage. His revenues were substantial and growing, from England running in the last decade of his life at over £20,000 per annum. But there remained intractable problems. His sons champed at the bit of his continuing authority. A new king of France, Philip II (1180-1223), would prove a more skilled adversary than his father Louis VII in the unending fencing match between Capetain king and Angevin vassal. In 1183, a major rebellion by the Young Henry was only averted by his death. In 1185, John's attempt to enforce his lordship in Ireland ended in fiasco. To many observers there appeared a weakening of Henry's grip. Gerald of Wales, who was close to Henry at this time, recognised this, fancifully attributing it to Henry's refusal to go to aid the Holy Land or accept the crown of Jerusalem (itself arguably a family possession; its kings were the direct descendants of Henry's grandfather Fulk of Anjou). In 1188, Henry did take the cross and was rewarded by the chance to levy a highly efficient tax, the Saladin Tithe, on all those of his free subjects who had not followed suit. The money helped pay for the wars of his last months.

The fundamental cause of Henry's troubles in his later years were his children. Even the deaths of Henry (1183) and Geoffrey (1186) did not remove the problem of the succession. After some years of increasing strain, in 1188-9 Richard of Poitou openly rebelled to assert his claim to the full Angevin inheritance, fearful, perhaps, lest Henry disinherit him for his younger brother John. With the support of Philip of France, Richard brought Henry to bay. Illness, age and political odds forced Henry to surrender the initiative. At the end, he simply gave up the struggle, dismissing his army, withdrawing to die at Chinon. The last act of the drama was played out, appropriately, in Anjou. Henry, however conscious of being the legitimate king of England was not, in any meaningful sense, English. His kingdom was just one of many possessions which he claimed as of right and to the control and exploitation of which he expended his immense vitality.

Inevitably, Henry's person and character attracted immense interest. If not quite the cynosure of all eyes, he was reputed to have introduced the short cloak of Anjou into England, prompting his nickname of Curtmantle. Contemporaries described him as dressing simply and rejecting the trappings of pomp. He rarely appeared at formal crown-wearings, unlike his Norman predecessors. Of medium height, powerfully if stockily built, with grey-blue eyes, bow-legs, rough hands and a ruddy and freckled complexion, he tended to look rather unkempt and grubby. Obsessed by hunting, his physical restlessness some attributed to this fear of getting fat, a fate he combatted by vigorous exercise. Whatever the cause, his impatience of repose, apart from presenting appalling logistical problems for his household staff who trailed along in his wake, 'disturbed almost half Christendom'. Most vividly, to Becket's disciple Herbert of Bosham, Henry was a human chariot, drawing all after him.

Admired, Henry was not well liked. Politically, he earned a reputation as an oath-breaker. Personally, he got on notoriously badly with his immediate family. Although he was affectionate towards his cousins, he kept his two brothers Geoffrey and William out of any significant possessions. His wife, the formidable Eleanor of Aquitaine, he kept under house arrest for the last fifteen years of their marriage. His indulgence of his sons was returned by treachery and hatred. Perhaps Henry was too much his own man to admit intimacy; perhaps as a father he expected too much character and too little independence. According to Gerald of Wales, Henry had had painted in Winchester castle a picture of an eagle being attacked by four young ones who, he explained to his friends, represented his four sons 'persecuting me even unto death'. Henry had a number of mistresses throughout his life, notably Rosamund Clifford (d.1176) whom he openly acknowledged after 1174. It is ironic that, in the final crisis of his reign, such an obsessive dynast should find loyalty only in an illegitimate son, his chancellor Geoffrey.

Yet where he chose to bestow it, his friendship was strong. Those he liked and admired most were often his opposites, men of inflexibility and calm: Hugh of Avalon; Baldwin of Ford; William Marshal; and Thomas Becket. All showed independence of mind and courage in the face of Henry's will. The difference between them was that the first three were embraced for their integrity, however awkward. But Becket, the friend of his youth, mentor, companion, guide, attractive, worldly but not corrupt, intelligent and seemingly loyal, had, in Henry's eyes, betrayed affection and friendship. For that there was no forgiveness.

Of all his personal traits, the image of Henry's anger is most indelible. His rages were Homeric. When opponents talked of the *ira* of the king, perhaps they had in mind more than a term for political or legal impropriety. Henry's tantrums were awesome, transcending mere petulance. When roused, he tore his clothes and literally chewed the carpet (easier to do then as they were made of straw). Such was the mood that condemned Becket: 'Will nobody rid me of this turbulent priest?'. Yet at other times he could be judicious, witty, generous, eager to understand the problems or people he encountered. He suffered from always being the centre of others' attention, which may explain why in his household he often withdrew in private, in marked contrast to his public accessibility. He held unexpected, even awkward views. He disdained the fashion of chivalry and tournaments. Brave in battle and a campaigner of renowned and proven stamina, he disliked battles and was distressed by casualties. A thoughtful monarch, his recorded conversation suggests a man of some humanity. When the patriarch of Jerusalem tried to persuade Henry to lead an army to the Holy Land in 1185, Henry remarked in private 'These clerks can incite us boldly to arms and danger since they themselves will receive no blows in the struggle, nor will they undertake any burdens which they can avoid'.

A war-hating warrior, Henry's piety presents a similar paradox. An unenthusiastic attender at services, he spent over twenty years toying with going on crusade before taking the Cross in 1188. Yet he quietly sent treasure for use in the defence of Jerusalem. A critic of secular clerks, he was a patron of the strict orders of Grandmont and Chartreuse and promoted the Cistercian Baldwin of Ford and the Carthusian Hugh of Avalon. Impatient with hypocrisy, Henry admired faithfulness and clarity; yet he himself was a notorious perjuror and dissembler. His interest in legal procedures, which gave rise to the thirteenth century story of him spending sleepless nights with his advisers perfecting the wording of the writ of novel desseisin, may have sprung from his intellectual self-confidence. As Peter of Blois optimistically put it 'with the king of England it is school every day'. This sits ill with the impression derived from others of a court seething with low life as well as the great and of a lord who delighted in inconveniencing his servants and courtiers. It is impossible to know what Henry was like, how much of his undoubted charisma was derived from his personality or his position. That is why historians have been able to cast him in their own image.

Henry's rule marked no great epoch. He presided over social and cultural developments on which he could, in the nature of things, exert little control. His achievements were pragmatic, in response to events and circumstance, the greatest of them being survival. There were no great triumphs to match those of the first William, Richard or Edward. What made Henry remarkable was the hold he kept over remarkably diverse lands for a remarkably long time. Above all, for contemporaries, he knew how to act regally. As Walter Map put it, he 'brought honour on good men'. When Henry compensated sailors of his fleet who had lost their ships during a Channel crossing, Map added 'perchance another king would not have paid this just debt'.

W. L. Warren, *Henry II*, 1973.
J. Gillingham, *The Angevin Empire*, 1984.

**ELEANOR OF AQUITAINE** (*c*.1122-1204) epitomised the constrained role allotted to medieval heiresses. Although by inheritance from her father, William X of Aquitaine, she was in her own right duchess of the largest duchy in France, stretching from Poitou to the Pyrenees, for sixty-seven years (1137-1204) her authority was exercised first by her two husbands, then by two of her sons. She merely conveyed and validated power. Her importance lay in her dynastic value which, in turn, depended on her ability to produce sons and heirs. In 1137, she married Louis VII of France (king 1137-80), but after fifteen years they had

*Eleanor of Aquitaine*
(From her effigy at Fontevrault Abbey in Anjou)

only had two daughters. Louis, despite the risk of losing such a large province, divorced Eleanor. There had been rumours of her sexual indiscretions with Geoffrey of Anjou (Henry II's father) and, most notoriously, with her uncle, Raymond of Poitiers, prince of Antioch, during the Second Crusade, on which Eleanor accompanied her husband (1147-9). This last piece of gossip may well have been embroidered as a *post facto* justification for the divorce in 1152. However, Eleanor's position and marital career(s) encouraged such talk, the more so when, a few weeks after her divorce from Louis, she married, around Whitsun 1152, his most powerful vassal, Henry of Anjou, who was only nineteen.

Not only did she bring her vast inheritance to extend the Angevin dominions from the Channel to the Spanish marches (to which England was added in 1154), but she bore Henry five sons, as well as three daughters (William, 1153-56; Henry 1155-83; Matilda 1156-89; Richard 1157-99; Geoffrey 1158-86; Eleanor 1163-1215; Joan 1165-99; and John 1167-1216). Yet during Henry II's life, her political role was formal, except for one disastrous intervention in 1173 when she joined her elder sons in their plot to depose their father. Eleanor was arrested as she tried to escape Henry's court at Chinon disguised as a man. For the rest of Henry's reign, she was virtually under house-arrest. But even before 1173, she was only a cypher, acting as titular head of the royal administration in England during some of Henry's absences, and agreeing to the investiture of her son Richard as count of Poitou and Aquitaine in 1170.

This impotence had, it seems, little to do with personality. As the young queen of France, she had been notably vivacious and, after Henry II's death, she assumed, for the first time, a prominent political role. As in 1173, she acted in her sons' interests, securing Richard I's succession in England in 1189 and John's in Anjou in 1199. In 1191, she escorted Berengaria of Navarre to Sicily to be married to Richard before returning to France: one crusade was, perhaps, enough to last a lifetime. In 1192-4 she tried to preserve Richard's rule in France, against Philip II (1180-1223), and in England against John. She saw herself, or was cleverly manipulated by the justiciar, Hubert Walter, to be seen as the guarantor of Angevin legitimacy. As such Eleanor was instrumental in raising the huge ransom for Richard in 1193-4 and in receiving the king from his captor, Henry VI of Germany, in February 1194. As she grew older, she may have begun to operate a dynastic policy of her own, with the aim of securing Aquitaine for her descendants — Angevin; Castilian; Toulousain; or French. She helped John secure his throne, not least by laying waste parts of rebellious Anjou in 1199 with Richard I's mercenary captain Mercadier, and, in 1202, held Mirebeau against her grandson Arthur of Brittany for long enough to allow John to relieve the castle. But Eleanor also arranged, in 1200, for another grandchild, Blanche of Castille, to marry the heir to the king of France, the future Louis VIII (1223-26). Until the birth of John's first son in 1207, any marriage of Eleanor's grandchildren was of potential significance for the succession to Angevin lands. In extreme old age, Eleanor retired to the abbey of Fontevrault where she died and was buried, appropriately enough, beside Henry II and Richard I. In death, as in life, Eleanor was defined by her relationship with husband and son.

Yet her life was sufficiently long and occasionally dramatic to have spawned a myth which placed her, with her daughter by

Louis VII, Marie of Champagne, at the centre of a cult of courtly love which was supposed to have grown up at her court in Poitiers between 1167 and 1173. Fostered by these independent feminine spirits and nurtured by troubadours under the leadership of the great Champagnois poet Chrétien de Troyes, the essence of this cult was the glorification of adulterous love of a man, usually unmarried, for a married woman, attainable (as with Guinivere in Chrétien de Troyes' Lancelot) or not. In a treatise *De Amore* or *The Art of Courtly Love*, written c.1186 by Andrew, a Champagne court chaplain, Eleanor and Marie are shown at Poitiers adjudicating lovers' quarrels. The whole paraphernalia has been seen as essentially seditious, undermining male dominance and authority as well as the teachings of the church. Unfortunately for romantics and feminists alike, it is all fiction. Eleanor was not at Poitiers consistently from 1167-73. There is no evidence that Marie or Chrétien visited her there or anywhere else. Andrew's treatise was written after he had left Marie's service and was composed in the spirit of irony, especially when depicting the aged Eleanor condemning consanguineous marriages (of which she made two) and marriage to worthless younger husbands (Henry was eleven years her junior). Marie of Champagne's notorious denial that love in marriage is impossible was dated by Andrew to May 1174 — when Eleanor was a prisoner of her husband at Chinon. If Eleanor was a patron of artists, her husband was more so. If she had a liking for formalised smut, we do not know of it. That she attracted such stories was perhaps explicable in terms of her marital adventures and her position as the last representative of the old, independent line of Aquitainian/Poitevin counts. Many of the Arthurian stories were hostile to the authority not only of husbands but of kings: Eleanor, countess of Poitou and duchess of Aquitaine would have been a suitable, if fictitious patroness. The reality was that she lived and died an appendage to her father, husbands, sons (and lovers, if she had any). Her resting place lay not in the pages of romance but beside her second husband and her favourite son in the abbey of Fontevrault. Eleanor's personal legacy were her descendants: her grandchildren included an emperor of Germany, Otto IV, as well as a king of England, Henry III. From her, all subsequent English monarchs were descended as were all French kings from Louis IX (1226-70) to Louis Philippe (1830-48). Impersonally, her legacy was even greater. Through her, Gascony was attached to the English crown until 1453, a source of constant tension and lengthy wars with the kings of France. With Gascony came Bordeaux, its wine trade, prosperity for Bristol and Southampton and the uniquely English, or rather Anglo-French word for red Bordeaux wine. In claret, Eleanor of Aquitaine's inheritance still lives.

W. W. Kibler, ed. *Eleanor of Aquitaine: Patron and Politician*, 1976.

J. F. Benton, 'The Court of Champagne as a Literary Center' in *Speculum* xxxvi, 1961.

**GILBERT FOLIOT** (1105/10-1188; abbot of Gloucester 1139-48; bishop of Hereford 1148-63; bishop of London 1163-88) has emerged from the polemics of the Becket dispute as a cold, devious, envious pharasaical church politician. The murder of his rival turned an ecclesiastical dispute into a cosmic judgement against Foliot and what he represented. Yet he had all the qualities of a remarkable bishop, more, in fact, than Becket: intelligence; education; good connections; literary skill; legal expertise; political sensitivity; personal piety; and monastic austerity.

Foliot's family were tenants of the earls of Huntingdon who were, for much of the twelfth century, also kings of Scotland, which might explain Gilbert's association with Ailred of Rievaulx, to whom he may have dedicated his *Homilies* (1163/67). Other relatives included Miles of Gloucester, earl of Hereford and Richard of Ilchester, a leading royal clerk under Henry II. In the 1130s, after a thorough education in the liberal arts, scriptural exegesis and canon law, which possibly took him to Paris and Bologna, Gilbert entered the great Burgundian monastery of Cluny, rising to be its prior and then abbot of its daughter house at Abbeville. Appointed by Miles of Gloucester to the abbacy at Gloucester (1139), he followed his patron in support of the Angevin claim although, when promoted to the see of Hereford by the pope in 1148, he proved a successful navigator of the political shoals of support for the future Henry II and public allegiance to King Stephen. As abbot and bishop Foliot was noted for combining personal austerity with administrative skill, which extended to condoning some important forgeries in support of his abbey's claims (a not uncommon twelfth century monastic pastime). Characteristically, he wanted to retain his abbacy when bishop: pluralist greed, or a yearning for the company of monks? Perhaps a bit of both.

In 1162, Thomas Becket, the king's chancellor, was chosen by Henry as archbishop of Canterbury. The only evidence that Foliot was a disappointed candidate comes from his enemies, and is unlikely. Translation between sees was uncommon, Foliot's own to London in 1163 requiring a special papal licence. Henry may, however, have regarded Foliot's promotion as balancing the preferment of a royal clerk with a distinctly secular reputation. Foliot was supposed to have complained at Becket's appointment that Henry had performed a miracle by transforming a soldier into an archbishop. The witness is hostile, but the sentiments may be genuine enough. Foliot, with his impeccable religious credentials, never fully believed in the sincerity of Becket's transformation from royal stooge to champion of the church. Events did little to alter his assessment.

The bitterness between Foliot and Becket was personal and political. From the start there was conflict, with Becket trying to insist that Foliot renew his oath of allegiance to Canterbury as bishop of London, while Foliot, with precedent and law on his side, argued that he was still bound by his profession of obedience as bishop of Hereford. Foliot thought Becket tactless and foolish in his handling of the king over clerical immunities in 1163-4. For Foliot, the issues at stake were not doctrinal or moral but administrative. Accommodation was possible without compromising principles or confrontation with the king. Becket managed to do both at the council of Clarendon (1164). For three days, the bishops had remained united in the face of verbal abuse and physical threats when, unilaterally, Becket capitulated to the king's demands that the bishops swear an oath to abide by the customs of the realm regarding church and state relations. As Foliot later put it: 'it was the general of our army who deserted, the captain who fled'. He did not trust Becket again. At Northampton, he tried to force Becket to accept the secular authority of the king's council and to allow the bishops to mediate. In the face of the archbishop's intransigence, Foliot shouted 'you always have been a fool, and always will be'. With Becket in exile, Foliot became the king's leading ecclesiastical adviser on how to handle the controversy. He was skilled at gaining clerical support, including that of Becket's former tutor and theological expert Robert of Melun, bishop of Hereford (1163-7), and marshelling arguments to present to the pope. The invective and mutual recriminations intensified, not least because Foliot had been assigned the administration of the Canterbury see. Becket may not have been an effective archbishop, but he was an excellent propagandist, supported as he was by most fashionable donnish opinion.

Foliot's response to the calumnies against him came in his letter *Multiplicem* written in 1166. On the principle that attack is the best method of defence, this was a stinging and savage indictment of Becket as a simoniac (which was untrue), a coward and a traitor to his fellow bishops. Foliot argued that Henry was best handled by quiet remonstrance not violent insults. Crucially, but, except for Becket, uncontroversially, Foliot admitted the royal right to judge bishops in secular cases (an argument accepted by Lanfranc in 1088), as well as the king's quasi-sacerdotal position by virtue of being annointed with chrism at coronation. Accusations aside, *Multiplicem* sums up Foliot's basic belief that the two swords of church and state must and could cooperate. Whatever Becket's allies said, Foliot was personally and professionally committed to church reform and freedom from secular domination. The Cluniac ideal was of separation from but influence over the laity. Shouting across an unbridgeable divide of prejudice would achieve nothing. Throughout the controversy, Foliot sought to detach the Becket case from the wider issue of *libertas ecclesiae*, which he felt the archbishop had hijacked. More specifically, with slick legalism he pressed, as at Argentan in 1167, for the pope to depose the archbishop, at the same time protecting his own back from possible excommunication. To achieve his ends, Foliot was as ready as his opponent to stoop into the gutter, as his self-seeking, disingenuous charges against Becket in *Multiplicem* showed.

Becket's language also became more personal and intemper-ate. In 1167, he wrote to Foliot: 'Your aim has all along been to effect the downfall of the Church and myself' (the association is typical). In 1169, he excommunicated Foliot. On the pope absolving him in 1170, Becket exclaimed: 'Satan is unloosed for the destruction of the Church'. On hearing that Foliot had assisted at the coronation of the Young Henry, Becket again excommunicated him. This time, because of Becket's murder (December 1170), Foliot was not released until 1172. In 1174, at Henry's public penance at Canterbury, it was appropriately Foliot who preached the sermon; not surprisingly he protested the king's innocence of blame for the murder. Unfortunately for the bishop, the Becket cult and the attendant cottage industry of histories of the controversy were already in full swing, with Foliot cast as a leading villain, a new Achitophel, corrupter of princes. After all, some of the pro-Becket writers still hoped for preferment from the king.

Carrying such uncomfortable baggage, Foliot could not resume a prominent political role. Although not a great scholar, he was fluent in Latin, French and English, an apparently notable accomplishment. In his later years he wrote commentaries on the *Pater noster* and the *Canticles*. He lingered on into extreme old age, but not as a representative of a past age. The English church of the 1180s bore more similarities with that of the 1150s than Becket's apologists would have welcomed. Foliot, a clerical grandee who, in his thirty-nine years as a bishop, appointed five archdeacons and every one a relative, was not out of place on an episcopal bench sporting names such as de Lucy, Ridel, Bohun, FitzJocelin, another Foliot, let alone the king's cousin, Roger, and son, Geoffrey. In one sense, Gilbert Foliot had lost the battle but won the war or, rather, hostilities had been suspended. On all sides, moderation and accommodation had prevailed after the histrionics of the 1160s. The ambitious prelate would have felt his defeat keenly; the austere monk may have been satisfied with Walter Map's description of him, when old and blind, as 'a treasure-house of goodness and wisdom'.

A. Morey and C. N. L. Brooke, *Gilbert Foliot and his Letters*, 1965.

**THOMAS BECKET** (*c*.1120-1170; archbishop of Canterbury 1162-70; canonised 1173) was the most famous Englishman of the Middle Ages. He remains perhaps the most controversial. Chaucer's 'holy, blissful martyr' redeemed a life of fame, conflict, vanity, pride and failure by being hacked to bits by four probably rather drunk knights one dark December evening in Canterbury Cathedral. His most famous death transformed his life into something beyond biography; for believers beyond history. His life and death became Providential, his sacrifice a lesson in the mysterious workings of God. The reality, however, if not the stuff of legend, is almost that of fiction.

Becket was born around 1120 in London the son of a merchant, perhaps a mercer, Gilbert Becket, and his wife, Matilda. Both parents were Norman, Gilbert originating from the Eure region of Lower Normandy. The surname Becket was Gilbert's and was never used by Thomas himself, who preferred to style himself 'Thomas of London'. (Nobody until the Reformation concocted 'à Becket'.) The acquisitive entrepreneurial spirit of a self-made London merchant may have influenced Thomas. Certainly, his background — urban, non-noble, commercial — forced him to live on his wits and personality as something of an outsider, not part of the established social hierarchy, nor in the traditional channel of social betterment, a monastic order. Although educated at the Augustinian Priory at Merton, at a London grammar-school and briefly at the Schools in Paris, Thomas was never part of the ambitious, self-congratulatory clerisy of schoolmen who so dominated later twelfth century church and state. Intelligent, but no scholar, a late entrant into clerical orders, Thomas never lost a secular air, to the suspicion of his critics and the unease of his supporters.

Becket's adult life falls into distinct periods, a fact which itself aroused contemporary comment on the fickleness of his personal and professional allegiances. Handsome, tall, thin, with pale skin, dark hair, a big nose and bright eyes, his personality invited friendship: he attracted people. But there were also signs of an inner nervousness. He was susceptible to stress-related illnesses and he had a slight stammer. A young man on the make, from a prosperous London mercantile family, it was perhaps

*The murder of Thomas Becket*
(From a Canterbury manuscript of John of Salisbury's account
of the martyrdom)

natural that his first attempt at a career (*c.*1143-45) was as
accountant to a leading London banker Osbert Huitdeniers (*i.e.*
Eightpence — perhaps his rate of interest in the pound?) In
1145/6 Becket found a greater patron when he joined the household of Archbishop Theobald of Canterbury, where he stayed
until 1155, rising to become archdeacon of Canterbury in 1154.
With Theobald, Becket gained his entrée to the world of politics.
He made contacts with future leaders of the church, such Roger

of Pont l'Evêque. Accompanying Theobald to the Council of Rheims (1148) he would have had the chance to meet the likes of Bernard of Clairvaux, Suger of St Denis and Peter Lombard, each of them pivotal figures in their respective fields of government, spirituality and theology. In the early 1150s Theobald sent Thomas for a year's study of civil and canon law at Bologna and Auxerre. He was introduced to diplomacy on visits to the papal Curia. His capacity to charm and talent for inspiring devotion in others was thoroughly exercised on Theobald and his colleagues in the archbishop's household.

Another Knight's Move, to become, on Theobald's recommendation, chancellor to the new, foreign and untried Henry II, opened up a fresh heady career which lasted from 1155 until his elevation to the see of Canterbury in 1162. He became the young king's intimate councillor and close friend. Although he performed official duties, witnessing royal letters and charters, sitting occasionally at the Exchequer and infrequently acting as a royal judge, it was his informal influence that counted. He and the king were inseparable: which of them learnt or benefited more is impossible to gauge.

Still in minor orders, Becket steadily amassed ecclesiastical benefices and was rewarded for his professional services by the king with a number of estates. As a sign of especial favour, the king excused his chancellor from rendering account at the Exchequer on lands he held in custody, i.e. on behalf of the king. This was potentially dangerous as Becket revealed a taste for outward magnificence which was fuelled by these royal grants of custodies which included vacant bishoprics and secular baronies such as the extensive Honor of Eye. Henry's assessment in 1164 that Becket had made £30,000 out of these lands was probably an exaggeration, but of the chancellor's wealth there can be no doubt. One of his biographers states that most of his fifty-two clerks were assigned to administer his estates. He had a military household of 700 knights. On an embassy to Paris in 1158, he took with him two hundred and fifty servants; eight large waggons laden with furnishings, plate and provisions; and twenty-four changes of clothes. Small wonder locals were astonished: 'What a wonderful king he must be to have such a great chancellor'. The effect was no doubt deliberate, but the extravagance went beyond diplomatic point-scoring: in Paris a single dish of eels eaten by Becket cost 100 shillings.

As well as a taste for the good life, Becket absorbed secular manners even to the extent of actively campaigning with his troops. In 1159, on Henry II's ill-fated expedition to subdue Toulouse, Becket, in full armour, led successful attacks on three towns. On the Vexin campaign of 1161, commanding a retinue of, according to one biographer, nearly six thousand cavalry and infantry, Becket led the royal vanguard. On one occasion he defeated a French knight, Engelram of Trie, at a joust, claiming his charger for his prize. Few Archbishops of Canterbury until Dr Robert Runcie (MC) could claim as much. Becket could play the great magnate, but his wealth and position was entirely dependent on the king. That had been his opportunity and still offered hope of advancement. But it spelt his doom.

When Archbishop Theobald died in 1161, Henry appointed Becket in his place, a characteristically bold yet pragmatic act. The tradition of monks being appointed to Canterbury had been strong since the tenth century, the sole royal clerk being the infamous Stigand. Becket's reputation and lifestyle were bizarre, if not offensive qualifications. Yet Theobald had favoured him, not least because of his knowledge of Canterbury and his close relationship with the king. In making the appointment, Henry did not intend to dominate the church, merely continue to cooperate with it. If he also wished to reclaim royal rights lost under Stephen, Becket was an even more ideal choice. There were continental precedents and parallels, most obviously in Germany where Frederick Barbarossa had appointed Rainald von Dassel his chancellor in 1156 and archbishop of Cologne in 1159: Rainald, an almost exact contemporary of Becket's who shared his delight in military exploits, continued to serve his temporal and spiritual masters without conflict or strain. Henry expected Thomas to do the same.

The final priod of Becket's life, as archbishop 1162-70, forms an apparent contrast to what had gone before. Yet, psychologically, his reaction to his changed circumstances is perhaps not so inconsistent. Once he had identified the nature of his responsibilities, he tried to suit them. Historians, then and now, have insisted on a transformation between the worldly chancellor and the ascetic champion of the church. In fact, Becket's perspective depended, not unnaturally, on his position: thus his advocacy in the king's interest of the harsh scutage of 1159 matches his later insistence on ecclesiastical immunities. Theobald had taught him that the church and the state were dependent but separate; Theobald's career had been conditioned by his attempt to retain independence in order best to protect the interests of his church, English or Canterbury (not always synonymous). Whatever and whenever internal conversion occurred, Becket was keen to act as fully the archbishop as he had the chancellor. If the externals required were different, so be it. Equally, if they were the same, Becket was not unwilling to comply. His hospitality as prelate was little changed in lavishness to that as royal favourite, his table no less luxurious.

What had definitely altered was Becket's status. As archbishop he was, for the first time, his own master. The sense of authority and liberation proved too much for what discretion he may have possessed. On receiving the *pallium* from the pope, he surrendered the chancellorship and almost immediately began to adopt extreme and provocative stands on ecclesiastical immunities and jurisdiction, to the annoyance of the king. Becket's initial posturing may have been designed to win acceptance and respect from the Canterbury monks and his fellow bishops suspicious of this royal nominee. Just as, when chancellor, he had aggressively pursued royal rights, so, as archbishop, he argued for the protection and recovery of all traditional rights belonging to Canterbury. One difficulty was Becket's style. He was tactless and aggressive, over-eager to assert himself, too sensitive to the possibility of being ignored.

Wider issues soon precipitated open conflict with the king, but personal hostility coloured all their dealings. By the autumn of 1163, relations with the king had disintegrated. In October, Becket was stripped of all secular honours acquired as chancellor: it is perhaps significant that he had not resigned them previously. At Westminster in October 1163, Henry raised the issue of the immunity of convicted criminous clerks from secular punishment. He argued tht secular crimes should be punished in secular not ecclesiastical courts. With the support of the other bishops, Becket insisted on clerical immunity and condemned the concept of double jeopardy, trial and punishment by two courts of the same offence. They only agreed to existing royal customs 'saving their order'. Attempts to find a compromise were unsuccessful. Relations with the king were further damaged at Clarendon in January 1164 when Henry tried to force the bishops to accept existing customs unconditionally. After three days'intransigence, Becket unexpectedly capitulated, to the shocked surprise of his episcopal colleagues. But Henry pressed his advantage by enshrining what he saw as the existing conventions in writing in the Constitutions of Clarendon. Further conflict was inevitable.

By now Becket's arrogance and inconsistency had alienated many of his colleagues, notably Archbishop Roger of York and Bishop Gilbert Foliot of London, and had aroused vindictive fury in the king who now plotted Becket's ruin. The archbishop was summoned to Northampton in October 1164 ostensibly to answer a charge brought against him by John the Marshal of unlawfully withholding property. Once there, Becket faced additional charges of peculation, dating back to his chancellorship, and treason. He was threatened with deprivation. Ignoring the legal and physical threats and the angry pleadings of the bishops, Becket defied his critics. On the day of his trial, with a characteristic sense of drama carrying his own cross, he denied the jurisdiction of the royal court, declared that the issue was one of ecclesiastical independence and appealed to Rome. He then fled in disguise into exile.

The six years Becket spent in exile turned what had been a local dispute into an international *cause célèbre*. This was no accident. To garner international support, Becket played on French political hostility to Henry and the weak position of Pope Alexander III, to whom he loudly protested his allegiance, somewhat to that cautious man's disquiet. He waged a relentless and increasingly heated and extravagant propaganda campaign. To further his cause he immersed himself in canon law and recruited sympathetic academics in the Schools. As is their wont, these intellectuals were happy to discuss the cosmic principles behind what others, such as Bishop Foliot and King Henry, regarded as matters of practical policy and administration. For all his protestations, Becket could not rely on the English church for support. Most bishops opposed his methods which, as Foliot pointed out in an acerbic attack in 1166, achieved nothing except to weaken the church. However, the king could not entirely ignore the controversy. Like his predecessor, Henry was keen to see his son crowned king in his lifetime to secure the new dynasty and was reluctant to close the door completely on compromise, whatever his personal feelings towards his former friend. The dispute had all the makings of drama: observers were not to be disappointed.

As if to emphasise his rightness as well as righteousness, in his private life Becket began to assume more recognisable features of rigorous piety. From 1165, he seems to have worn some form of monastic habit, perhaps adopted at the Cistercian house of Pontigny where he stayed 1164-66. About this time he also began to wear a hair shirt next to his skin and to indulge in violent flagellation. Once more, chameleon-like, he assumed the appearance most fitting his station: not the flamboyant royal *familiaris*, nor yet the primate of England, but now a symbol of persecution.

Frequent attempts at reconciliation organised by the pope or Louis VII of France foundered on the obstinacy of both parties. In 1169, with the dispute in stalemate, personal interviews between Henry and Becket at Montmirail and Montmartre failed to achieve anything: king and archbishop were alike in their obstinacy and their hatred of losing face. However, in June 1170 Henry II had his eldest son, Henry, crowned king by the archbishop of York, in blatant contravention of one of the most cherished rights of Canterbury. Ironically, this blow to Becket's position led to a reconciliation with Henry at Fréteval in July 1170 which restored Becket's lands, allowed his return to England but left the substantive issues of dispute untouched. The agreement had little chance of success.

Returning to England to a mixed reception in December 1170, Becket proceeded with a typical lack of tact, travelling ostentatiously across southern England and refusing to lift the excommunication of the bishops involved in the coronation of the young Henry. Angered by news of this, and possibly alarmed at reports of Becket's popularity, King Henry, in Normandy for Christmas, lost his temper. In one of his notorious passions, possibly exacerbated by seasonable junketings, Henry was reputed to have declared 'What miserable drones and traitors have I nourished and promoted in my household who let their lord be treated with such shameful contempt by a low-born clerk' or, more popularly and more succinctly, but less reliably, 'will nobody rid me of this turbulent priest?' This was the cue for four knights, Hugh de Moreville, William de Tracey, Reginald FitzUrse and Richard le Breton to embark for England. Their motive may have been simply to arrest the archbishop, but, once they reached Canterbury on 29 December, events slid out of control. Argument turned to anger and anger into violence. Becket's last moments were the noblest of his life, heroic, even if we discount the embellishments of the many hagiographers who retold the tale. He was unafraid of death and remained calm amid the confusion and horror. Uncompromising to the end, his pride and rashness were transmuted into a steely resolve to meet his fate. Refusing to go with the knights, he was cut down and butchered in the north transept of his cathedral, the second of five archbishops of Canterbury to meet a violent end.

The manner of his murder ensured for Becket a possibly desired martyr's crown. His was the single most chronicled death in English history, its impact and legacy matched only, perhaps, by that of Charles I. There are five accounts of the martyrdom written by those actually in the cathedral at the time of Becket's death, including John of Salisbury (who hid behind the altars); Benedict of Peterborough (who collected the first stories of miracles); and Edward Grim who, in trying to protect his master, had his arm sliced through to the bone by a blow from Reginald FitzUrse's sword. What confirmed the unique significnce of the assassination were the miracles which began within days. Within a decade, 703 miracles were recorded. In 1173, Becket was canonised, by which time his tomb had already become a focus of pilgrimage and healing. Becket's cult and shrine rapidly gained international popularity which survived to the Reformation. Apart from its carefully documented efficacy, the cult was sustained by the production of Canterbury Water, allegedly an inexhaustible supply of the martyr's diluted blood, but probably a sort of medieval Ribena, which pilgrims would carry away with them in specially crafted ampullae which the monks sold to the faithful. Whatever the transcendent benefits of Becket's cult, materially it secured the prosperity of Canterbury and its tourist trade for more than three and a half centuries.

His death transformed Becket's career and achievement. In life he had proved one of the least successful archbishops in English history. Effectively he performed his duties for under two and a half years. He alienated former friends, such as Roger of York and Arnold of Lisieux; exasperated allies, including Pope Alexander III; and convinced enemies such as Foliot of his unsuitability. Proud, inflexible, sincere but unimaginative, Becket had a love of the grand gesture but a weakness for exaggeration. His assessment of issues was unsubtle, if vigorously and skilfully defended. The mess he made of his great opportunity in 1162 suggests that he was promoted beyond his abilities: an excellent lieutenant, a poor leader. Unable to compromise, as archbishop his frenetic behaviour and nervous outbursts mark him as being overwhelmed. Intelligent, he lacked schooling; efficient in the ways of the world, he never mastered patience. Perhaps he would have been a better soldier than statesman.

The great issues for which he claimed he fought were resolved after his death by negotiation, not confrontation. A chastened Henry II, who did penance at Becket's tomb in 1174, agreed to the principles of free elections to bishoprics, the right of appeal to Rome, independent ecclesiastical jurisdiction and clerical immunity. However, over the subsequent twenty years, less exclusive perameters of cooperation were settled: for instance civil secular suits involving clergy were heard in royal courts and, crucially, the king retained a decisive voice in episcopal appointments. Henry II saw the problem of criminous clerks as one of law and order, legal equity, perhaps royal sovereignty; Becket defined it as a central to *libertas ecclesiae*, freedom of the church, the old battle cry of church reformers for the past century and more. Others interpreted that freedom as more complex than Becket would allow. Developments in canon and civil law made tension inevitable but accommodation imperative for the well-being of both church and state. This Becket failed to understand. No less damaging was his habit of regarding his defence of the particular rights of his church of Canterbury as synonymous with the universal contest: both his arraignment at

Northampton and his fury over the coronation of the Young Henry actually concerned the privileges of his diocese, not the whole clerical order, as he pretended. The violence of his language, the obstinacy of his opinions and the narrowness of his vision gained his cause little but publicity. Even his death was a triumph for the Faith rather than a vindication of his policies. By the end, he had come to identify his cause with himself: in his dying agony he murmured: 'For the name of Jesus and the protection of the church I am ready to embrace death'.

F. Barlow, *Thomas Becket*, 1985.
B. Smalley, *The Becket Controversy in the Schools*, 1973.

**RICHARD DE LUCY** (*d*.1179) was the most prominent royal administrator of mid-twelfth century England. He came from a knightly family with land in Kent and East Anglia which originated from Lucé on the Normandy/Maine border, an area in which Henry I had interests before he became king. Although modern observers emphasise his lack of baronial background, Richard's family had significant connections, one of his relatives being the successful Abbot Geoffrey of St Albans (1119-46). By the early years of Stephen's reign, Richard was castellan of Falaise, while his brother Walter, with some help from Queen Matilda, had been appointed abbot of Battle (1139-71).

Richard remained in Stephen's service throughout his reign, by the end of which he had acted as local jucticiar in Essex and was castellan of the Tower and Windsor, two of the three most important castles in south-east England (Dover being the third), Richard's position being recognised in the Treaty of Winchester which secured the end of the civil war in 1153. After 1154, despite his continued association with Stephen's surviving son, William, Richard, with Robert, earl of Leicester, was made jointly responsible for the supervision of the royal administration. Henry II was careful neither to alienate those who had run the country under Stephen nor to create another viceroy like Roger of Salisbury. Both justiciars had been supporters of Stephen, and while Robert of Leicester was one of the most powerful barons in his own right, Richard owed his growing landed fortune to loyal service to the king, continuing the tradition of secular advisers drawn from the lesser nobility which had been a notorious feature of the rule of Henry I.

In the early years of Henry II's reign, Richard concentrated on the administration, rather than politics, where Earl Robert took precedence, possibly because he remained in England while Richard followed the court. During this period the justiciars acted as intermediaries rather than viceroys, particularly during the king's visits to England. Nonetheless, Richard was involved in a wide variety of business, financial, judicial and diplomatic. In 1162, he managed the appointment of his friend and colleague, the chancellor, Thomas Becket, as archbishop of Canterbury which, in the careful handling of the Canterbury monks and the other bishops, required tact and authority. Richard's concern with ecclesiastical issues was recurrent. No doubt well briefed by his brother, in 1157 he advised the king to uphold the franchises of Battle Abbey in a dispute over the jurisdiction of the bishop of Chichester. In 1164, at least so Becket believed, Richard helped draft the Constitutions of Clarendon, being excommunicated for his pains in 1166.

With the defection of Becket as chancellor (1162) and the retirement of the veteran treasurer, Nigel of Ely (1164/5), the justiciars' influence grew. Increasingly, Richard took the lead in implementing policy, at the exchequer and in supervising royal justice. In 1164, he unsuccessfully tried to persuade the exiled Becket to come to terms with the king. In 1166, in order to enforce the Assize of Clarendon, Richard and Geoffrey de Mandeville visited seventeen counties before Geoffrey's death that October. The Clarendon assize had instructed sheriffs to apprehend and try felons through juries of presentment and trial by water, sheriffs being allowed to hunt down criminals regardless of local franchises. Convicted felons forfeited their lands to their lords and their chattels to the king. The presence of Richard and Geoffrey was highly effective, the Pipe Roll showing that sheriffs were markedly more vigilant in those counties the royal justices visited than the rest. The 1166 visitation set the pattern for regular judicial circuits — or eyres — conducted by teams of justices which began in 1168. It also demonstrated the failure of many sheriffs to carry out royal instructions without supervision: this was one motive for the general Inquest of the

Sheriffs of 1170, which led to twenty out of twenty-six being replaced. Thus both administratively and judicially, Richard's 1166 visitation marked a significant step towards greater central scrutiny of provincial royal agents and barons. Richard was probably also closely concerned with the establishment of procedures by which non-baronial freemen could resolve litigation over possession and ownership of property, the so-called possessory assizes *novel disseisin* and *mort d'ancestor*. Thus, though no legal expert himself, Richard presided over the inception and administration of a judicial system that profoundly enhanced the role of the crown in the affairs of its subjects. This proved a double-edged weapon. The reforms were popular: by 1176-8, the general eyres were overloaded with work. But they were equally seen by some — not unjustly — as vehicles for royal extortion and rapacity.

In royal service, Richard had become a baron of some consequence, his estates being assessed in 1166 at thirty knights' fees, centred upon Ongar in Essex. His political authority, which had been increasing steadily, was confirmed after the death of Robert of Leicester in 1168, when he was left the sole justiciar. However, his power, and, in consequence, that of his office, was transformed by the rebellion of 1173-4 when for some months he held England for the king, vigorously combating the military manoeuvres of the new earl of Leicester and the king of Scots. Earlier in the reign, in the king's absences abroad, the regency had been filled by members of the royal family: Henry's mother, wife or son Henry. In 1173, Matilda was dead and Eleanor and the Young Henry ranged against the king. Richard was left in sole charge and his energy and loyalty in large measure saved England for Henry. Richard's rewards were territorial and political.

After 1174, he acted as the king's *alter ego* in the manner of Roger of Salisbury. On his own authority he could issue writs and command expenditure. He dominated the exchequer; acted as a justice in the north; assessed tallages in the Midlands and the south; implemented the new possessory assizes; fortified castles; organised defence against the Welsh; and acted generally as the king's paymaster and chief executive. Even then, he remained the king's servant. It was the king's presence that prompted the Assize of Northampton, which dealt with enforcing criminal and civil law, in 1176. In the same year, Richard argued unavailingly against Henry's retrospective cancellation of the suspension of the Forest Laws granted during the rebellion of 1173 and, in common with other barons, had to surrender his main castle at Ongar. Furthermore, he had powerful and influential colleagues such as Richard of Ilchester, bishop of Winchester, and Geoffrey Ridel, bishop of Ely. Even so, between 1173 and 1178, Richard set the pattern for the justiciarship elaborated and perfected by his successors Ranulf Glanvill, Hubert Walter, Geoffrey FitzPeter, Peter des Roches and Hubert de Burgh. Significantly, all of them depended on the king. As ambitious clerics and knights with backgrounds in the lesser nobility of the Angevin dominions, they were royal creatures.

Richard de Lucy had shown his frequently absent king the usefulness of a chief official in England, dependent on royal favour and command but with status as great as any baron, whose prime qualification was that, as proxy, he used the king's power in relentless pursuit of royal rights and interests. Henry regretted Richard's resignation in the winter of 1178-9 for he had lost a minister who, however personally ambitious, deserved the nickname the king gave him: Richard the Loyal.

At his retirement, Richard was probably an old man. He had been active in government for forty years. He withdrew to the house of Augustinian canons he had founded at Lesnes, in Kent, where, before his death in 1179, he adopted the habit of the order. Such gestures were not uncommon, but Richard appears to have possessed a high degree of conventional piety. In 1164, he apparently went on pilgrimage to Compostella and, in reaction to the Becket dispute, he may have taken the cross, and even gone to the Holy Land. More certainly, whatever the state of his soul, Richard died leaving both a barony — inherited by his grandson — and a political dynasty: one son, Godfrey, became bishop of Winchester (1189-1204); his grandson was prominent under John and Henry III. However, like the other lay justiciars (Glanvill, FitzPeter, de Burgh), he failed to found a dynasty that could sustain itself at the top of the English baronage for more than a couple of generations.

Richard's career was, in one way, replicated across twelfth century Europe. With the growth of written records, the study of law and developments in accounting, monarchs increasingly trusted their affairs to curial knights rather than risk conflicts of interests and time inevitable with ministers drawn from the upper nobility. However, the scope of administrative activity over which Richard presided and to some extent initiated was peculiar to England: the regular central audit; the control of localities through itinerant justices, confiscations of castles and supervising sheriffs; the inauguration of legal mechanisms to resolve the social dislocation of persistent litigation over land; the imposition of rules to govern the apprehension and trial of felons; and the institution of national inquiries as a means of government. Royal authority — as Richard himself showed in 1173-4 — was based on the skilful or fortunate manipulation of force and patronage, on politics and people not bureaucracy and parchment. But Richard de Lucy and his colleagues gave Henry II weapons with which he could take unusual advantage of whatever political success he achieved.

W. L. Warren, *Henry II*, 1973.

F. J. West, *The Justiciarship in England*, 1966.

**ROGER OF PONT L'EVEQUE** (*d*.1181; archbishop of York 1154-81) has suffered from being judged by his role in the Becket controversy. Although this perspective aptly reflects the corrosive embrace of the affair, it does not give Roger his due. A well educated Norman, a good Latinist and able church lawyer, Roger was one of the talented group of erudite secular clerks Archbishop Theobald gathered around him in the 1140s. Later hostile gossip suggested that Roger was condescending and antagonistic to the less academically groomed Thomas Becket. Yet until the parting of the ways in 1162-4, there was no especial antagonism between Roger and Thomas, beyond perhaps inevitable rivalry for preferment and attention in the competitive, self-consciously superior hot-house of Theobald's household, the twelfth century's equivalent of Jowett's Balliol, just as Bayeux was the eleventh's. Roger, indeed, had little to be jealous about. One of Theobald's favourites, in 1148 Roger became archdeacon of Canterbury and in 1154, largely through Theobald's influence, archbishop of York.

Theobald may have hoped that in Roger he would have a pliant archbishop of York who, with his Canterbury background, would forego the usual disputes with the southern metropolitan. In fact Roger turned native, becoming an aggressive and skilful advocate of York's claims to equality with Canterbury and authority over the Scottish episcopacy. In York itself he extended the Minster with the construction of a new choir, east end and lavishly endowed chapel of St Sepulchre, as well as building himself a substantial palace. To his scholarly interests may be attributed surviving twelfth century manuscripts still in the Minster Library. Perhaps it was because of his benefactions, made possible by the considerable fortune he amassed, or his absences on national business that he retained good relations with his chapter. His household included the renowned Italian canon lawyer Master Vacarius, another old boy of Theobald's entourage. He accompanied Roger north in 1154 and never went back, his presence testimony to Roger's stature and the attractions, under his rule, of the northern province. Roger brought to the province of York a stability not seen for more than a decade before his election and not witnessed again for another thirty-five years after his death.

As archbishop of York, Roger's finest hour should have been when he crowned Henry II's son king in June 1170. Instead, this formed a prime charge in the indictment levelled at him by the supporters of Becket for whom Roger had been an invader of the rights of his superior metropolitan, a malicious inciter of royal anger and, even, a conspirator and paymaster of the saint's murderers. By 1162, when Becket was appointed archbishop of Canterbury, Roger was already an experienced prelate. Outside his diocese he served as a papal judge-delegate; he undertook diplomatic missions for the king; he regularly attended the king's court; and, in the Canterbury vacancy after the death of Theobald in 1161, he had acted, with papal approval, as head of the English church. Historically and perhaps personally, tension with the new archbishop of Canterbury was likely, if not inevitable. After 1163, Roger sided with the king — as in the end did all his brother bishops. Appointed a papal legate in 1164, Roger's connivance at the Young Henry's coronation was unsurprising, but it attracted Becket's especial wrath and his disciples' particular venom. It was Becket's excommunication, on the eve of his return to England in November 1170, of Roger and two colleagues for their part in the coronation that prompted Roger's visit to Henry at Bar-le-Roi over Christmas; the king's outburst of rage at his former chancellor; and the retaliation of the four knights. Some later said that Roger helped plan the knights' attack. This probably owes more to the hysteria of Becket's bereaved followers than truth. Although he was suspended by the pope, by the end of 1171 he had been rehabilitated: the charges of the Becket faction had not stuck.

Throughout the Becket controversy, Roger had played his own game. While Foliot took the polemical lead, Roger exploited the situation to consolidate, where possible, the rights of York. He disagreed with Becket's position; deplored his methods; and had little regard for his powers of argument, but he was motivated not by personal spite or ideological disagreement but institutional advantage. In the aftermath of the martyrdom, such expedient opportunism was damned by hindsight but was more representative of how the church operated than Becket's histrionics. Roger persisted with his attempts to establish York's independence from Canterbury under Becket's successor, Richard of Dover, and continued to assert his claims over Scotland. He played a significant role on the king's side in the rebellion of 1173-4. Looked at from his new palace, his career was neither blighted nor peripheral.

Dangerously for the historian, Roger's opposition to Becket ensured that his personality received close and unflattering scrutiny from the martyr's apologists. Even the high-minded John of Salisbury in 1172 dragged up a twenty-year-old scandal about Roger's sex life. In the early 1150s Roger apparently had a homosexual affair with a beautiful boy, possibly an oblate, called Walter. When Walter later told others about the liaison, Roger, perhaps fearing blackmail and the ruin of a career so promisingly launched, used his authority as archdeacon to have the unfortunate Walter's eyes put out. Then, to silence him for good, Roger persuaded some secular judges to convict Walter as a felon and have him hanged. There followed a cover-up, smoothly orchestrated by Archbishop Theobald, ending with absolution from the pope. As a story, it had much to titillate:

illicit sex; the abuse of power; the murky private lives of the great; the establishment closing ranks. How much, if any of it, is true is impossible to estimate. It is hard to credit that Roger, so soon after these events, would have been selected by Theobald as archbishop of York, nor that he could, as he did, have kept on such civil terms with the rest of Theobald's high-minded, priggish protégés. John of Salisbury's salacious story probably tells us more about him and the sort of scabrous tale popular in twelfth century educated circles than it does about Roger. Nevertheless, Roger would not have been the last archbishop of York whose sexuality was a grey area.

F. Barlow, *Thomas Becket*, 1986.
A. Aylmer and R. Cant, *A History of York Minster*, 1977.

ROSAMUND CLIFFORD (*d.c.*1176) was the most favoured of Henry II's mistresses. Daughter of Walter de Clifford, a marcher lord, Rosamund appears to have been openly acknowledged by Henry after the Great Rebellion of 1173-4 and the consequent disgrace of his wife, Eleanor of Aquitaine. Legends soon began to cluster around Rosamund, including romantic tales of her seclusion at Woodstock and her poisoning by a jealous queen. What is certain is that she did not long enjoy her status as Henry's *maîtresse en titre*, dying perhaps as early as 1176. She was buried at Godstow nunnery near Oxford, with which her family had connections and on which a devastated Henry lavished donations for her shrine. In 1191, a convenient four years after her lover's death, Rosamund's tomb was removed from before the altar at Godstow by an outraged Hugh, bishop of Lincoln. Immune from the censure of Henry II, the moralising bishop had Rosamund's body reburied in the cemetery because 'she was a harlot'. Described on the inscription on her grave as 'Rose of the world', Rosamund appears to have been, in the words of Henry's most recent biographer, 'the great love of his life', prominent enough to excite rumour and gossip among contemporaries and to feature in salacious stories a century after her death. Discernable political influence she had none, as Henry recognised in not divorcing Eleanor in 1175, which he was rumoured to be contemplating. The inadequate evidence concerning 'Fair Rosamund' is a reminder of how little can be reconstructed of the private lives even of the most famous medieval people. Henry II had a number of mistresses, and at least two bastards, Geoffrey FitzRoy, archbishop of York and William Longsword, earl of Salisbury, their mother possibly being an Englishwoman, called Ykenai, with whom Henry had a liaison in the early 1150s. We know nothing of Henry's, or his mistresses', emotions, although the king was probably a generous lover. The Pipe Roll of 1184 records payment of £55 17s for 'clothes and hoods and cloaks and for the trimming for two capes of samite and for the clothes of the queen and of Belle-belle, for the king's use'.

W. L. Warren, *Henry II*, 1973.


HUGH BIGOD (*c.*1094-1177), second son of Roger Bigod, on the death of his elder brother William in the White Ship disaster (1120) inherited vast estates especially in East Anglia, a region he bent most of his energies over an exceptionally long and active political career to dominate. Where his father had been a loyal servant of successive kings, Hugh, although a hereditary steward in the royal household, exploited the civil war under Stephen to try to establish quasi-autonomous power in East Anglia, a policy which, when pursued in more settled times under Henry II, led to conflict with the king and near ruin. Hugh's priorities were the reverse of his father's. Roger Bigod had served his king well and had in consequence been created a great provincial magnate; Hugh had inherited a great provincial position and, therefore, expected to play a part in national politics. His loyalty was conditional on what suited his local interests. Thus Hugh regarded Stephen, who possessed extensive personal lands in eastern England, as a local competitor as much as king. Hugh's defection to Matilda in 1141 was to serve his own ambitions, not hers: he received the title of earl of Norfolk as a reward. Under Henry II, rivalry with Stephen's son, William, continued until 1157 when the king confiscated the castles of both men. Hugh bought only partial restitution on payment of a large fine in 1165. This grievance made Hugh well-disposed towards the rebellion against Henry in 1173-4 but, despite capturing Norwich, he was forced to submit, with his stronghold of Framlingham being dismantled. Hugh's failure to escape royal control was, in one way, ironic, as in 1135 he had played kingmaker when he swore — almost certainly falsely — that the dying Henry I had designated Stephen his successor. That one moment of influence typified Hugh's career of earnest, not always prescient and often frustrated seeking after personal and dynastic advantage.

W. L. Warren, *Henry II,* 1973.

**THOMAS BROWN** (*d.c.*1180), an Englishman by birth, had a remarkable career as a leading counsellor and administrator to two of the dominant rulers of twelfth century Europe, Roger II of Sicily (1105-54) and Henry II of England. He appears in Sicilian charters as a royal chaplain possibly as early as 1137. A cleric, customarily called 'Master' (*Magister*), he is also mentioned as 'familiaris regis' and, in a Greek charter (Roger's scriptorium being trilingual: Latin; Greek and Arabic), 'Thomas the Brown' (θωμα τοῦ Βρουνου). Later described as being 'almost at the head of King Roger's confidential business', apparently his fame was such that there were 'many kingdoms in which he would have been received with honour'. It was said that Henry II repeatedly offered Thomas a post in his native England. But it was only the death of Roger II and the subsequent persecution of the late king's servants by his son, William I, that forced Thomas to flee in search of new employment. His international reputation may be testimony to the cosmopolitan world of the Norman connection and of court gossip throughout western Europe. Alternatively, Thomas's fame may have been embroidered by his colleague, Richard FitzNeal, from whose book, *The Dialogue of the Exchequer* (1178), most of the information comes. Whatever the means of his preferment at the Angevin court, Thomas, who was in England by 1159, rapidly moved to the centre of the royal administration. He appears as Henry II's almoner (officially the royal officer who distributed alms on behalf of the king) in 1166, having been appointed perhaps some years earlier. His actual importance was far greater. According to FitzNeal, Thomas had a special privileged seat at the Exchequer audit, with his own clerk who noted down all Treasury receipts and expenses. Thomas's competence seems to have ranged across all royal business. He kept a third roll to complement those of the Treasurer (the so-called Pipe roll) and the Chancellor, an innovation in customary Exchequer practice devised uniquely for Thomas. With his 'lynx-eyed' clerk scrutinising all Treasury transactions, his own association with all important Exchequer decisions and his private roll containing, says FitzNeal, 'the laws of the realm and the secrets of the king', Thomas appears to have acted as Henry's personal representative, presumably briefed to check on how the audit was conducted. As the later troubles of Angevin government illustrate, how equitably or efficiently the Exchequer operated was of prime political as well as financial significance for the king. Thomas's position was entirely personal and unofficial. The king may have been eager to have his own ears and eyes in an institution which, as FitzNeal's description of it hints, had already developed a sense of corporate tradition, even self-importance. FitzNeal's rather prim comment that Thomas's private roll was contrary to the Exchequer's 'ancient custom' may show a recognition of this intrusion, which itself reveals that royal government was still not rigidly bureaucratised. Furthermore, the ease with which Thomas, and others in the twelfth century, moved between courts, argues either for similarity or simplicity of governmental procedure. Thomas's administrative career provides a mirror to those of aristocratic opportunists such as William Marshal: mobile; cosmopolitan; precarious; dependent on personal ability, luck and the friendship and trust of princes; crowned by great rewards in profit, influence and power. Thomas was a knight-errant and an aristocrat of civil servants.

**HERBERT OF BOSHAM** (*d*.1194) was a notable scholar, a pupil of Peter Lombard in Paris and a Hebraist whose career was devoured by his loyalty and devotion to Thomas Becket. He first worked for Becket before 1157 as a royal clerk when the future archbishop was Henry II's chancellor. There developed a close bond between them, Herbert remaining with Becket after 1162. In the archbishop's household, Herbert was Becket's teacher, counsellor and, on a number of occasions, his confidential agent. At Becket's side at Clarendon and Northampton in 1164, he shared the archbishop's exile. Others in Becket's entourage found him rather trying. He was difficult, obstinate, intemperate and extreme in the advice he offered. Devastated at not being present at Becket's murder, he found it almost impossible to reconcile himself to the compromises necessary afterwards. In 1172, he complained hysterically to the pope of shabby treatment, but his inflexible hostility to all who were not as fanatical in honouring Becket's memory as he made it difficult for him to be treated any differently. In 1184-6, he wrote his *Life of St. Thomas of Canterbury*, dedicated to Archbishop Baldwin, which, although containing the best account of Becket's exile, relies heavily on turgid sermonising. In 1189 he briefly entered the household of William Longchamp, regent for Richard I, but he clearly was past holding down any responsible post. He spent his last years in a Cistercian abbey in Artois writing a commentary on Jerome's *Hebrew Psalter* to make ends meet. Herbert, who thought of himself as privileged to have served Becket, was a victim of the conflict. It had been the most exciting period of his life; he could not cope with the drabber days that followed. He felt betrayed. To the trimmers who inherited Becket's legacy, he was an awkward reminder of the saint's own extremism and passion.

E. Barlow, *Thomas Becket*, 1986.
A. Gransden, *Historical Writing in England c.550-c.1307*, 1974.

**AILNOTH INGENIATOR,** or the Engineer (*fl*.1157-90), was one of, if not the most expert of Henry II's overseers of royal buildings. For over thirty years, from 1157/8 until 1189, he drew a salary of 7d a day (£10 12s 11d a year). His main position was that of Keeper of the Palace of Westminster, but this minimises the variety of tasks entrusted to him as well as his own versatility. At Westminster, his responsibilities included repairs of the fabric of the complex of houses which comprised the royal palace, cleaning them, providing fresh rushes, replacing broken windows (in 1179, early evidence for royal houses of domestic glazing), erecting a cloister linking the king's chambers, and the planning and construction of a new wharf and landing stair. At

Westminster Abbey he repaired the refectory in 1175, built a stone arch in 1187 and possibly designed the Chapel of St. Catherine in 1160. Elsewhere, Ailnoth supervised the building of the Fleet gaol in London during the 1170s and 1180s and was regularly engaged on work at the Tower where he provided lead for the Chapel roof (1176) and hired carpenters to find timber for building work there in 1175. He was also active at various times at Windsor Castle, Woodstock and Rayleigh. It is probable that Ailnoth was involved with, perhaps even designed Orford Castle, with its novel polygonal keep, built between 1165 and 1173. Certainly his duties were not confined to civil works alone. In 1175 and 1176 he led a team of royal carpenters and masons who pulled down the motte and bailey castle at Framlingham, stronghold of Hugh Bigod, earl of Norfolk and one of the defeated leaders of the Great Rebellion against Henry II in 1173-4. As with many contemporary engineers, although he dealt with lead, glass and stone, he had probably begun his career as a carpenter and had most likely worked on war- and siege-machines, useful talents in a country recovering from civil war, as England was in the 1150s. It is only in the twelfth century, with the financial record of payments made at the Exchequer recorded on the Pipe Rolls, that we are able to trace careers of men like Ailnoth. But whether he acted as a superviser, designer, architect, builder or manager of the king's works is impossible to say. Ailnoth seems to have retired in 1189/90, as his wages in 1190 were recorded as being only £2 10s. He was certainly dead by 1197, when his wife Maud is described as a widow. He seems to have acquired or was given property in Westminster and was probably the father of Roger Enganet, who was active in Westminster c.1177-1216. It was on men like Ailnoth that the grander facade of Angevin government depended if only for the reason that kings needed experts to maintain their palaces, build their castles and tear down those of their enemies.

J. Harvey, *English Mediaeval Architects*, 1987.

**GEOFFREY FITZROY** (1151/3-1212), illegitimate son of the future Henry II and an Englishwoman, Ykenai, possessed much of the ability of the Angevins, not least their capacity to make enemies. Destined for the church, he was elected bishop of Lincoln in 1173, although not yet a priest. For nine years, Geoffrey enjoyed the revenues as bishop-elect but made no moves to be consecrated, which says much for the ineffectiveness of the ideals of the martyred Thomas Becket. In all, Lincoln remained vacant for over sixteen years (1166-1183), although Geoffrey was a benefactor, as when he redeemed cathedral ornaments for £300 from the banker Aaron of Lincoln. Politically, Geoffrey proved more loyal to his father than his legitimate half-brothers, especially during the Great Rebellion of 1173-4 and the civil war in France with Richard (1187-9). In 1182, he became his father's chancellor. Alone of Henry's sons he was at his father's deathbed at Chinon in 1189. Richard I put an end to Geoffrey's lingering political ambitions by sacking him as chancellor and having him forcibly made a priest in 1189 shortly after nominating him as archbishop of York. After a challenge from the York chapter, Geoffrey was consecrated in 1191. Although reconciled with Richard, Geoffrey was regarded by most, including his half-brother John and the justiciar Hubert Walter, as a troublemaker. The rest of his career was spent fending off ecclesiastical challenges to his position and dabbling ineffectually in national politics. An educated man, possibly with a speech impediment, his career as absentee and pluralist sits oddly beside the respectability and, in a few cases, vocation of his contemporary bishops. Geoffrey did not take Holy Orders very seriously but they were all that were left. Any political ambitions were stifled by his illegitimacy, a comment less on his talents than on the effectiveness of the church over the previous century in changing secular attitudes to marriage. Thus Geoffrey was condemned to obscurity or notorious frustration. He chose the latter, with, it seems, his father's approval. After the Great Rebellion by his other sons the king reputedly declared of Geoffrey: 'Baseborn indeed have my other children shown themselves; this alone is my true son'. Unsurprisingly, the 'other children' disagreed.

Gerald of Wales, *Vita Galfridi* in *Opera*, ed. J. S. Brewer, J. F. Dimock & G. F. Warner, 1861-91, vol iv.

**HENRY** (1155-83; crowned king of England 1170) was the eldest son of Henry II and Eleanor of Aquitaine. To secure his dynasty, the elder Henry followed French practice by having the Young Henry crowned in his lifetime. Although the ceremony itself, performed by the archbishop of York at the height of the conflict with Becket, proved controversial, its validity was unchallenged, thus creating a situation unique since the Conquest of there being simultaneously two crowned kings of England. In 1169, Henry II had assigned the succession to his dominions to his three eldest sons: Henry was to inherit the patrimonial lands of England, Normandy and Anjou; Richard his mother's duchy of Aquitaine; and Geoffrey the county of Brittany. In the event the Old King was compromised by the very thoroughness of the arrangement. His sons, as legally constituted rulers, wished for actual power which their father denied them. This was especially true of the Young King. Richard was given an increasingly free hand in Aquitaine and Geoffrey in Brittany, but Henry, despite his title of king, was left with no political authority and no lands to rule as his own. This anomaly was largely his father's fault, but was also a consequence of the Young Henry's personality. Like other heirs to forceful royal parents, Robert Curthose, the Prince Regent, Edward VII or Edward VIII, Henry's charm was vitiated by restless shallowness, a bored pursuit of pleasure rather than duty. Refusing to play a constructive role in government as his father's subordinate or representative, Henry sought vicarious excitement in an obsession with tournaments and the burgeoning fashion of chivalry. At no stage did he suggest anything but political fecklessness and incompetence; his influence was almost wholly destructive. Impatient for power, if not responsibility, Henry fomented the Great Rebellion against his father of 1173-4 in alliance with his two elder brothers, the king of France and the count of Flanders. Despite reconciliation with his father in 1174, Henry remained dilatory in performing even the modest political tasks entrusted to him while maintaining a taste for disruptive intrigue. In the months before his death, with Geoffrey of Brittany and Philip II of France, he once more unavailingly confronted his father, dying unreconciled and unsuccessful. His political failure was balanced by his contemporary popularity. Open-handed

chivalric poseurs won more plaudits than tight-fisted administrators. Yet it is significant that even his tutor-in-arms, William
Marshal, lost patience and favour. Whether Henry's fickleness
came from stupidity or petulence, his career as a gilded playboy
touched pathos. Energetically, even desperately convivial, flat-
tered, cosseted and irresponsible, Henry was heir to a destiny
too great for him to grasp. For all his heart-winning generosity,
capacity for friendship, ambition and pretensions, in the end
Henry ruled nothing, not even his own appetites.

W. Warren, *Henry II*, 1973.

GEOFFREY OF BRITTANY (1158-86) was the fourth son of
Henry II and Eleanor of Aquitaine. As part of his father's plans
to secure and extend his family lands in France, as a child he was
betrothed (1166/7) to Constance, the heiress to the count of Brittany (Conan the Little, d.1171). At the family settlement at
Montmirail on 1169, Geoffrey did homage for Brittany to his
eldest brother, the Young Henry, who, in turn, did homage to
Louis VII of France. With his elder brothers, he allied with the
French king against his father in 1173-4. In 1175, he began his
rule in Brittany, doing homage for the county to the new French
king, Philip II, in 1179. He finally married Constance in 1181. In
1183, he goaded the Young Henry into revolt against the old
king and Richard of Poitou, the future Richard I; a year later, he
allied with his younger brother John against Richard, disappointed, perhaps, at not being given Anjou on the Young
Henry's death (1183): it had gone to Richard. In Brittany he promulgated the so-called 'Assize of Geoffrey' (1185) which was
aimed at protecting lords' rights. Knighted by his father in 1178,
Geoffrey developed a passion for tournament and intrigue which
finally killed him. It was at a tournament in Paris, whither he
had gone to plot with Philip II in 1186, that he was mortally
wounded. His son, Arthur, who was to contest as unsuccessfully
as his father for the Anjevin inheritance (1199-1203), was born
posthumously. The contemporary royal clerk and historian,
Roger of Howden, called Geoffrey 'that son of perdition'.
Gerald of Wales, with his acute dislike of all the Angevins,
described Geoffrey as 'of tireless endeavour, a hypocrite in

everything, a deceiver and a dissembler' 'able to corrupt two kingdoms with his tongue'. Geoffrey's career testifies to the ambition and the weakness of Henry II's schemes.

**WILLIAM CADE** (*d*.1166) was a financier of Flemish origins whose business activities reveal the existence and something of the extent of the credit market of twelfth century England. A moneylender on a massive scale, in the 1150s and 1160s he numbered among his clients some of the greatest in the land, including the king. At his death, he was owed around £5,000. Although his surviving accounts are not explicit about the interest he charged, it is probable that, as with contemporary banking transactions by monasteries, the sums outstanding include hidden usury. His Flemish background could point to a mercantile base for his operations, as England traded extensively with the Low Countries. The size of his loans, and those of other twelfth century Christian moneylenders, such as the merchant Gervase of Southampton, combined with the banking activities of religious houses and the growing Jewish community indicate one central difficulty confronting contemporary social elites. How could extensive landed wealth and rights over markets, trade, and tenants be converted into ready cash to meet the rising costs of aristocratic life, in particular the expenses of military retinues in peace as well as war, and the price of land. Few historical orthodoxies are as bogus as that which suggests that in a so-called 'feudal' society all land, in a sort of tenurial pyramid, was held ultimately of the king in return for personal military service and that all armies were raised by a feudal levy of knights provided by tenants according to a fixed quota, the knight's fee. Such appearances were, at best, legal fictions. Thus the *Cartae Baronum* of 1166, which purported to be a survey of the knights' fees possessed by all tenants-in-chief was designed to reveal not how many troops Henry II could call upon but the basis for a fiscal re-assessment of the scutage tax. Just as soldiers had been paid, even where they owed homage and fealty, so too had land changed hands after financial transactions, at least since the eighth century. Wages and purchase prices rose while fixed rents lost value in the twelfth century, on top of which many families had to suffer the often crippling costs of crusading, high taxation, and heavy feudal incidents (*e.g.* reliefs and wardships). The cycle of debt, encouraged in some instances by Angevin government, or so believed the instigators of *Magna Carta*, offered scope and, no doubt, rich pickings for those with access to bullion and cash. Despite ecclesiastical prohibitions, lending money for profit was flourishing among the Christian as well as Jewish community, with monks as well as merchants leading the way. Men like Cade provided an essential service to a society and economy which refused to be pinned down by church dogma or modest and laboriously realised annual rates of return on land.

H. Jenkinson, 'William Cade' in *English Historical Review*, xxviii (1913) and in *Essays in History Presented to R. L. Poole.*

**RALPH OF BETHLEHEM** (*d.*1174; bishop of Bethlehem 1156-74), an Englishman, was chancellor of the Latin Kingdom of Jerusalem for the last thirty years of his life. The Queen Regnant Melisende, his patroness, had tried unsuccessfully to appoint him archbishop of Tyre, the second see in the kingdom, in 1146. It was said by his successor as chancellor that Ralph owed his promotion to Bethlehem in 1156 to being a fellow countryman to the then pope, Hadrian IV. A learned but worldly man, Ralph played a significant role in the affairs of the kingdom as administrator, diplomat, even military commander: he was wounded on campaign in Egypt in 1165. Under Bishop Ralph the remarkable Byzantine mosaics were installed in the Church of the Nativity in Bethlehem, which survive to this day: Greek designs, commissioned by an English bishop for a Latin church in Palestine, symbols of the cosmopolitan world which allowed Ralph to find employment two thousand miles from his homeland. Ralph was a Levantine counterpart to Thomas Brown, the English minister of Roger II of Sicily. It is likely that Ralph came from a noble family who, frustrated by career prospects in Europe, sought his fortune in the less congested ecclesiastical world of Outremer where western also-rans could come in winners. Ralph was not the only successful Englishman in the east. Another was William, prior of the chapter of the Holy Sepulchre who became the first Latin archbishop of Tyre in 1128. The horizons of twelfth century Europe were widening, offering, as Ralph's career showed, new and attractive opportunities for the educated, well-connected and pushy.

B. Hamilton, *The Latin Church in the Crusader States: The Secular Church*, 1980.

**RICHARD OF CLARE** (*d*.1176), nicknamed by some contemporaries 'Strongbow' (a play on one of his titles, lord of Striguil), was the most prominent of the Anglo-Norman lords who began to colonize Ireland in the reign of Henry II. The son of Gilbert, earl of Pembroke, he inherited his father's estates in south Wales in 1148. His loyalty to King Stephen cost him his earldom on Henry II's accession. In consequence, as Gerald of Wales commented, 'his pedigree was longer than his purse'. In common with many disinherited noblemen, Richard was open to any proposal likely to restore his fortune. Ireland offered just such an opportunity.

As with England in the 1060s and Scotland in the 1090s, internal Irish political tensions attracted foreign intervention. There had been ecclesiastical pressure on Henry II to consider extending his overlordship to Ireland since the 1150s, but it was only on the invitation of Dermot, king of Leinster, that intervention began. In 1167, Henry II gave Dermot permission to recruit supporters to help him win back control of Dublin from the king of Connaught. A few Marcher lords, led by Robert FitzStephen and Maurice FitzGerald landed at Wexford in 1169. Richard of Clare joined them in August 1170 having reached a very favourable deal with Dermot: Richard was to marry Dermot's daughter and in due course inherit his kindom.

The Anglo-Normans were immediately effective, using military techniques new to Ireland, such as the motte-and-bailey castle, and mounted knights operating in conjunction with archers and infantry. In September 1170, Dublin was taken and by the time Dermot died in 1171, his power over Leinster had been restored. Richard of Clare now asserted his claim to Leinster. This not only ran counter to Irish law but also aroused the suspicion of Henry II, anxious lest any vassal of his dare establish himself as a ruler independent of his authority. In the autumn of 1171, therefore, Richard was faced by a siege of Dublin by Rory

O'Connor, king of Connaught; withdrawal of royal aid from England; and the imminent arrival of Henry himself armed to conquer all, including Richard, who stood against him. Richard defeated King Rory, but had to obey Henry. Paying homage for his Irish lands, Richard was confirmed in control of Leinster, but only received the key towns of Waterford, Wexford, and Dublin in 1174. From 1173 to 1176, he seemed to have acted as Henry's viceroy in Ireland, a position he adopted from Henry's initial agent, Hugh de Lacy who was established as lord of Meath. However, if Henry had hoped that by formally imposing his lordship on Irish and Anglo-Normans alike (Rory O'Connor submitted in 1175) he had solved the problem of his authority in Ireland, he was wrong. But the violence and instability in Ireland, which had attracted Richard of Clare in the first place, cannot be seen in nationalist terms. The Irish kings fought each other; they fought the Anglo-Normans; they allied with the Anglo-Normans against Irish rivals. It is true that beneath this carapace of feuding and flouted legality, Anglo-Norman settlement began, especially in the east, adding yet another fault-line along which Irish society could tear and break. But it must be remembered, when any facile condemnations about English involvement in Ireland are trotted out, that opportunists like Richard of Clare had been given their chance and their stake in Ireland by indigenous Irish leaders. Henry II reluctantly became involved only when Richard of Clare's success seemed to threaten his interests elsewhere.

**WILLIAM OF SENS** (*d*.1180) has often been credited with introducing French Gothic style into English ecclesiastical architecture when he was placed in charge of the extensive remodelling of Canterbury Cathedral between 1174 and 1177. A fire had conveniently gutted the cathedral choir, giving the monks the opportunity to redesign it as a monument to Thomas Becket. To find the right mason, the monks held a medieval equivalent of an architects' competition. A number of master masons were interviewed before William of Sens was chosen. Our main source for the rebuilding, the eye-witness Gervase of Canterbury, described William as 'the most cunning craftsman in wood and stone'. One of his techniques was to make moulds which were then sent to the individual masons for cutting the stones. William oversaw the rebuilding for about three years before badly injuring his back in a fall of fifty feet from the wooden scaffolding. Crippled and bed-ridden, William struggled on for a short time giving instructions to a young monk (possibly Gervase himself) who supervised the work. This arrangement proved unsatisfactory. William soon relinquished his post to his namesake, William the Englishman, returning to France where he died on 11 August 1180.

While there are evident similarities between the new design of Canterbury in the 1170s and the cathedral of Sens, begun in the 1140s and one of the earliest to be built in the new Gothic style, the most stylistically innovative parts of the rebuilding, for example the Trinity Chapel and Corona, date from after William of Sens had departed and must be credited to William the Englishman who completed the work in 1184. The latter was, according to Gervase, 'small in body, but in workmanship of many kinds acute and honest' and may have pursued a career as architect, engineer or carpenter at Canterbury and for the king until 1214. As for William of Sens, he was evidently widely travelled and experienced before 1174. It is possible he was attracted to Canterbury by the link between Sens and Becket, who had stayed there during his exile. It is as likely that he was on the look out for lucrative employment. William of Sens's appearance at Canterbury indicates a lively international traffic in masons and thus in artistic and architectural influences. However, the contribution of William the Englishman is a reminder of the equally significant role of local inspiration.

J. Harvey, *English Mediaeval Architects,* 1987.

**RICHARD OF DOVER** (*d.*1184: archbishop of Canterbury 1173-84) was the unlikely choice as Becket's successor. A previously obscure mediocrity, he nevertheless demonstrated, to the anger of the Becketeers, that effective cooperation with the king was possible. Although not glamorous, Richard's credentials were appropriate. He had been a monk at Canterbury and, unusual in a household dominated by secular clerks, one of Archbishop Theobald's chaplains before being promoted as prior of St Martin's, Dover in 1157. His suitability for the primacy seems to have become apparent on a visit he made to Henry II in 1173 as part of a delegation to discuss the election of a new archbishop. While the form of a free election was preserved, as, in the circumstances of the king's submission to the pope earlier in the year at Avranches was essential, it represented a deal struck between Henry, his Justiciar, Richard de Lucy, and the prior of the Canterbury monks, Odo. Such outward compliance with canonical precept and practical compromise with secular authority set the tone for Richard's tenure of Canterbury. The contrast in style and concerns between Richard and his predecessor could hardly have been greater. Richard was interested in the reform of the clergy. A canonist of some enthusiasm, he collected papal decretals for circulation in England and acted as a papal judge-delegate. But he was also a royalist. In 1173-4, he went along with the appeal against his election by the Young King Henry because he knew that he had the Old King and the bishops on his side: this appeal to Rome looked good but was wholly ineffectual. He consistently defended the king's role in episcopal elections (to the irritation of Pope Alexander III); he allowed the king to sit in on his judgements as papal delegate; he approved of the use of bishops as royal justices; he argued for the trials of murderers of clerics to be held in secular courts; and he specifically repudiated Becket's hostility to what he had called double punishment in cases where clerks were tried by secular as well as ecclesiastical courts. In a letter of 1176, Richard put forward the view that if one court 'supplements the other's insufficiency, that is not a double punishment but a combined punishment'. Such opinions provoked accusations that he lost for the church every point for which Becket had fought. But it was Richard's policies, not Becket's, which charted the relationship between the English church and state for the rest of the Middle Ages.

H. Mayr-Harting, 'Henry II and the Papacy', *Journal of Ecclesiastical History*, 1965.

**MAURICE** (*fl.*1174-87) was probably responsible for building two of the most impressive English stone keeps of the twelfth

century, at Newcastle-upon-Tyne and Dover. Described in
1174-5 as a *cementarius* (mason) at Newcastle, he may have been
involved throughout its building 1171-77. Between 1181 and
1187 he was in charge of construction at Dover as an *ingeniator*
(engineer), being paid at the unusually high rate of one shilling a
day. In 1181, he received over £3 as a gift from the king. This
value placed on his work and the similarities of design between
Newcastle and Dover points to Maurice as their architect. In
style, both are dominated by traditional donjons: regular, rect-
angular stone towers, like the Tower of London of the previous
century. These were being superseded by polygonal keeps (such
as at Orford 1165-73) which gave defenders greater coverage of
besiegers. Nevertheless, Maurice's keeps were impressive
defences. They were also very expensive: Newcastle cost up to
£1,000, while the price for Dover was nearly £4,000, perhaps a
quater of the English king's annual income. Maurice has been
described as 'the greatest, as he was the last, of the exponents of
the square donjon'.

That financially hard-pressed monarchs were prepared to
spend such vast sums on castles demonstrates their importance
as centres of administration, political control, military garrisons
and defence. From William the Conqueror's makeshift pallisades
at Pevensey and Hastings in 1066, to the motte and baileys which
helped secure the French conquest of England, to the great stone
fortifications at London, Colchester, Rochester, Windsor,
Winchester, Nottingham or Norwich, castles played a crucial
role in English political life. Henry II spent over £20,000 on some
ninety castles over thirty-three years. Much more than success in
set-piece battles, control of castles formed the pivotal objectives
of kings and their opponents in every major crisis of the period,
for example the establishment of William I's power 1066-1069
and Henry II's in the 1150s or the civil wars of 1088, 1139-53,
1173-4, 1215-17 and 1263-65. The royal garrison at Orford effectively hampered Hugh Bigod's manoeuvres in East Anglia in
1173-4, while, on the other hand, Brian FitzCount's castle at
Wallingford in Stephen's reign, Falkes de Bréauté's fortress at
Bedford in 1224 and the Montfort stronghold at Kenilworth in
1265-66 proved intractible obstacles to royal supremacy. Thus
the work of servants such as Maurice was central to royal

government, a role brought to its apogee by the building of the Edwardian castles in North Wales, symbols of almost imperial might, by the Savoyard James of St George in the 1270s and 1280s.

J. Harvey, *English Mediaeval Architects,* 1987.

**AARON OF LINCOLN** (*d.*1185/6) was a leading banker in twelfth century England, a prominent member of the modest but significant Jewish community which had established itself in the second half of the twelfth century. Given the formal restrictions on Jewish commercial and civil rights, the scale and scope of Aaron's business was remarkable. On his death, his property, including outstanding debts owed him, escheated to the Crown. The amounts owing were so great that a special government office was established to chase them up, the *scaccarium Aaronis* — 'Aaron's exchequer': it took more than twenty years to finish its work. Aaron's deals were spread across the kingdom and throughout the secular and lay establishment. He had clients in twenty-five counties; they included the king of Scotland, the archbishop of Canterbury as well as nine Cistercian abbeys, who owed Aaron 6,400 marks. He arranged funding for the new cathedral at Lincoln and the abbeys at Peterborough and St Alban's. He also took on debts owed to other Jews, presumably because of his larger and more effective operation for administering and collecting debts. It is sometimes said that Jews made so much money out of lending because of their high interest rates, 43½%, even 60% in some instances. The inflexibility in the land market and the chronic problem of liquidity in an economy based on the exploitation of land, made such rates acceptable, attractive even, especially when compared to what was offered by others. Although sometimes in need of liquid capital themselves, monasteries were another source of cash. Some of them actually had agents scouring the land touting for trade at propitious moments, such as an impending crusade. However, unlike transactions with the Jews, monastic loans were hedged around with legal fictions or pious facts about grants for the good of the monastery and the debtor's soul. Monkish interest rates, however disguised, were definitely competitive: for example in the

1140s St Benet's Holme (Norfolk) made at least a profit of 133%
over seven years on a deal with a departing crusader. The problem of debt was endemic amongst the ruling classes, despite, or
perhaps because of an expanding economy. The costs of capital
projects, such as constructing castles or churches, and war
required immediate payments out of reach of even the most
grasping landlord or government. The Jewish success in this
market depended ultimately on their usefulness to the Crown
whose special protection they alternately enjoyed and suffered.
The king regularly received offerings from Jews *pro recto debiti
sui, i.e.* to help them recover their debts. Jews could be tallaged
at will by monarchs (as with the massive levy of £60,000
imposed at Guildford in 1186); but in consequence the Jews had
to be allowed to prosper for the king to profit. When, in the thirteenth century, the wealth of the Jewish communities declined,
they became more vulnerable. It was their poverty not their
riches which led to their expulsion by Edward I in 1290. Aaron of
Lincoln, however, prospered relatively unhindered, free at least
from the worst excesses of visceral prejudice which emerged
with destructive force in 1190. Whether feared or respected, he
performed a vital service in Angevin England.

C. Roth, *A History of the Jews in England,* 1978.
R. B. Dobson, *The Jews of Medieval York and the Massacre of
1190* (Borthwick Papers No 45), 1974.


**RANULF GLANVILL** (1120/30-1190), one of Henry II's chief
ministers, came from a family of Suffolk landowners. His father,
Hervey, had been one of the leaders of the English fleet which
had helped capture Lisbon in 1147 during the Second Crusade.
His uncle, Roger, also had a successful career in royal service,
and his wife's nephew, Hubert Walter, having begun his career in
Ranulf's household, rose to become justiciar 1193-98 and chancellor 1199-1205. Ranulf seems early to have been destined for
an official career, his first appearance in the records (1144/54)
being as a witness to a charter of Nigel, bishop of Ely, Henry I's
treasurer and restorer of the Exchequer after 1154. He also witnessed charters in the 1150s of King Stephen's second son,

William (*d*.1159). His early official career was centred on the north, as sheriff of Yorkshire (1163-70; 1175-89), and, at various times, custodian of Richmond, Westmorland and Lancaster. Although he lost his shrievalty in the Inquest of Sheriffs in 1170, he retained royal favour, which he cemented with his victory at Alnwick over William the Lion, king of Scots, in 1174 during the Great Rebellion against Henry II. Thereafter, Ranulf moved to the centre of affairs as a justice-in-eyre, diplomat and, from 1180 at the latest, justiciar in succession to Richard de Lucy, a man of similar background and dependence on royal patronage with whom Ranulf may have been associated since the 1150s. Ranulf, by all accounts, became one of Henry's closest personal advisers, as well as his leading official in England. Apart from financial, administrative and military responsibilities, Ranulf was especially active as a judge, both centrally and, unusually, in the provinces. His tenure of the justiciarship coincided with the definition of the judicial organisation required by Henry II's legal reforms, particularly the possessory assizes. Ranulf gained a reputation as an effective judge, eager to settle cases rapidly, although a number of observers close to the court noted that he was not above twisting the law and his position to his own advantage. It was under his auspices, although not by his own pen, that the law-book associated with his name, *Tractatus de legibus et consuetudinibus regni Angliae* (1187/89), was composed. The *Tractatus* is both a statement of principles and a guide to what was evidently still tentative practices. The main thrust of Henry's legal innovations had been to guarantee royal justice to all freemen in matters of land tenure and property rights. To make this anything more than pious hope or arbitrary interference, a system of coherent procedures and consistent judgements was essential. Ranulf, as justiciar, was central to this process to which the *Tractatus* bears authoritative witness. But Ranulf's authority depended on his ability and usefulness as a politician more than as a jurist. His loyalty to Henry II never wavered, as commander of campaigns against the Welsh; negotiator with Philip II of France; executor of the king's will; or supporter of Henry against his sons in 1188-9. Ranulf did not make policy; he executed it with the full freedom of royal favour. His rewards were tangible, from royal grants to the profits of office: in 1176/77, he was allowed to keep over £1,500 in cash, valuable horses and silver plate acquired in the course of his duties as sheriff of Yorkshire. Although he founded no dynasty, he was an important patron of the church in his native Suffolk where he founded an Augustinian priory at Butley (1171) and a Premonstratensian abbey at Leiston (1182). Given his support for Henry II, it was inevitable that, when the king died in 1189, Ranulf would be sacked, a fall accompanied by the usual charges of peculation which hounded finance ministers of dead monarchs throughout medieval Europe. In addition, it was said that the new king, Richard I, fined Ranulf the huge sums of £15,000; if true a tribute to the avarice of both parties. Although ruined politically, Ranulf retained enough power to follow his father's crusading example and lead a contingent on the Third Crusade. With him was his nephew Hubert Walter, newly promoted to the see of Salisbury, a fact which may suggest Ranulf's fall was not as complete as some contemporaries would have us believe. With Archbishop Baldwin of Canterbury, Ranulf left the king's army at Marseilles and hurried to Palestine in the autumn of 1190 as an advance-guard to the main English force which wintered in Sicily. There, in the appalling conditions of the besiegers' camp outside Acre, Ranulf died in October 1190. His life can be treated as typical of the Angevin lay civil servant, raised not from the dust but from the lesser nobility; supported by a network of patrons, family and protégés; lining his own and his master's pockets; loyal, energetic, and flexible as judge, financier, administrator and general. Ranulf's personality is irrecoverable, but his use to Henry appears to have been not simply that of the efficient bureaucrat but as a trusted adviser. Something of the atmosphere he created and the personal and political talent the king valued may be caught in the description of Ranulf by a close observer of Angevin government in the 1180s, Richard of Devizes. According to him, Ranulf was 'the king's eye'.

R. Mortimer, 'The Family of Ranulf de Glanville' *Bulletin of the Institute of Historical Research liv, 1981*
Glanvill, *Tractatus de legibus et consuetudines regni Angliae* ed G. D. G. Hall, 1965.

**BALDWIN OF FORD** (*d*.1190; bishop of Worcester 1180-84; archbishop of Canterbury 1184-90) combined a secular clerk's knowledge of worldly affairs with a Cistercian's exclusive moral rectitude. Depending on occasion or point of view he was fearless or tactless in the pursuit of his aims. Although one of the less famous or notorious twelfth century archbishops, neither a saint nor a great scholar, his career throws light more evenly than those of more glamorous figures on a number of salient features of the church infra-diocesan feuding; the practical problems of implementing canon law; the relations of church and state, kings and churchmen; and the crusade, its preaching, organisation and conduct. For these alone, Baldwin's life repays attention.

Born at Exeter, he received a good education, probably at the cathedral school in his native town, earning by 1150 an international reputation as a teacher. He became an expert in canon law under the patronage of Bishop Bartholomew of Exeter (1162-84) who appointed him archdeacon of Totnes. A satisfying career in the service of church and state seemed to beckon. However, Baldwin, as a number of mildly surprised contemporaries noted, took his religion very seriously and, in about 1170, abandoned his prospects as a secular clerk and entered the Cistercian monastery at Ford on the Devon/Dorset border. It was while a monk at Ford that Baldwin produced most of his surviving works, including a *Penitential*, various sermons and treatises on the Sacraments and the Scriptures. His literary output was orthodox, conventional, even mundane. His particular interest in the anchorite Wulfric of Haselbury, also his later commitment to the Third Crusade, may suggest an inner spiritual life of some force. Whatever the power of his vocation, he soon resumed a successful public career. By 1175, he had become abbot of Ford and, in 1180, he was raised to the see of Worcester. In 1184, he intervened to prevent the execution at Worcester of Gilbert of Plumpton, a convicted robber, kidnapper, seducer of a royal ward and a victim of Justiciar Glanvill's particular hatred. Instead of anger at having his justice deflected, Henry II, displaying a penchant for stiff-necked prelates he repeated two years later by his preferment to the see of Lincoln of Hugh of Avalon, insisted on Baldwin's election as archbishop of Canterbury.

Independence of spirit may have counted with the king for less than Baldwin's unique perspective on ecclesiastical politics. As a Cistercian whose reputation was laid as a secular clerk specialising in canon law, Baldwin could be expected to keep his distance from the vested interests of the Benedictine monks of Christ Church, Canterbury, who acted as the cathedral chapter, as well as holding credentials for piety and administrative acumen. Given the internecine feuds and jealousies between the competing religious orders of the later twelfth century, the appointment of a Cistercian to Benedictine Canterbury, especially one intellectually suspicious of monastic as opposed to secular cathedral chapters, was provocative, not least as the Canterbury monks' preferred choices had been three Benedictines. Henry may have calculated that Baldwin would not, as had so many of his predecessors, 'turn native' and, thus dependent on royal patronage, would be willing to make Canterbury resources available for royal causes, as indeed happened in 1187/8 for the crusade. In fact, Baldwin's pontificate was marked by spectacular rows with the monks that threw into relief the long-standing eccentricity of the English tradition of monastic cathedral chapters whose relationships with their bishops were nowhere defined by increasingly rigid continental (*i.e.* universal) canon law. Baldwin's policies, not surprisingly, attracted the institutional hostility of contemporary monastic writers, especially exciting the venom of Gervase of Canterbury whose relentless bias against Baldwin stands in striking contrast to Eadmer's eulogies on Anselm. Our views of twelfth century archbishops are conditioned more than is sometimes acknowledged by the acceptability of the prelates to their clerical constituencies rather than to their effectiveness or holiness.

Baldwin began by wresting some estates from the control of the Canterbury monks who, he claimed, had degenerated into luxurious living in the first flush of the massive exploitation of the cult of Becket since 1170. There are echoes here of the long running twelfth century debate between Cistercians and Benedictines over the degree of asceticism required by the Rule of St. Benedict. Such controversies were marked by justice and hypocrisy on both sides. However, the question of estates and revenues paled into insignificance in the face of Baldwin's scheme to found a college of secular canons at Hackington, on the outskirts of Canterbury, dedicated to St. Stephen and St. Thomas. The monks of Christ Church regarded this not only as a threat to their prestige but also as providing a model and an excuse for replacing them with secular canons in the cathedral chapter, as both the king and most of his bishops apparently desired. Baldwin reacted vigorously to the sustained monastic opposition to his plans, at one period imprisoning the monks in their own buildings for over eighteen months (January 1188-August 1189) and later imposing on them a prior of his choice. The new king, Richard I, eager to resolve such conflicts before embarking on crusade, imposed a settlement on the disputants in November 1189 which largely favoured Christ Church, Baldwin transferring his plans for a college to land he acquired at Lambeth. The dispute had drawn much attention to it throughout western Christendom and was to rumble on in some form or another for years after Baldwin's death. His conduct is difficult to judge given that the most detailed account of it, by Gervase of Canterbury, is eloquently hostile, but his actions show Baldwin as provocative, reluctant to compromise, aggressive and dictatorial. The end of the dispute in 1189 also suggests that royal approval and support was crucial and its withdrawal fatal. One thing that Becket's death had failed to achieve was archiepiscopal independence from the crown: the position was too important for that.

Not all Baldwin's energies were expended on his dispute with the monks of Christ Church. He played an active role as adviser and diplomat for the king, one which he combined with his ecclesiastical position most famously during Lent 1188 when he lead a tour of Wales to preach the Third Crusade. One of Baldwin's companions was Gerald of Wales who wrote a detailed account of the trip, *The Journey through Wales*. Part preaching, part recruiting, part diplomatic mission to secure Angevin overlordship over the Welsh church and princelings, Baldwin's tour was ostensibly a success, even though, on Gerald's self-serving evidence, Baldwin was an indifferent and uninspiring preacher. As an organiser, though, Baldwin was careful and thorough. In 1188 he insisted that his unfit entourage dismount, lead their mounts and walk the steep valleys of mid-Wales in preparation for the arduous journey to Jerusalem. On his new estate at Lambeth in 1189 he erected the tents he intended to take east with him, presumably to test their suitability or to practise putting them up. One of only two English bishops to fulfil their crusade vows(the other was Hubert Walter, bishop of Salisbury who later succeeded Baldwin at Canterbury), Baldwin played a brief but significant role in the campaign. Leaving Richard I at Marseilles in August 1190, he, Ranulf Glanvill and Hubert Walter led an advance party of the Angevin army to the Holy Land arriving at the siege of Acre in October. With the Patriarch of Jerusalem ill, Baldwin found himself the most important cleric among the besiegers. As such he made strenuous efforts to prevent the erosion of the power of King Guy of Jerusalem who, as a Lusignan, had been a vassal of King Richard. However, conditions in the crusader camp were atrocious and Baldwin died on 19 November 1190. In his will he left some money to provide wages for twenty knights and fifty sergeants to act as sentries, the remainder going to the central fund established to look after the increasing number of impoverished and destitute crusaders.

Whatever his faults and limitations as a pastor, Baldwin's noble death probably tempered more adverse judgements by contemporary chroniclers. Gerald of Wales, who had observed him at close range, thought him gloomy and highly-strung but patient, without malice and scholarly; a somewhat grey figure. All commentators outside Christ Church, Canterbury agreed on his religious sincerity, but there hung about him a whiff of failure. For one in his position, piety was not enough. Pope Urban III (1185-87) was said to have described Baldwin as 'a most fervent monk, a zealous abbot, a lukewarm bishop and a careless archbishop'. This rather jaundiced opinion, coming from an ageing pontiff who allegedly died of shock on the news of Saladin's victories in the Holy Land, may seem too glib, a reflection of a widely shared irritation at Baldwin's bellicose handling of his monkish chapter. Of Baldwin's capacity to inflame Benedictines there can be no doubt, a trace of such resentment even colouring Dom David Knowles's account of his career written in the 1940s. Baldwin lacked the heroic stature (or folly) or the clearly defined principle (or good press) that made memorable the careers of Anselm, Becket or Langton. He was no quietly efficient administrator in the Lanfranc or Hubert Walter mould. With these shortcomings he was fairly representative of the English episcopacy, clergy and church: a man of some firm beliefs who enjoyed good academic training and munificent secular patronage, but who still found the complexities of lay and ecclesiastical politics open to no simple solutions.

W. L. Warren, *Henry II*, 1973.
D. Knowles, *The Monastic Order in England*, 1949.

HUGH DU PUISET (*c.*1120/5-1195; bishop of Durham 1153-95; justiciar 1189-90), reputedly one of the most avaricious public figures in twelfth century England, owed his glittering career in church and state largely to his birth. A great-grandson of William the Conqueror, his mother was Agnes of Blois, sister of King Stephen; his father, Hugh III of Le Puiset, was a notorious gangster who terrorized wide areas of northern France before retiring to Jerusalem in 1128/9. Blois patronage brought the younger Hugh to England *c.*1130 and preferment in the church. Bishop Henry of Winchester, an uncle, made Hugh his archdeacon in 1139; in 1143 he became Treasurer of York and archdeacon of the East Riding under Archbishop William, another relation, whose cause he strenuously maintained against his surplanter, the Cistercian Archbishop Murdac. A taste of Hugh's arrogance is preserved in how he described himself at this time: 'By the Grace of God, treasurer and archdeacon'. He felt quite free to excommunicate his own archbishop: the feeling was mutual. Tactically withdrawing to assist his uncle at Winchester in 1149/50, he returned north as bishop of Durham, apparently a popular as well as royal choice, commending himself to locals and to the pope alike as an opponent of the increasingly abrasive Cistercian mafia which at the time looked set to dominate the northern church. Consecrated by Pope Anastasius IV himself at Rome in December 1153, he proved a moderately active diocesan, especially in periods when excluded from court in the 1150s and 1190s, although his most permanent legacy was in buildings rather than administration. Both his office and his background gave Hugh a certain independence, precariously so after the end of the power of the house of Blois in England in

1154. By the 1160s, he had ingratiated himself with Henry II, remaining in conditional favour for the rest of his reign. In some ways Hugh was an unlikely bishop. For royal service, although well-connected and adequately secular in outlook, he lacked learning or bureaucratic experience; for spiritual leadership, he possessed neither theological grasp nor monastic training. It is perhaps unsurprising that he held aloof during the Becket controversy. His diocese uneasily placed on the frontier, Hugh's loyalty was tested during the Scottish invasion of 1173-4, his policy of self-interest leading to the confiscation of his castles, the return of which remained a source of tension with Henry II for many years. However, he was increasingly regular in attending the king's court and in royal service. In 1188, he went to Scotland to try to extract the Saladin tithe. All the time he was assiduously expanding his wealth by purchase or exchange. When he took the cross (in 1185 or 1188), although temporarily adopting a hair shirt, he made rich preparations for his crusade. These came to nothing in 1189 when the death of Henry and the accession of Richard I opened new opportunities. Richard was desperate for money. Hugh, probably using the treasure he had raised for the crusade, obliged with a total of 3,600 marks for property, release from his crusade vow, a half share in the justiciarship and the earldom of Northumberland, prompting Richard to the sardonic quip that he had made a young earl out of an old bishop. Perhaps Hugh's promotion was made with a view to keeping Scotland quiet in the king's absence on crusade. However, Hugh's foray into national politics was brief and disastrous. The actual work was done by a committee of which Hugh was not a member. Appointed in September 1189, in March 1190 he was stripped of formal power in the south, and in June sacked altogether. He was no match for the ambitious chancellor William Longchamp, who effectively replaced him.

Although restored to uneasy favour after Longchamp's fall in 1191, his sphere of influence was largely confined to the north, where he remained loyal to Richard I's interests in the face of John's attempted *coup* of 1193-4. He died, after apparently overindulging at a Shrove Tuesday feast, in 1195, a not inappropriate end for a man who lived lavishly, surrounded by material luxury. He died immensely wealthy: after his debts had been paid, there was a surplus of at least £3,000. His domestic life was equally extravagant. His affair with Alice de Percy gave him four sons, one becoming chancellor of France, another a Yorkshire landowner, the others archdeacons. As William of Newburgh commented, his public career had seemingly been framed by his insatiable thirst for money. He found, however, that even if he could afford to buy favour, he could not purchase success. A prince of the church, he lacked the skills to rule.

G. V. Scammell, *Hugh du Puiset*, 1956.

**RICHARD FITZNEAL (or FITZNIGEL)** (*c*.1130-1198) was an illegitimate son of Nigel, bishop of Ely, treasurer of Henry I. A leading civil servant under Henry II, Richard's fame rests on his *Dialogue of the Exchequer*(1178), an account of the history and practices of the central royal accounting office. His whole life was bound up with the small administrative elite employed to run the king's household government. During the civil wars of the 1140s, Richard had been taken hostage by King Stephen to secure the good conduct of Bishop Nigel, who had been disgraced in 1139. In 1154, Nigel was restored to office by Henry II in order to revive the financial system of Henry I. Richard may then have become the Chief Writing Clerk. In 1156/8, Nigel bought his son the Treasurership from the king for £400, a post Richard held for most of the rest of his life (until 1195/6), In common with other royal officials, Richard's activities were not confined to one part of royal administration. He acted as a justice-in-eyre and a judge of Common Pleas at Westminster. In 1176, with his colleague Richard of Ilchester, Richard went to Normandy to reorganise the Rouen exchequer. Parallel to his bureaucratic career, Richard attracted the ecclesiastical preferment to be expected by a royal official in a period before substantial civil service salaries, pensions or systematic bribery. Archdeacon in his father's diocese of Ely in 1160, he added a canonry at St. Paul's and the archdeaconry of Colchester before becoming dean of Lincoln in 1184. Rejected as bishop of Lincoln in 1186 in favour of the dynamic Hugh of Avalon, Richard secured the bishopric of London during Richard I's initial orgy of patronage in 1189. Although adequately versed in the law,

a)

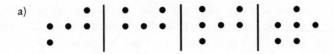

b)

| £ | | | £ | | | s | | | d | | |
|---|---|---|---|---|---|---|---|---|---|---|---|
| | | 100 | 10 | | 5 | 10 | | 5 | | | 6 |
| 20 | 20 | 20 | 1 | 1 | 1 | 1 | 1 | 1 | 1 | 1 | 1 |
| 20 | | | | | | 1 | | | 1 | 1 | |

How the Exchequer Board worked:

a) is how £198 19s 11d was shown on the board;
b) is the key.

Seating plan for the Exchequer Table

Richard was no scholar, and his ecclesiastical role did not extend beyond the administrative. As the *Dialogue* showed, his career and heart lay in the Exchequer and royal business.

Apart from his duties at the Exchequer in examining the accounts rendered each Michaelmas by the sheriffs and organising the annual audit, the Treasurer also controlled the royal treasuries, in which were stored the king's money, mainly in the form of barrels or sacks of £100 worth of silver pennies. Treasuries were located in convenient royal castles, such as Gloucester, Salisbury or Oxford, with larger depositories at Winchester (convenient for journeys across the Channel to Normandy) and London, near the Exchequer at Westminster, The Treasurer was a slightly detached figure in the king's household. Concerned with securing the king's treasure and valuables, collecting revenue and debts, and, through the audit, scrutinising the behaviour, loyalty and honesty of local officers, his job ensured long absences from the itinerant court and the presence of the king, where power lay. Yet his function was vital for royal government for he supervised the transfer of funds to the king's Chamber, the financial department of the royal household. The Chamber was the key financial office, through which huge sums were directed to warfare, the costs of the royal court and the king's entertainment. Yet, because Chamber accounts do not survive from before the thirteenth century, its role has been obscured by that of the Exchequer, whose records, the Pipe Rolls, survive from 1130 and, in a more or less continuous sequence, from 1155.

The *Dialogue* pioneered administrative and corporate history. In describing the working of the Exchequer, Richard details all sources of royal revenue for which account was rendered there and, in many instances (e.g. Danegeld and Domesday Book) provides historical accounts, often of doubtful accuracy, of the origins of payments and procedures. The *Dialogue* casts the bureaucrat as hero. In part this is because the history of the Exchequer was, for Richard, family history. The importance, perhaps even the existence of the Exchequer was due to Richard's great-uncle, Roger 'le Poer', bishop of Salisbury; its re-establishment under Henry II, to Richard's father. Writing of Bishop Roger, Richard remarked 'it is from the overflow of his learning that I have received, in my blood, the little I know'. As with most family histories , Richard's may not be as objective as it at first appears. For example, it is evident that the Exchequer was a place where important people met rather than, as Richard would have it, of great political importance *per se*. The *Dialogue* conveys a sense of corporate identity associated with the physical surroundings of the office, its halls, seating plans, tables etc. The Prologue begins 'In the twenty-third year of the reign of King Henry II (i.e. 1176-77), as I was sitting at a turret window overlooking the Thames . . .' Some things have changed little for the English mandarin.

The most famous item of office furniture in English history was the Exchequer board, a table covered with a chequered cloth which was used to show the figures being audited (see diagram). The board acted as a two-dimensional abacus, a device which probably was introduced to England c.1100. Of great interest to mathematicians, to whom it opened up calculation of high numbers, its adoption by royal financial officials is an early example of the application of information technology to government: the twelfth century Exchequer was the first English computerised department of state. Its efficiency was not lost on those who sat around the Exchequer board. One of them, Robert of Meulan (d.1118), Henry I's chief minister, had his own exchequer for revenues from his English estates. The Exchequer board provided the intimidating focal point of the annual Michaelmas audit of sheriff's accounts, which was conducted in front of an impressive array of officials and specially appointed experts, including *ex officio* the Justiciar, who presided; the Treasurer who led the scrutiny and supervised the compilation of the official record of the audit on the Pipe Rolls; and the Chancellor, who kept his own copy of the audit, the Chancellor's Roll, for use by the royal household and, presumably, the Chamber. (In the thirteenth century, when pressure of judicial work kept the Chancellor away, a deputy attended on his behalf, known as the Chancellor of the Exchequer.) Underlying this system, however, was an older method of keeping accounts and records, the tally stick. Notches representing the amounts rendered were cut in sticks which were then split, one being given to the renderer of the account, the other kept at the Exchequer. None of the latter survive, as in 1834, during a fit of bureaucratic efficiency, the Exchequer tallies were burnt. The resulting conflagration of timber, some of it dried over eight centuries, not only carried off an irreplacable historical archive, but destroyed the old Palace of Westminster too. As one who revered tradition (even where spurious), Richard might have thought it served his successors right.

C. Johnson, ed., *The Dialogue of the Exchequer*, 1950.

**RICHARD I** (1157-99; king of England 1189-99) was one of the most glamorous of medieval monarchs and, judged by what mattered at the time, one of the greatest. Yet, admired and feared by contemporaries, he has been reviled by modern historians. No English king has had more legends woven about him, by scholars no less than romancers. Until the seventeenth century, he was a hero. Since then, while retaining a popular image as a knight, he has been condemned as an absentee warlord who capriciously milked England of its wealth to fund campaigns in France and the Mediterranean, by implication far away places of which good Englishmen know nothing. Yet for more than a century after his death, his aura lent lustre to his successors. Henry III was proud to dine beneath his uncle's shield and decorated his palaces with murals and titles depicting Richard's heroic exploits on crusade. Edward I's crusading provoked the comparison: 'Behold he shines like a new Richard'. Another observer contrasted the uneasy first six years of Edward II's reign with the drama and success of Richard's first three. Far from being a shameful example of royal neglect and princely self-indulgence, Richard I was the yardstick for admirable English monarchy.

Born in Oxford, the third son of Henry II and Eleanor of Aquitaine, Richard spent most of his early years in England. Whether acquired then or later, in adult life Richard displayed particular affection for the insular saints Alban and Edmund of East Anglia. He had some fond memories of childhood: when king in 1189, he gave estates in Wiltshire to his former wet-nurse, Hodierna, whose reward is recalled in the parish of Knoyle Hodierne. Apart from military training, Richard received an excellent education. Belying his popular image as being little

Richard Cœur de Lion

*Richard I*
(From his effigy at Fontevrault Abbey in Anjou)

more than an effective killing machine, Richard was a talented linguist. He could tell jokes in Latin and recite poetry in French and Provençal. He exhibited interest and skill in choral music. For all his passion for tournaments, the trappings of chivalry and the reality of fighting, Richard was no mindless thug. He brought his intellect and insight to the conduct of war, initially in consolidating his rule in Aquitaine then, as king, in launching a massive amphibious force on the Third Crusade and subsequently in regaining territory in France. There was more to successful warfare than mastery of riding, holding the lance and sword-play. Raising money, men, ships and supplies for the crusade; building castles; and, above all, leading men and convincing them to fight, demanded skills of a high order. Richard's own family history was littered with those unequal to such tasks: Robert Curthose; Stephen; John.

In 1167, it was decided that Richard should inherit the lands of his mother, the county of Poitou and the duchy of Aquitaine, for which he did homage to the king of France in 1169. From 1172, when he was formally installed as duke, Richard's career was chiefly spent in asserting ducal power over a recalcitrant nobility in a large and diverse province: excellent training for kingship. Politically, Richard faced tensions within his family: he joined his mother and brothers in the Great Rebellion against Henry II in 1173-4 during which he held his first independent command; in 1182-3 his authority was challlenged by his elder brother Henry; finally, in 1187-9, he was heavily engaged in securing inheritance to all the Angevin lands. Throughout, Richard showed himself energetic, single-minded and resourceful. A sign of his self-confidence is shown by his willingness to ally with Philip II of France in order to secure his inheritance. Philip's price was Richard's public acceptance of Capetian overlordship. As king, whatever the political favours, personal obligation or legal status, Richard felt no constraints in dealing with Philip. As ever, the effectiveness of Capetian attempts to exploit their overlordship depended on the behaviour of their vassals rather than their own efforts.

Richard's accession as king of England, for all the uncertainties of 1187-9, was the most harmonious and least challenged of any English king between 1042 and 1272. His coronation at Westminster, the first for which we have a detailed account, was lavish, the feast afterwards even more so. Behind such ceremonies lay atavistic traditions of sacral kingship — the centrepiece of the coronation being the anointing of the king on his head, hands and bare chest — and the assertion of power. Richard had especial need to signal his authority as he had determined to lead an army to the Holy Land to recapture Jerusalem. Richard needed to establish an effective regency and raise vast sums of money. It is no small tribute to Richard as a political leader that Angevin authority survived his absence and his people contributed to his crusade in almost unprecedented amounts.

Few things reveal the absolute gulf between the Middle Ages and our own time more than the crusades. Modern experience of war has stripped away the last vestiges of noble, chivalric veneer. The squalid ends of empires have cast suspicion over stereotypes based upon cultural or racial superiority and antagonism. Religious wars have too often contradicted the Faith ostensibly in dispute. Yet, for many of Richard I's contemporaries, few ideals were nobler, for the layman none more meritorious than taking the sign of the cross to defend or recapture the scene of Man's Redemption, the Holy Sepulchre and the Holy City of

Jerusalem. To achieve either required personal commitment of a very high order: many failed to reach their destination; more did not return. Crusading demanded material resources and organisation usually beyond an individual. The First Crusade (1096-99), which captured Jerusalem, had attracted only sparse support from Englishmen, although many from the Anglo-Norman aristocracy took part. The second large-scale expedition (1146-9) elicited a more widespread response. Nobles used it as a respectable excuse to escape political dilemmas at home. Contingents from London, East Anglia and the Channel ports made a significant contribution to the crusading fleets which succesfully besieged Lisbon in 1147. By 1187, a tradition of interest in and visits to the Holy Land had become well-stablished in England. News that the armies of the Christian king of Jerusalem had been annihilated by the Egyptian sultan Saladin at the battle of Hattin (July 1187) and that Jerusalem itself had fallen (October) galvanized the West. The Angevin lands, including England, were swept up in the huge military effort now known as the Third Crusade. In November 1187, Richard was the first prince north of the Alps to take the cross.

The Third Crusade became a central pre-occupation of Angevin government and a major dimension of English politics. Where Henry II had temporized for decades, Richard acted decisively: nine months after his coronation and just under a year after his father's death, Richard set out on crusade from Vézelay in northern Burgundy. On the evidence of his organis-ation and conduct of the crusade alone, Richard is revealed as a most formidable politician and administrator, as well as a com-mander of stature. An experienced general, Richard realised that there was no limit to the treasure needed for the crusade: its first year cost at least as much as the king's annual income. Roger of Howden, a royal clerk and former justice who himself went on Richard's crusade, recalled that the new king 'put up for sale all he had, offices, lordships, earldoms, sheriffdoms, castles, towns, lands, everything.' Officials of his father, including the justiciar Ranulf Glanvill, were sacked and heavily fined, their offices auc-tioned to the highest bidder. Episcopal sees, such as London and Ely; forest rights; town charters; even his own demesne lands were all sold off. Richard told his friends that he would have sold London itself if he could have found a buyer.

Richard's preparations were precise, effective and breathtakingly large. He raised and pre-paid a fleet of over a hundred ships, carrying perhaps 8,000 men. His own land army which met the fleet at the pre-arranged rendezvous ports of Marseilles and Messina, may have totalled as much as 9,000. Having wintered in Sicily, but for a storm which blew his huge fleet off-course (allowing him, with typical aggression, to capture Cyprus) Richard would have arrived in Palestine as he had planned, a year after embarkation. To exert such control over logistics and strategy by land and sea over the length of a continent is a feat unparalleled in previous English history. Although from 1189 significant private contingents departed for the Holy Land, notably from London, the core of the English response to the crusade was very much that of central government, from the hiring of ships from Cinque Port merchants to the ordering of horse-shoes from the Forest of Dean, cheeses from Hampshire and bacon from Warwickshire. The dynamism behind such operations was that of the king himself. Where other crusader princes — the king of France or the emperor of Germany — relied on leading a coalition of self-financing vassals, Richard made sure that his leadership was supported by a massive force in his direct control and pay. The Third Crusade was a triumph of Angevin organisation, in scope, imagination and execution, one of the most remarkable governmental achievements of the Middle Ages.

To medieval observers, Richard's crusading exploits confirmed him as the ideal prince. Modern criticism, by contrast, condemns Richard for leaving his lands dangerously exposed to internal wrangling and external threat. Dynastically, Richard was taking a risk. Like Louis VII of France before him (in 1146), he set out for the East without a male heir. He compounded possible confusion by recognising, for immediate diplomatic advantage, his infant nephew Arthur of Brittany as his successor at Messina in October 1190, whilst having only recently built up the landed position of his brother John to almost viceregal status in parts of England. However, the regency arrangements worked, with the little local difficulty of the fall of his chosen viceroy Longchamp being smoothly resolved by his replacement with Walter of Coutances, archbishop of Rouen (1191) and, finally, by the appointment of Hubert Walter as archbishop of Canterbury and justiciar in 1193. If Richard had returned, as planned, in the spring of 1193, all would have been well, Furthermore, Richard did not cut himself off from problems at home. On rumours of political tensions in England, Walter of Coutances was despached as royal troubleshooter from Sicily early in 1191. Richard was kept in close touch by a stream of messengers: in return he sent regular newsletters announcing his triumphs, such as the capture of Acre (July 1191) and the defeat of Saladin at Arsuf (September 1191). News from England could have reached the Holy Land in little more than two months: the king knew of Longchamp's deposition in October 1191 by the following January. For England, Richard on crusade was only different from Richard in Aquitaine by degree.

The problem was Richard's failure to return in 1193. He had begun his journey East in July 1190. Having sent an advance guard to the siege of Acre in the autumn of 1190, Richard and the bulk of his army wintered at Messina in Sicily before embarking for Palestine. Having almost casually overrun Cyprus, Richard arrived at Acre in July 1191: the city fell a month later, after a siege of two years. Philip II of France left for the West three weeks later, leaving Richard as the dominant commander. After repulsing Saladin and occupying Jaffa, Richard twice tried an assault on Jerusalem, each time withdrawing a few miles from the Holy City because of the vulnerability of his supply lines and the realisation that, even if he could take Jerusalem, he would not be able to hold it. Such careful campaigning and agonising, but militarily enlightened decisions mark Richard as an outstanding general. Persuading his followers to obey him, to have the prize of their efforts dashed from them at the last moment, reveals a remarkable leader of men. As 1192 progressed, military stalemate forced a three-year truce to be agreed between Richard and Saladin in August 1192 (they never actually met, *pace* thirteenth century myth-makers and twentieth century Ladybird books). Although the Holy City remained in Muslim hands, the littoral of Palestine was restored to an attenuated Christian kingdom of Jerusalem. Part of the deal was that crusaders were allowed to fulfil their vows and pray at the church of Holy Sepulchre under Saladin's safe-conduct, no doubt the source of his laudatory reputation in the West thereafter. Richard declined the offer, prefering to leave his own vow unfulfilled for future redemption. Richard sailed from Acre in October 1192. So far, so good.

What transformed Richard's crusade from orderly and digni-fied, if limited success into potentially fatal personal and politi-cal disaster was his capture on his way home in December 1192 by Leopold of Austria, whom Richard had insulted during the siege of Acre. Within a few weeks, Leopold had sold Richard to Henry VI of Germany. Richard stayed in captivity for a year while Henry conducted an auction for the king's release. One side of the bidding was Richard, backed by the resources of the Angevin empire. On the other were Philip of France and Prince John, in 1193-4 allies in a partially successful attempt to dis-member Richard's continental possessions. Richard won, offer-ing a ransom of 100,000 marks, the bulk of which was paid before the king's release in February 1194. Such was the impor-tance of Richard's freedom that, on hearing of the deal with Henry VI, Philip II wrote to John: 'Look to yourself: the devil is loose'.

But the damage had already been done. Although the regency in England held firm under Eleanor of Aquitaine, Walter of Coutances and Hubert Walter, strategically important parts of Normandy were lost to the French king in the year of Richard's captivity, the recovery of which dominated the last five years of the reign. Imprisonment of medieval rulers was not unknown, but, as in the cases of Stephen, Henry III, Edward II, Richard II, Henry VI *etc.* was usually the result of internal discord. Not all precedents were reassuring. Richard's great-great-uncle, Robert Curthose, duke of Normandy, spent twenty-eight years in prison. Like him, Richard took to poetry to while away the time, although there is no truth in the legends of his being sought out and discovered by a faithful minstrel Blondel. Observers were impressed at Richard's demeanour. One usually hostile French writer enthused that Richard bore himself in adversity as if 'seated on the throne of his ancestors at Lincoln or Caen'. Even at the nadir of his fortunes, Richard knew how to

cut an impressive figure. But part of the blame for his predicament must be his. Alone of the great leaders of the major crusades, he had failed to arrange safe passage home. If the
consequences for his power and dominions were limited partly
by his own effort, the severity of the threat was no less his
responsiblity. The obverse of his self-confidence was a streak of
recklessness.

During his brief, and as it transpired final visit to the land of
his birth (March-May 1194), he ostentatiously rededicated his
rule to two national saints closely identified with English crusaders, Thomas Becket and Edmund. Like Stephen on his release
in 1141, at Winchester in April 1194 he revived the custom of
ceremonially wearing his crown. But Richard never fully escaped
the repercussions of his captivity. One of the terms of his release
was that he had to perform homage to Henry VI for England,
technically thus reduced to a fief of the empire. Richard was able
to ignore any practical implications of this, helped by the early
death of Henry (1197) and subsequent German civil war. His
homage had only personal advantage, easing the speed of his
freedom. By contrast, when John, in a move much criticised by
later commentators, submitted England to the overlordship of
the papacy in 1213, he gained practical support from successive
popes which proved vital in keeping the Angevin dynasty on the
English throne. More seriously, the loss of lands in France, particularly in the Seine valley, significantly weakened the external
defences of his lands, as well as showing how continental loyalties, at least, could be swayed away from the Angevins, a lesson
repeated more devastatingly a decade later.

Richard's ransom and consequent wars with Philip of France
cost his subjects a fortune. The ransom of 1193 necessitated the
levy throughout the Angevin lands of a tax on moveables and
25% on incomes. A year's wool crop was requisitioned from the
great Cistercian sheep ranches of upland England, as well as
ecclesiastical gold and silver plate. The speed of collection — at
least 70,000 marks were paid in six months before Richard's
release — is testimony to the efficiency of royal administration
and, more strikingly, the loyalty of taxpayers. Richard's officials
could not have coerced such sums from an unwilling populace:
the support, particularly, of the baronage was vital, fiscally as it

was politically, in resisting the schemes of John. Richard was alert to the political dimension. Even in his German prison, he wanted to know how much each baron had contributed to the ransom 'so that we may judge how far we must return the compliment'. Angevin kings forgot nothing but learnt much.

No less remarkable were the sums raised 1194-99 for Richard's French wars realising tens of thousands of pounds and necessitating a new land tax — the carucage — in 1194. Typically, Richard's officials, in a manner powerfully reminiscent of his father's reign, took the opportunity of the king's return to launch an extensive general investigation into what they called 'royal pleas' , meaning all the king's potentially lucrative rights. Whatever else, Richard's reign saw no slackening of the grip of Angevin government. Apart from the characteristic ploy of extracting protection money from wealthy individuals, towns and the vulnerable Jewish community, those who had bought offices in 1189 were now informed that they had in fact only purchased a short lease and had to pay a further sum to retain possesion. Richard understood that success in war which revolved around sieges and scorched-earth campaigns, went to the general with the most money. Wages, food, siege engines: all were expensive. Castle-building was astronomically so: Château Gaillard, built on the Seine as an offensive bastion against the French, in two years (1196-98) cost £11,500. (The total royal expenditure on English castles for the whole reign was only £7,000.)

The question often posed is whether Richard's military enterprises bled his dominions white, leaving them vulnerable to French attack after his death. Evidence from England and Normandy for the early years of John's reign suggest that these milch cows were by no means exhausted. What differed was the willingness to shoulder the burden which was related directly to the popularity of the ruler and his success or, in John's case, lack of it. Richard's exploitation of his resources depended as much on perceptions of him as a ruler as on the bureaucratic skills of his officials. Thanks to both, Richard's rule went unchallenged despite his extravagant demands on his subjects. By 1199, almost all the lands lost to Philip II had been recaptured, with some others added. Richard's supreme ability to harnass men and materials to specific political objectives continued to pay rich dividends.

Richard died on 6 April 1199 from a crossbow wound suffered during a siege of the castle of Chalus-Chabrol, near Limoges in Aquitaine. He is one of eight post-conquest kings so far who have died violent deaths, This alone makes the event notable. But the manner of it has encapsulated much of the criticism of Richard: foolhardy in pursuit of ephemeral, capricious greed. It was later claimed that Richard believed that Chalus-Chabrol housed hidden treasure. Such claims miss the mark. His death was in keeping with his adult life but not in the way his insular critics imagine. Apart from the years of the crusade, Richard's career was largely spent in maintaining, protecting and extending his inherited lands and jurisdiction, chiefly on the continent where they were most vulnerable. For Richard, England demanded no especial attention. At Chalus he was policing a troublesome rebellion in a strategically vital part of his dominions.

However, Richard received his fatal wound because he exposed himself to enemy fire without the protection of armour. Richard's personal bravery and recklessness in battle was no small part of his reputation. It is also remarkable how many medieval commanders died because they could not bear to wear full armour in the front line (testimony to quite how uncomfortable it all was). Richard's lack of caution may have been part of his political personality. Literary convention urged enjoyment of war, well expressed by Richard's own protégé Bertrand of Born: 'once he has entered the fray let each man of high birth think of nothing but the breaking of heads and arms; for it is better to die than to be vanquished and live'. The reality may have been less gung ho. Henry II, for one, was circumspect about fighting and revolted by casualties in which Bertrand seemed to delight: 'I find no such pleasure in food, wine or sleep as . . . in seeing men great and small go down on the grass by the ditches; and in seeing the dead, with the pennoned stumps of lances in their sides'. Richard appears a creature inhabiting Bertrand's world. Yet he consistently refused to impose his own foolhardy heroism on his troops. Richard fought in the front line, as when he famously waded ashore at the head of a relief force to save

Jaffa falling to Saladin in 1192, beacuse that is where leaders who expected to be obeyed fought. Such behaviour was deliberate. The example was not one to follow but to inspire. Richard's personality, as opposed to his legend, has left scant trace. Indifferent to personal safety, he was capable of calculated cruelty, as when he had executed 3,000 Muslim captives after the fall of Acre. His crusade testifies to militant piety. A man of few but decisive words, he could be eloquent when occasion demanded, as in his defence of himself at Speyer in 1193. He lacked pettiness and vindictiveness. Many of his father's loyal servants found in him a generous master. He forgave the crossbowman who fired the fatal shot at Chalus. Richard can be considered negligent in failing to produce an heir after eight years of marriage to Berengaria of Navarre, but there is little evidence to support accusations of homosexuality. These reflect misunderstandings of medieval habits, where sharing a bed, which Richard is said to have done with Philip II, was a symbol of brotherhood, of a contractual rather than erotic relationship. In any case, almost nobody suggested Richard was a homosexual until the mid-twentieth century. A maverick hermit in 1195 accused him of 'illicit acts' and reminded him of the fate of Sodom, but other observers criticised his voracious appetite for girls, even on his deathbed. Richard's one acknowledged bastard was sufficiently well-known for Shakespeare to give him the leading role in his *King John*, where Richard — complete with the thirteenth century story of ripping out and eating the heart of a lion — is held up in heroic contrast to his shifty brother.

Richard ruled England in his own interests, as did all medieval kings. The difference was that, unlike so many of them, he did it rather well. His captivity was partly his fault, The uncertainty about his preference for Arthur or John allowed Philip II to cause trouble after his death. But while he lived he held most of his vast territories together, bequeathing his successor the most extensive inheritance in western Europe. It was hardly Richard's fault that John squandered it. His early death can be counted a blessing, as in the case of Henry V. But Richard achieved a huge amount in a brief decade. Supremely, he won the acquiescence of his subjects and the respect of his enemies. A French chronicler called his performance in captivity 'lionhearted'; a thirteenth century Muslim observer called him the most remarkable ruler of his times.

J. Gillingham, *Richard the Lionheart*, 1978.

**WILLIAM LONGCHAMP** (*d*.1197; bishop of Ely 1189-97), who briefly ruled England during Richard I's absence on crusade 1190-1, was one of the most vilified public figures of the Middle Ages. Not content to demolish his policies and motives, his enemies portrayed him as a physically grotesque, ugly, misshapen, dwarfish, leering, pot-bellied pederast. Whether or not Longchamp resembled a gargoyle or could not, as some alleged, be trusted with the sons of the nobility, his chief failings were political tactlessness and personal arrogance which, in the eyes of his employer King Richard, were, initially at least, outweighed by his effectiveness in conducting royal business. A Norman clerk and expert in civil law, he graduated from Henry II's chancery to the service of the future Richard I, rising to be his chancellor before 1189. After Richard's accession, Longchamp, now the royal chancellor in England, was selected as the king's chief representative in England, being appointed joint justiciar and bishop of Ely, the traditional civil servant's see. The following year Longchamp ousted his colleague, Hugh of Le Puiset, bishop of Durham, leaving himself supreme. Richard clearly calculated that he needed a viceroy of complete personal loyalty, without existing potentially conflicting ties of interest. To provide the necessary institutional status, Richard not only agreed to the demotion of Le Puiset but secured (for a cool 1500 marks) Longchamp's appointment as papal legate. This concentration of authority was no irresponsible whim: Longchamp's power over church and state was replicated after 1194 in Richard's appointment of Hubert Walter as archbishop of Canterbury and justiciar.

In his eighteen months in power (March 1190-October 1191), Longchamp proved himself vigorous and effective. The central administration continued to function smoothly, Longchamp's management even provoking what passed for humour from one of his bureaucrats compiling the Pipe Roll:

The bishop of Ely owes £20 of that (*i.e.* Welsh) scutage on account of his knights. But he had them and a great many more in that same army in the king's service. And therefore with angels and archangels he is quit.

Longchamp pursued royal rights energetically, especially in controlling strategic castles. In 1190, he toured the north, disciplining royal officials who had allowed the massacre of the Jews in York and dissidents at Lincoln. He twice campaigned in the Welsh Marches. He held a church council at Westminster in 1190. As measure of his success, the majority of the bishops supported his petition to the new pope Celestine III in 1191 for his legation to be renewed and he retained the support of senior barons, such as the earls of Warenne and Aumale.

Longchamp's tactics were no more draconian than those of Henry II's servants, but in the absence of the king he was vulnerable. Office had not yet been divorced from person, and baronial resentment at government action could express itself more easily against a parvenu minister rather than the king. Longchamp fell foul of the xenophobic snobbery of the English elite, which, rather than nascent constitutionalism, was an increasingly marked feature of this period. Longchamp also had to contend with the restless ambition of Richard's surviving brother and adult heir presumptive, John, to whom the king had alloted considerable estates in England. Together, John and discontented barons set out to destroy the chancellor, whose highhanded methods proved poor politics. In the summer of 1191, civil war was only averted by a treaty between Longchamp and John mediated at Winchester by the king's special envoy, Walter of Coutances. The compromise included criticism of arbitrary disseisin by royal officers, an anxiety which reached mature expression in Clause 39 of *Magna Carta*. Certainly, Longchamp had, with Hugh of Le Puiset, Gerard de Camville or Roger Mortimer, acted ruthlessly on his own authority, but it could be argued that was what he had been appointed to do. His opponents talked of his disregard of what they described as the legitimate customs of the realm, but their motives were hardly altruistic. John wanted to run England by and for himself. His chief propagandist, Hugh of Nonant, bishop of Coventry, was a self-important, opportunist turn-coat whose main talent, it seems, lay in the invention of colourfully venomous anecdotes about the chancellor.

Longchamp's fall was dramatic. In trying to prevent the king's half-brother, Geoffrey, archbishop of York, from entering the country, some of Longchamp's men had violently dragged him from sanctuary into custody. Geoffrey and his allies ensured that no-one would miss the parallels with Becket's murder. Although politically trivial in itself, the incident provided an excuse for all Longchamp's enemies to combine to force him from office. This they achieved by mid-October 1191, when Longchamp surrendered the seal. According to Hugh of Nonant, Longchamp's initial attempt to flee the country disguised as a woman — 'a sex which he always hated' — ended in humiliating farce: waiting on Dover beach, he was picked up by a fisherman whose attempted rape was only thwarted after he lifted Longchamp's skirts.

Although excluded from England, Longchamp retained Richard's favour and continued to show his worth. In 1193, he arranged terms for the king's release from captivity in Germany and visited England to arrange payment of the ransom of 100,000 marks. He was in England again during the king's visit in 1194. As a servant of the king, Longchamp showed skill and tenacity, two traits which especially irritated the factious barons and prelates he so conspicuously failed to control during his period of office in England.

W. Appleby, *England without Richard,* 1965.
J. Gillingham, *Richard the Lionheart,* 1978.

**HUBERT WALTER** (?c.1140/5-1205; bishop of Salisbury 1189-1193; archbishop of Canterbury 1193-1205; justiciar 1193-1198; chancellor 1199-1205) has been described as 'one of the greatest royal ministers of all time'. In organising royal justice, finance, warfare or administration, he was supreme, his authority matched by his competence. For more than a decade, as chief minister, primate of England and papal legate, he dominated church and state with a thoroughness unmatched until Thomas Wolsey three centuries later. While his reputation among modern historians has been enhanced by his instituting efficient government record-keeping of lawsuits and official correspondence, of his achievement there is no doubt. Fifty years afterwards, the inventive Matthew Paris had King John exclaim on hearing of Hubert's death 'Now, for the first time am I truly king of England'. Although apocryphal, the sentiment was not inappropriate: if a litigant went over Justiciar Hubert's head directly to King Richard, he was liable to be punished; and in 1205, Chancellor Hubert effectively scuppered King John's projected invasion of France. Wherever he was active, Hubert, combining efficiency with ruthlessness, was a force to be reckoned with.

Born, probably at West Dereham, Norfolk, into the ranks of the lesser baronage, Hubert was educated in the household of his uncle, the powerful royal official Ranulf Glanvill (justiciar 1180-89), whose right-hand-man Hubert became in the 1180s. First appearing as a witness to royal charters in 1181/2, Hubert's rise was swift. A justice from 1184 and dean of York in 1185, Hubert worked in the Exchequer and chancery. In 1189, Richard I elevated him to the bishopric of Salisbury, a move perhaps not uninfluenced by the presence at Salisbury of the depository of the Saladin Tithe. The Third Crusade was the making of Hubert. Accompanying his uncle Ranulf with the English advance-guard to Acre in 1190, the deaths of the other leaders left him in effective control of the beleaguered English force in the winter and spring of 1190-1. He rose to the challenge: he conducted the tortuous diplomacy with other contingents; administered a central fund to pay soldiers and provide for the provisioning of the destitute; and even led forays against the Muslims. On Richard's arrival in 1191, he became his close adviser, acting as his chief negotiator with Saladin and leading the first group of crusaders allowed to visit the Holy Sepulchre in Jerusalem under the terms of the treaty of 1192. Hearing of Richard's captivity on his way home, Hubert visited the king in Germany in 1193 and was sent to England to supervise the collection of the massive ransom. His reward was the archbishopric of Canterbury and the justiciarship, becoming, in effect, Richard's viceroy.

The justiciarship had elastic powers but two specific functions: the control of royal finances and the administration of justice. As a finance minister, Hubert was notoriously

*Hubert Walter (left) anointing King John at his coronation*
(From mid-thirteenth century drawing)

successful. The Ransom of 1193 raised 100,000 marks; scutages were extracted in 1195 and 1196; tallages on royal demesnes, including towns, in successive years from 1194; levies on wool were imposed on the sheep-ranches of the Gilbertines and

Cistercians; and in 1194 a new land tax, the carucage, was instituted. According to the former royal justice Roger of Howden, Hubert raised 1,100,000 marks in two years 1194-96. Allowing for taxpayers' exaggeration, Hubert was collecting huge sums to pay for wars in Wales and France. Additional revenue came from feudal dues; miscellaneous, often large, debts to the Exchequer; and the profits of justice. These latter included fines (often levied as security for good behaviour), payments for writs and hearings, as well as innumerable *douceurs* from anxious litigants eager to ensure prompt and/or favourable judgements. Thus, Hubert's judicial role was linked to the financial. The general judicial eyres he organised in 1194 and 1198 were occasions to call in money owing as well as to dispense royal justice. Hubert also gained a reputation for his knowledge of legal custom. The permanent *curia regis* which sat at Westminster was attracting more business and the justices, inevitably, grew more professional than their predecessors whose activities had ranged more widely across royal business. Increasingly, *curiales* specialised in finance or law. A symptom of the increase in legal work may have been the introduction under Hubert of formal records of *curia regis* cases on rolls of parchment. With more business, the need to establish precedent and case law became more pressing. These rolls formed the basis of the first legal text-books in the following century. It is also true that Hubert had a tidy mind. The appearance of newly detailed evidence should not automatically persuade historians of significant developments in practice: Hubert's changes may have been motivated by considerations of bureaucratic efficiency, not more work. The same can be said of the enrollment of royal letters and patents during Hubert's period as chancellor under King John.

Away from Westminster, Hubert was involved in general royal policy. His major political achievement as justiciar was the pacification of the realm after the turmoil of Richard's absence, the opposition to Longchamp and the rebellion of Prince John. Involved in Richard's continental diplomacy, as well as providing for the king's wars, he also fought some of them. As at Acre in 1190-1, Hubert directed military operations at the sieges of Marlborough (1194); the Welsh campaigns of 1196 and 1197; and he helped raise the relief force for the siege of Painscastle shortly-before he retired from the justiciarship in 1198. Hubert was not a desk-bound bureaucrat: he was the king's chief agent, executive and minister.

Hubert was also archbishop and, from 1195 to 1198, papal legate. Most contemporaries were fairly sure where his priorities lay, especially those clergy whom he taxed. When secular circumstances demanded, Hubert ignored clerical privileges. But he worked with characteristic energy as an ecclesiastical judge; he conducted diocesan visitations; he chased up recalcitrant crusaders from Cornwall to Lincolnshire; he held a legatine council for the Northern province in 1195, and a council for the south in 1200. In John's reign he protected monastic immunities and helped in the canonisation of Wulfstan of Worcester and Gilbert of Sempringham (1203 and 1202 respectively). Unlike many, including perhaps Pope Innocent III (1198-1216), Hubert saw no contradiction in wielding the two swords of *regnum* and *sacerdotium*. He embodied the normal practice of twelfth century Europe. In a sense, Hubert was what Henry II had hoped Becket would be. It was frankly hypocritical for Roger of Howden, a royal clerk who had spent years in government service instead of tending his flock in the East Riding, to condemn Hubert for prefering worldly office to spiritual ministry. Hubert was not a great religious leader and was no theologian, but he was efficient and thorough in church business, which is more than can be said of some other primates, more inspired, intelligent or passionate than he. At least in his ferocious conflict with the monks of Canterbury over his scheme to establish a college of secular canons at Lambeth, Hubert maintained the highest traditions of his office.

This is not to deny to Hubert a spiritual life. He embraced a variety of religious insurance policies. In 1193, he adopted the habit of an Augustinian canon at Merton priory, a gesture which may or may not have been prompted by the new archbishop's desire to associate himself with his famous predecessor Thomas Becket who had gone to school there. In 1195, he became a *confrater* (*i.e.* an associate member) of the Cistercians, a connection which paid dividends when he persuaded the Cistercian abbots in England to write him a glowing testimonial to the pope. More intriguing was his reaction to a visit to the Carthusian house at Witham where he was so impressed by the sanctity of the monk

Adam of Dryburgh that he insisted on receiving from him 'discipline with the rod'. What either party made of this scene where an obscure holy man beat the naked body of the most powerful man in England is not recorded.

Hubert's resignation as justiciar in 1198 scarcely interrupted his influence, if it lessened his load. His protégé Geoffrey FitzPeter succeeded him and he remained an intimate adviser of the king. In 1199, although initially reluctant, he decisively supported the accession of John, receiving the chancellorship as immediate reward. To consolidate his hold on England John, whose main interests were then continental, may have wished to recruit Hubert as an ally as much as a servant. Either way, it signalled that there would be little change in the tenor of English government which, in the long term, John may have regretted. Only after Hubert's death did John promote his own clients into posts of great influence. Immediately, Hubert displayed his talents in the chancery. Within a month, a fixed schedule of fees for documents issued under the Great Seal was produced and chancery writs and charters began to be enrolled. His experience and relationship with other leading officials gave the new chancellor a brief far beyond his formal duties. He was active in diplomacy; in May 1202 he was sent to England to convey the king's commands to officials and to lead their counsels; in 1203, he was in charge of levying a seventh from the clergy; he continued to sit as a judge; he advised the king on all matters fiscal, political and administrative; he kept the church quiescent. The defeat in France in 1204 may have led to a cooling of relations with the king, but Hubert retained enough clout to dissuade John from his 1205 campaign. It may be that, at the end, within weeks of his own death, Hubert felt doubts or even remorse at the rapacity which was the inevitable accompaniment to war. Perhaps he saw that the administrative and political costs were proving too high. Perhaps he knew that John was no Richard, and that another French defeat could fatally compromise his position in England, especially as there was at the time no direct heir. Whatever the motive, the old minister prevailed; a familar circumstance.

If a definition of a great minister is that he fulfils his master's wishes, Hubert Walter was one of the greatest. Seemingly unencumbered by sophisticated education or lofty ideals, he was a practical genius who could organise anything, anywhere, anytime. Contemporaries noted his lack of learning: his Latin was apparently poor and he was an indifferent public speaker. But he had a clear mind and a huge capacity for work. His brilliance as an administrator, first prominently displayed in the unlikely surroundings of a disease-ridden army camp in Palestine, underpinned his success as a finance minister and judge. He knew how things — and presumably people — worked; he knew what he and his masters wanted. In relations with his monarchs he showed conspicuous skill, unassuming and indispensible. He carefully built up a network of contacts in government service and, with equal care, and unlike his potential rival William Longchamp, did not dabble in politics on his own account. He made sure that his enemies were the king's. Despite his high ecclesiastical office, he espoused no political independence; not for him the mistakes of Henry of Blois or Stephen Langton. Loyalty, as he knew better than any, had its own reward.

His *modus operandi* was quietly and effectively self-interested. From the number of disseisins he had perpetrated which needed special investigation after his death, it is clear he used his judicial position for personal gain. In office, he had the use of large sums which passed through his hands for which rendering account could be delayed for years. He received money direct which normally went to the Exchequer. Although one modern apologist talks of Hubert's 'speculative investment' in royal wardships, corruption is a better word. In 1203, he paid 1,000 marks down, with a promise of a 3,000 more over three years for a rich royal wardship which netted 2,000 marks a year. In a sense, as justiciar and chancellor, he was dealing with himself, and so could make profits for all concerned, except the ward's family. Hubert used his public position to strike private deals as well. Thanks to his official intervention, the abbot of Bury St. Edmund's secured control of the wardship of Adam de Cokefield's grand-daughter, which he then sold (freely?) to Hubert for 150 marks, although the going rate was 300. Hubert then sold the wardship on for 500 marks. Such manipulation of rank allowed Hubert to live lavishly and ostentatiously. He died a very wealthy man.

At its height, Hubert's power was awesome, but not invulnerable. When threatened, he showed his steel. In 1196, complaints that Hubert's regime was corrupt and rife with official peculation were directed at the king from two sources: William Fitz-Osbert, a prominent London citizen and rabblerouser, and Robert, abbot of St. Stephen's, Caen. The latter was sent by Richard to London to head an investigation into the conduct of the Exchequer and the honesty of the sheriffs rendering account there. The day before Abbot Robert arrived in London, Fitz-Osbert was hanged on the justiciar's orders for resisting arrest (by Hubert's men), causing an affray and manslaughter. At dinner with Hubert the following day, the newly arrived abbot was taken ill: he died five days later. William of Newburgh commented 'those who feared his coming, did not mourn his going'. The inquiry was cancelled.

Tall, handsome, diffident on the public stage, relentless behind it, Hubert Walter may appear the archetypal English mandarin. Yet he was a ruthless and effective politician too, not in the sense of competing with the baronial magnates in loud gestures of support or opposition to royal acts or in open, bitterly fought land disputes, but rather in council, on the bench and in administration. He provided the king with money and solutions to problems. Familiar with Exchequer, chancery, the court, the church, the siege and the battlefield, his versatility and command over the whole range of government business made him much more than a serviceable bureaucrat. It was Hubert's voice which was crucial in the acceptance of John as king in 1199. Hubert was formidable, unscrupulous but, it was said, sensitive to criticism. Many suffered at his regime's bullying, often vindictive pursuit of royal rights, fiscal exploitation and personal greed. Yet he set a standard of efficiency that his successors could but try to emulate. In his capacity for official business; administrative expertise and imagination; determined financial management; skill at handling kings, politicians and opponents; personal venality; political ruthlessness; and success, Hubert Walter bears comparison with another Norfolk man — Robert Walpole.

C. R. Cheney, *Hubert Walter*, 1967.

**HUGH OF AVALON** (*c*.1135-1200; bishop of Lincoln 1186-1200) combined noble birth, spiritual integrity and unusually outspoken self-confidence to become one of the most distinguished prelates of his age. His life was commemorated in two contemproary biographies, a character sketch by Gerald of Wales and a more hagiographic account by his own chaplain, Adam of Eynsham. A nobleman from the Burgundy/Savoy region of France, Hugh had tried various religious vocations before joining the Carthusian order *c*.1160, attracted by its eremitic strictness and refusal to compromise its original principles. Unlike the Cistercians, the Carthusians remained few in number, an elite group the rigour of whose life, based on solitary devotions rather than communal ceremony, was never weakened to accommodate popularity. Although protesting his dislike of official business, Hugh was good at it, becoming successively *procurator* (*i.e.* bursar) of the Grande Chartreuse, the mother house of the Order; prior of Witham (Somerset); and bishop of Lincoln. Hugh was an ascetic, but not a contemplative. He fulfilled his stern vocation in ruling and guiding others. Hugh owed his career in England, however, to being well-connected. Henry II was looking for a prior to rescue his under-endowed foundation of Witham; Hugh was recommended by a neighbour of the Grande Chartreuse, the count of Maurienne. Immediately, Hugh improved conditions and appealed — impressively but not very successfully — for more royal funds. Hugh's plain speaking avoided the common pitfall of clerical admonition by never being hysterically vituperative. There was always some specific point to his famed obstinacy, a practical purpose behind his inflexible determination. He was no Thomas Becket. To the surprise of many, Henry II lapped this up. He took Hugh's rebukes so well that rumours circulated that Hugh was Henry's bastard son. In fact, in 1186, Henry replaced his actual bastard, Geoffrey, bishop-elect of Lincoln, with Hugh, who thus became the only Carthusian directly to become an English bishop. As bishop, Hugh successfully juggled his vocation as monk, diocesan and self-appointed moral censor of secular, especially court politics. Whilst retreating at least twice a year to Witham, he issued reform decrees; instituted regular alms to lepers and the poor; took a keen interest in the rebuilding of the cathedral after the earthquake of 1185; insisted on a high standard in the clergy he licensed; resisted attempts to instal unworthy courtiers into lucrative prebends; attacked, even excommunicated, royal officials he regarded as guilty of excessive exploitation, people not hard to find in Angevin England. Nationally he sat as a papal judge-delegate, sometimes with that very different monastic leader, Abbot Samson of Bury St. Edmund's; he opposed the rule of Longchamp and the attempted *coup d'etat* of Prince John in 1194; in 1197 he refused Hubert Walter's demand for a clerical aid; in 1199 he assisted at Richard I's burial at Fontevrault. There were many anecdotes of his idiosyncratic treatment of his monarchs: turning Henry II's anger to laughter with a jibe at the king's illegitimate ancestry; manhandling Richard I into giving him the kiss of peace; forcing John to delay his dinner by a lengthy sermon. He delighted in exposing the vanity and hypocrisy of power. His principles were adamantine. He returned Henry II's gift to Witham of the Winchester Bible, one of the finest twelfth century manuscripts, because the king had purloined it from St. Swithun's, Winchester. When Hubert Walter sought the dying Hugh's repentence for his harsh words about the archbishop, all he received was regret that they had not been stronger. Although like an Old Testament prophet, a scourge of backsliding kings, Hugh's reputation depended as much on his wide human sympathy. Unlike many monks, he was no misogynist, allowing a place in Heaven for married women; he liked babies; he was sceptical of miracles and uninterested in apparent natural prodigies. Hugh's consistent impatience with human foibles made him an irritable chairman of Chapter meetings at Lincoln as well as a prickly courtier. It may also explain why his most famous companion was the swan he adopted at his estate at Stow, near Lincoln. One of the more distinctive and unusual bishops of his time, he was canonised in 1220.

H. Mayr-Harting, ed., *St. Hugh of Lincoln*, 1986.

**WILLIAM FITZOSBERT** (*d.*1196), nicknamed 'Longbeard', came from a prominent London family, members of which, according to a thirteenth century legend, affected beards 'as a mark of their hatred of the Normans'. In 1190 he and a fellow

Londoner, Geoffrey the Goldsmith, fitted out and commanded a ship for the Third Crusade. On his return, FitzOsbert placed himself at the head of a popular party, critical and suspicious of the ruling oligarchy which ran London's affairs after the establishment of a Commune in London in 1191. FitzOsbert repeatedly complained that the Commune was hand in glove with the government, to the detriment of the ordinary Londoners. Litigous and demogogic, in 1194 he accused his own brother of treason when he was refused a loan and campaigned vigorously against what he saw as the underpayment of the King's ransom by the City fathers who, reluctantly, were forced to accept him on the City council. Extravagant in behaviour and language, FitzOsbert used his prominent position to oppose the harsh financial regime of the justiciar Hubert Walter, complaining against government corruption, especially in the form of unequal tax assessments in which he suspected the connivance of the City elite. His tactic was to use the regular folkmoots at St. Paul's Cross to condemn the justiciar while claiming that he was protecting the interests of the king. That Hubert Walter almost certainly had things to hide made FitzOsbert's attacks more dangerous. In 1196, FitzOsbert took his grievances to the king in Normandy and Richard, possibly coincidentally, appointed the abbot of Caen to investigate charges of peculation at the Exchequer. Threatened with FitzOsbert's popular agitation and an official enquiry, the justiciar's position was precarious. His reaction was characteristically thorough. His agents provoked an affray when trying to arrest FitzOsbert. After futile resistance, FitzOsbert fled to the sanctuary of Bow church whence he was dragged to a summary trial and execution at Smithfield. As for the abbot of Caen, he died suddenly soon after arriving in London to investigate the justiciar, and before he had had time to start inquiries, let alone report to the king. The inquiry was dropped. Events had fallen out remarkably conveniently for Hubert Walter, whether by accident or not.

FitzOsbert's posthumous repuation was mixed. To some, he was a martyr, to others a rabble-rouser. His career provides a revealing footnote to the methods and impact of Angevin government and to the history of the development of self-government in London. Successive post-Conquest kings had tried to retain control of London while granting certain fiscal privileges and administrative autonomy. Whenever royal power was weak, Londoners took advantage. In 1141, they declared themselves to be a Commune, a sworn body sovereign unto itself. Although this was crushed under Henry II, the need for good relations with the rich merchants and bankers of the city tempered government hostility. In 1191, with the king on crusade and the regency government of William Longchamp in tatters, another Commune was established, with a leading merchant Henry FitzAilwin as mayor. This marked the beginning of London's continuous tradition of self-government. The London Commune was in no sense egalitarian, whatever the suspicions of the more traditional powers of king, church and nobility. Fitz-Osbert's actions exposed the reality of a tight-knit, wealthy oligarchy who maintained their independence for their own narrow self-interest, not that of the citizenry or inhabitants as a whole. Then, as now, there was little democratic about the City of London.

G. Williams, *Medieval London*, 1963.


ODO (*d*.1200; abbot of Battle 1175-1200) provides an example of the two faces medieval abbots can show posterity. For the writer of the *Chronicle of Battle Abbey*, Odo was a figure of spiritual power, simplicity, eloquence, humility and learning, the leader who worked and ate with his community and only refrained from sleeping in the common dormitory because of an unpleasant bowel condition. It is of this man that Dom David Knowles waxed lyrical: 'one of the most attractive of all those that appear in the literature of the time . . . had others cultivated the simplicity and sobriety of Odo the subsequent history of the monastic order in England would have been happier and more peaceful'. Yet Odo, as sub-prior and prior of the monks of Christ Church, Canterbury, played an active and distinctly equivocal, if minor role in the Becket affair. It was his business acumen as much as his sanctity that appealed to the monks of Battle when they elected him abbot in 1175. No man who twice was considered for the archbishopric of Canterbury or who provoked papal accusations of conspiracy to murder was entirely unworldly.

Already prominent in Canterbury circles by 1159, Odo became the leading figure in the Canterbury priory at a time when all the attention was sought and taken by the secular clerks of the households of Archbishops Theobald and Becket. Yet Odo was not overawed in such company. John of Salisbury respected his quality and, in 1163, as sub-prior, Odo acted as Becket's proctor in Rome in the dispute with York. Becket's absence (1164-70) presented the monks with a severe conflict of loyalty, to their archbishop or convent. Odo seems to have been faithful to his institution. In 1166-7, he cooperated with the king's agent Richard of Ilchester and in 1167 was chosen as prior without Becket's approval. Although Odo temporarily withdrew from Christ Church in 1169, this did not spare him from coming under suspicion of collusion with the archbishop's enemies in 1170. Yet Becket's disciples were predominantly members of his household without permanent status or affiliation at Canterbury, so during the vacancy 1170-73, the convent, led by Odo, once again assumed prominence. Although passed over for Richard of Dover in 1173, Odo continued to act as Christ Church's business manager and legal spokesman. As such he attracted the notice of the monks of Battle. The abbey of Battle acted as both a war memorial and, as the justiciar Richard de Lucy observed, a symbol of Norman victory and legitimacy. As abbot, Odo continued his predecessors' defence against the bishop of Chichester's claims to jurisdiction. Although again losing out at Canterbury to Baldwin of Ford in 1184, Odo established a reputation for holiness partly through his public sermons, in which he expounded the scriptures with clarity and style. To his monks he spoke in Latin or French; to the people he spoke in English. That we think of Odo as a saint rather than a man of affairs reflects not a dichotomy in twelfth century monasticism so much as the slant of our records. Odo may have been an admirable man — although not all contemporaries thought so — but he was also an effective manager of a monastic community and its secular interests.

D. Knowles, *The Monastic Orders in England,* 1949.

**DANIEL OF MORLEY** (*fl.*1180-1200) was one of a growing number of western European scholars who devoted themselves to transmitting Arabic learning to Christendom. Having studied in Paris, perhaps after Oxford, Daniel spent twenty years or so in Toledo, where he studied under an Italian scholar and translator, Gerard of Cremona. Daniel was primarily interested in mathematics and science, subjects which naturally drew him to the work of Islamic writers. In Toledo he attended Gerard's lectures on astronomy (*i.e.* what would now be called astrology) and engaged in translation of Arabic works perhaps, like Gerard, on medicine, astronomy, alchemy, mathematics, philosophy and logic. He probably did not have a reading knowledge of Arabic, relying instead on locals, probably Mozarabs (*i.e.* Arabic speaking Christians), to translate the texts into Spanish which he could then turn into Latin. Daniel wrote at least two books himself, one on Philosophy and one on Natural Science. To the latter, the *Liber de Naturis inferiorum et superiorum,* he appended an autobiographical preface. Apparently he returned to England with a collection of translated texts, but found the intellectual life of his native country sterile. He was especially disappointed at the quality of science, which is ironic as it was to science that one of the most original English medieval thinkers, Robert Grosseteste, made some of his more significant contributions in the next generation. Daniel was, however, persuaded to stay by John of Oxford, bishop of Norwich. It was on the almost professional teams of translators like Daniel, working in Spain, Southern Italy and Sicily, that the great triumphs of Scholastic synthesis of Albert the Great and Aquinas were based.

J. Catto, ed, *History of Oxford University,* volume i, 1984.

**ROGER OF HOWDEN** (*d.*1201/2) a Yorkshireman from the East Riding, was vicar of Howden from 1173/6. A royal clerk by 1174, he was involved in diplomatic missions, led an inquiry into vacant abbeys (1175) and was an itinerant justice 1185-90. In 1190, he accompanied Richard I on crusade. At the siege of Acre he was in close touch with a group of crusaders from his part of Yorkshire. In 1191, Richard sent Roger back to Europe to keep an eye on Philip II of France. One of Roger's patrons was Hugh du Puiset, bishop of Durham whose fall from power as justiciar in 1190 may have led to Roger's exclusion from office in the 1190s as he retained close links with the bishop, who died in Howden in 1195. Roger wrote two major chronicles, the *Gesta Henrici II et Ricardi (Deeds of Henry II and Richard)*, which covered events to 1192 and a *Chronica*, which revised and edited the *Gesta*, extending it to cover a wider span, 732-1201. The *Gesta* has been attributed to another chronicler, the so-called 'Benedict of Peterborough', but it is now clear that Roger wrote both. For the reigns of Henry II and Richard I, Roger is an indispensible source. Drawing heavily on official records, Roger provides a detailed account of central government, diplomacy, international affairs and high politics, while keeping an eye on local events in south Yorkshire. He preserves a detailed itinerary of Richard I's journey to Sicily and Palestine in 1190-1, and an eye-witness account of the siege of Acre. Reflecting his own career and interests, Roger copied into his text Henry II's assises, the law book attributed to Ranulf Glanvill, names of Henry's justices, papal letters and diplomatic treaties. Roger set a standard for dispassionate narrative and official history not often met by other chroniclers of the political scene. His private life may have been more turbulent. A story did the rounds in the late 1180s of the parson of Howden's mistress (his *belle amie*) whose immorality was exposed by a miracle at a local shrine which led to her being publicly beaten up. Perhaps Roger's crusade was of penitence or escape.

D. Corner, 'The *Gesta Regis Henrici Sewind'* and *Chronica* of Roger parson of Howden, *Bulletin of the Institute of Historical Research,* LVI, 1983.

J. Gillingham, 'Roger of Howden on Crusade', *Medieval Historical Writing*, ed. D. O. Morgan (1983).

**RALPH DICETO** (1120/30-1201) spent most of his career at St Paul's Cathedral, London, as canon in the 1140s, archdeacon of Middlesex (1152/3) and dean (1180/1). He was active in reorganising the cathedral archives and, as dean, conducted a survey of churches owned by St Paul's. A secular clerk, his energies were not confined to the cathedral chapter. He spent time in

Paris and knew other parts of France well, particularly Anjou. He may have been born there, although, alternatively, 'Diceto' could have derived from Diss in Norfolk. As a prominent member of the St Paul's chapter, Ralph was inevitably involved in politics. In the 1160s he was closely associated with Gilbert Foliot's opposition to Becket and, through Foliot, gained an entré to Henry II's court. He came to know most of the church leaders of his time, men who also ran the state: Hubert Walter, William Longchamp, Walter of Coutances, Richard FitzNeal as well as Foliot. Towards the end of the 1180s, Ralph began writing history. His main works are the *Abbreviationes Chronicorum,* a potted history of the world from the Creation to 1148, and the *Ymagines Historiarum (Images of History),* which dealt with the years 1148 to 1202, from 1188 written contemporaneously. Ralph also composed short digests of historical information, *opuscula,* as he was concerned to communicate his material in acceptable form: hence the *Abbreviationes;* the summary of events which prefaced the *Ymagines*; and his system of marginal signs to indicate certain subjects. Well-informed, not least by his extensive political contacts, Ralph's perspective is broad. He is equally at home describing French affairs, Sicilian politics, the plight of crusaders in the dire winter at Acre in 1190-1 or the machinations at the English court. His portrait of Henry II is flattering, emphasising the king's generosity, love of justice and his legal reforms. Ralph applauds the appointment of leading churchmen to secular positions of judicial or political power. In this, Ralph was no more than acknowledging an established fact. For all the rhetoric, usually monkish, of separation of functions, the church provided the state with its rulers and, Ralph thought, a good thing too.

A. Gransden, *Historical Writing in England c.550-c.1307,* 1974.

**PETER OF BLOIS** (*c.*1130-1212) was one of the most popular western writers of the Middle Ages: over five hundred manuscripts of his works survive. After a conventional upper class education in law, at Bologna, and theology, at Paris, Peter became a freelance tutor, lawyer, and attendant cleric to any household willing to employ him. His story was that he spent his time warding off would-be patrons. He held an influential post at the Sicilian court (1166-8), acting as keeper of the royal seal and tutor to the young William II. In the 1170s he was attached to the households of the archbishop of Rouen; Reginald Fitz-Jocelin, archdeacon of Salisbury; and, from 1174, the archbishop of Canterbury, Richard of Dover, whose chancellor Peter became. He also made contact with the royal court. In 1182, FitzJocelin, now bishop of Bath, appointed Peter his archdeacon. Between 1184 and 1190, Peter worked for the new archbishop of Canterbury, Baldwin of Ford. He was closely involved in presenting Baldwin's legal case against the monks of Canterbury, in which cause he was prepared to lie in court and tamper with evidence. He accompanied Baldwin on crusade in 1190. Thereafter, he drifted between service to Eleanor of Aquitaine, Hubert Walter and Archbishop Geoffrey of York. Further preferment came with the deanery of Wolverhampton and the archdeaconry of London, but despite these and other benefices, Peter complained of poverty and neglect. What he really wanted was a bishopric. His inability to speak English — and his refusal to learn — may have played a part in this.

Peter was in the second or third rank of secular clerks, competing for but never achieving high office. Perhaps because of this, he became a more or less professional writer of letters, pamphlets and short treatises. Some, such as the panegyric on Henry II c.1174, were designed to impress potential patrons. Others, such as his three tracts on the Third Crusade, had a wider purpose, to influence opinion. In 1184 he compiled a collection of his letters to which he added over the next decade. They formed the basis of his posthumous reputation, and were read into the fifteenth century as models of style as much as anything more profound. Peter was not an original thinker: for his treatise on friendship he plagiarised Ailred of Rievaulx. His strength was rhetoric. In many of his letters he advocated moral reform, a return to individual apostolic poverty as a protection against the evils consequent on material extravagance. Whether this implied indigence or humility is not entirely clear, nor is it plain to what extent Peter's arguments were personally felt or literary exercises. Well-travelled, vain, self-righteous, a regular in the ante-chambers of the great, Peter was a twelfth century pundit, a sort of proto-journalist. Like a modern leader-writer, he took an event, for instance the rebellion of 1173-4 or the death of Raynald of Châtillon at the hands of Saladin (*Passio Reginaldi* 1187/90), and proceeded to tell his audience what its significance was and what they should think and do about it. He articulated ideas for others to use.

R. W. Southern in *Medieval Humanism,* 1970.

**GERALD OF WALES** (1146-1223), royal clerk, chronicler, ethnographer, polemicist, observer of nature and frustrated careerist, was one of the most prolific writers of his generation. The central theme of his life was his uneasy position as a member of a mixed, frontier Franco-Welsh aristocracy. Too French for the Welsh; too Welsh for the Angevin rulers of England; too cosmopolitan to have anything but contempt for the English, his intellectual inquisitiveness was matched by a political restlessness which ultimately secured for him a position of marginal impotence from which he railed at his erstwhile patrons. With justice he has been compared with Jonathan Swift: 'another disappointed man with literary and invective talent who suffered from the ambiguities of his national position'.

Gerald was the grandson of Nesta, daughter of Rhys ap Tewdwr, prince of South Wales. A remarkable woman, a mistress of Henry I and twice married thereafter, her descendants littered the higher reaches of the Welsh marcher nobility and the Anglo-Norman colonists in Ireland. Gerald, the son of Nesta's daughter Angharad and William of Barry, was, in fact, only a quarter Welsh by blood. This inheritance bred in Gerald an almost schizophrenic attitude towards the kings of England. On the one hand, they offered the path to preferment; on the other they threatened the independence of Welsh marcher lords and their cousins in Ireland. Between these two stools of loyalty and resentment, Gerald leapt and fell.

Educated at Brecon, Gloucester and Paris he was appointed, *c.*1175, archdeacon of Brecon. He cannot then have dreamt that this was the highest post his talent and his family's influence would obtain for him. As a churchman, Gerald displayed the intellectual's inflexible adherence to principle and blindness to hypocrisy. A provocative reformist, he nonetheless condoned nepotism when he was exercising it. The central goal of his clerical life was, however, to secure the diocese of St David's, which had been held by an uncle. Three times, in 1176, 1198-1203 and 1214, the prize eluded him. His background and conduct were against him. In 1199, his one serious chance, although gaining election from the chapter, his insistence on the independence of St David's from Canterbury ensured the opposition of Hubert Walter and, through his influence, the pope. Gerald's pursuit of his claim in Wales merely served to enrage King John, who outlawed him, while failing to secure the see. With only the support of Welsh princes, he was regarded as a proponent of dangerous autonomy. Yet this was the man who had spent a decade or more ingratiating himself with the great of the English church and state; the man who, in 1188, had accompanied the then archbishop of Canterbury on a tour of Wales which included a very public assertion of the supremacy of Canterbury over St David's. What counted against him were his contacts with the Marcher families who repeatedly in the twelfth and early thirteenth century threatened the power of the Angevin kings.

Gerald was attached to the royal court from 1184 to 1194, where his contacts were fully exploited. In 1185, he accompanied Prince John on his ill-fated journey to Ireland and in 1188 he helped Archbishop Baldwin preach the Third Crusade throughout Wales. In the early years of Richard I, he was sent more than once to protect royal interests in Wales. His withdrawal from court in 1194 may have been connected with the failure of John's *coup* and the appointment of Hubert Walter as justiciar, a man who showed himself no friend to Marcher lords. Gerald's alienation from the Angevins was complete after his defeat at St David's, but it had begun in the mid-1190s when, in his disappointment at the lack of patronage, he called the court 'that image of death and model of Hell'. There is no evidence that Gerald possessed any administrative ability. He does not seem to have had any particular legal skills, still less political aptitude. Cleverness and literary ability alone were not enough to gain preferment from the Angevin kings who perhaps looked askance at this provincial *manqué*, this middle-aged *enfant terrible*. In time, as so often, disappointment turned to hate. After his retirement to Lincoln in 1207, Gerald's pen poured forth vitriol against the Angevins culminating in 1216 with a declaration of loyalty to Louis of France.

If his later work is saturated by self-pity and hate, Gerald's writings nevertheless reveal a talent for observation and description, whether in chronicle narratives, political polemics, or accounts of peoples and places. His output was prodigious and his curiosity protean: substantial chronicles dealing with high politics; descriptions of Wales and Ireland; works of semi-autobiography; biography; saints' lives; pamphlets in support of the rights of St David's; poems; a map of Wales; and a book on tides. Many of these works were revised and rewritten over decades. He worked on his most popular book, the *Topographia Hibernica* for over thirty years. His polemical history of the rise and fall of Henry II, misleadingly hiding under the title *De Principis Instructione (Concerning the Education of Princes)* was begun *c.*1190 and completed *c.*1217. His chronicles, although widely quoted, are more expressions of spite than balanced history. What sets him apart from his contemporaries are his works on the topography and ethnography of Ireland and Wales, the *Topographia Hibernica* (1188); the *Expugnatione Hibernica* (1189), the *Descriptio Kambriae* (*c.*1194) and, to a lesser extent, the account of his preaching tour of 1188, the *Itinerarium Kambriae* (*c.*1191). In these Gerald not only describes the natural world as he saw it, with, for the time, rare, as well as vivid, empirical, almost scientific detachment. He also analyses the societies he found. A man of many nations and, ultimately, none, Gerald was sensitive to differences in culture and social behaviour. His work reminds us that twelfth century Europe was a place of frontiers, of strangers, of ethnic and cultural clashes beside which the Norman Conquest of England appears a squabble amongst siblings.

Gerald's own position was, typically, equivocal and occasionally disingenuous. Strident about his Welshness, he spoke no Welsh, only French and Latin. A champion of Welsh national aspirations, at least ecclesiastical, he despised the Welsh. His contempt for the native Irish was even greater. The indigenous Irish Christian tradition was second to none in western Europe. Only by portraying them as barbarians could Gerald hope to justify, in the name of civilisation and the church, the invasion of Ireland and its attempted subjugation by, amongst others, his own relatives. Gerald of Wales was rarely neutral. He wrote for a purpose as much controlled by vanity and prejudice as intellect. He dropped names with professional intensity, to vilify them later. He glorified his own deeds (we only have his word for his exceptional preaching talent). In 1187 or 1188, he took the unusual step for a twelfth century author of promoting his own book. On three consecutive days, he gave public readings from his *Topographia Hibernica* in Oxford. Yet for all his pride and venom, Gerald was one of the most distinguished and original writers of his day, widely quoted in subsequent generations. His vision of the new frontiers of Ireland and Wales, as much as of the old drama of princes and power, was highly individual because, to his deep hurt, he never ceased to be an outsider when being 'one of us' was never more important.

R. Bartlett, *Gerald of Wales*, 1982.

**SAMSON OF BURY** (1135-1211; abbot of Bury St. Edmund's 1182-1211) was perhaps a more typical abbot than the saints and scholars who are so often taken to represent twelfth and thirteenth century religious and monastic life. Unusual for his time in having an intimate biography written of him which is far from unthinkingly or consistently laudatory, Samson's spirituality, whatever it was, is hidden behind practical affairs. Yet such mundane matters as balancing accounts and managing estates were fundamental to contemporary monasticism. Without the sometimes predatory acquisitive instinct none of the great monastic revivals would have been possible, nor would the exercise of learning or holiness. The successful man of God had to be adept in dealing with Mammon, Few were more energetic or notorious in their pursuit of the essential material basis for the spiritual life than Samson of Bury.

The chronicle written by another monk at Bury, Jocelin of Brakelond, presents a uniquely rounded portrait of Samson; its richness of texture prompted Thomas Carlyle to celebrate Samson's life in his popular *Past and Present* (1843). Jocelin's biography reflects the author's own changing relationship with his subject. From Samson's election as abbot in 1182 until 1187 Jocelin was his chaplain and acted as his secretary; thereafter he became more closely involved in other areas of the abbey's life, becaming guestmaster in 1200. As Samson spent much of his time trying to restrict the monks' administrative freedom, control of property and independence of action, Jocelin's tone became increasingly critical, at times even hostile towards his former hero. Although his *Chronicle* ends in 1202, Jocelin's picture of Bury and its abbot is one of the most vivid medieval accounts of monastic life.

Samson, like a number of twelfth century abbots (*e.g.* Baldwin of Ford), began his career as a secular clerk. A Norfolk man, he followed the fashion of studying in Paris. He first served the great local Benedictine house of Bury St. Edmunds in 1160, ironically as spokesman for the monks in an appeal to Rome against the abbot: this earned him a spell in the abbatial prison at Castle Acre. Seeing, perhaps, the opportunity for advancement within a protected corporate structure, Samson took monastic vows at Bury in 1166. He soon proved himself an effective administrator, holding a series of offices, including, in the 1170s, that of novice master. Jocelin of Brakelond was one of his charges. This wide experience of how the abbey was organised not only helped build for Samson support among the monks, in whose interests he had once more been confined briefly to Castle Acre, but also was ideal preparation for his period as abbot. He knew, none better, where lay the monks' interests, weaknesses and inefficiencies.

On his election as a compromise candidate in 1182, Samson's objectives were clear: the restoration of the abbey's finances through a recovery of temporal rights and vigorous management of property. A thorough investigation of abbey estates was conducted. Within two years, all debts had been paid off and by 1186 a book, known as *Abbot Samson's Kalendar,* had been completed listing all the rights and revenues owed to the monastery from each of its holdings. The increased revenues that ensued were used by Samson to pursue contested rights, for instance in the 1190s over the number of knights' fees attached to the monastery, and to rebuilding the abbey church and other monastic quarters (he had been master of the workmen 1180-82 when the choir of the church was rebuilt). Although vigilant in protecting the abbey's privileges and immunities, Samson also encouraged the liberties of the town of Bury, not least as a counterweight to the pretensions of his monks. Similarly, as had his predecesors, he allied with the king to control the aspirations of the Bury monks. It was little wonder that their resentment at his autocratic manner and behaviour, as well as to the detail of his policy, grew. At one stage, in 1199, Samson feared for his life. The sustained opposition was based on legitimate anxieties as well as corporate self-interest. Samson saw his responsibility in running Bury as that of a royal tenant-in-chief accountable to the king for his barony: hence his determination to control as much of the community's property as possible. The monks, on the other hand, feared that, during any protracted abbatial vacancy (as occurred in 1180-2 and 1211-15) the lands that the abbot had taken from the community would be dealt with by the king as part of the abbot's barony and controlled by the crown. However, it is also clear from Jocelin's politically alert account that the monastic body itself was a network of disputing factions, based on age and personal loyalties. Where other writers give only the merest hint of such institutional discord, Jocelin exposes in detail what must, nevertheless, have been a commonplace of life in such wealthy, cloistered communities of men or women, where pettiness could be interpreted as principle and prejudice as piety.

Inevitably, by taste and position, Samson was heavily engaged in national secular as well as local ecclesiastical politics. Perhaps his most memorable intervention was in the 1190s when he defended Richard I's administration from John's attempted *coup*. In 1193 he excommunicated John and the other rebels and, with his military retinue, besieged John at Windsor. Later he visited Richard in Germany. As with his policies towards his abbey, Samson's characteristically firm stand suggests not only a strong personality but a substratum of principle and conviction beneath his actions. However, Samson realised the importance of royal favour and was reconciled to John after he became king in 1199.

Samson was no saint. An effective administrator, he was more at home with the intricacies of politics and estate management than with ascetic rigour or spiritual endeavour. Jocelin describes him as disliking introverted scholarly monks, preferring good organisers. Apparently he harboured the unfulfilled wish to have been the abbey's accountant. Although adequately versed in-Latin, he preached in French and English, the latter with a Norfolk dialect, a habit he shared with another expert administrator, Robert Walpole. Something approaching local pride may be deduced from his devotion to St. Edmund, on whose miracles he compiled a largely derivative treatise between 1166 and 1182 and whose body he examined in 1198 while constructing a new shrine for the saint. Although, on hearing of the loss of Jerusalem and the True Cross in 1187, he took to wearing hair shirts and drawers and abandoned eating meat, he was not noted for personal privation. and, in any case, he preferred 'fresh milk and honey and such like to any other food'. Energetic, at times almost frenetic, he could be impulsive or showy, as when he appeared in front of his guest Henry II in 1188 carrying a needle, thread and a cloth cross and demanding to be allowed to go on crusade. The king refused.

Jocelin's detailed physical description of Samson is a mirror of his personality:

> Abbot Samson was of middle height, and almost entirely bald; his face was neither round nor long, his nose prominent, his lips thick, his eyes clear as crystal and of penetrating glance; his hearing of the sharpest; his eyebrows grew long and were often clipped; a slight cold made him soon hoarse. He had a few white hairs in a red beard and a very few in the hair on his head, which was black and rather curly; but within fourteen years of his election he was white as snow. He was a man of extreme sobriety, never given to sloth, extremely strong and ever ready to go either on horseback or on foot, until old age prevailed and tempered his eagerness.

Jocelin of Brakelond, *Chronicle*, ed. and trans. H. E. Butler, 1949.

**JOCELIN OF BRAKELOND** (*fl.*1180s-after1200) became a monk at Bury St Edmund's in Suffolk in 1173. Shortly after 1202 he completed a *Chronicle* of events in the abbey from 1180 to

1202, effectively a biography of Abbot Samson (abbot 1182-1211), who had been Jocelin's novice master in the 1170s. Jocelin was ideally placed for his work, as he had been Samson's chaplain and secretary (1182-7). At the time of writing, Jocelin was the abbey's guestmaster. Adequately trained in the Latin classics (Virgil, Horace, Ovid *etc.*), Jocelin kept abreast of contemporary historical writing, quoting Ralph Diceto's *Ymagines Historiarum* (finished by 1200), and included considerable information about the customs, administration and tenants of the abbey. His account of Samson is tinged with hagiography, although, when considering the events after he had ceased to be the abbot's secretary, Jocelin allows a more objective, occasionally critical tone to intrude. Most striking, however, is the vivid description of Samson's physique and personality which, unlike most monastic chroniclers, is convincingly drawn from life, not from an honoured exemplar. The accounts of the internal factions; the struggles over Samson's administrative and financial reforms; and the tensions between young and old in the monastery are sharply observed, conveying a sense of reality. Jocelin's purpose may have been to praise Samson and, ultimately, the patronal saint, Edmund, but in the process he left the clearest and most lively description of the life and aspirations within a community of monks written in the medieval England. Jocelin also wrote a now lost *Life of St Robert,* a boy supposedly killed by Jews in Bury in 1181. Jocelin and his *Chronicle* were popularised by Thomas Carlyle's *Past and Present* (1843) as evidence of the virtues of a pre-industrial society run by heroic individuals, a sentimental view wholly of the nineteenth not the thirteenth century.

*The Chronicle of Jocelin de Brakelond* ed & trans H. E. Butler, 1949.

**WILLIAM MARSHAL** (1147-1219) had a most remarkable career. Born the son of a prosperous minor baron, he made his name first as a roistering but shrewd manager of a team of tournament fighters. With good looks and a loyal disposition, he established an enviable reputation for the newly fashionable qualities of courtliness and chivalry. The protégé successively of

Eleanor of Aquitaine, her son the Young King Henry and Henry II, the originally landless William netted one of the greatest heiresses in the Angevin Empire. Prominent in the service of Richard I and John, despite the latter's ingratitude, William stood firm in support of the king in the years of disaster for the Angevins 1213-16, so much so that when John died, leaving as heir a child of nine, the septugenarian William became the young Henry III's protector and regent of England for the last three years of his life.

William's distinctive life was nonetheless a palimpsest upon which were successively written the obsessions of his age and class: war; tournaments; courtly intrigue; the caprice and generosity of the great; pilgrimage to the Holy Land; the hunt for heiresses; the hard choices of men with more than one lord; loyalty; dynastic greed; and the balance of rule between monarchs and their nobles. That William, despite nasty setbacks, emerged triumphant in most of these itself deserved notice: he was clearly more than a pretty face, a silver tongue and a strong right arm. There is a tenacity of ambition and ruthless determination which framed and lent purpose to the outward glitter of his life.

No less remarkable is that William was the subject of the first medieval biography of a layman who was not a king. The *Histoire de Guillaume le Maréchal,* a vernacular poem of over 19,000 lines finished between 1226 and 1229, was written by a member of the Marshal's circle, called John. The author is hardly objective; but he is informative. Behind the glamorous veneer, a man considerably less of a bland archetype can be detected, one whose deeds nevertheless inspired enough interest and devotion to warrant such a unique surviving tribute.

Although not from one of the great landed dynasties of Anglo-Norman England, William spent his whole life in or near royal courts. In 1152, still a very young boy, his pro-Angevin father, John Marshal, gave him as a hostage to King Stephen to buy more time at the siege of Newbury. William later recalled that in his tent Stephen played him at 'knights', a tournament game with straw men, a scene which says much about the amiability of king and the charm of the child.

In the decade before his death in 1165, John Marshal's fortunes declined so much so that William was left nothing.

Entering the household of William de Tancarville, in 1167 he was knighted, and for the first time saw action (at the battle of Neufchâtel-en-Bray) and fought in a tournament. Despite earning praise for his courtliness, William lacked cultural refinement. Nicknamed 'gaste-viande' (*i.e.* 'guzzle-guts'), he was unusual for one of his background in never learning to read or write. His education was more or less exclusively fitted for a career as a professional soldier. Yet he was quick-witted enough to spend his life extracting profit from tournaments and royal service.

After spending a couple of years attached to the court of Eleanor of Aquitaine, in 1170 William joined the extravagant and glamorous entourage of the Young King Henry, where, while keeping up his semi-professional tournament business, he fulfilled the role as the prince's tutor-in-arms. Henry was a tournament fanatic, so William's place in his favour was sure. In 1173, William's prestige was singularly recognised when he knighted the Young King, a ceremony which he repeated in vastly different circumstances for young Henry's nephew and namesake forty-three years later. Except for a brief period in the early 1180s, William remained close to the Young King, but Henry's death in 1183 transformed prospects. Entrusted with carrying the dead prince's cloak bearing his crusader's cross to the Holy Land, William received a promise of employment on his return from Henry II. William brought back with him in 1186 the rich cloth which was to serve as his own pall thirty-three years later.

Having lost the reversionary interest of the Young Henry, William rapidly compensated by service to the Old Henry. The secure foundations of his later grandeur were laid in 1186-89. He made close contacts with influential members of the king's household, such as the future Justiciar Geoffrey FitzPeter and began to receive patronage, in the form of lands, lucrative wardships and the promise of the hand of Isabel, heiress to the extensive lands in the Marches, Wales and Ireland of Earl Richard of Striguil. On Henry II's death in 1189, despite having been unhorsed by William in a recent encounter at Le Mans, the new king, Richard I, confirmed and extended his father's grants on both sides of the Channel. On his marriage to Isabel of Striguil, William at last entered the baronage and independence.

However, he owed his fortune to his loyalty. Richard I had elevated him for a purpose, to help guard his dominions during his absence on the Third Crusade. This proved a test of William's political skill and prescience, as the conflict between the Chancellor Longchamp and Prince John careered towards civil war. William backed John and led the movement which ousted Longchamp in October 1191. Although faithful to King Richard, remaining at his side through his French campaigns of 1194-99, William kept in with John. In 1194, he refused homage to Richard for his Irish lands, instead reserving it for John, as Lord of Ireland. Such ambivalence had a precise purpose. As his enemy Longchamp acutely remarked 'Planting vines, Marshal?'

After Richard's unexpected death in 1199, William harvested the fruits of his husbandry. Instrumental in securing John's succession, he was rewarded with the earldom of Pembroke and a significant extension of his estates, especially in Wales and Ireland. Enjoying the favour of a new and grateful king and the friendship of both justiciar (Geoffrey FitzPeter) and chancellor (Hubert Walter), William appeared at the summit of his career. But his self-interest could not long remain compatible with that of a monarch whose power was crumbling and whose suspicion was pervasive and venomous. William played a vigorous if unavailing part in the defence of Normandy. But when Philip II gained control of the duchy in 1204, William looked to his own, managing to negotiate a deal with Philip in 1205 whereby he did the king liege homage for his French lands. This implied that William would be unable, on risk of forfeiture, to fight Philip in France. As the recapture of his French lands was King John's central policy, William's homage to Philip at one stroke questioned his loyalty and negated his usefulness. Between 1205 and 1212, William suffered the humiliations and political insecurity of loss of royal favour. Initially, he was not even allowed to retire peacefully to his possessions in Ireland, as John was fearful for his own lordship there. When summoned to court in 1207-8, it was to be publicly humiliated, personally teased, politically undermined and legally threatened. From 1208, William lived in retirement in Kilkenny, for the first time acting as a settled ruler of his estates, as well as indulging in a favoured pastime of beating

up the native Irish: as the imaginative Matthew Paris put it a
generation later, he was 'a Saturn to Ireland'.

The extraordinary transformation of William's fortunes
between 1212 and 1216 from distrusted exile to regent of England reveals the extent of the collapse of John's authority as well
as the Marshal's almost robotic loyalty. Yet even in his late sixties, William never altered his conviction that the greatest
rewards were to be found at the hands of the richest provider, the
king. He, as very few then did, remembered the failure of the
1173-4 rebellion and the ultimate futility of hoping for preferment in opposition to the monarch. If he had been tempted to
forget, his experiences of 1205-12 served as a raw reminder.
When, in 1212, magnate discontent with John's methods of rule
expressed themselves through an ill-concealed assassination
plot, William ensured that Ireland stayed loyal. In a sense he had
no option: a successful *coup* would not have advantaged him
much more than a vengeful king. As for John, the plot of 1212
and the opposition to the French campaign of 1213-14 demonstrated that there were fewer and fewer men of substance and
experience on whom he could rely. Patronage in the Middle Ages
was never entirely efficient in binding the loyalty of subjects, but
it was with William Marshal, perhaps because he had started
with nothing.

Returning to England in 1213, William immediately began to
reap the landed rewards of service. He also emerged, with the
earl of Chester, as the leading loyalists among the magnates as
the English baronage slid from the defeat in France in 1214, to
the failed compromise of *Magna Carta* and open civil war in
1215. Nevertheless, whether by accident or design, family interests were protected by William's eldest son's support for the
baronial side. As the crisis deepened for the Angevins, William's
importance grew. He organised the royalists in the southern
Marches and Wales. In 1216 he unsuccessfully tried to dissuade
Philip II from sending his son Louis to England: such an invasion
obviously placed William in a uniquely difficult position. But he
did not flinch in his adherence to John. After the king's death in
October, when to many it must have seemed that a Capetian triumph was inevitable, William assumed guardianship of the
young Henry III and, with the approval of the earl of Chester,

the regency: 'rector noster et regni nostri' as he was styled in royal documents. The sight of the venerable warrior, who had buried three kings (four if you include the Young Henry), whose memories stretched back to King Stephen, with the boy-king were the stuff of romance — and maybe of actual emotion. There is a Churchillian sentimentality in William's recorded remarks to three friends the evening of his acceptance of the regency: 'If everyone abandons the boy but me, do you know what I shall do? I will carry him on my back, and if I can hold him up, I will hop from island to island, from country to country, even if I have to beg for my bread'.

The first task facing the new regent was survival. This William achieved in 1217 primarily through military victories over the French and the rebels at Lincoln and in the Channel. At Lincoln, William himself fought energetically, forgetting his helmet in his eagerness for the fray in which he killed Robert of Roppesley. The naval battle off Sandwich he merely observed with the king from the cliff-tops. But the royalist success was consolidated by a lack of vindictiveness. Already in November 1216 he had *Magna Carta* reissued, a symbol of a fresh start and a more consensual method of governing. Now, after the French defeat, William negotiated the withdrawl of Prince Louis for the sum of 10,000 marks. As Louis was the son of William's French overlord, perhaps this generosity was not wholly altruistic.

In the last two years of his life, William laid the foundations for the rebuilding of royal authority. Given the poverty of the crown and the divisions of the civil war, it was inevitable that he had to conciliate rather than coerce. *Magna Carta* was again reissued in 1217; the Exchequer was restored; the judicial bench returned to Westminster in 1217, with salaried justices to minimise corruption; a general eyre was instituted in 1218-19; and regular councils gave the magnates the impression that they were involved in rule through common consent. Helping the regent were the papal legates, Guala and Pandulph; the Justiciar Hubert de Burgh; and the bishop of Winchester, Peter des Roches. But none of them could (or were to) inspire wide enough confidence, especially vital as there was no prospect of effective independent royal government dealing with intransigent rebels or grasping partisans of the late king, not least because of the failure to restore royal finances. Of course, William never ignored the interests of his family: in 1217 he recovered Marlborough which his father had lost almost sixty years before. But whatever the limitations of his rule, William had kept the centre intact. By the time he died in 1219, there was a system of royal government for others to expand and develop.

The verse biography of William Marshal makes it both easier and more difficult to approach the man as an individual. Opinions and remarks attributed to him have to be treated with care. But something of the private man can be detected. He seems to have been a faithful and certainly uxorious husband: he and Isabel had ten children. Although over forty when he married, he left no recorded bastards. He was a brave, vigorous and deadly fighter into his seventies. He turned his prodigious skill at tournaments (he claimed to have taken prisoner over 500 knights) into a thriving business in the 1170s, with his Flemish partner Richard de Gaugy: they had a disciplined team with a deliberate strategy calculated to maximise captives and minimise risk of injury, all conducted on a professionally commercial footing. Of his dynastic ambition there can be no doubt: it provided the most prominent *leitmotif* of his life. His success can be judged that when he died, possibly of cancer, on his own manor, surrounded by his own extended household, he had made his family one of the greatest in the British Isles. His loyalty was not disinterested. Neither, presumably, were his extensive religious donations. He died, in the habit of a Templar, the model of a good Christian lord and knight, firm in his Faith and his social position. Rather typically, the biographer's account ignored the inconvenient detail that William died still under excommunication by the Irish bishop of Ferns, a penalty dating back to some Irish-bashing of 1212.

William's political apotheosis was the result of longevity — he knew personally all the kings who ruled England from 1135 to 1272 — and clear political vision. It may also have been because he was liked. William had the qualities contemporaries admired and a personality to match. He was no routine toady: on his deathbed, holding Henry III by the hand, he prayed that the king's life might be short if he followed the example of 'alcun felon ancestre' ('a certain criminal ancestor'). Famously impassive in public, here the dying courtier perhaps let slip his true feelings for at least one of his Angevin masters. William's life shows that there was more to being a courtier than literature might imply. In warfare, chivalry, politics, faction, intrigue and self-advancement, William Marshal fought his way to the top and managed to stay there. As Richard I once said of him, he was indeed 'molt corteis', most courtly.

D. Crouch, *William Marshal*, 1990.

**WALTER MAP** (*c.*1130/5-1209/10) was a successful royal clerk and church administrator who gained a great reputation as a *reconteur*. Many of his stories are preserved in his *De Nugis Curialium (Courtiers' Trifles)* compiled between 1181 and the early 1190s. Born in the Welsh Marches (Map = ap = son of in Welsh), his family had served Henry II before 1154. Educated at Gloucester and in Paris, he became a canon of Hereford under the patronage of Gilbert Foliot. In the king's service by 1173, when he was an itinerant justice in Gloucestershire, he remained a prominent royal clerk for the rest of Henry II's reign. Walter attended the Third Lateran Council in 1179 as one of Henry's representatives and was attached to the household of the Young Henry until the prince's death in 1183. As his official career developed, he amassed a comfortable living as a pluralist. Already a canon, in 1186 he became chancellor of Lincoln and precentor in 1189. In 1196 he was appointed archdeacon of Oxford. By this time, he had finished *De Nugis*, a rambling compendium of court gossip and satirical anecdotes, with as much organisation, Walter himself admitted, as a timber yard. At its serious moments it compares with a parody of the *Mirror of Princes* genre supported by edifying moral or cautionary tales. Walter attempted some historical portraits, all worthless except his vivid, surprisingly unbiased and convincing description of his patron Henry II — an objectivity which may account for Walter not publishing it. *De Nugis* sheds light on the rather chaotic mind of a leading member of the chattering classes of the late twelfth century. His interests are human; his eduction classical; his style urbane, witty, informed and spacious, devoid of the portentous anxiety or academic pretentiousness displayed by so many of his contemporaries. One curiosity is that *De Nugis* is the earliest known work to nickname Ethelred II 'the Unready' or, more properly 'un-raed', bad counsel, a pun which would have been right up Walter's street.

Walter Map, *De Nugis Curialium* ed M. R. James, C. N. L. Brooke and R. A. Mynors, 1983.

**GEOFFREY FITZPETER** (*d*.1213) was the epitome of the successful and versatile royal servant. His rise from holding one knight's fee to the earldom of Essex demonstrated how great were the rewards of office in Angevin England. Soldier, administrator, politician, landowner and judge, he played an increasingly important role in Henry II's and Richard I's administrations until succeeding his close associate Hubert Walter as justicar in 1198, a post he held until his death. Although not of 'grant linage', his promotion to the highest ranks of the nobility did not arouse such hostility as did that of another modestly born justiciar, Hubert de Burgh. It may be that, from his activities as judge and tax collector, the enemies he made were the king's enemies, the friends his own. He was fortunate not to have lived to witness the near-collapse of Angevin control of England, his posthumous reputation being enhanced by the chaos after 1213. Matthew Paris lamented: 'after his death England was like a ship in a storm without a navigator'.

Originally from Wiltshire, where in 1166 he held a knight's fee at Cherhill, Geoffrey entered royal service in the late 1160s, perhaps as a household knight. How he caught the king's attention is unknown, although in the household he may have attracted the interest and patronage of Ranulf Glanvill, himself a future justicar (1180-89), whose nephew, Hubert Walter, became one of Geoffrey's closest colleagues. Geoffrey's progress was swift. He witnessed royal charters from 1181; in 1184 he was appointed sheriff of Northamptonshire and Chief Forester (which meant that he led the regular Forest eyres to uphold royal rights, collect dues and hear grievances); by 1189, he had been a justice-in-eyre and sat on the bench of justices at Westminster. Geoffrey's importance was recognised when the pope allowed him to postpone his crusade vow in 1189 on the grounds of his being indispensible to the government of England in Richard's absence.

Office brought riches. Before 1185, Geoffrey had married Beatrice de Say (*d*.1197), one of the heiresses to the wealthy earldom of Essex; various royal wards were assigned to him; and his own estates were, by 1189, worth at least twelve knights' fees. Throughout the 1190s, Geoffrey continued to hold sheriffdoms, act as an itinerant justice and sit on the central bench of justices at Westminster. Opposed to the wilful rule of Longchamp, he was a member of the regency council which replaced him in 1191. On Hubert Walter's appointment as justiciar in 1193, Geoffrey's influence grew further. So regularly did he witness Hubert Walter's writs that court clerks tended simply to abbreviate his name to 'G. fil. P.'. When Walter resigned in 1198, Geoffrey was a natural successor, ensuring continuity.

Retained in 1199 by John, whose claim he had supported, Geoffrey continued to supervise the exchequer; the collection of taxes; the justices at Westminster; and the general eyres. In 1204, he organised an overhaul of the system of raising money from the shires, replacing sheriff farms (agreed annual fixed sums payable to the Exchequer by the sheriffs in lieu of royal dues, any surplus being kept by the sheriff) by custodian sheriffs (the actual, varying amounts owing to the crown being payable). This involved replacing twenty-two out of thirty-one sheriffs, a major political undertaking. Geoffrey was the king's regent in his absences and chief executive when John was in England, which he was increasingly after 1204. The king's presence reduced Geoffrey's independent political role and, unsurprisingly, led to tension. After granting Geoffrey the title of earl of Essex and showering him with gifts (including fifteen tuns of wine) in 1199 in gratitude for his support, and lavishing property on him in the awkward aftermath of the loss of Normandy in 1204, John seems to have cooled towards his minister. In 1209, cases for the justices at Westminster were diverted to the *coram rege* for the king to adjudicate. After 1210, John introduced more of his own officials into government, such as Peter des Roches. In 1212, Geoffrey was implicated, by association, in the plot to kill the king: two of his daughters had married sons of the archtraitor Robert FitzWalter. As an inducement to loyalty, John allowed the dispute over the succession to the lands of William de Mandeville, earl of Essex (*d*.1189) to be reopened. The case was a politico-legal *cause célèbre*. In 1189, Geoffrey de Say had won the Mandeville inheritance against Geoffrey PitzPeter's claim on payment of a relief of 7,000 marks. When, however, Geoffrey de Say defaulted, Geoffrey FitzPeter secured the inheritance with 3,000 marks. Even to withstand a new legal assault on his claim opened the prospect of massive new payments to the king: the loss of the lands themselves was hardly to be contemplated by one so avaricious and successful in pursuit of property. John seemed to be harassing his justiciar. There were policy disagreements, as in 1209 when Geoffrey tried to engineer a reconciliation with Innocent III. By the time of Geoffrey's death, John had reportedly lost confidence in him. Hearing the news, the king remarked: 'when he enters Hell let him salute Hubert, archbishop of Canterbury, whom no doubt he will find there'. A good story, but laced with the possibly accurate sense of royal dissillusion with the men who had ruled England in the king's name for a generation.

Geoffrey was a man of many parts. A *miles literatus,* he knew Latin and was interested in mathematics. He kept his own file of copies of his charters and, with Hubert Walter, presided over the increasingly efficient system of government record-keeping. He was a conscientious and meticulous judge, one of those who established a system of law which provided a relatively stable and unified framework within which the expanding political nation could operate. Immensely industrious, Geoffrey used the Tower of London as a permanent office. But he was not just a desk-bound official. His career had begun in military service for Henry II and, even at the height of his administrative and judicial responsibilities, he led campaigns in Wales in 1192, 1198 and 1210. On one level, his career appears successful, effective, even beneficent. This was far from true. Geoffrey was one of the architects of the system which broke down in 1215. At the centre of public business for thirty years, he tenaciously pursued royal rights; closely supervised payments to the Exchequer: ruthlessly imposed and collected scutages and carucages, all of which, allied to political failure, precipitated the near-collapse of Angevin government after his death. There is little evidence that he could have prevented it. Geoffrey conducted a regime increasingly perceived as rapacious; and in the process lined his own pockets. Not as glamorous or lurid as other leading figures in the dramatic events of the reigns of Richard I and John, he was no less responsible for what happened.

R. V. Turner, *Men Raised from the Dust*, 1988.
F. J. West, *The Justiciarship in England*, 1966.

JOHN (1167-1216; king of England 1199-1216) is the most notorious English king, one of the most unfairly maligned but also one of the least successful. The legend of his awfulness as a person as well as a ruler dates from his own lifetime. Even now, when his positive qualities as a conscientious judge, a careful adminstrator, a man of culture and a ruler of energy are widely recognised, his personality and style leave a nasty taste in the mouth. 'Foul as it is . . . Hell itself is defiled by the fouler presence of King John'. This verdict of Matthew Paris of St. Albans in the thirteenth and J. R. Green in the nineteenth century sums up the 'Bad King John' theory, investigated with more pathos and psychological sympathy by A. A. Milne in his wistful poem 'King John's Christmas' where the monster is reduced to loneliness, self-knowledge and child-like yearning. Other opinion portrays John as able but flawed, 'the ablest and most ruthless of the Angevins' (J. R. Green again) with, in the words of a post-war biographer, W. L. Warren, 'the mental abilities of a great king, but the inclinations of a petty tyrant'. This interpretation too has a long pedigree. In the 1220s, the annalist of Barnwell priory near Cambridge, commented 'he was a great prince certainly but hardly a happy one'. For Shakespeare in the 1590s, John was the unprincely prince, the schemer whose schemes all came unstuck, whose outward show of regality and power concealed a character unstable and deceitful but not monstrous.

More recently, the arguments have moved away from John's character — more or less irrecoverable — to his rule. Thus John's arbitrary government has been studied by J. A. Jolliffe without going down the *cul-de-sac* of moral judgment. Rehabilitation has come with scrutiny of offical records, from which John appears hard-working and competent. J. C. Holt has even

*John*
(From his effigy at Worcester Cathedral *c*.1225-30)

compared John's administrative achievement with that of Henry II or Edward I. This has drawn the retort from J. Gillingham that 'John is the most overrated king in English history', only the accident of record-keeping making him seem busier and more industrious than his predecessors. After all, the contemporary Ralph, abbot of Coggeshall, awarded only faint praise: John governed 'satis laboriose', with enough effort. The problem with assessing King John is that he presents an image of contradictions: energetic and slothful; judicious and corrupt; sensitive and myopic; intelligent and brutish; cultured and violent. Such, to the confusion of contemporaries and historians, was the sum of John's humanity.

Critics and apologists are faced with one supreme fact. Tactically successful — in gaining the throne, defeating his rival Arthur of Brittany, exploiting the fiscal potential of England, gathering a coalition against France, supervising English administration, recruiting vital political and material aid from the pope when he needed it most — as a whole John's reign was a disaster. Having lost much of his continental inheritance by 1204, by his death he had forfetied the loyalty of most of the English baronage and was facing civil war and a foreign invasion. He left his dynasty's future in the hazard, its survival dependent on the repudiation of John and his style of rule. Even King Stephen had retained more support than John. His responsibility for this is related to why his personality inspired such a loathesome reputation. The vilification of John is comparable in English history only to the Protestant slander of Mary I. Other kings had angered the church by their policies, yet clerical and monastic chroniclers reacted much more violently to John and the Interdict than to Henry II and Becket's murder. Why did the normally sober William of Newburgh call John 'nature's enemy'?

John was born in 1167, like his brother Richard at Oxford, the last child of Henry II and Eleanor of Aquitaine, who was forty-seven at the time of John's birth. Significantly younger than his brothers, John was excluded from the dynastic settlement of 1169, but in the 1170s various schemes for John's endowment were proposed. Interestingly, with four healthy sons, Henry II ignored the option of directing any of them to the church. A plan for John to marry the heiress to the county of Maurienne, which controlled the western Alpine passes vital for access to Rome and the Mediterranean, came to nothing. (Both John's sons, Henry III and Richard of Cornwall, actually did marry into the family which controlled this strategically important region.) In 1177, John was created lord of Ireland, an empty title carrying opportunity and risk rather than authority or profit. This was especially true after John's unsuccessful visit in 1185 designed to establish his position. With hindsight, chroniclers saw a pattern in John's political adventures. In Ireland, he frittered away the money his father had provided and indulged with his young friends in luxurious living and mockery of the locals: ridicule of the hairy Irish; disdain for the Anglo-Norman settlers. John was not the last insensitive and futile English proconsul in Ireland. But a reputation for failure clings.

The Irish fisaco of 1185 did not prompt Henry to moderate his devotion to his youngest child, There were rumours — which the future Richard I believed — that Henry was contemplating making John his heir. None of this prevented John from deserting his father at the last, a betrayal that caught the disgust of contemporaries. Small wonder the well-informed Richard of Devizes thought him flighty, an habitual traitor. On his accession in 1189, Richard I provided John with an heiress to marry — Isabella of Gloucester — and vast estates in England, the honour of Lancaster and the counties of Nottingham, Derby, Dorset, Somerset, Devon and Cornwall; in Normandy the county of Mortain which the young Henry I had held. There was no doubt that John was then regarded as Richard's heir. In the king's absence on crusade, he set about reinforcing his position. Almost in defiance of the regency government under Longchamp, John established his own court complete with justiciar, chancellor, *etc.* Nobles earlier in the century had had their own exchequers, but John's establishment had the air of a rival government. Perhaps resentful at not being given the regency himself, John led opposition which forced Longchamp's removal in 1191. Continued exclusion from power thereafter, combined with his brother's designation at the treaty of Messina (1191) of their nephew Arthur of Brittany as his heir, drove John to take advantage of the king's captivity in Germany (1193-4) to ally with

Philip II in dismembering Richard's continental lands. This second betrayal, especially of a crusader, did little to enhance John's reputation: nor did his subsequent *volte face*. In 1194, John had been given Evreux by Philip; after submitting to a remarkably forgiving Richard, he returned to Evreux and massacred his French garrison. Henry II had been a notorious liar and cheat, and yet earned grudging respect. The same traits in John just made him appear shifty.

Richard I's sudden death in April 1199 propelled John to his inheritance. In a possibly apocryphal story circulating twenty years later, William Marshal and Hubert Walter, archbishop of Canterbury, debated whether to support Arthur of Brittany or John as king of England. William persuaded Hubert that legally and politically John should be prefered, but the archbishop warned: 'So be it . . . but mark my words, Marshal, you will never regret anything in your life as much as this'. Yet the early signs must have encouraged both. After a vigorous diplomatic and military campaign, by September John had been accepted by all the Angevin provinces in France and had been crowned king of England; Arthur of Brittany and his mother Constance had submitted; and Philip of France had agreed to parley. At the treaty of Le Goulet (May 1200) Philip recognised John as rightful heir to all Richard's lands in return for a relief (payment to a lord by a vassal entering into possession of an inherited fief) of 20,000 marks. The fact of acknowledging Capetian overlordship was neither novel nor degrading. Henry II and Richard I had openly acknowledged it, as had, tacitly, Henry I. What the Capetians made of their recognised suzerainty depended less on them than on their vassals, Angevin, Burgundian, Flemish or Champagnois. Here lay the difference between John and his predecessors: they coped with Capetian overlordship; John did not. The relief, however, was new, and an added drain on John's finances. There is little evidence that John's, or Richard's, demands exhausted Angevin territories. However, whereas Richard's demands led to results that were popular — the crusade; the king's release; the counterattack in France — John's exactions, heavy from the start of his reign, produced no such positive results. Furthermore, where Richard could persuade English nobles to support his continental wars, John had much greater difficulty. The elusive element of personality was central. The task of a medieval monarch was to convince a few hundred men, and a few women, to follow his lead. Richard could do it; John could not.

John's reign had three distinct phases. During the policing and ultimate loss of Normandy and Anjou to 1204, John was as absent from England as much any of his predecessors. Between 1204 and 1214 most of his energies went in amassing the funds to recapture his continental lands, his presence in England presenting novel circumstances for a political nation used to an absentee overlord, The failure of the reconquest led directly to the final challenge to his authority, the civil war and French invasion 1215-16. It is largely a consequence of the clerical monopoly on chronicles and later attempts to place John's resistance to the papacy in a suitably Anglican light that have exaggerated the importance of the papal Interdict (1208-13), making John a monster of godless depravity or, as in *The troublesome reign of King John* (1591), a flawed Protestant champion. In fact, as far as John's control over the church and his nobility, the Interdict made little difference; its resolution if anything strengthening John's position by gaining a useful ally against enemies both foreign and domestic.

Throughout his reign, John showed vigour and intelligence comparable to his father and brother. His hurried divorce and subsequent marriage to the twelve-year-old Isabella of Angoulême in 1200 secured a strategically important alliance in Aquitaine. In 1202, decisive military action and a forced march of eighty miles in less than two days out-manoeuvred his enemies at Mirebeau, where Arthur of Brittany was captured. Angevin control of Poitou was consolidated by the limited expedition of 1206. Careful naval preparations were rewarded by the first major English victory at sea at the battle of Damme in 1213. During the dark days of civil war in the winter of 1215-16, John wrong-footed the rebels with a lightening three-month campaign through their territory, his march from Winchester to Berwick taking less than five weeks. This was coercive warfare in the best style of Henry II. Elsewhere in the British Isles, with only the threat of force, John imposed a harsh treaty on the inveterate troublemaker, William the Lion, king of Scots, in

1209. In 1210, a brief expedition to Ireland established royal authority over the Anglo-Irish barons in the east. In 1211, Llywelyn, prince of north Wales was subdued so that, in the words of the Barnwell chronicler, 'now no one in Ireland, Scotland or Wales . . . did not bow to his nod'. From such successes, John derived not only political clout but substantial booty.

John was no slouch as an administrator. He personally supervised the work of the Exchequer. He was an assiduous judge: in 1209-12, the central judicial bench which customarily sat at Westminster was suspended, the justices following the king around the country. During the reign there were significant developments in bureaucracy: household offices became increasingly specialised; systematic collection of administrative and judicial records was instituted; a royal privy seal was employed to expedite business; the distinction was established between the civil (Common Pleas) and criminal (King's Bench) jurisdiction of the Westminster judges. John presided over the creation of a national customs system based upon standardized weights and measures and the organisation of a royally funded and built navy. The tone of John's government is captured in his instructions to agents in Southampton in 1206 to carry out his orders with 'immediate haste', whether 'night or day' 'as you love us, our honour, the peace of our kingdom, and regard your own safety and welfare'. All the ingredients of Angevin success and failure are present: urgency; attention to detail; authority; menace.

Yet John was no bureaucrat. His close involvement in the government of England was largely enforced by the loss of Normandy and Anjou. Thereafter, John, whose restlessness was notorious (only once in his reign staying more than a month in any one place), travelled incessantly in his kingdom, as some saw it meddling in his subjects' affairs. In areas such as the north, rarely visited by kings since the tenth century (indeed even Henry III only went north three times in fifty-six years), the presence of an inquisitive and acquisitive monarch on the doorstep came as a rude shock. It was no accident that the rebellion of 1215 was initiated by a group known as 'the Northerners'. The impression of John's conscientiousness, no less than that of a more specialised household, may simply reflect the creation of new ways of recording business which coincided with John's reign. Consequently, by accident, John can be studied in far greater detail than any of his predecessors. The administrative initiatives probably owe more to John's civil servants than to the king. Under John England was run by veterans of Angevin service who had been ruling the kingdom for years before 1199, such as the justicar, Geoffrey FitzPeter, and the chancellor, Hubert Walter. It was for political rather than bureaucratic reasons that John introduced his own men into English government, such as the Tourainers Peter des Roches (bishop of Winchester from 1205; justicar 1213-15), Peter de Mauley, Engelard de Cigogné and Gerard d'Athée and the Norman Falkes de Bréauté.

Whatever his achievements, John consistently undermined them. The nickname 'Softsword' stuck because of a willingness to give up a cause before decisive action. John left Normandy in December 1203, six months before the fall of Rouen, and three before the fall of Château Gaillard. The month before Rouen capitulated in June 1204, the archives of Norman government were shipped to England and taken to London in carts provided by the king, hardly an encouraging sign to those still at their posts in the duchy. In 1214, on the news of the defeat of his allies at Bouvines, John withdrew. Eighteen months later, instead of combating the invasion of Prince Louis of France, John allowed him to land without resistance. With the exception of the Welsh campaign of 1211, John, in marked contrast to his father and brother, lacked tenacity in adversity. On each occasion, however, he feared treachery and would not expose himself to the risk of battle or campaigns against the odds.

Suspicion ate at the heart of John's personality and rule, vitiating his triumphs. In 1200, instead of compensating Hugh of Lusignan for the loss of his intended bride, Isabella of Angoulême, John siezed his duchy of La Marche. This prompted Hugh to appeal to his and John's overlord, Philip of France, thus setting in train the formal confiscation of John's continental lands and the loss of Normandy and Anjou between 1202 and 1204. After the spectacular *coup* at Mirebeau in 1202, John willfully alienated William des Roches, seneschal of Anjou. There-

after, John could no longer rely on the loyalty of the barons of
Anjou. Most damaging was the disappearance and presumed
murder inside one of John's prisons of Arthur of Brittany in
1202-3. Rumours swirled around Arthur's death. Hubert de
Burgh, custodian of Falaise where Arthur may have been held,
denied responsibility for his death. Some accused John's henchman Peter de Mauley of the murder. One account, possibly
derived from an eye-witness, accused John in person, saying that
he murdered Arthur in a post-prandial alcoholic rage at Rouen
at Easter 1203, disposing of the body in the Seine. Whatever the
truth, Arthur's fate and John's inability to produce him, lent
Philip II a telling propaganda weapon and ensured the hostility
of the Bretons.

In dealings with English nobles, John was no less malevolent.
Even the loyalist earls of Chester and Pembroke were harried
and threatened for no better reason than that they were powerful. More notoriously, John's former favourite, William de
Briouze, was ruined and exiled, his wife and son starved to death
in prison. Such violence fostered an atmosphere of fear. It was
one thing to execute thirty Welsh hostages in 1212 or allow captives from Mirebeau to starve to death in Corfe Castle after a
failed attempt at a mass break-out. But the persecution, without
trial, of English barons was different.

Yet this is precisely what John's policy seemed often to be. At
every turn he exploited wardship, relief, and his sovereignty as
king to discipline his nobles. A favoured technique was to force
barons to become royal debtors. Again, the Briouze family provides a most dramatic example, Matilda de Briouze being compelled to offer the huge sum of 50,000 marks (equivalent to the
Exchequer revenue for one year) for the king's grace (*i.e.* protection money) when her assets amounted to 24 marks and some
gold pieces. Geoffrey de Mandeville forced to offer 20,000 marks
for John's ex-wife and the earldom of Gloucester. Reliefs varied
according to loyalty. 10,000 marks were imposed on William
FitzAlan and Nicholas Stuteville, but William de Forz, the son of
John's mistress the dowager countess of Aumale, inherited for
free. The purpose was political control not financial profit.
Stuteville had, by 1230, almost £10,000 still outstanding on debts
contracted under John. Given the average annual baronial

income of £200, very few being worth even as much as £400, the threat of foreclosure was potentially ruinous. If the debtor had recourse to Jewish bankers for a loan, he again confronted the king who regularly taxed the Jews and received all their property — including notes of credit — on their deaths. Other avenues of extortion were explored. The venality of Angevin justice and adminstration, exactly matching its pretentions, could be turned to the king's advantage. William Mowbray was encouraged to offer a bribe of 2,000 marks to the king to obtain a favourable outcome in a land suit. John accepted the bribe — and allowed Mowbray to lose the case, insisting he pay up nonetheless. It is unsurprising that the sale of justice, judgement without trial and the cost of reliefs and wardships appeared prominently in *Magna Carta*

John's unpopularity went further. His style of rule and his personality repelled affection and loyalty. Even his gambling and drinking crony, his half-brother William of Salisbury, briefly deserted him in 1216. John's suspicious nature was matched by gracelessness and the insensitivity of a cunning, introverted cleverness. Many of his hobbies were innocuous enough. John was an avid collector of jewels, which he liked to wear round his neck. He drank and gambled and, like his father, was an obsessive huntsman. Well-read and cultivated, he read both French and Latin, possessing his own portable library, including a copy of Pliny. John was also a predatory lecher, with a repuation for seducing his nobles' sisters, daughters and wives. He had numerous mistresses and at least five bastards. Outrage at John's sexual licentiousness may have added an edge of bitternees to political resentment. One of John's alleged intended victims was the wife of the northern baron Eustace de Vesci who for no obvious political reason played a central role in stirring rebellion in 1215. John also had a penchant for blackmailing others for their sexual adventures, accepting bribes as 'hush-money'. He may have had a dirty sense of humour, which may explain the famous, if enigmatic entry on the Oblate Roll of 1204: 'The wife of Hugh Neville promises the lord king two hundred chickens that she might lie one night with her husband'. Whether or not John was a smutty-minded groper, it does seem that many thought him personally unsavoury. In a world where private relationships were the stuff of high politics, that was a distinct problem.

John had a gift for making enemies, but policies as much as personal quirks caused friction. John was determined to recapture his inheritance. Money was raised by any means possible. There were national property taxes in 1203 and 1207. As the latter raised £60,000 it is difficult to argue that the fiscal exactions of the 1190s had bled England dry. However, the political price was high, there being considerable resistance to the 1207 levy. Thereafter, John was forced to more piece-meal expedients. As feudal overlord, John levied reliefs, wardships and scutages at unprecedentedly high rates. On top of the scutage, a tax in lieu of military service, calculated on the number of knights owed, each baron had to pay a fine for personal exemption. This was hardly popular. Sheriffs were required to account for every penny owed the crown instead of, as previously, paying an agreed lump sum (or 'farm'). Inevitably, this encouraged sheriffs to greater rapacity (or efficiency as Exchequer clerks no doubt saw it). Towns were encouraged to purchase mercantile privileges. Infringements of the onerous Forest Laws were assiduously pursued, as were more general profits of justice and the ubiquitous imposition of amercements, fines for petty misdemeanours, often merely protection money. To such sources of income were added the profitable campaigns of 1209-11, Jewish legacies and tallages, and the proceeds of the deserted benefices during the Interdict. Small wonder John was accused of being 'a pillager of his subjects'. More dangerous than the pious clichés of monastic chroniclers, such high and persistent demands for money excited concerted resistance and, in 1213-14, refusal to pay the scutage. In the insistence that aids and scutages be levied with the consent of the barons (Clause 12), *Magna Carta* was passing political judgement on John's preparations for the great reconquest in France. But by then John's hopes had been dashed. The road from Bouvines to Runnymede was direct.

The last years of John's reign were some of the most extraordinary in English history. Confident in his treasure and his own leadership, two obstacles to a return to Normandy remained. To forestall a projected French invasion blessed by the church, in 1213 John submitted his kingdom to the pope to remove both his personal excommunication and the country's Interdict. When Richard I had done homage for England to the Emperor Henry VI in 1194, he gained merely his own freedom. John, by becoming a papal vassal for his kingdom, acquired a staunchly loyal ally which played a crucial role in sustaining the Angevin dynasty. The root of the dispute had been the king's traditional right to appoint the archbishop of Canterbury, which the pope had contradicted by appointing Stephen Langton archbishop in 1206. Although not overtly a pious man (again like his father), John's response had little to do with religion. At stake was royal control over church appointments which, given the irrevocable increase in the church's estates, was essential for royal authority to be maintained. An independent church or one wholly controlled by an ultramontane papacy would present immense difficulties in ruling England. As it was, the settlement of 1213 acknowledged the pope's legal authority, but with Innocent III (and his successors) committed to support of their newly repentent vassal, there ceased to be any challenge to royal wishes. For most practical purposes, provided the king and pope cooperated, royal manipulation of the church could continue.

Less tractable was the mounting irritation of sections of the baronage. In 1212, there was a plot to assassinate the king. It is significant of what John had to face that one of the ring leaders, Robert FitzWalter, had surrendered the vital town of Vaudreuil to the French in 1204. John's enemies were champions of no liberty except their own. In 1215, FitzWalter trumpeted himself as 'Marshal of the Army of God', yet personal vendetta and grievance not constitutional, still less religious principle lay at the heart of opposition to John. Neither side could claim the moral advantage. Robert's fellow traitor of Vaudreuil, Saer de Quincy, was another to rebel in 1215. John was confronted by men exasperated but no less duplicitous and self-seeking than he. John's failure was to woo enough interests and individuals to his side. One problem was that his interests and those of his leading barons increasingly diverged. In 1205 and 1213 he was prevented by magnate indifference and hostilty from attacking Normandy. In 1213, his attempt to circumvent the higher nobility and widen the scope of political action by summoning knights from the shires to a national assembly backfired: they were as unenthusiastic as the barons about the French wars. All might have been transformed by victory in 1214. Failure, however, is contagious.

The civil war of 1215-16 showed John at his best and worst. A master of tactics, he wrong-footed his enemies, led by a hard core of northern malcontents, by assuming the protection of the crusader when he took the Cross at Easter. At Runnymede in June, *Magna Carta*, into which all the baronial fear and distaste for the operation of Angevin government was untidily poured, provided some basis for compromise, except that its final clause (61) provided for a committee of twenty-five barons to supervise government. If implemented (which inevitably it was not), this would have placed the English crown into commission. Yet at the very time he was ordering his sheriffs to execute the terms of the charter, John was seeking its annulment by the pope. Militarily, John had the beating of the rebels until the invasion on their behalf by Louis of France, son of Philip II, in the summer of 1216. John's characteristic refusal to challenge Louis on the field led to a haemorrage in his support. Misfortune, such as the loss of some of his treasure near the Wash, and illness took its toll. John himself recognised the desperation of his plight. In his will, dictated on his deathbed, he urged his executors to 'render assistance to my sons for the recovery and defence of their inheritance'.

By October 1216, the central issue in the civil war was no longer Angevin government but John himself. Immediately after his death, the regency, on behalf of the nine-year-old Henry III, issued a modified *Magna Carta* signalling a new, more consensual style of rule. Already, the image of Bad King John was abroad. Ironically, John is most remembered for *Magna Carta*, in the drafting of which he was little involved and whose content he quickly repudiated. The true measure of John's reign is not in the temporary truce between two mercenary and self-interested factions, which the charter represented. It lies in the contrast between the magnificent inheritance of 1199 and the legacy of 1216, with the enemy already within the gates and almost ready to take possession. John may not have been the worst English monarch, nor yet the most tyrannical; but it hard not to judge him, on any terms other than his own, as one of the most unsuccessful. However, John's family did not entirely reject his memory. Fifty years after his death on a windy October night at Newark, John's grandson, the future Edward I, named his first-born son John.

W. L. Warren, *King John*, 1961.
J. C. Holt, *King John* (Historical Association Pamphlet), 1963.
R. V. Turner, *King John*, 1994.

**ARTHUR OF BRITTANY** (1187-?1203) was one of the many kings England almost but never had. His father was Henry II's fourth son, Geoffrey, who died after a tournament accident some months before Arthur's birth; his mother was Constance, heiress to the county of Brittany. In 1190, at Messina, on his way to the Holy Land, Richard I designated his young nephew heir to all the Angevin lands, a move that helped provoke Arthur's other surviving uncle, John, into rebellion. Richard's gesture was probably merely symbolic, as he was about to marry and could have expected heirs of his own. In April 1199, however, on Richard's sudden death, Anjou, Maine and Touraine declared for Arthur and he had the support, so it is said, of Archbishop Hubert Walter for the succession to England and Normandy. Whether John or Arthur was the rightful heir was unclear in contemporary English law, and different areas of the Angevin Empire had their own inheritance customs. The matter was resolved by force and diplomacy. By September Arthur had been deserted by his Angevin followers and compelled, with his mother, to make peace and accept John as overlord. In 1202, Arthur seized the opportunity of Philip II's formal confiscation of John's French dominions by doing homage to the French king for all Angevin fiefs except Normandy, which Philip was determined to keep for himself. Philip also knighted Arthur. However, in the ensuing campaign Arthur was captured in Mirebeau where he was beseiging his grandmother, Eleanor of Aquitaine, and incarcerated at Falaise. He then vanishes from view. How, when and where he died was at the time and has remained ever since a source of speculation and debate. The Annals of Margam Abbey in Glamorgan have John killing Arthur in a drunken fury one evening at Rouen in April 1203, a story which may have come from the abbey's patron, William of Briouze, Arthur's captor at Mirebeau. John is known to have been at Rouen at the time. However, John's later barbaric treatment of the Briouze family may have coloured the tale. Other sources adopt a very different line, insisting that Arthur was a traitor and oathbreaker who deserved his obscure and shameful death. Both the reliable Barnwell Chronicle and the *Life* of William Marshal mention Arthur's pride, leaving an image far removed from the innocent, beguiling and rather nauseating child depicted by Shakespeare in his play *King John*. Most of Arthur's life was spent as a pawn in others' political and dynastic contests. On the threshold of manhood, he was no match for his generous-seeming patron, Philip of France, nor his determined rival, King John. Arthur's significance, in fact, may lie elsewhere, as a symbol of the creation of national identify myths. A common twelfth century phenomenon, these fantasies were fuelled by distorted or invented histories which constructed fabulous and honourable pasts to confirm present aspirations. The greatest pseudo-history of the twelfth, perhaps any post-Classical century, was Geoffrey of Monmouth's *History of the Kings of Britain*, after whose central hero Constance of Brittany deliberately named her son.

W. L. Warren, *King John*.

**ISABELLA OF ANGOULÊME** (*c*.1188-1246) was the daughter and heiress of Aymer (*d*.1213), count of Angoulême, a strategically important county in south-west France. Although betrothed to Hugh IX, count of Lusignan, Isabella was married to King John in 1200. Whether diplomacy or an allegedly uncontrollable passion for the twelve-year-old were uppermost in John's motives, it proved an expensive move. His subsequent hostility to Hugh led to the count's appeal to the king of France which was the pretext for the formal confiscation of John's French lands in 1202. From 1213, when she inherited Angoulême, Isabella attracted rumours about her infidelity. John may have believed them, as there is a story he placed her under house arrest at Gloucester in December 1214. After John's death, and the establishment of a stable regency for her son Henry III in 1217, she returned to her county. In 1220 she married Hugh X of

Isabelle d'Angoulême

*Isabella of Angoulême*
(From her effigy at Fontevrault Abbey in Anjou)

Lusignan, the son of her suitor of 1200. For the rest of her life she was perched precariously between the interests of her two families. Her Poitevin sons may have sought their fortunes at Henry III's court, to that king's ultimate detriment, but Hugh betrayed him at Taillebourg in 1240. She died and was buried at Fontevrault in 1246, beside Henry II, Eleanor of Aquitaine and Richard I. From her perspective, the collapse of the Angevin empire was not a defining moment of national history, but one episode in French comital relations in which her role was that of territorial pawn. At least until the 1250s, it was a perspective shared by her sons in England.

**WILLIAM OF BRIOUZE** or Braose (*d*.1211) was at the centre of one of the most damaging *cause célèbres* of John's reign. After succeeding to his father's lands in Sussex, Devon and Wales in 1180, he proved himself a tough and ruthless fighter in the Angevin cause in the Welsh Marches and France. He was with Richard I at Chalus in 1199 and with John in Normandy 1202-3, when he captured Arthur of Brittany at Mirebeau in 1202. An arrogant and unpopular man, with a shrewish wife,

William was showered with favour by John, receiving the extensive Irish lordship of Limerick in 1200-1, more castles in 1205 and lucrative marriages for his many children. For reasons not entirely clear, from 1205 John began to harry his former favourite, perhaps out of fear of his independent spirit or a desire to show that even those powerful by royal creation were subject to the king's will. It is certain that John determined to make an example of William and that William reacted with obstinacy, rashness and incompetence. The weapon William had placed in John's hands were his pledges of huge sums in return for royal grants (5,000 marks for Limerick in 1201; 800 marks for the castles in 1205) on which he subsequently defaulted. Not only did John undermine William's position in Ireland and deprive him of offices in England, he also had a legal case against him at the Exchequer. When the king demanded hostages in 1208, William initially blustered and his wife, Matilda, fatally for her, apparently excused her refusal to deliver her sons as hostages by accusing John of murdering his nephew Arthur. This was particularly provocative as William was probably one of the few who actually knew what had happened to Arthur and who could lend credence to the rumours that John himself had murdered his nephew in a drunken rage at Rouen in April 1203. Whatever the personal edge, John proceeded vigorously. In 1209, William's chattels were distrained, castles surrendered, hostages promised and his English and Welsh lands pledged as security for repayment of his loan. To add pressure, John sent troops to attack William's Marcher lands. William and his family fled to Ireland, but returned in 1210 to avoid John's armies there. This was unavailing. Matilda and her eldest son were captured, taken to Windsor Castle where, despite offers of ransom, they were starved to death. William fled to France, where he died a broken man in 1211, his funeral being conducted by another exile from John's anger, Stephen Langton.

It was not William's harassment which shocked. As the king, supported by many leading barons, insisted in 1210, William was a contumacious debtor and rebel. It was the inexorable quality of the pursuit and the obscene cruelty of the treatment of Matilda and her son, attested by contemporaries, which made the case notorious. William could be said to have brought about his own ruin by failing to submit. There is little objective evidence that John was especially vindictive in the early stages of his attack. In the campaign to increase the effectiveness of the Exchequer's collection of revenue owing to the crown, William's fate was to show other barons that none were immune from royal authority. Whether John's subsequent cruelty was informed by personal spite or misjudged sternness is impossible to say. However, the case of William and Matilda de Briouze showed an increasingly resentful baronage the lengths to which the king could go and, in time, would stand as a major indictment of John's policy, judgement and personality, a significant part of the myth of 'Bad King John'.

W. L. Warren, *King John*, 1961.
J. C. Holt, *The Northerners*, 1961.

**ROBERT FITZWALTER** (*c.*?1170-1235) was an irascible baronial troublemaker who attempted to elevate treason and personal spite into a crusade for liberty. A bully who threatened violence when faced with the workings of the law and surrendered a vital fortress when confronted with a fight, his career makes the rapacity, paranoia and brutality of King John's government explicable. With impeccable credentials (one grandfather was Henry II's justiciar, Richard de Lucy, another, Robert, had been Henry I's steward; one uncle was bishop of Winchester), he held important lands in the south, including the lordship of Dunmow (Essex) and Baynard's Castle in London, as well as extensive estates in northern England through his wife. Perhaps because of his London base, he was involved in the wine trade, owning a number of wine ships. In John's reign he was soon notorious. In 1203, he surrendered the castle of Vaudreuil in Normandy to Philip II of France without a fight. In the circumstances, John's refusal to pay Robert's ransom was understandable, although it made him an enemy for life as Robert had to sell land to raise the money himself. There is a story of Robert arriving at the trial of his son-in-law for murder with five hundred armed men, a reflection if not of the truth then of his reputation for violence and wealth. In 1212, he had to flee the country when a plot he instigated to assassinate the king was

*Robert Fitzwalter*
(From his seal)

discovered. In exile in France, he made contacts with the French
court which proved useful during the English civil war 1215-17.
Robert managed to convince enough influential people on the
continent that he was a martyr to the harsh regime of an excommunicate monarch with such success that he was named as one
with whom the king must be reconciled in the treaty of 1213
between John and the pope which ended the Interdict. From
1214, Robert was a militant leader of the rebels. Even after the

compromise at Runnymede, Robert, now calling himself Marshal of the Army of God (perhaps as a counter to John's status as a crusader), kept a baronial force in being under the guise of holding tournaments. In the subsequent civil war, his influence in London was important, as were his links with the French which he used in 1215-16 to secure the intervention of Prince Louis, to whom he and the other baronial leaders swore allegiance. Taken prisoner at Lincoln in 1217, he was soon released. Rehabilitated in a general political amnesty in 1218, his departure in 1219 on crusade suggests that he was content in the protection of his lands during his absence. It is ironic that in 1223-4, when the justiciar, Hubert de Burgh, was destroying Robert's old adversary, Falkes de Bréauté, Robert appeared at court at Hubert's side. The link may have been Archbishop Langton, a fellow opponent of King John, but if Hubert was going to assert his authority over veterans of John's administration, such as Peter des Roches, all aid was welcome. For Robert, the justiciar's favour helped the security of his lands. He may have appreciated the further irony in 1225 when he, one of the committee of twenty five set up by *Magna Carta* to control royal actions, witnessed the royal re-issue of the Charter in 1225. Perhaps he had mellowed with age. Only, however, one blinded by hysterical hatred of John and fanatical devotion to an anachronistic view of *Magna Carta* as the foundation of English liberty, law and parliamentary democracy could share T. F. Tout's view that Robert had been 'the first champion of English liberty'.

Robert's *D.N.B.* entry was by Tout.
J. C. Holt, *The Northerners*, 1961.

**EUSTACE DE VESCI** (1169-1216) was one of the leaders of the so-called 'Northerners', who provided the nucleus of the rebellion against King John in 1215. The son of a substantial northern landowner who had served Henry II as a sheriff, Eustace held estates in Northumberland, Durham and Yorkshire, with his principal castles at Alnwick and Malton. In 1193, by marrying Margaret, the illegitimate daughter of William the Lion, king of Scots, he added lands in the Scottish Borders. Under Richard I and John he appears as a loyal and frugal baron, employed in diplomacy with Scotland and paying military service and scutage as demanded. Unlike other barons, he avoided running up large debts at the Exchequer; perhaps having to pay off his relief of 1,300 marks in 1190 taught him a useful lesson. Nonetheless, he stood as pledge for the debts of others, and so was involved in what became under John a major source of grievance against the crown as the Exchequer increasingly insisted on strict terms of repayment. Whereas his father had benefited from the beginnings of systematic royal intervention into northern affairs, Eustace never served as a sheriff or profited from the king's closer exploitation of revenue and justice after 1204. Yet even in the face of the increase in the weight of government in the north 1204-14, there is no obvious explanation for Eustace's career of treachery and rebellion between 1212 and 1216. The records suggest a cautious character who spent modestly in litigation or purchases of land and franchises. In one recorded action, Eustace secured the manor of Rotherham at a cost of only 100 marks — and a successful duel. Independent, unafraid to match his claims with physical violence, careful with money, resentful of southern interference, Eustace emerges as something close to the stereotype of the touchy, blunt northerner.

For whatever reason, in 1212 Eustace joined a widespread baronial conspiracy to assassinate King John. The motive behind the plot may have been connected with a proposed Inquest on baronial tenures and obligations. Eustace was not the most prominent of the conspirators, but he, like Robert Fitz-Walter, was the most important to be found out. Eustace fled to Scotland (actually only a few miles from his Northumberland estates); he was outlawed and his English lands confiscated. Rather skilfully, he managed to persuade the circle around archbishop Langton that his exile was because of his opposition to the Interdict, so as part of the settlement between pope and king in 1213 he regained his estates. However, John was not so easily taken in: Eustace's compensation was paltry and the castles of Alnwick and Malton were razed to the ground. Restoration left Eustace unreconciled. In 1214, with a group of fellow northern barons, he refused military service or scutage for the Poitou expedition. After the failure of John's continental campaign, these 'Northerners' became the focus of armed opposition to John which led to *Magna Carta*. Eustace's role was recognised by his being named as one of the baronial committee of Twenty-Five set up by the charter to supervise royal policy. More practically, he managed to have restored his right to hunt his dogs in the forest of Northumberland. With the collapse of the *Magna Carta* compromise and the outbreak of full-scale civil war, Eustace took an active part in operations in the north, helping negotiate the entry on the baronial side of Alexander II king of Scots, his brother-in-law, with whom he campaigned in the summer of 1216, meeting his death at the siege of Barnard's Castle on the Tees.

Eustace appears the model of an irreconcilable, self-interested provincial baron. His treason is evident; his unforgiving rebellious nature attested by the pope himself in 1214. But his career should not be seen solely through the prism of royal interests. There is no denying Eustace's violent and aggressive nature. It was rumoured, not entirely convincingly, that his hatred of John sprang from the king's lecherous advances to his wife. Such stories may be more credible as metaphors. Eustace may have thought rebellion the only price to pay for what he regarded as direct, insidious attacks less on his wife's virtue but on his own traditional way of political life in the north. Almost alone of those opposed to John, there was no evident financial grudge, although he may have regretted exclusion from the royal gravy-train. Eustace's actions reveal that the disturber of the king's peace may also be the defender of regional independence. But medieval history has tended to be written by admirers of the state, for whom local thuggery is condemned with far greater acerbity than the violence of central government.

J. C. Holt, *The Northerners*, 1961.

**FALKES (or FAWKES) DE BRÉAUTÉ** (*d*.1226) has suffered from nationalist prejudice from his own time to this. An entrepreneurial soldier and self-made politician, loyal to John but ultimately unable to find a settled role in the apparently more respectable regime of Henry III's minority, Falkes, as much as any, was responsible for there being a King Henry at all. Much of the hostility directed at Falkes was due to endemic snobbery: he was foreign and he lacked pedigree. Equally damaging to his reputation, he offended the abbey of St Alban's, home to two of the most influential historians of the thirteenth century, Roger of Wendover and Matthew Paris, who embellished his account of Falkes's death from food poisoning by drawing a picture of the devil shoving the offending bad fish into his mouth.

Falkes was the illegitimate son of a Norman knight. According to a contemporary story his first name alluded to a falx, or scythe, with which he had killed a knight on his father's land. He entered the service of King John as a serjeant, but rose to become one of his most trusted associates, whose loyalty was as unquestioned as his fortune was dependent upon royal favour. He acquired a reputation for brutality as sheriff of Glamorgan and, by 1217, had amassed a number of other shrievalties as well as the custody of six important castles: Bedford, Buckingham, Cambridge, Hertford, Northampton and Oxford. In the civil was of 1215-16, he was one of the leading royalist commanders. In 1216 he captured and plundered Worcester and attacked Ely; in 1217 it was the turn of St Alban's. He played a conspicuous part in the royalist victory at Lincoln (1217). His rewards were great, being assigned the heiress of the earldom of Devon, the lands (although not the title) of which he received as his wife's dower in 1218. During the regency, he cut a substantial figure, often in alliance with Peter des Roches, the bishop of Winchester, with whom he abortively planned to go on crusade in 1221. However useful his considerable military skills, Falkes was politically vulnerable. He was resented as a parvenu who openly disdained royal letters and accused 'all native-born Englishmen' of being traitors. Most of all, he had no patrimony of his own in England, his lands and offices depending on his wife, who had a son by a previous marriage; royal grants, which could be revoked; and his own acquisitions, each achieved at a political cost. His vulnerability was demonstrated by a series of suits of disseisin against him, many successful. More used to the independence of the war years, Falkes was impatient at the attempts of the justiciar Hubert de Burgh to regulate his activities in the shires under his control. Although he cooperated with the justiciar in quelling riots in London in 1222, Falkes was increasingly alienated by the government policy of resumption of the royal demesne (1222), royal castles and sheriffdoms (1223-4). His anxiety was in proportion to what he stood to lose. It was, however, his other land deals which precipitated his fall, when in 1224 he lost sixteen suits of disseisin. The kidnap of one of the justices by Falkes's brother, William led to the siege and capture of Falkes's castle at Bedford; the execution of William; and the ruin of Falkes himself. After pleading his case before the pope and composing an ingenious complaint at his treatment (known ∴ his *querimonia*), he died in exile in Rome in 1226. Falkes had been a mainstay of Angevin government who sunk in the shifting political sands of the Minority. No more ambitious than his rivals, he lacked their established positions in the church or the English baronage. Self-made, he self-destructed. An arrogant man, in his pomp called by one chronicler 'more than a king in England', his turbulent career was a product of his dependence on royal patronage: it created him and ruined him. So far from being an over-mighty subject, Falkes demonstrated the difficulties facing the political adventurer: it is hard to buck the established order. Falkes seemed to have had an idea of this. His son was given the English name of Thomas and became an Oxfordshire county knight, a respectability his father, for all his fame and wealth, never quite achieved.

W. L. Warren, *King John,* 1961.
D. Carpenter, *The Minority of Henry III,* 1990.

**STEPHEN LANGTON** (*c.*1165-1228; archbishop of Canterbury 1207-28), one of the foremost Biblical scholars of his time, found himself, through little fault of his own, one of the most controversial archbishops of Canterbury at the centre of the most serious and acrimonious dispute between the king of England and the pope in the Middle Ages. Born in Lincolnshire, Langton studied in Paris in the 1180s, remaining there to teach and write. The schools of Paris then attracted the intellectual and ambitious elite of western Europe. One of Langton's fellow students was a well-connected Italian nobleman, Lothar dei Conti of Segni who, as Pope Innocent III (1198-1216), was to determine the course of his later career. Together, the two of them may well have visited the Canterbury shrine of Thomas Becket, a saint for whom Langton held a persistent, patriotic admiration. Langton's academic studies were mainly scriptural. Although his *Quaestiones*, which revealed a practical mind when applied to textual or theological problems, were popular, his fame rested upon his preaching and his work as a Biblical commentator, his re-organisation of the chapters of the Bible in the late 1190s gradually winning general acceptance across the whole of western Christendom. His other works included religious verses such as the hymn *Veni, Sancta Spiritus*. A later English chronicler ascribed to Langton, somewhat improbably, a life of Richard I. Orthodox and unoriginal, it is unlikely that it was his pedagogic influence that led to his only pupil known by name, one Master Guerin of Corbeil, to be condemned for heresy in 1210. Langton, whose academic reputation was recognised by preferment to canonries at Paris and York, was typical of a group of his Paris contemporaries, including fellow Englishman Robert of Courçon (*i.e.* Curzon). Not satisfied with purely speculative theology, Langton and his colleagues were concerned with the systematizing of doctrine and its application to the actual world: one of his own famous sermons was on usury. Of particular relevance to the future was Langton's teaching at Paris that it was lawful to resist a tyrannical king who acted by his own will, not the law, a precept he had to defend in practice as King John's archbishop.

This pragmatic quality, allied to occasionally inflexible intellectual rigour, was characteristic of a generation of ecclesiastics which came to the fore under Innocent III. Among these Langton was prominent. In 1206, he was appointed Cardinal Priest of St Chrysogonus (an obscure, possibly fictional martyr of the early fourth century), testimony to his Parisian eminence. The timing was fortuitous. By the end of the year. Langton had been elected archbishop of Canterbury after an almost unprecedented display of papal authority. After the death of the previous archbishop, Hubert Walter, in 1205, one faction among the monks of Christ Church, Canterbury had elected their fellow monk Reginald, another the king's candidate John de Gray. The parties appealed to Rome, where Innocent set aside both candidates and presided over the election, by the Canterbury monks present at the Papal

*Stephen Langton re-crowning Henry III in 1220*
(From Matthew Paris's Chronica Majora)

Curia, of Cardinal Langton who was in Rome at the time. The new archbishop was consecrated by the pope at Viterbo in June 1207. According to the agreements reached between English kings and the papacy over the previous century, although the election by the monks was canonical, the consecration, without royal assent, broke accepted precedent. King John felt his rights of patronage and hence control over the English church, were threatened; he refused to recognise Langton as archbishop.

This led to a bitter six-year conflict, with Langton, except for a brief foray to Dover in 1209, exiled from England. Significantly and deliberately, he spent much of this period at the Cistercian monastery at Pontigny where Becket had stayed in the 1160s. King John was excommunicated and England placed under a papal Interdict. Deadlock was only ended in 1213 by the pope's threat to depose John at the very time the king's plans to recover his lost patrimony in France were nearing fruition. Faced by a possible papally sponsored French invasion, King John yielded in May 1213, receiving absolution from Langton himself in July. Having been a symbol of a papal vision of ecclesiastical authority, Langton in office proved to be his own man. From 1213-15, he clashed with successive papal legates, a result of the novel and anomalous circumstance of the king having submitted his kingdom to papal overlordship as a price of reconciliation in 1213. From being the traditional head of the church, the archbishop now had to contend with a papal representative whose main brief was to support a now-faithful papal vassal, the king. In 1213/14, Langton clashed with Legate Nicholas over the extent of royal patronage. During the early months of 1215, Langton attempted to mediate between John and the rebellious magnates. According to the unreliable St Alban's chronicler, Roger of Wendover, Langton suggested the Coronation Charter of Henry I as a legitimate basis for the baronial demands against the king. This is credible, if only because two years earlier Langton had presided over the council of St Alban's where John had sworn to abide by the laws of Henry I, by which may have meant the Coronation Charter. Whatever his role in drafting *Magna Carta*, Langton's failure to support the king wholeheartedly excited the anger of the pope and led to the archbishop's suspension by Legate Pandulf and summons to Rome. After attending the Fourth Lateran Council, Langton remained abroad from 1215 until 1218. He had demonstrated that, like other occupants of the chair of St Augustine, he possessed inconvenient single-mindedness.

The political landscape to which he returned was very different from that which he had left. The Minority government of William Marshal operated on the basis of consent rather than coercion. After the Marshal's death in 1219, Langton continued as an ally of the justiciar, Hubert de Burgh, in protecting the authority of the crown, in particular against former partisans of King John such as Falkes de Bréauté. He remained wedded to finding just agreement between magnates and king: between 1221 and 1223, he played a leading role in mediating between the young Henry III's counsellors; in 1223, he called for the reissuing of *Magna Carta*, as he did again in 1225 in return for support for a fifteenth for a campaign in Poitou. In 1223, in order to bolster the independent effectiveness of the king's government, he helped secure the papal bull which granted Henry III control of his own seal.

As archbishop, Langton proved loyal to the traditions of his office and the national church. He recrowned Henry in 1220 (the Legate Guala and the bishop of Winchester had performed an unavoidably perfunctory ceremony in the dark days of 1216). In 1221, he persuaded Pope Honorius III (1216-27) to remove the resident papal legate; to limit papal provisions in England, a system whereby the pope imposed candidates to benefices, often absentees or papal cronies; and to restate the superiority of Canterbury over York. In 1226, Langton further emphasised his independence by resisting an attempt to reserve a prebend in each collegiate church for papal funds. In tune with the reforms encouraged by Innocent III at the Fourth Lateran Council, probably at an assembly held at Osney Abbey near Oxford in 1222, Langton issues a set of Constitutions concerning ecclesiastical discipline and organisation which were widely imitated across the English dioceses over the next generation.

By the time of his death in 1228, Langton had shown himself as a constructive church leader and a politician of pragmatism. He was no Becket. Unlike the martyr, whose relics he moved to a new shrine amidst great ceremony in 1220, he sought to translate general principles into effective practice. If he lacked the silken skills of the adept political infighter, he also lacked the brittle prigishness of many intellectuals in public life. It is rare for such a distinguished academic to cope even as well as Langton with the pressures of political leadership, but in this, as in much else, Langton conformed to the reforming approach and programme of his circle of Parisian scholars and of Innocent III in particular. It is often said that Innocent's pontificate marked the apogee of papal monarchy in the Middle Ages. If so, his success and lasting influence depended on men of the calibre of Stephen Langton.

But Langton was not simply a general in the papal army, however much he came to symbolise the pope's claims to authority in Christendom during the dispute with King John. As a figurehead for Innocent III's vision of the world order, he could encounter trouble, as on the occasion one of his sermons was heckled shortly after his return to England in 1213. But in contrast to any identification with the ultramontane implications of Innocent's policies, Langton was proud of his Englishness. Like many exiles through choice or compulsion (and Langton was both), he lauded his love of his country. In 1207 he declared that 'from our tender years we have loved our kingdom with a natural love'. This may have been no more than politic for the newly appointed ex-patriot archbishop establishing his local credentials. But it was a theme to which he returned. At the translation of Becket's relics in 1220 he talked of 'the triumph of an Englishman' and in a sermon of 1224 he refered to men like Falkes de Bréauté as 'the affliction of the natives to whom the people of England were so often given over as booty . . . take heed so that aliens are no longer permitted to act against you'. The thirteenth century saw a growing awareness amongst the political elite of national identity. It is entirely in keeping with this development that Langton, one of the most cosmopolitan of archbishops, should have issued, in January 1215, a charter in Anglo-Norman French, one of the first such documents not written in Latin, the universal language of government, law and religion, since the reign of William I.

Stephen Langton was neither a hero nor a saint. He was at times as much a victim as a champion of the cause he was chosen to represent. From his politics, sermons and writings, he emerges as a highly practical man, of sharp but flexible intellect, who prefered to achieve than to strike propagandist poses or escape into intellectual obscurantism. To have helped compose *Magna Carta* or to have re-organised the Vulgate text of the Bible would each have been notable: to have done both was remarkable.

F. M. Powicke, *Stephen Langton*, 1928.

**PETER DES ROCHES** (*d.*1238; bishop of Winchester 1205-1238; Justiciar 1213-15) was a central figure in English politics for over thirty years. He acquired an awesome reputation as a hard-faced and ruthless exponent of unrestricted royal authority. Many observers, from the thirteenth to the twentieth century,

*Peter des Roches blessing the royalist fleet
at the battle of Sandwich 1217*
(From Matthew Paris's Chronica Majora)

have seen him as head of a sinister invasion of 'aliens', derisively
described by contemporaries as 'Poitevins' (*i.e.* notoriously
untrustworthy) who were held to have conspired, over half a century, against the interests of native-born Englishmen. In fact,
Peter, who was actually from Touraine, was an extremely effective administrator on behalf of John and Henry III whose chief
political fault was that he did not suffer gladly or silently the
self-interested posturing of the English baronage or their greedy
attempts to feed on the carcass of royal rights. The idea that the
magnates could provide good government he brusquely dismissed on intellectual and pragmatic grounds. As a foreigner, his
views were less obscured by local sentiment, family networks
and group solidarity. Peter's career was international, embracing
Italy and the Holy Land as well as France and England. Like any
other great lord, he surrounded himself with and promoted
those he found congenial and useful, often men who literally
spoke his own language, a group which included his three royal
masters, Richard I, John and Henry III. To them, Peter was certainly not an alien; rather he was very much 'one of us'. Therein
lay the secret of his tenacious influence.

Although the hostile Roger of Wendover described him as
having been in youth a 'knight, expert in warfare', this may be
wishful thinking: Peter was not the only cleric who showed
military aptitude. His early career was as a clerk in the house-

hold of Richard I, firmly rooted in the ecclesiastical aristocracy of his native region and Poitou where he held a number of significant benefices. As treasurer of Poitiers, he may have impressed Richard with his financial abilities, because it was in household finance that he first made his mark. Retained by John as one of his clerks after 1199, he worked closely with the king, authorizing payments to and from the Chamber, the royal household's financial office. Until 1205, the chamberlain was Hubert de Burgh, but Peter's role became increasingly important. It may be that Peter des Roches was one of King John's few genuine friends (*pace* A. A. Milne). By 1204, he was working alongside great barons and leading ministers. After Hubert's removal to France from 1202, Peter progressively took over the running of the household finances, being rewarded with custody of the English lands of the court of La Perche and the vacant bishoprics of Chichester and Winchester.

In 1205, John appointed Peter to the see of Winchester, perhaps the richest in England. Although hardly the model of the concerned reforming diocesan so energetically promoted by the pope at the time, Peter found in Winchester a power-base that was to give him invaluable political security. Ironically, in view of the exactly contemporary disputed election at Canterbury, in order to render his appointment incontestable, John sent Peter to Rome to receive consecration by Pope Innocent III. The importance John attached to Peter's elevation is indicated by his gift to the new bishop on the day of his enthronement at Winchester in 1206 of gorgeous vestments and chapel ornaments belonging to the recently deceased Hubert Walter.

Peter returned John's favour with interest. Despite the papal Interdict and the king's excommunication, Peter remained at his post, by the end of 1209 the only bishop left resident in England. Both in the king's household and at the Exchequer he extended his activities. A satire from this period sums up one view of his activities:

> 'The warrior of Winchester, presiding at the exchequer, keen at accounting, slack at Scripture, unrolling the king's roll, ignoring Luke for lucre, valuing marks more than Mark and putting money above books.'

Peter acted both as one of the king's finance ministers and his personal financial agent. His enthusiasm for this sort of work is reflected in the pipe roll for the Winchester estates he had compiled.

As one of the small group of advisers who ran the central institutions of government, Peter's power was considerable, especially as John's main policy in these years was to acquire sufficient treasure for the reconquest of his French lands. Peter displayed political as well as financial skills during the negotiations to end the Interdict. Despite his lack of any legal experience or expertise, on Geoffrey FitzPeter's death in 1213 Peter was a logical choice as justiciar. The appointment was, however, double-edged. In his handling of the regency in John's absence in France, in overseeing the 1214 scutage, the more sensitive law suits at Westminster and the disposal of castles and patronage, Peter proved himself capable but aggressive. It was not simply that he presided over some of the most notorious incidents of the king's manipulation of his rights, such as the infamous Mandeville inheritance case where it appeared superficially that Geoffrey de Say (15,000 marks) and Geoffrey de Mandeville (20,000 marks) had both paid the king huge sums for the same property. It was Peter's peremptory viceregal manner which added insult to injury, at least in the eyes of barons sensitive about the deference due to their eminence. A flavour of Peter's style is to be found in this summons to David, earl of Huntingdon to appear at a council in 1214 (David, it should be noted, was the brother of the king of Scots):

'Know that we have many things to say to you concerning the business of the lord king and of his kingdom, wherefore we order you, as you love his honour and yourself and your hostages and whatsoever you hold of him, that, without delay or excuse, you shall be in the neighbourhood of London, wherever you hear we are, about the octave of the Assumption of the Blessed Mary (*i.e.* 22 August) to treat concerning his aforesaid business.'

It is no surprise that Peter was a casualty of the compromise reached between the king and the rebellious barons at Runnymede in 1215, being replaced as justiciar by the less abrasive

Hubert de Burgh. Peter regarded the proceedings and *Magna Carta* itself with some contempt. However, his loss was not, in practice, so very great. The civil war of 1215-17 effectively suspended the justiciar's traditional duties. Peter retained his wealthy bishopric and his position at court. But he was never again to hold formal office, a measure of the lack of trust his behaviour as justiciar 1213-15 generated among the English magnates in whose favour the balance of power shifted during Henry III's minority. Writing perhaps in 1219, the Waverley Annalist remembered Peter's policy as justiciar was that 'little by little he might subject the most powerful men of the land to the will of the king', adding that anger against him 'is sedated not even now'.

This made little or no difference to Peter's attitudes or conduct. Ironically, it was he who imposed the papal suspension of Langton from office in 1215. In 1216, under the direction of the Legate Guala, he crowned Henry III. The following year he played an active and crucial role in the victory at Lincoln. In pursuing royal rights, he had not changed his spots: in 1218 he imposed extortionate terms on some Lincolnshire debtors. From 1216 Peter had the guardianship of the king, a sign of the trust placed in him at least by the king's mother, the Poitevin Isabella of Angoulême. Although after 1219 he retained considerable influence as well as the tutorship of King Henry, his position was gradually undermined by Hubert de Burgh. In 1221, Peter's ally, Peter de Mauley, was exiled and he himself accused of treason and deprived of the royal tutorship, although some may argue that his views on kingship had already left their mark on the teenage monarch. His political eclipse became almost total in 1223-4 when, with other former servants of King John, he lost castles and the shrievalties and was again accused of treason by Hubert de Burgh who apparently blamed the bishop for all the evils of John's reign and the Minority. Peter vowed vengeance: 'if it cost him all he had, he would cause the justiciar to be removed from power'.

Despite this exclusion from power, Peter lost none of his ambition or resourcefulness. His horizons were international. It was reported even that he had been elected, *in absentia,* bishop of the Egyptian port of Damietta after its capture by crusaders in 1219. He had taken the Cross in 1221: after 1224 he prepared to fulfil his vow. His crusade of 1227-29 greatly enhanced his reputation. Even the xenophobic Matthew Paris had a good word to say, praising the bishop's expedition as being 'to the salvation and honour of many, especially of all Englishmen'. Paris may have been influenced by Peter's gift, on his return, of a book on the marvels of the East. On crusade, Peter struck up a close relationship with the German Emperor Frederick II, witnessing his treaty with the Sultan of Cairo (18 February 1229) which restored Jerusalem to Christian rule. Equipped with considerable funds, Peter supervised the rebuilding of Jaffa and militarized the English Order of St Thomas of Acre by giving it a new rule, based upon that of the Teutonic Knights. A lasting monument to Peter's crusade may be the chapel of the Holy Sepulchre in Winchester cathedral which has been associated with the bishop. Peter stayed at Frederick II's side on his return to the West, helping negotiate the peace of Ceperano between the emperor and Pope Gregory IX in 1230. On his way back to England, he assisted in arranging a truce between Louis IX and Henry III. There was far more to Peter des Roches than his English critics allowed.

After a triumphant return to England, Peter capitalized on the increasing problems of Hubert de Burgh and the king's growing impatience with his justiciar. Supported by a coalition of disparate magnates, including the earls of Cornwall, Chester and Pembroke, Peter managed to secure the appointment of his son, Peter des Rivaux, as head of royal finances in March 1232 and the overthrow of Hubert a few months later. Between 1232 and 1234, Peter was dominant. Peter des Rivaux held the shrievalties of twenty-one counties; old companions such as Peter de Mauley and Engelard de Cigogné, returned from exile; strategic castles were manned by dependable Flemish and Breton mercenaries. A series of disseisins were effected 'per voluntatem regis', in contradiction of Clause 39 of *Magna Carta* which had guaranteed judgement by peers not royal whim. Peter justified such acts by referring to the king's 'plenitude of power' over his subjects, an idea fashionable in many royal courts at the time, including the pope's and Frederick II's whose most grandiloquent statement of a ruler's authority, the *Liber Augustalis,* appeared shortly after Bishop Peter had left him in 1231.

As two decades before, Peter's methods aroused hostility, fear and revolt, led by Richard Marshal, earl of Pembroke, son of Peter's former colleague, the regent. In response to Richard's complaint that he had suffered judgement without trial by peers, Peter sneeringly repudiated the idea that there were peers in England, as there were in France (where Richard had spent most of his time). Peter insisted that the king could sentence anyone on the judgement of whomsoever he wished to appoint as judge. While the barons saw Clause 39 of *Magna Carta* as a defence of liberties, Peter saw it as protection of sectional privilege. The lesson he drew from recent legal history was that all free Englishmen were equal before the law, the king's law, obedient to the monarch. He was not tolerant of special interests. However, politics prevailed over ideological niceties. After baronial threats of deposition and royal demands for special oaths of fealty, open war flared up on the Welsh Marches in 1233, as Richard allied with Llewelyn of Wales. Attempted ecclesiastical mediation in 1234 was overtaken by the death, in Ireland, of the Marshal. Suspicion clung to Peter des Roches, leaving the king little option but to repudiate the bishop and his allies in June 1234. For the last time, Peter had fallen foul of the factional politics of the English nobility he professed to despise. Peter had himself become the obstacle to the implementation of his own policies. These were not solely concerned with the forceful assertion of royal rights. More quietly, but effectively, his associates began reforming the procedures of the Exchequer and other financial institutions to bring them more firmly under royal control. If the politics of Hubert de Burgh allowed Henry III to survive the Minority, the reforms of Peter des Roches enabled him to rule as king. It is significant that three central figures in the bishop's administration of 1232-34, Peter des Rivaux, Robert Passelew and Stephen Segrave, all returned to office in 1236.

Once more rejected by his adopted homeland, Peter found an outlet for his restless energy abroad. In 1235-6 he was again in Italy, placing his military skills at Gregory IX's disposal. In 1236, with the count of Toulouse, he defeated the pope's Roman enemies at Viterbo. Back in England later that year, he died at his castle of Farnham in 1238.

Peter's career was, by any standard, remarkable in its length and scope. Yet precisely the qualities that made it distinctive rendered it unintelligible to English observers who inhabited a more constricted universe. Viewed from his own perspective, the association of Peter with an 'alien' conspiracy in England was no less incomprehensible. His masters were French, if his estates were English. His ecclesiastical offices stradled the Channel. His career exemplified the practical unity of Christendom, from the British Isles to Syria, where a man of talent, contacts and ambition could play many parts. Diplomat, bishop, statesman, civil servant, minister, general, crusader and courtier, Peter des Roches, far from the malign intriguer of English legend, proved himself a loyal servant and a valuable colleague. His taste for magnificence, his generosity to relatives and clients, fidelity to his *familia* and companions mark him as possessing the attractive qualities of an admirable lord. Like all effective medieval rulers, he was feared, yet his consistency stands in marked contrast to the shifting allegiances of his fiercest critics. Those who criticised Peter and the other 'aliens' were the very same who queued up to swear allegiance to Louis of France. Peter's loyalty was based not on spurious nationalism but faithful service to a succession of demanding masters — Richard I, John, Henry III, Frederick II — in whose service he was not found wanting. But there was more. With many clerics of his generation he identified principles of authority behind political action. Furthermore, there was an observed strand of lordly faith; he was an active crusader and his last public words were of the extirpation of all infidels and the triumph of the one catholic church. Whatever the truth of Peter's personality, it is hard to disagree with the punning monks of St Swithin's, Winchester, who described him as 'hard as rocks'.

D. Carpenter, *The Minority of Henry III*, 1990.
F. J. West, *The Justiciarship in England*, 1966.
N. Vincent's magisterial study on Peter des Roches is forthcoming.

**RALPH OF COGGESHALL** (*d.* after 1224) was abbot of the Cistercian abbey of Coggeshall in Essex from 1207 until ill-health forced him to resign in 1218. He gave his name to a *Chronicon Anglicanum,* covering the years 1066-1223, the last section of which, 1187-1223, he wrote himself. Although head of an obscure provincial house, through extensive personal contacts with the nobility and the international Cistercian network, Ralph was well-informed. His information about the Third and Fourth Crusades, for instance, came from returning crusaders and monks. Much of his chronicle is based on oral evidence, which lends it a diffuse character. Not a witness of political standing or academic distinction, Ralph displays the orthodox prejudices of a conventional monk content to follow the harsh judgemental view of a sinful world familiar to his predecessors. The great, Richard I or Hubert Walter, are punished for their vanities or sins; the Jews deserved death in the massacres of 1190. His portraits of Richard I and John may represent a barometer of contemporary opinion, moulded by the hindsight of events. Richard is a flawed hero, his chivalric reputation sullied by greed and anger. Ralph's dislike of John grew as his reign progressed, until by 1216, he is shown as a bad-tempered liar, cheat, glutton and coward. Henry III's minority, however, is regarded more positively, perhaps because of the reconciliation between royalists and most of the baronial opposition between 1217 and 1219. Ralph's description of the ravages of the civil war of 1215-17 explains his enthusiasm at the return of peace. He, like many others, transferred their loyalties from the baronial faction to the royalists, a conversion tinged with overt nationalism. Just as Ralph was suspicious of John's foreign officials, such as Peter des Roches, so he scorns the French Prince Louis as one 'who had come to destroy the English people'. Such xenophobia, initially useful in rallying support behind Henry III, was to grow to deafening, irrational proportions in the hands of later writers, such as Matthew Paris, and some discontented politicians in the late 1250s. Ralph's nationalism suggests that the future of an Anglo-French Angevin empire would have been precarious regardless of the outcome of John's battles with Philip II of France, a fact largely lost on the cosmopolitan courtiers of Henry III.

A. Gransden, *Historical Writing in England c.550-c.1307,* 1974.

**RANULF III**, earl of Chester (c.1170-1232) was one of the old school of Anglo-Norman barons whose loyalty to the Angevin dynasty was consistent but contingent on the receipt of lucrative favours. Bishop Stubbs described him as 'almost the last relic of the great feudal aristocracy of the Conquest' and, however his career is viewed, he was — and thought himself — very grand. Small in physical stature, he was a giant in terms of family relationships and estates, the twin pillars of his ambition and political career. Succeeding to the earldom as a minor in 1181 and attaining majority and control of his estates in England and Normandy in 1187, in 1189 he married Constance of Brittany, widow of Henry II's son Geoffrey (d.1186) and mother of Arthur of Brittany, with whom King John contested the Angevin succession 1199-1202. Although bringing Ranulf control of the honour of Richmond in England as well as the duchy of Brittany, the marriage was not a success, being finally dissolved in 1199. The following year Ranulf cemented his power in Normandy by marrying Clemencia of Fougères. Relations with John were initially tentative. Ranulf had opposed John's attempted *coup* of 1193-4; he retained many contacts with partisans of his former stepson, Arthur; and his second wife's family joined Philip II. Spending most of 1199-1204 in France, Ranulf's continued loyalty was bought by John with further patronage. But the king was suspicious of Ranulf (as, indeed, he was of most people), perhaps with reason. In the winter of 1204-5, Ranulf, suspected of dealings with the rebellious Welsh and of contemplating revolt himself, had extensive estates temporarily confiscated by the king. The episode demonstrated the limits of independent action even by the most powerful English magnate, which may have persuaded Ranulf that loyalty was good business. Thereafter, Ranulf basked in an uninterrupted flow of royal favours. In return, he fought John's Welsh wars 1209-12; helped secure the peace with the pope in 1213-14; and was with the king in Poitou in 1214. Loyal to John in 1215-16, one of the few barons to witness *Magna Carta* of 1215 *ex parte regis*, Ranulf played a leading military role in the civil war by virtue of his extensive estates and numerous castles. On John's death, Ranulf's influence increased further. Although he stood aside to allow William Marshal to assume the regency for the young

Henry III, he put his political weight behind the reissuing of *Magna Carta* (1216 and 1217); his military experience in defeating the rebels at Lincoln (1217); and his diplomatic skill in negotiating the treaty with Louis of France (1217) and peace with the Welsh (1217/8). His rewards from the government he partly ran were immense, including the earldom of Lincoln, a clutch of sheriffdoms and estates in the north, East Midlands and East Anglia. In 1218, his decision to honour the crusade vow he had taken in 1215 may point to a genuine piety beyond that of the customary ecclesiastical patronage expected of the great. It may also reflect a degree of thwarted ambition: relations with the regent were not always easy. In the East, Ranulf played a leading role in the Fifth Crusade's siege and occupation of Damietta (1218-19). On the Crusade's failure, he returned to England in 1220, to find William Marshal dead and the government in the hands of Hubert de Burgh. Ranulf was not alone in finding the shoals of faction difficult to navigate in 1220-1224 as tensions grew between government officials and old John loyalists. These flared into open conflict in the winter of 1223-4 when Ranulf, among others, briefly tried to resist de Burgh's policy of resumption of sheriffdoms and royal castles. Ranulf's final years saw him acting as an elder statesman, witnessing the 1225 re-issue of *Magna Carta*; playing a prominent role in the dispute in 1227 over Forest Laws; and, as a veteran, leading Henry III's army on the ill-fated Poitou expedition of 1230-1. He never lost sight of his private advantage. In 1220, some of his estates avoided the carucage; the 1225 Aid was not levied in Cheshire; and in 1229, he successfully resisted the ecclesiastical tax collector. It may have been a sign of age and declining influence that he failed to stop the levy of the 1232 Fortieth on his lands. The whole of Ranulf's career had been determined by the maintenance and acquisition of rights and property. It must therefore have been galling that he had no heir, on his death his estates being divided between his four sisters. Ranulf's political career reinforces the folly of historical periodisation. Knighted by Henry II, with estates on both sides of the Channel, Ranulf cut a European figure after 1204, on crusade 1218-20 and on two campaigns in Poitou, 1214 and 1230-1. A witness to all first four issues of *Magna Carta*, he had little thought of running his estates according to new constraints of political or legal behaviour. Historians seek the origins of change: in Ranulf III of Chester they have a good example of the tenacity of tradition.

J. W. Alexander, *Ranulf of Chester*, 1983.

**HENRY III** (1207-72; king of England 1216-72) reigned for longer than any other English monarch until the eighteenth century. Yet his personality has often been obscured by the rush of events, his achievements clouded by the incessant problems of sustaining royal power. To nationalist and constitutional historians of the last century or more, Henry has appeared as a tyrannical hindrance to the progress of parliamentary government or as a cosmopolitan traitor to the growth of English independence. Henry has tended to be overshadowed by the stronger personalities of his own courtiers and contemporaries: Hubert de Burgh, Peter des Roches, Robert Grosseteste, Louis IX, Simon de Montfort and the Lord Edward. He has suffered at the hands of chroniclers opposed to foreigners or sympathetic to the reform movement of 1258-65. Even royalist writers seem lukewarm, his son attracting the credit for the successes of his final years.

Henry III is the first English king whose daily life can be followed through the sources. He is also the first of whom we have a clue of what he looked like. Henry had a drooping eyelid which shadowed one eye; it was genetic: his son Edward had one too. Henry was a ruler of stature who defied the maxim that all political careers end in failure: his end was physically pathetic, but politically triumphant. He suffered humiliations at the hands of his own subjects beyond those of any king since the Conquest, but his policy ultimately prevailed. In 1216, he ascended the throne as the child figurehead of a beleaguered faction of baronial oligarchs. When he died, royal authority was such that his son succeeded without a murmur, even though he was hundreds of miles away.

Henry was the first monarch since Harthacnut (1040-42) born to be king; he was the only king until the late fourteenth century to be educated as king. Publicly and privately his Minority (1216-27) shaped his future. The restoration of the monarchy through resumption of estates and administrative and judicial functions was achieved by consensual government where magnates and royal officials joined together to decide policy and household appointments. The principles were those of the re-issued *Magna Carta* of 1216, 1217 and 1225. The crown was expected to operate through consultation and within agreed limits of custom and law. However, it was not resolved how this system could work when there was an adult, sane monarch. The clause placing the king under the scrutiny of twenty-five barons (Clause 61 of the 1215 charter) had been dropped in 1216. There was no agreed mechanism to interpret law and custom. Even the stipulation of trial by peers (Clause 39)could be challenged, as by the pugnacious Peter des Roches in 1233 when he questioned what was meant by peers: all freemen or a privileged elite of barons? The charter contained no rules for appointing royal officials, still seen for what they still were, personal agents of the king not officers of an impersonal state. The behaviour of sheriffs and justices were conditioned in certain circumstances, but not their recuitment or terms of service. The insistence that the king do justice to his people and respect their liberties was as flexible as each lawsuit was individual. On royal patronage, the very stuff of politics, the charter was silent.

Yet the repeated re-drafting, re-issuing and confirmation of the Charter (or Charters, as clauses dealing with Forest law were published separately from 1217) created expectations of baronial consultation and control, particularly over policy. During the Minority, successive regents had carefully balanced the factions and consulted widely in order to make policy acceptable. In any case, men such as William Marshal (regent 1216-19) and Hubert de Burgh (justiciar 1215-32) were themselves barons. Problems arose when, of age, Henry wished, perfectly legitimately, to restore the royal prerogative in areas traditionally governed by it: patronage; foreign policy; justice; appointment of household officials. There was nothing except the experience of the Minority to suggest that the king, like any other lord, had not full freedom in these areas. After 1216, the king may have been seen as being under the law. But resurrecting the prerogative was a political not a legal matter and, inevitably, caused friction with baronial interests. Henry III was happy to confirm the

*Henry III*
(From his effigy at Westminster Abbey finished in 1291)

Charters in 1237 and 1253; he had no wish to rule as a tyrant, nor in general did he. The problem was that there remained the desire of many barons to influence the exercise of the royal prerogative to their collective or individual advantage. The Minority left the Charters fundamental to political debate, positively, in the parameters of behaviour they set and negatively, in what they left unsaid.

Henry provoked anger because he behaved as king not as chairman of a baronial Round Table. Thus much criticism was directed at his appointments, his distribution of patronage and, as in 1238, 1242 and 1255-8, his failure to consult over controversial, expensive or disastrous decisions, respectively the marriage of his sister Eleanor to Simon de Montfort, his botched attempt to recapture Poitou and the Sicilian business. There were two possible solutions to this inherent tension. Formal baronial control of the royal prerogative; or the strengthening of royal authority as the undisputed head of the community of the realm supported by consent and obedience. The verdict of Henry's reign, uneasily and bloodily reached, was clear. The connundrums bequeathed by the Minority were resolved by 1272 in the monarchy's favour.

Privately, Henry's experiences and education during his minority were also formative. Whatever he learnt from the grammarian Hugh of Avranches, whose enthusiasm to show off his skills led him to produce a primer 2,200 lines long, Henry grew up on politics and administration. His mentor was Peter des Roches, the most dynamic royal official of his generation. Throughout his reign Henry understood how government worked and often manipulated it skilfully. Gradually brought into political prominence, crowned for the second time in 1220, given the use of his own seal in 1223 and formally declaring himself of age in 1227, Henry had his own household and was consulted on matters of state from an early age, as in 1220 over Welsh affairs. There were even suggestions that his majority would be declared on his fourteenth birthday. Unlike the young Henry VI, Henry III clearly showed some aptitude. From whatever source, Henry imbibed a heightened ideology of kingship, fashionable among the rulers of the time. The king was God's minister who had responsibilites to all his people; whose

liberties transcended sectional interests but whose prerogative
was untrammelled by other terrestrial jurisdictions, lay or ecclesiastical; to whom obdience must be unconditonal and absolute.
Henry was fond of insisting on the majesty of his office; and
keen to accuse those he disliked of treason. He increased the
occasions on which the *laudes regiae* (chants praising the king)
were sung. But, unlike his father, King John, his rhetoric was not
matched by deeds. His concept of his office was grand but his
use of the prerogative bounded by practical limits. He may have
learnt from Peter des Roches,who he made his first minister of
his personal rule (1232-4) and whose son, Peter des Rievaux,
remained an influential advisor and servant for two decades.

How far the  circumstances of his youth affected Henry's personality is impossible to say. Matthew Paris recorded him saying
once 'You English want to hurl me from my throne as you did
my father'. He harboured a lifelong and not unjustified suspicion of the selfishness of the English baronage, just as he
retained a devotion, sometimes more sincere than sensible, to the
papacy which had sustained his monarchy in his youth. Henry
grew up to be a petulant, injudicious man, quick-witted with a
waspish, unguarded tongue. Possibly as a consequence of youthful isolation, Henry was lavish with affection, but over-sensitive
to betrayal. Impetuous, lacking wisdom, Henry was, however,
neither especially vindictive nor did he share the taste for violence showed by his father and son. In government, he was
industrious and alert. He understood how to articulate his policies if less able to implement them. He was not a good general.
In public he cut a figure lacking *gravitas* or self-possession. The
chronicles are full of his rude, aggressive and provocative outbursts. But as he got as good as he gave, he evidently did not
inspire fear or even respect from those who knew him. He seems
to have been a nervy chairman of meetings of his council or
assemblies, often with good reason. But he was not unpersua-
sive, on more than one occasion, for example, using private
blandishment to encourage abbots to part with their money.

Henry was famously pious, in a rather showy way, a hostile
witness commenting: 'the less he was clever in his actions on
earth the more he indulged in a display of humility before God'.
An addicted pilgrim, he regularly toured English shrines such as

Bromholm, Walsingham, Bury St Edmund's and St Alban's He adored ceremonies, such as the reception in Westminster Abbey of a relic of the Holy Blood in 1247 which the overexcited Henry insisted Matthew Paris, who was in the audience, record for posterity. Extravagant in lifestyle, Henry, like his brother-in-law Louis IX, was obsessed by the poor. Like many devout rich people in the Middle Ages, Henry confronted the criticism inherent in the Gospel stories of the wealthy man's path to Heaven, or Lazarus and Dives, by using charity to the poor as a passport to redemption. Riches used in this way could circumvent the apparent clarity of Christ's teaching. In religion as in politics, Henry's motto was that he had inscribed over the gable in the Painted Chamber of Westminster Palace: 'He who does not give what he holds does not receive what he desires'.

In fact, Henry had a childlike passion for presents. A generous giver, he loved receiving them. At his eldest son's baptism, his relish in the christening gifts prompted a courtier to remark: 'God has given us this child, but the lord King is selling it'. Unusually for his family, Henry was chaste, a loyal and faithful husband. He directed much energy into a love of artefacts. Like his father, he delighted in jewels. He took an interest in all aspects of public display: vestments, sacred vessels, pictures, interior decoration, sculpture and architecture, as witnessed by his rebuilding of Westminster Abbey (completed 1269) and his work on his residences, for example Westminster Palace or Clarendon. His love of books does not seem to have extended far beyond their bindings or illuminations. A moody, affectionate, excitable, energetic, thoughtful and devout man, Henry was unfortunate that his virtues were unheroic and his weaknesses damaging. Yet, while there may have been better monarchs to rule England, there have been few better men.

In one aspect of his rule, Henry's youth was probably decisive. His father had enjoined his executors in 1216 to assist Henry and his brother Richard regain their inheritance. Henry's titles were king of England, lord of Ireland, duke of Normandy and Aquitaine and count of Anjou. Even as late as the 1230s, he styled himself in official documents, such as the statute of Merton (1236), 'king Henry son of King John'. Under the guidance of Peter des Roches and his father's former Poitevin cronies such as Peter de Mauley, Henry grew up with a firm sense of his inheritance and the inescapable obligation to reconquer those lordships lost under John (Normandy and Anjou) and during the Minority (Poitou in 1224). Henry saw himself as a European figure. If anything, he extended his continental interests by marrying, in 1236, Eleanor of Provence, giving him a link to the western Alpine passes, and, in the 1250s, bidding to establish his own family in place of the Hohenstaufen. In 1255, he accepted, on behalf of his second son, Edmund, the crown of southern Italy and Sicily. In 1257, his brother, Richard of Cornwall, bought himself the crown of Germany. For thirty years, first through military means, the invasion of Brittany in 1230 and Poitou in 1242, then by diplomacy, Henry tried to regain the Angevin provinces in France. These claims were only abandoned at the treaty of Paris (1259) when Henry needed a French alliance to extricate himself from the Sicilian mire and against pressing foes at home. The surviving possession of Gascony was defended at huge and often fruitless expense, a major priority as well as financial drain, and the scene of Henry's one successful military expedition in 1253-4.

However, Henry's cosmopolitan interests were not shared by his English magnates to whom he had to turn for assistance to achieve his ambitions. Almost none of the barons had any concern with lands in France and those who did, such as Richard Marshal (d.1233) and Simon de Montfort, were just as likely to be leading the oppostion. This lack of sympathy with Henry's dearest schemes underpinned much of the mutual suspicion between king and noble. There was an even wider gulf separating royal concerns and those of the increasingly influential lesser baronage, knights and shire gentry, whose anxieties probably lie behind the repeated refusal of assemblies in the 1240s and 1250s to taxation. While Henry surrounded himself with foreigners speaking southern French (*langue d'oc*) and dreamt of an Angevin empire stretching across France to Germany, Italy and the Mediterrean, his subjects saw no further than the Channel. In 1258 the Provisions of Oxford were circulated to the shires in Latin, French — and English.

Such tensions were exacerbated by Henry's penchant for advisers and favourites from southern France who were seen as either imposing alien rule or syphoning off decreasingly available royal patronage. Between 1232 and 1234, the government was run by Peter des Roches. In the years after his marriage in 1236, Henry welcomed his wife's uncles from Savoy: in 1236-7, William, bishop-elect of Valence was prominent at court; Peter of Savoy became lord of Richmond in 1240 and remained a major figure at court for two decades; in 1241, Boniface of Savoy was appointed archbishop of Canterbury. With them came other Savoyards: Peter d'Aigueblanche, given the see of Hereford in 1239; or Henry de Susa, the celebrated canon lawyer, better known as Hostiensis, who was the king's proctor in ecclesiastical cases until 1243. Such men were not only useful in Henry's continental diplomacy, but provided loyal service in England as magnate and official factions on whose loyalty the king could rely. They also had the advantage, perhaps, of being more congenial to the king, who seems to have a liking, again possibly dating from childhood, for Occitans (people from southern France). In 1247, Henry welcomed his Lusignan half-brothers, sons of his mother Isabelle, who had married, as her second husband in 1220, Hugh de Lusignan. They were showered with lucrative favour: William of Valence was given the heiress to the earldom of Pembroke; Aymer received the see of Winchester, one of the richest in the kingdom; Guy and Geoffrey were richly provided for.

This policy of promoting foreigners aroused widespread dismay. Many, lay and clerical, saw it as proof that the king, by depriving natives and prefering aliens, was intent on imposing absolutist tyranny. Henry was accused of having a distorted — i.e. selfish — view of national priorities. This feeling was most keenly voiced by clergy who associated it with Henry's willingness to allow the pope to interfere in church appointments and, most worrying to the comfortably beneficed or cosily cloistered, to levy church taxes. If anything, Henry was being rather conservative. He saw government in terms of pursuing his and his family's rights. His lands were possesssions to be ruled fairly to serve his ends. Kingship was personal, even if elevated by doctrines at once theocratic and Roman. Ruling was nobody else's business. Ideas of power being derived from the community, that there was a test of justice beyond his own or that his lands

constituted a unitary state would have had little meaning for
Henry, not least because they had little practical reality. Ironically, this dislocation between Henry's cosmopolitan, conservative, pesonal kingship and the concerns of a widening political
nation did more than anything to implant such ideas into English politics. Henry's internationlism was a powerful force in
developing English national identity. Henry had no intention of
subverting his own realm, although his failure to communicate
and gain the approval of his magnates and their vassals almost
destroyed his regime. Henry's failings were less tyrannical than
imaginative.

Unlike other child-kings, Richard II or Henry VI, Henry III
was an effective monarch for a quarter of a century. Although
the Poitevin *coup* of 1232, which released Henry from the tute-
lage of Hubert de Burgh and marked his political emancipation,
was unsustainable in the face of united baronial and episcopal
opposition, there was no return to limited monarchy. From 1234,
Henry was master of the government. Away from high politics,
he restored royal administration. Despite his public pronouncements, he wisely left baronial adminstration of their affairs
alone, concentrating on enforcing royal rights, through the
reform of the Exchequer, scrutiny of sheriffs, increased regularity of judicial eyres, and use of the central courts at Westminster.
A sign of Henry's refusal to challenge the maladminstration of
the magnates in the localities is found in the wave of complaints
against baronial officials which emerged in 1258-9. By 1250,
Henry was solvent and at peace, he (or rather his cleverer and
more dynamic brother Richard) had reformed the coinage and
he was even salting away a considerable fortune in gold preparatory to going on crusade.

There had been difficulties with the barons over policy, the
appointment of officials, and taxation. Despite regular meetings
of what came to be called parliaments, in 1242, 1244, 1248, 1252,
1255 and 1257 lay subsidies were refused. Anger over their exclusion from administration and policy-making led to baronial
schemes for controlling the crown such as the 'Paper' Constitution of 1244. However, the recovery of royal government since
1232 was real, significant and unchallenged. But Henry's
manipulation of his magnates was less effective than his

exploitation of his rights. Henry was not a particularly good soldier. His campaigns in France in 1230 and 1242 had been fiascos; his expeditions to Wales hardly decisive. That he could maintain his authority being so militarily limp says much for the efficiency of his bureaucracy. However, relations with many of the nobles were poor or equivocal and his handling of the church vitiated by his alliance with the papacy with whose fiscal demands he generally concurred.

Three things led to the temporary collapse of Henry's power in 1258: foreign policy; finance; and the Lusignans. Maintaining Gascony was massively expensive, as were the campaigns there in 1253-4 and in Wales in 1257. The need to pay for these expeditons in the absence of lay subsisdies forced royal officials to exert greater pressure on the localities, already burdened by poor harvests. The Sicilian business seemed to encapsulate Henry's faults as a ruler: lack of consultation; subservience to the pope; wild fantasies of international power; and financial idiocy. The agreement called for Henry to provide, as a sort of entry fee, over £90,000. Although Henry hoped this would come from the church, there was the cost of the actual campaign to conquer Sicily. The idea may not have been absurd: indeed one of Henry's brothers-in-law, Charles of Anjou, achieved in the 1260s precisely what Henry had hoped for in the 1250s. But the commitment had been made without any consultation of those on whom the burden of sustaining the enterprise would fall. In addition, Henry was in the undignified position of promising to go on three crusades at once: to Palestine (according to his vow of 1250); North Africa (with the king of Castile); and Sicily (elevated by the pope to crusade status to ease funding and recruitment). Perhaps typically, he went on none.

The Sicilian obligation came at precisely the moment Henry was increasingly strapped for cash. This had a direct political effect. Some of his magnates were his creditors. If the king wanted subsidies he had to agree to greater baronial involvement in government. Traditionally, kings bought support by patronage, but Henry's policy was here myopic and provocative. In the 1250s, the land available to the king to give out to his nobles was severely limited, yet he continued to shower the Lusignans with whatever was available, to the fury of those, like Simon de

Montfort, who regarded their own claims to a place at the trough as superior. Equally, if not more damaging, was the riotous and rapacious behaviour of the Lusignans themselves and Henry's willingness to protect them even to the point of denying justice to those who entered pleas against them. Such actions held strong echoes of John's reign. As a sign of Henry's failure to manage his barons and the essential factionalism, rather than nationalism, that lay behind the baronial coup of 1258, among the seven who banded together against the king in April 1258 were Peter of Savoy and Simon de Montfort, both aliens who had done well out of the king — but not as well as the threatening Lusignans.

The reform programme known as the Provisions of Oxford, devised between 1258 and 1259 at parliaments at Oxford and Westminster, effectively placed the crown into commission. Policy and offical appointments were to be conducted by a standing council, regularly answerable to parliaments. Grievances of knights and gentry were to be met in a new general eyre which ostensibly was to investigate baronial as well as royal administration. Affecting to solve the problems left outstanding in *Magna Carta*, the Provisions solved little. Control of the king lay at the heart of the scheme, a matter of authority not law. By skilful use of a loyal bureaucracy and playing off baronial factions, Henry easily outmanoeuvred the reformers, a success which should not be overlooked in assessing his political ability. By 1261 he was back in power. In the unrest of 1263-4, especially after the Mise of Amiens vindicated his position, the king could even appear as the best guarantor of justice against the hot-headed self-interested rebels. But whatever the failings of Montfort and his allies, without Henry's duplicity, misjudgements and mismanagement of the 1250s, there would have been no need for such a conflict.

The outcome was settled by force of arms. In May 1264, Henry was unexpectedly defeated at Lewes and captured. In some senses this marked the end of his rule. Montfort's prisoner, he played no part in the royalist victory in 1265, narrowly avoiding being killed by friendly troops at Evesham. Thereafter his son, Edward, and his friends increasingly controlled events. But the final settlement, enshrined in the Dictum of Kenilworth

(1266) and the Statute of Marlborough (1267) owed not a little to Henry's careful handling of his opponents in 1260-3. Whilst rejecting any control of the prerogative, Henry nonetheless had not closed the door on judicial changes directed especially at answering the grievances of the wider political nation. Henry was always suspicious of baronial hegemony: now he was quite happy to assert royal justice as the defence of the commuity against the rapacity of men like Simon de Montfort.

Henry's achievement was mixed. To allow the restoration of the royal prerogative in the 1230s and 1240s, he was prepared to loosen the hold on baronial power in the localities in return for an extension of royal authority elsewhere. Yet, from Henry III's reign, the Common Law administered and protected by royal judges and royal courts became the medium through which Englishmen perceived — often wrongly — their rights and liberties. Despite the fine words of 1258-9, it was the crown not the barons which summoned the new political classes to redress the self-interested factionalism of the old. Henry's personal rule had ended in bloody civil war and near-deposition. To survive, Henry had abandoned, in 1259, all his cherished hopes of recovering his birthright in France. The victory of 1265-7 established the undisputed authority of the crown, if not the person of the king, for the next three and a half centuries, in some part the result of Henry's fixed dermination not to compromise the royal prerogative, even when it seemed possible, an attitude in marked contrast to the vacillating caprice of his son, Edward. Both Matthew Paris and Dante, who had little else in common, characterised Henry III as 'simple'. The legend underestimates the fact.

More widely, Henry III instituted a new image of monarchy, one deliberately theatrical, associated with gorgeous public ceremonies, surrounded not by the trappings of the hunt or battlefield but the paraphenalia of quasi-ecclesiatical ritual. Although plotting a continental future, Henry was devoted to English saints. He called his sons after two of them, Edward and Edmund. His special concern was the building of the new shrine of Edward the Confessor. The king damned for corrupting his realm with aliens made being English respectable. Although kings of England held French ambitions for another three centuries, Henry III's reign marked the parting of the ways.

Henceforward, the kings of England were English rather than Frenchmen or men of princely lineage for whom the kingdom was just one part of their accidental but legitimate inheritance. Before 1259, such a position would have been unthinkable, not least to Henry himself.

Henry's final years witnessed increasing infirmity. Even in his son's absence on crusade, Henry does not seem to have given the lead. Seriously ill for much of the time, in April 1271 the council emphasised his decline by restricting his access to his revenues to 6/8d a day pocket money. He was still trundled about to symbolise authority, but he played little active part in affairs. His death, in November 1272, severed a link with a distant and now foreign past. As a boy, Henry had been protected by William Marshal who, when a child, had played games with King Stephen, grandson of the Conqueror. Almost as a requiem for an age, Henry III's body went to Westminster Abbey, his new national shrine. But his heart went to lie beside his mother, his uncle and his grandfather, at Fontevrault, in Anjou.

D. Carpenter, 'The personal rule of Henry III', *Speculum*, 1985.
F. M. Powicke, *Henry III and the Lord Edward*, 1947.

**GUALA BICCHIERI** (*d*.1227), cardinal priest of St Martin, was papal legate to England from May 1216 to November 1218, a period crucial for the survival of the Angevin dynasty. One of Innocent III's inner circle of advisers, Guala was effectively head of the church in England as the pope's agent. His role became immeasurably more important on the death of King John in October 1216 in the midst of civil war. Since 1213, John had been a papal vassal, England a papal fief. With John dead, Guala, whose name headed John's chosen executors, immediately presided over the coronation of the young Henry III which was preceded by the young king's homage to the legate for his kingdom. Although leaving routine administration to the regent, William Marshal, and Peter des Roches, bishop of Winchester, Guala, representating the king's temporal as well as spiritual overlord, lent legitimacy and active support to the regime, whose plight was further endangered by the invasion of Louis of France. In the winter of 1216-17, with the approval of the new pope, Honorius III, Guala turned the royalist cause into a crusade, allowing supporters of the king the same privileges and indulgences as those who fought the infidel. At the very least this boosted morale and gave waverers an incentive and a justification for throwing in their lot with the king's party. In the aftermath of the civil war, Guala, keeping out of factious politics, avoided vindictiveness, although he selectively disciplined certain clerical rebel sympathisers. Nonetheless, he found his influence over ecclesiastical patronage useful in rewarding members of his household, including a number of his nephews, while at the same time disapproving of indigenous pluralists. In 1218, however, the return of fellow cardinal Archbishop Stephen Langton compromised Guala's position and he was allowed to resign his legation. Guala's role in helping save Henry III was one of the clearest demonstrations of effective papal monarchy in the Middle Ages. His achievement was recalled with admiration fifty years later when in 1264 a successor, Cardinal Gui Foulquois, was trying to gain entry to a kingdom once more in the hands of rebels.

**HUBERT DE BURGH** (*d.*1243; Justiciar of England 1215-32) was one of the most powerful royal ministers of the thirteenth century, dominating government from 1219 until his fall in 1232, a period when, it was said by a contemporary chronicler, 'he lacked nothing of royal power save the dignity of a royal diadem'. Yet Hubert's career was founded on a series of paradoxes. One of the richest men in the kingdom by 1232, he failed to establish a solid dynastic base. A noted commander and brave warrior, he could also read. A public advocate of the *Magna Carta* principles of protection against arbitrary judgements and disseisins, he used his office as the king's *alter ego* to feather his nest. Built up (not without his own connivance) as a champion of England and Englishness, his advancement owed much to his service in the continental interests of his Angevin masters. One of the most authoritarian of justiciars, he lacked the legal training or experience of his predecessors. In his hands the power of his office had never been greater; after his fall, it rapidly disappeared from English government.

Hubert belonged to a Norfolk gentry family. His elder brother served Prince John in Ireland in 1185. In the mid-1190s, Hubert was himself attached to the prince's household, serving as chamberlain by 1198. After John's accession, Hubert continued as chamberlain to the king's household until 1205, amassing the fruits of royal service, including numerous sheriffdoms and the custody of castles, such as Windsor, Wallingford and Dunster. He was employed on diplomatic embassies to Portugal (1200) and Philip II of France (1203). Tangible proof of his standing is seen in 1201 when he received the wardenship of the Welsh Marches, three important castles in Gwent, the wardenship of the Cinque Ports and the custody of Dover castle. In 1202, he was transferred to helping John in France, becoming successively castellan of Falaise and Chinon. The famous story of Hubert's refusal to mutilate Arthur of Brittany, then in his keeping at Falaise, was certainly current in own lifetime, and may have been given to the chronicler Ralph of Coggeshall by Hubert himself, presumably to avoid implication in John's most notorious crime. The legend embodied in Shakespeare's *King John* was thus of contemporary manufacture. At Chinon, Hubert defended the castle heroically against the French months after the rest of Normandy and Anjou had been lost, his resistance ending with his being severely wounded and taken prisoner.

Hubert's captivity from 1205 to 1207 proved in the long term not to be as severe a setback as it appeared at the time. Although he lost most of what he had been granted since 1199, a lesson in royal gratitude and the fragility of his own fortune which was not lost on him, Hubert was equally not implicated in the worst excesses of John's rule. Even as sheriff of Lincolnshire from 1208, he operated through a deputy. Although by 1212 his holdings were assessed at fifty knights' fees, only in 1213 was he recalled to active royal service, as seneschal of Poitou, a potentially vital appointment in view of John's impending campaign in France. Whatever his administrative skills, it was as a soldier that Hubert was conspicuous. In the face of baronial opposition to the king in 1214-15, Hubert remained loyal. In some ways his position resembled that of William Marshal who had also been recalled to the colours in 1213: both were able to preserve a reputation for loyalty untarnished by association with tyranny. In Hubert's case this made him an acceptable compromise choice for king and barons as justiciar, which he was appointed at Runnymede at the same time as *Magna Carta* was sealed.

Hubert's justiciarship falls into distinct phases. During the civil war of 1215-17, the central administration, Exchequer and the exploitation of royal financial and judicial rights through sheriffs and eyres, over which the justiciar traditionally presided, ceased to function. Given wide authority in Kent, East Anglia and London, Hubert's role was primarily military. With the invasion of Louis of France, his defence of Dover was crucial, especially his refusal to surrender the castle on hearing of John's death. In May 1217, Hubert engineered the defeat of the relief French fleet off Sandwich, thereby convincing Louis to come to terms.

Between 1217 and 1219, Hubert's power was overshadowed by that of the regent, William Marshal, the papal legates, Guala and Pandulf, and his predecessor as justiciar and later fierce rival, the bishop of Winchester, Peter des Roches. Until the Marshal's death in 1219, Hubert was one of a group who acted to re-establish royal government through cooperation with the magnates according to the principles of *Magna Carta*, which was reissued, with Hubert's approval, in 1216 and 1217. To his rising eminence he probably owed his marriage in 1217 to Isabella, widow of Geoffrey de Mandeville, divorced first wife of King John and heiress of the earldom of Gloucester.

Hubert's ascent to political dominance began after the Marshal's death in 1219, when, as one of a triumvirate with the legate Pandulf and Peter des Roches, he assumed the day to day running of the government, symbolised by his custody of the Great Seal. This accretion of power was probably due to his perceived political moderation. Although conscious of having to restore royal rights, as justiciar he respected the need to proceed within limits acceptable to the majority of magnates. The gibe that this was government by the magnates for the magnates is not entirely misleading. He was quite prepared to repudiate the actions of John's government (in which, of course, Peter des Roches had figured prominently). Equally, as he still lacked a sizeable heritable patrimony, he had to conciliate to survive. Ironically, this insecurity which made him politcially acceptable to the baronial power-brokers also made Hubert socially suspect in their eyes. Although originally coming from a background by no means inferior to his predecessor but one, Geoffrey FitzPeter, unlike him Hubert was regarded as a *novus homo*, a parvenu, a man on the make. It was only in 1227 that he was created earl of Kent and even then his estates barely survived his political fall and his title died with him. It may also be the case that Hubert was suspected because he was disliked. If the anecdotes about him are remotely true, there may have been an unattractive edginess about his character which, combined with a degree of self-righteousness and pride, leaves a rather unappealing impression. Unfortunately, although personalities are the stuff of politics, beyond outlines drawn by others they are irrecoverable.

The central task of the Minority administration was the resumption of royal property and rights and the provision of legal and political arbitration. As justiciar, Hubert was central to these efforts. As his power grew, so that of the other triumvirs declined until in 1221, with the support of Archbishop Langton and the bishops, Hubert got Pandulf withdrawn by the pope and Peter des Roches's guardianship of the young Henry III ended. A final confrontation with former partisans of John, led by Falkes de Bréauté, in 1223-4, culminating in the siege of Bedford, left Hubert triumphant. He had also, in 1221, managed to net, as his third and grandest wife, Margaret, eldest sister of Alexander II, king of Scots.

Hubert's victory seemed complete. He had the ear of the young king; eased Peter des Roches out of favour; and purged the administration, Peter des Roches's son (or nephew) Peter des Rivaux being sacked as senior clerk of the Wardobe. But the victory was won at a price. Although Bishop Peter spent most of the next few years abroad, he had vowed revenge, a pursuit which would attract the support of a number of other dissidents of 1223-4, such as the earl of Chester. With the king's attainment of majority in 1227, Hubert's political position became even more narrowly based, a vulnerability tacitly acknowledged by his appointment as justiciar for life in 1228.

The king's majority in 1227 shifted the priorities of government. Hitherto, the direction had been towards the restoration of royal rights and income, but without a return to the authoritarian methods of John's reign. Politically, this had depended on allowing baronial supporters of the regime much latitude, not least the justiciar himself. The effectiveness of Hubert's rule was haphazard, dependent upon shifting coalitions of self-interest and, as in 1221 and 1223-4, *ad hoc* victimisation of opponents. Financially, Hubert's rule was at least a partial success. From 1220, royal income accounted at the exchequer grew steadily, while expenditure remained more or less constant, at a modest level compared to the large amounts amassed and spent on the foreign and domestic wars of 1213-17. But in the 1220s, income was far less than it had been under John and did not allow for any expansive or aggressive policies which a new king might have in mind.

Politics and finance were inseparable. In 1225, in order to gain agreement to a fifteenth, Hubert consented to re-issuing *Magna Carta*. But such gestures could only work occasionally. More serious still for the justiciar was Henry III's own ambitions. Brought up by Peter des Roches with a clear sense of his continental inheritance and his lost legacy there, Henry was eager to attempt to win back his French lands. Hubert's administration had been unable to stop the conquest of Poitou in 1224. Worse the fiasco of the failed preparations for a Poitou campaign in 1229 were laid by the king squarely,and perhaps fairly, at Hubert's door. On top of the expense, Hubert, with the caution of the veteran of Chinon, who had seen war achieve little of benefit in a long career, may have thought the enterprise futile. The subsequent disastrous expedition to Brittany of 1230 did little for Hubert's reputation or his relations with the king. However, despite such problems, Hubert's fall was sudden and unexpected.

By 1232, with Peter des Roches back in England, Hubert lacked the depth of baronial or episcopal support that he had enjoyed a decade earlier. Langton had died in 1228 and some of the leading magnates — the earls of Chester, Cornwall and Pembroke — were either neutral or hostile. Politically his grip was loosening; his attempt to defeat the Welsh came to nothing and he failed to secure a subsidy at a great council in 1232. In the Spring of that year, the king appointed Peter des Rivaux treasurer of the household. Already there had been damaging attacks on Hubert's cherished marriage, on the grounds of consanguinity. But Hubert was an experienced player in the game of faction. In June and early July 1232 he seemed to have restored royal confidence in him, being appointed justiciar for Ireland and having the king confirm charters granted to him and his wife. But in July his enemies struck with accusations that Hubert was behind a series of coordinated attacks on papal tax collectors and Italian clergy in England. On 29 July, he was stripped of the justiciarship and, in the next few months, of his estates, title, treasure and liberty. Although the new government of Peter des Roches and Peter des Rivaux collapsed in 1234, for Hubert there was only the partial restoration of lands and title: office, favour and power were gone for ever.

Even in retirement, Hubert was occasionally harassed by the king, who was no doubt nervous of such an eminent political outcast. He might have been more nervous if he had known that, in a manner made familiar by twentieth century fallen ministers, Hubert had been telling his story, or parts of it, to the voracious consumer of anecdotes, Matthew Paris. Hubert cast himself in heroic mould, the defender of Dover and the victor of Sandwich. It is from Paris that comes an image of Hubert as a national hero, champion of 'England for the English'. There may have lain some truth behind this rehearsal of the chronicler's own prejudices. Foreign entanglements had almost cost Hubert his life in 1205; foreigners, Peter des Roches and Peter des Rivaux, had cost him his job in 1232. There may be substance to the allegations of incitement of the anti-Italian riots of 1231-2. But if Hubert was wary of 'aliens', it was for politics not sentiment. Factional rivalry and military conflict dictated Hubert's attitude. To see him as harbinger of nationalism is to view his career through a monocle of hindsight.

What is more certain is that Hubert's period in office revealed that the English political scene had changed significantly and, as it turned out, permanently. These changes led to greater insularity of attitude and personnel, but were hardly caused by them. The loss of Normandy, Anjou and Poitou severed the continental connection for all but the king's own relatives. This could lead to a dislocation of interests between an increasingly insular baronage and cosmopolitan kings. But this should not be exaggerated: Henry III, for all his continental longings, chose an

Anglo-Saxon saint as his patron and named his two surviving sons after Old English king-saints. More specifically, the consequent presence of the king more or less permanently in the realm had profound effects on politics and government. Simply put, the king was there to do his own business: there was less or no need for an *alter ego*. However, the justiciarship was decreasingly effective as an insititution anyway, because of the growing bureaucratic specialisation and departmental separation within the royal administration. Unlike in the twelfth century, it was inconceivable that one man could have the range of knowledge or time efficiently to oversee or control all the legal, financial and clerical activities of the king. The triumph of the written word and the keeping of records were causes and symptoms of these developments.

Hubert de Burgh transcended the changes because of the unique political circumstances of the long minority of Henry III. It would be harsh to condemn him as an anachronism. His personal behaviour may have included favouritism and peculation, although he failed to secure the dynastic patrimony he craved. But he seems to have recognised that the methods of Richard I and John were counterproductive for all except the narrow royalist interest. In his conduct of business, he appears to have taken seriously both the lessons of 1213-17 and the general principle which lay behind *Magna Carta*, that monarch and magnate, king and subject have to rule and be ruled by mutual interest, protection and security. Royal rights had to be asserted within a framework of consent and the support of the powerful. He proved as much after 1219; he learnt as much in 1232. *Magna Carta* of 1215 had been a failed expedient. By reissuing it three times, Hubert, the justiciar appointed at Runnymede, ensured the charter's permanence in English politics.

D. Carpenter, *The Minority of Henry III*, 1990.
D. Carpenter, 'The Fall of Hubert de Burgh', *Journal of British Studies*, xix, 1980.

**PANDULF MASCA** (*d*.1226) was an Italian papal official who, between 1219 and 1221, in the words of T. F. Tout, 'almost acted as king of England' and, unlike some who actually wore

the crown in this period, did so with considerable skill and success. A sub-deacon of the Roman church, Pandulf first came to
England in 1211 on an unsuccessful mission to negotiate an end
to the Interdict, earning notoriety and praise for apparently
resisting John's attempts at physical intimidation. Two years
later, in very different circumstances, Pandulf was back to
receive John's submission and cession of the kingdom to the
pope. From 1213 to 1215, Pandulf continued to act as a papal
agent in England, for some of the time under the Legate
Nicholas (1213-14). His reward, illustrating the new Angevin-
papal alliance, was his election to the see of Norwich in 1215. In
the same year he returned to Rome to attend the Lateran Council and resume work in the papal chamber. Although in the confidence of the new pope, Honorius III, with whom he may have
worked at the Curia, Pandulf never became a cardinal. When, in
1218, he was appointed to succeed the distinguished Cardinal
Guala as Legate to England, he had to rely on his personality,
ability and the full papal authority ('plenarium potestatem')
Honorius granted him in matters spiritual and temporal.

In the first few months as legate, Pandulf made such a good
impression that in April 1219 the dying regent, William Marshal,
commended the young Henry III to his guardianship, despite the
furious protestations of the king's tutor, Peter des Roches. After
the regent's death, a governing triumvirate emerged of the
legate, Peter des Roches and the justiciar, Hubert de Burgh.
Unlike Guala, Pandulf was an experienced administrator who
concerned himself closely in government. While consulting
meticulously with his colleagues, as legate and guardian of the
king he took the lead. It was his implementation of the papally
inspired policy of resumption of royal castles, lands and rights
and renewed control over local agents of the crown that gave the
Minority government its direction and objective. Under the slo-
gan Pandulf used to the justices of the bench in 1220 'royal
rights are to be preserved' and publically stated in repeated papal
bulls of 1219, 1220 and 1221, this policy provided the foundation upon which Angevin government could be rebuilt.

Pandulf was not shy in getting involved in specific cases, but
his activity was inevitably wide. He initiated talks leading to
peace with the Welsh and the 1220 truce with Scotland. To

underpin the campaign for restitution of the king's rights, he organised Henry III's second coronation in 1220 in a more orthodox ceremony than the hugger-mugger affair of 1216. Typical of his diplomatic treatment of colleagues, Pandulf allowed the sensitive Archbishop Langton to exercise his traditional right to crown the king. As legate, as well as controlling ecclesiastical patronage, Pandulf lent material support to the regime. Where lay taxation, such as the scutage of 1217 or the 1220 carucage, produced meagre sums, his profitable tax for the crusade allowed him to give loans to the government, thus, in D. Carpenter's words, becoming its paymaster as well as director.

By 1221, central authority was becoming more accepted; the policy of resumption was beginning to bear fruit and, especially important, royal income was at last rising substantially (the £8,000 raised in 1220 was £3,000 more than the previous year): and it never looked back. Politically, however, Pandulf's position in both church and state was becoming increasingly anomalous in the face of the growing authority of Langton and Hubert de Burgh, or so, at least, Langton on a visit to Rome seems to have persuaded the pope. On the archbishop's return to England in July 1221, Pandulf resigned, not to be replaced. Back in Rome in 1222, he was finally consecrated bishop of Norwich. His interest in English affairs remained to the end. In 1225, he was encouraging Hubert de Burgh in his handling of the rebels of 1223-4, urging him to ensure that 'the pride of the traitors does not ascend further than is expedient'. However, Pandulf did not meddle after his retirement. He was in no position to, as his authority had always been that of a representative, never wielded in his own right. He remained simply a bishop *in absentia*. In 1226 his body was brought to Norwich for burial in the cathedral he had never entered as bishop in life. Like so many of his contemporaries, Pandulf's career knew no nationalities. With his predecessor Guala, Pandulf, despite his relatively modest status, put into practice the rhetoric of papal monarchy as effectively as anyone in the Middle Ages. This may explain his relative neglect by champions of an insular reading of English history. It is ironic that so many of those who in these years stood between England and factional anarchy were not natives. But unlike many of the

others, Pandulf earned the accolade of local praise: even
Matthew Paris had a good word to say for him.

D. Carpenter, *The Minority of Henry III*, 1990.

**ROGER OF WENDOVER** (*d*.1236) was a monk of St.
Alban's. He rose to be prior of the dependent cell at Belvoir but
had to be removed in 1219 for financial mismanagement. Sometime after 1202, perhaps as late as 1231, he began writing a history from the Creation to his own day, the *Flores Historiarum
(Flowers of History)*. Unoriginal to 1202, from then until he finished writing in 1234 Roger used no surviving chronicle. Unfortunately, he seemed to have relied heavily on his own imagination
or gossip to fill the gap. The black reputation, almost gothic horror that surrounds the posthumous reputation of King John
derives largely from Roger's account written a decade or so after
the king's death. His anecdotes establishing the image of John as
lecherous, idle and sadistic, as far as they can be checked, appear
to have been invented. His picture of the young Henry III is more
sympathetic, perhaps because royal policy was less destructive of
church interests; perhaps because, in retrospect, anyone was better than John. Roger has Henry declare 'I prefer to be considered
a stupid king rather than a cruel or tyrannical one'. Roger took
his stand with the barons, and was virulent in opposition both to
royal exactions and the intrusive authority of the pope (who had
in 1215 supported the royalists). Roger's attitudes were partisan.
His portrait of John, however, may accurately reflect what was
said of the late king in the years after the civil war and the often
uneasy minority of Henry III. Roger was, in fact, a dull story-
teller, loading his tales with circumstantial evidence in a pedes-
trian literary style. His fame, and the currency of his stories,
depend largely on his successor as chief historiographer at
St. Alban's, Matthew Paris, who incorporated, edited and
'improved' Roger's account in his *Chronica majora*.

A. Gransden, *Historical Writing in England c.550-c.1307*, 1979.

**EDMUND RICH OF ABINGDON** (*c*.1170-1240; archbishop
of Canterbury 1234-40; canonised 1246) provides an example of

how the best men often made ineffective prelates, political failure nonetheless being a qualification for sainthood. Born near and educated at Oxford, Edmund's intense personal piety was fostered by his forceful mother, Mabel (his father having escaped into Eynsham Abbey). For the rest of his life Edmund wore a particularly painful hair-shirt. In 1192, Edmund went to Paris, whence he returned to teach the Quadrivium before turning to theology. At Oxford, Edmund gained a reputation as a popular preacher and teacher famed for the slickness of his expositions, some of which so defied logical explanation that they were ascribed to divine inspiration. Seemingly a model don, Edmund occasionally dozed off while teaching, a result, perhaps, of his inability to lie down to sleep at night because of his hair-shirt. In 1222, he abandoned lecturing on theology, allegedly because he found the fashionable disputation method of teaching and learning, by which pupils and masters orally exchanged competing arguments and texts in a combative search for truth, conducive to vanity. As canon and treasurer of Salisbury, Edmund displayed administrative skills. These, with his contacts with the royal family as a spiritual adviser to the king's sister, Eleanor and his achievements as a scholar recommended him as archbishop after Pope Gregory IX had rejected three other candidates. As a spiritual guide, Edmund set an impressive example; as a politician, he was handicapped by a tender conscience without the stomach for confrontation of his colleague Robert Grosseteste of Lincoln. After playing a pivotal eirenic role in the removal of Peter des Roches's government in 1234, Edmund suffered consistent disappointment and rebuff, both from the king and the pope. In 1236, he acquiesced in the decision of the council at Merton on bastardy although it ran counter to canon law; 1238 saw his impotent outrage at the marriage of Simon de Montfort to Princess Eleanor, in contradiction to her oath of chastity he had witnessed; the political crisis of 1238 exposed the loss of episcopal influence in the previous four years. Edmund resisted papal demands for taxation for the war against Frederick II and the scheme to reserve three hundred English benefices for papal appointment. This championing of the rights of the indigenous church won him the approval of Matthew Paris who composed a respectful biography of Edmund after his death. But Archbishop

Edmund ran aground on the shallows of detail. Unlike Grosseteste he failed to articulate clear principles and strategies. A sympathiser with the reforming attitudes of Langton, Edmund
lacked the skill to assert ecclesiastical interests in the secular
world or implement change within the church. In 1237, as a
recognition of his exposed weakness, a papal legate, Otto, was
appointed to pursue both papal interests and church reform.
Edmund's position was severely compromised. An unsuccessful
appeal to the papacy in 1237 over the rights of Canterbury was
followed by continued failure to resolve his conflict with the
monks of Canterbury over a clutch of vested interests, including
his foundation of a house of secular canons at Maidstone. In
1240, he withdrew again, ostensibly to visit the pope. Seeking
the shades of Becket and Langton at Pontigny, he died at nearby
Soissy In death, his personal qualities soon obscuring his public
failure, Edmund became an ideal subject for canonisation by a
papacy eager to claim martyrs for ecclesiastical rights. Miracles
of healing soon began to be ascribed to him, his tomb becoming
a place of veneration. In 1246 he became the last archbishop of
Canterbury to be canonised. His cult was immediately popular,
especially among Englishmen, including those who thwarted
him in life such as Henry III, who visited the shrine in 1254.
Richard of Cornwall, Edmund's ally in 1238, was especially
devoted, visiting Edmund's shrine in 1247 and naming his second
son after him. Such was the ubiquitous appeal of the dead archbishop that he was admired by royalists and rebels alike in the
1260s, including Simon de Montfort whose marriage Edmund
had so vigorously opposed. His shrine continued to attract English pilgrims, including Edward I in 1286. In England the cult
was maintained at Catesby, in Northamptonshire, a house reputedly founded by Edmund for his equally ascetic sisters. Edmund
conformed in aspiration to the academic reforming prelates of
the age of Innocent III, scholars, administrators, spiritual advisers and statesmen. Although failing to put these ideals into
effective practice, Edmund's personality left its mark on contemporaries. He combined scholarship with piety: the mystical *Mirror of the Holy Church* has been ascribed to him. He believed in
personal conversion and the supremacy of private conscience: an
unlikely archbishop and an unlikely saint. His most lasting

memorial is appropriately where he achieved most unalloyed renown, in the community of students and scholars named after him at Oxford, St. Edmund Hall.

C. H. Lawrence, *Edmund of Abingdon*, 1960.

**ELIAS OF DEREHAM** (*fl.*1188-*d.*1245) presided over the building of the new Salisbury Cathedral for the first twenty-five years of its construction, 1220-45. A secular clerk, later rector of Melton Mowbray and Harrow and canon of Salisbury and Wells, he seems to have begun his career in East Anglia as a protégé of Hubert Walter in the 1180s. This connection gave him his introduction to royal administration and the world of ecclesiastical and high politics. He was an executor of the wills of Hubert Walter himself (1205); Walter's successor as archbishop of Canterbury, Stephen Langton (1228); and Peter des Roches, bishop of Winchester and a former justiciar (1238). He acted as steward of the archiepiscopal estates under both Walter and Langton and may have acted as the archbishop's attorney in a suit in the king's courts in 1204. In 1215, he was present at the signing of *Magna Carta* at Runnymede, being appointed one of the commissioners to distribute copies of the charter. During the Interdict and later he was associated with Bishop Jocelyn of Bath (1206-42), mentioned as his steward in 1229. But his particular administrative skills lay, apparently, in art, architecture and design. His Canterbury connection was underlined in 1220 when he played a leading role ('by counsel and invention' says Matthew Paris) in the construction of a new shrine to receive the body of Thomas Becket and again in 1237 when he advised Archbishop Rich on a suitable site for his proposed college of secular canons. Elias seems to have been eclectic in his pursuits. Apart from supervising buildings for kings and bishops, in 1238 he was responsible for constructing a marble tomb for Henry III's sister, Joan, queen of Scotland and in 1244 he was given £20 by the king to make a hanging pyx for the High Altar at Salisbury. His main occupation in his later years, as far as his career has left traces in surviving records, was in connection with the King's Works and Salisbury Cathedral. In the 1230s, he was in charge of work for the king at Winchester and Clarendon. At

Salisbury, his position was unique in medieval England. The new cathedral was the only one to be built on a green field site, initially away even from a major settlement. Although it is unlikely that Elias was what would today be called an architect, it is possible that the theoretically satisfying but architecturally strained homogenous proportions of Salisbury were his contribution. In a cosmographical St. Alban's manuscript, his interest in theories of proportion is attested by a diagram of the world being labelled 'according to Master Eyas de Derham'. At Salisbury, he would have supervised the building of the Lady chapel (completed 1225) and the east arm of the church (completed by 1237). Presumably to be near his work, Elias built himself a house in the Close (known as Leadenhall). From what survives of his interests, he appears something of a dilettante, an amateur artist or decorator, a designer whose administrative skills allowed him to try his hand at architecture. Alternatively, he was simply another well-connected, intellectually alert civil servant who specialised in buildings and furnishing buildings not as a creator but as an administrator. Perhaps personal taste determined the projects he managed, but it may have been his efficiency and experience in organising men, materials and money not his taste, let alone genius, that secured him his position.

J. Harvey, *English Mediaeval Architects*, 1987.


**RICHARD, EARL OF CORNWALL** (1209-72; king of the Romans 1257-72) was the second son of King John and younger brother of Henry III. His career exemplifies the ambition and reality of Angevin rule in the mid-thirteenth century. Claimant to the county of Poitou (1225), the duchy of Gascony (1242-3) and the Holy Roman Empire (1257-72), and repeatedly refusing to accept the papally-proffered title of king of Sicily, by contrast Richard's material power rested on his estates in the Thames valley and East Anglia, his earldom of Cornwall, his control of the Cornish tin mining industry and his position in the English baronage and court. Angevin dreams remained international: Richard himself was an active crusader. Angevin authority, however, rested on control of England. Richard's failure to give

*Richard of Cornwall agreeing a treaty*
*with Nazir Lord of Kerak*
(From Matthew Paris's Chronica Majora)

substance to his foreign aspirations underlined this withdrawal to insular, national preoccupations. Few individuals more neatly illustrate how the rulers of England, in spite of themselves, became English monarchs. Richard of Cornwall even notoriously spoke good English.

Richard was a tremendous swell, a lover of ceremonies, titles, pomp, luxury, pretty women and fine clothes: even in prison he insisted on wearing scarlet robes. But he lacked one essential element to complete the perfect image of what he spent his life being, a king-in-waiting. A puny child, Richard's poor physique denied him a proper training in arms. For all his pride and tenacity in defending or asserting his rights, Richard was a talker, not a fighter. Never was this better displayed than on his crusade of 1240-1. No battles were fought, still less victories achieved. The treaty Richard negotiated with the sultan of Cairo was less realistic than that signed the year before with the sultan of Damascus by the count of Champagne. Yet Richard's reputation soared at what contemporaries saw as his success, hardly surprising as he handled his own publicity. The story of his triumphs depended on his own newsletter and carefully targeted reminiscences with well-placed chroniclers, such as Matthew Paris. The whole exercise was a masterpiece of self-promotion. There was another, equally characteristic side to Richard's crusade. He secured the release of French prisoners and the burial of Christian soldiers killed in a rout at Gaza in 1239. Gestures and diplomacy, rather than blood and iron, won for Richard the admiration of western chivalry, and more. At a very tricky moment at Taillebourg in 1242, Richard managed by negotiation to extricate his brother from an untenable military position because the French were grateful at his having secured the release of their compatriots the year before.

From 1215 until 1223, Richard was educated at Corfe Castle by an obscure royalist backwoodsman, Roger d'Acastre, under the aegis of the influential Poitevin Peter de Mauley. Roger may not have been the ideal gentleman scholar to act as Richard's tutor. Much of the tuition may have been unfashionably in English and Richard never developed an interest in any of the arts, apart from the sartorial, either directly or as a patron. His concern in the construction of his religious foundations, notably at Hailes in Gloucestershire, did not stretch beyond the financial and pious. The contrast with his brother Henry, the refined mastermind of Westminster Abbey, is plain. What Richard's education does seem to have provided — or at least not impeded — was an excellent head for finance and business acumen, what would now be called management skills, *i.e.* the ability to deal with people, to strike bargains, to achieve through negotiation and personal contact simultaneously public consensus and private advantage.

The position of the king's brother was rarely enviable. Although in the hundred and fifty years before Henry III's accession, two out of seven kings had succeeded brothers, the awkward, hand-to-mouth experiences of Henry I or John before ascending the throne were less than encouraging precedents. For more than twenty years, until 1239, Richard was the heir presumptive during which time his relations with the king were often strained. Ironically, after the birth of the future Edward I, Richard's position at court was increasingly important, his influence more consistent and significant. Before 1239, Richard could be seen by some as a potential leader of disaffected barons and, on more than one occasion, acted as such, in 1233 and 1238, for example. Thereafter, his role was that of a mediator in crises whose loyalties were hardly in doubt. Oddly, and perhaps typical of Henry III, the barometer of Richard's loyalty was the grants he received rather than the services he performed. His loyalty was purchased at a high price, which, however, for the king was worth it.

Richard's public career began in 1225 when he was knighted and sent as figurehead of a successful campaign to secure continued Angevin overlordship, if not much practical control, over Gascony. In 1225, Richard was granted Cornwall, a traditional holding for cadets of the royal line since the Conquest: William I's brother Robert of Mortain; Reginald, bastard son of Henry I; and King John in the 1190s all held Cornwall. Although created earl of Cornwall in 1227, Richard only received his lands in fee (*i.e.* with tenure rather than at the king's pleasure) on his marriage in 1231. His first marriage points to Richard's disaffection with his brother, whom he did not consult. Isabel Marshal (*d.*1240) was the sister of the leader of baronial opposition to the regime of Hubert de Burgh. Richard spent the next decade running with the foxes of magnate discontent opposition and hunting with the hounds of royal favourites. On three occasions, 1227, 1233 and 1238, he challenged his brother, only to be bought off with lavish grants. As Richard's biographer, Denholm-Young put it, 'Richard never quarrelled with Henry without coming away a richer man'.

The years around 1240 were pivotal in Richard's career. The death of his first wife in 1240 loosened ties with the traditional opponents to royal authority, while his crusade won him an international fame and cosmopolitan contacts, a position reinforced by his friendship with the Emperor Frederick II and his second marriage to Sanchia of Provence (*d.*1262), sister to Henry III's wife Eleanor. He was provided with an income granted by the pope, from the money paid by those who had taken the

Cross but had redeemed their vows for cash rather than actually going on crusade. In England, Richard's importance was increasing. Politically, his contacts with the higher nobility and his proximity and influence over the king made him a ubiquitous arbiter of potentially damaging disputes between nobles and with the crown. In this capacity Richard acted between Simon de Montfort and Gilbert Marshal, both his brothers-in-law, and the king in 1239; in 1244 he negotiated a treaty with Scotland and sat on the committee to investigate baronial grievances against the crown in 1244; in the 1250s he acted as ambassador to France and settled disputes between Londoners and Westminster Abbey. In 1252, he determined the amount of Simon de Montfort's expenses when lieutenant in Gascony; in 1260 he mediated between the earl of Gloucester and the Lord Edward and the king; and in 1267 and 1270 he handed down awards to resolve the grievances of the new earl of Gloucester, especially with the Lord Edward. As a troubleshooter, Richard clearly set great store by his ability. What evidence we have, for example on the 1270 award, suggests that others did not share his self-esteem, Earl Gilbert forcefully exposing Richard's award as one-sided and short-sighted. Given the repeated difficulties faced by the court during Henry's reign, Richard's political and legal skills may have been exaggerated, but at least they appeared better than Henry's.

Richard was almost a sort of vice-king. He fought for his brother in Brittany in 1230; in Poitou in 1242-3 and against the barons in 1263-4. He was regent in 1253-4, 1264 and, *de facto*, 1270-72. At other times, in the words of the royalist chronicler Thomas Wykes, 'on his nod hung all the business of the realm'. Richard had little consistent political philosophy, unlike his verbose brother who was forever lauding the power of kingship. Some saw Richard as a trickster, a man who would do anything for the right price. In March 1246, he was strongly opposed to papal demands on the English church. By July he had completely changed his mind, adopting a pro-papal stance. Between these dates he had received the papal grant of crusade vow redemptions. Nonetheless, Richard's influence lent an element of cohesion to English politics and it is perhaps significant that the two major disasters for Henry III's regime, the Sicilian Business and the Provisions of Oxford, did not involve Richard, the first because he opposed the scheme from the start; the latter because he was out of the country. His reaction to the papal invitation to conquer Sicily suggests a man of realism: 'You might as well say: I will sell or give you the moon; go up and take it'.

What set Richard apart from other magnates, besides his birth, was his great wealth and the financial role which that allowed him to play. In addition to his very extensive estates centred on Cornwall, Wallingford, Berkhampstead and Eye, he enjoyed the monopoly on Cornish tin (the Stannaries) which alone brought in between 1,000 and 3,000 marks a year, the cash redemption of crusade vows and tallages from the Jews. Such were his resources that he was able to retain many of his noble followers on crusade. Between 1240 and 1271, he lent the crown just under £40,000. In 1256-7, he spent 28,000 marks buying the votes of three German electors. Most spectacularly, in 1247, he undertook the farm of the royal Mint for twelve years, during which time coinage worth £1 million was produced, and organised the first complete recoinage since 1180. For a capital outlay of 10,000 marks, Richard made profits of perhaps £20,000. The recoinage was perhaps Richard's most constructive act in government. At times, it appeared that Richard's finances and those of the state were synonymous, recognised in 1271 when his own treasurer, Philip of Eye, became the king's Treasurer.

This Croesus had political ambitions. He wanted to become a king. So, in keeping with the grandeur of his brother's foreign policy, in 1257 Richard bought himself one, the crown of Germany. For a few years it seemed possible that he would be able to persuade the pope to crown him emperor as well. In the event, although crowned king of the Romans (*i.e.* emperor-designate) at Aachen in May 1257, he was never more than king of the Rhineland and even that was largely honorific, his four brief visits (1257-9; 1260; 1262-3; 1268-9) having more ceremonial than political significance. It was through his German connections that in 1269 he married his third wife, Beatrice of Falkenburg (*d*.1277), like the other two a noted beauty.

After 1260, Richard saw that his imperial longings were as chimeric as his brother's Sicilian hopes had been. During the baronial wars of the 1260s, Richard, although again acting as mediator in trying to increase magnate support for the royalists, was a consistent advocate of his brother's cause. By 1264, he pushed for a military solution, although himself no warrior. After the surprise defeat of the royalists at Lewes, he was captured in a nearby windmill attempting to make good his escape. From May 1264 until September 1265 he was held in comfortable captivity. Thereafter, while profiting from grants of land from the disinherited rebels, he worked for compromise, but power had shifted to the next generation, to the Lord Edward and Richard's own son Henry, surnamed 'of Almain' in deference to his father's German crown. Only when Edward and Henry departed on crusade in 1270, did Richard again emerge as a leading political figure, his brother by then having slid into the shadows of senility. Ironically, Richard predeceased his brother, dying in April 1272 four months after a debilitating stroke. His passing, followed in November by Henry III, marks an epoch in English political history. They were the last of the Angevins, whose ambitions were neither predominantly English nor British.

N. Denholm-Young, *Richard of Cornwall*, 1947.


**SIMON DE MONTFORT** (*c*.1208-1265) is one of the most famous men in English history. Mistaken by Victorians as the founder of parliamentary government, Simon led the most concerted and radical attempt to control royal power and authority before the seventeenth century. For three months in 1263 and another fifteen in 1264-65, Simon ruled England ostensibly in the name of a programme of reform devised in 1258-9 which denied the free exercise of the royal prerogative, instead insisting on government by council, consent by parliament, accountable central and local administration, and justice equitable in recognising the interests and liberties of barons, knights, gentry, freemen and even peasants. Royalty was put into commission on behalf of the *communitas regni*, the community of the realm, led by barons but acting with regard to a wider political nation. Montfort's failure was personal, political and ideological. Later generations removed incompetent or malicious monarchs through deposition. His problem of limiting the authority of a sane, adult monarch was essentially the same faced by the Army and Parliament in 1648-9 when for the first time a solution was hit upon more revolutionary than that attempted by Simon de Montfort.

Simon was no plaster hero of liberty or constitutionalism. If, in Sir Maurice Powicke's words, he was a 'kind of saint', he was also 'a public nuisance'. Idealism was matched by avarice; conscience by harshness; piety by pride. He wore a hair-shirt, yet travelled in magnificence. By circumstance an adventurer and by instinct and ambition a ruler, he possessed adamantine principle and arrogant self-righteousness, a defender of liberties and a nepotist. Quick-witted, serious-minded, silver-tongued yet acerbic, his personality charmed, dazzled, confused, angered and frightened, his memory reviled by enemies and revered by pilgrims. For a generation after his arrival in England in 1230 a well-connected younger son with nothing to commend him but a famous name and a reputation as a good warrior, Simon scorched the political world of England and northern France in a career so dramatic, indeed improbable, that his violent and sordid end can almost appear classically tragic.

Simon de Montfort's father and namesake had a career every bit as remarkable as his son. The elder Simon (c.1170-1218), a cruel, pious man, had fought on the Fourth Crusade (1202-4) and in 1209 had assumed the leadership of the crusade against the Albigensians. With military command he ruled areas conquered from the heretics and their allies which he secured by a crushing victory at Muret (1213). Simon bore responsibility for the bestiality of the crusaders' treatment of opponents, heretics or Christians. In 1218, he met his death, crushed by a stone flung from a mangonel at the siege of Toulouse. Simon's connection with England was the part interest he had through his mother in the earldom of Leicester, a claim acknowledged in 1205/6 without any practical results. Such was Simon's fame that there were rumours that in 1210 or 1212 barons disaffected from King John thought of offering him the English crown. The younger Simon retained a keen and sometimes touchy loyalty to the memory of a father many of whose attitudes, abilities and ambitions he shared.

*Simon de Montfort's dismemberment*
*after the Battle of Evesham in 1265*
(From an early fourteenth century Rochester manuscript)

Young Simon's inheritance was crucial in forming his career. The third son of a famous father, he had close contacts throughout the highest reaches of the French nobility and church: both Louis IX and Eudes Rigaud, archbishop of Rouen were among his friends; but he had no patrimony of his own. His links with France and a ceaseless quest for patronage made Simon an unusual and often uncomfortable member of the English nobility. Unlike most mid-thirteenth century barons, Montfort could escape local political difficulties across the Channel and could, as with the county of Bigorre in the 1250s, seek estates outside England. In this international aspect, Simon and Henry III had more in common with each other than either had with the majority of the English baronage. However, until the last few years of his life, Simon never had the estates commensurate with his status and ambitions. Unmatched by financial stability, his political pretensions caused friction. The surprise is that, despite a consistent need for royal favour, Simon was able to be so much his own man. In that sense, Henry III only had himself to blame for creating and maintaining Montfort in power and influence, ultimately a fact not lost on the king. But, by skill and audacity, Simon forced himself into Henry's favour so far that he could not be removed without major disruption.

First arriving in England in 1230, Simon rapidly established himself as a prominent figure at Henry III's court. The young king, perhaps because of his experience with the litigious and dour native barons who ruled his youth, had a penchant for Frenchmen who shared his cosmopolitan outlook and whose political loyalties could be guaranteed. Successively he favoured Poitevin veterans of his father's reign, Savoyard relatives of his wife and his Lusignan half-brothers. Although Simon fitted this pattern, he retained his independence. Before joining Henry on the Breton campaign of 1230, he had earned fame as a soldier, possibly in Languedoc in 1228-9. Simon also sought his own alliances in the English nobility as claimant to the earldom of Leicester, to which end he attracted the patronage of the aged Ranulf of Chester, premier baron in England. Not the least of Simon's skills was that of impressing people.

In the 1230s, Montfort exerted powerful influence over King Henry, their relationship providing one of the most unusual political and personal confrontations in English history. Henry moved from affection to jealousy to suspicion to hatred, while Simon affected cooler emotions. Unafraid to exploit the king's friendship for gain, Simon frequently displayed open disdain and contempt for Henry, making their contacts increasingly uneasy. Yet they were yoked together by Simon's ambition and Henry's position as the man who could best further them. The final scene of their relationship, at Evesham in 1265, when Henry, captive and in borrowed armour, was forced into the field to see Simon butchered by the troops of his own son and Montfort's godson, Edward, is too dramatic for fiction.

Tangible rewards held Simon at the English court. In 1231, he was given the honour of Leicester. Rising in influence, by 1236-7 he was thought to be a dominant voice in royal counsels. In 1238, his prospects were transformed by his hasty marriage to the king's strong-minded sister, Eleanor (1215-75). She brought Simon lands (including her dowry from her first marriage to William Marshal (d.1231), loyalty and status. In 1239, Simon was invested with the earldom of Leicester. The marriage was a success. They had five sons and a daughter and Eleanor pursued their mutual interests with a vigour equalling her husband's. The liaison was not without scandal. Eleanor had taken vows of chastity after the death of her first husband and it was rumoured that Simon had seduced her before the wedding, which was conducted almost in secret.

By agreeing to the marriage, King Henry ensured his new brother-in-law a central role in English politics, an opportunity Simon grasped with enthusiasm. He fought alongside Henry in Poitou in 1242 and Wales in 1245. In 1248-52, he governed Gascony effectively if controversially. In 1253-4, he assisted the king in his successful campaign there. With his contacts at the French court, Simon was repeatedly used in diplomatic missions, especially in the negotiations preparatory to the Treaty of Paris (1259) in which his wife, as a child of King John, had a direct stake. In domestic politics, until the late 1250s, Simon tended to take the curial side: that was where the rewards in land, fees, pensions, wardships *etc.* came from. Out of self-interest, Montfort did not oppose Henry III's personal rule.

However, Simon's loyalty was neither without tension nor unconditional. In 1239, in a row over Simon's use of the king's name to borrow money, the king was only narrowly dissuaded from throwing him into the Tower. As it was the Montforts went into exile. In 1242, after the fiasco at Saintes, Simon's exasperation at Henry's amoebic military style, boiled over, telling the king he should be locked up, a gibe which Henry stored in bitterness for twenty years. In 1252, Simon was arraigned for being both too harsh and too extravagant in Gascony. Once again the dispute took a nasty personal turn, Henry accusing Montfort of being a traitor to which the earl replied by questioning the king's credentials as a Christian.

Another source of dispute which finally destroyed Simon's allegiance to Henry III was financial. As a parvenu with four healthy sons, Simon was desperate to establish a substantial patrimony of his own to endow his dynasty. Apart from Leicester, much of his property was not held in fee (i.e. heritable) and his wife's was primarily dower lands which would leave family control on her death. As the 1240s and 1250s progressed, Simon had three central grievances. First, the king owed him money; secondly, specifically, Eleanor was not receiving her due from her dower lands, in 1259 Simon claiming that the arrears amounted to over 36,000 marks; and thirdly the king refused to convert grants of money and tenancies into heritable lands. The

importance of these considerations to Simon was demonstrated
by the way Henry bought his support with grants and the manner in which Montfort exploited his political position in 1259-61
and 1263-5 to amass a vast patrimony. With Simon, private gain
always walked beside public policy. The two combined to dictate
resistance to the king in the late 1250s when Henry's concentration of patronage on the Lusignans aroused Simon's indignation. Ironically, in 1264-5, his concentration on his own nearest
relatives lost him baronial support just as surely as Henry's
identical policy had in 1258.

Away from England, Simon acquired a stature which suggests
qualities beyond those of an adept featherer of his own nest.
Like his father, he was a crusader, taking the cross twice, in 1236
and 1247, and visiting the Holy Land in 1240-1. One unexpected
result was the request in June 1241 by the 'barons, knights and
citizens' of the commune of Acre to the Emperor Frederick II to
appoint Simon as governor of the kingdom of Jerusalem. In
1253, the French nobility offered Simon the stewardship of
France in the continued absence of Louis IX in Palestine, ostensibly because of his father's reputation and the earl's own love of
France and French blood. During the first five years of the so-
called baronial reform movement, 1258-63, its supposed champion spent half his time across the Channel. This made his
political choices easier, as he did not have to stay in England to
cope with their consequences or compromise. It is equally
significant that in the final two years of his life, he only visited
the land of his birth for a few days.

Simon de Montfort's adherence to the baronial confederacy of
April 1258 which led to the Provisions of Oxford and the oath to
uphold them in June was a turning point in his life. Although he
had been driven into opposition by largely selfish motives concerning patronage and the fear of a military coup by the Lusignans, and continued to milk the reform movement and the king
for material gain, his commitment to the reform programme was
sincere. He took oaths seriously; he saw himself as religiously
obligated to abide by the terms agreed and sworn at Oxford. To
this oath, while never missing an opportunity to gain secular
advantage, he held firm. The combination of principle and self-
interest aroused cynicism in observers and it is a measure of

Simon's own self-assurance that he was able to suppress in his own mind the inevitable contradictions. Just before the battle of Evesham, knowing he was doomed, he apparently turned on his son Henry: 'your presumption and the pride of your brothers has brought me to this end'. In fact, it was Simon's own presumption and pride that had permitted the excesses of his children.

The importance Simon attached to the oath of 1258 is of a part with his spiritual life. Simon was more than a mercenary bully with a sharp wit and ready sword. He numbered among his close friends and mentors Robert Grosseteste, one of the sternest moralists of the day, the Franciscan Adam Marsh, who was his spiritual counsellor, and the saintly Cantelupes, Walter and Thomas. Through them he was in touch both with the theology and learning of the nascent university of Oxford, but also the fresh religious emphasis on lay piety through confession and the practices of personal devotion. Central to both were conscience and asceticism. It was King Henry's lack of these that Simon hurled in his face in 1252. The language of his will of 1259 reveals a man acutely aware of the reality of sin. It is shot through with the remorse of a troubled conscience, the more convincing because private, hidden, like his hair-shirt. Simon was nothing if not thoughtful. He appreciated the importance of learning. He had his sons well educated: the eldest Henry actually wrote out the 1259 will; Amaury later composed a treatise on alchemy a copy of which, in his own handwriting, survives in the Bodleian Library, Oxford. Simon's academic concerns were tinged with morality. From Grosseteste, he learned of the Aristotelian distinction between just and tyrannical rule; but by Adam Marsh he was told how to apply conscience and faith to his daily life. At least two independent sources, although with the historical disadvantage of hindsight, comment on how the oath of 1258 intensified Simon's already extensive private devotions and self-denial, even to the point of abstinence from sexual intercourse with his wife.

For one so committed to the 1258 oath, Simon's role was less prominent in the initial implementation of the reform programme in 1259. This established control of royal actions by a standing council, which also determined appointments. Abuses by local officials, royal and baronial, were to be investigated by a new judicial eyre and grievances redressed. The key concept was justice and the recognisition of the liberties (*i.e.* customary legal rights) of subjects. The king should be governed and govern according to established laws, rather than by his own volition. Such ideas had the virtue of being academically up-to-date and coinciding with the practical desires of a political nation which, for almost the first time, was acknowledged as including more than the nobility. What had begun as a factional move against royal favourites became a root and branch reform of government and the constitution.

In the conduct of this revolution, Simon's role was sporadic and occasionally inconsistent. In the autumn of 1260, for example, by allying himself with the Lord Edward and the earl of Gloucester, Montfort was re-admitted to influence at the price of watering down the Provisions' commitment to investigate baronial officials. However, when, in 1261, Henry III skilfully engineered himself back into power, persuading the pope to repudiate his oath to the Provisions, Simon was energetic in organising armed resistance to this *revanche*, to little avail. In doing so, he signalled what was to become a lasting legacy of the movement when in September 1261 he summoned three knights from each shire to meet him at St. Alban's. This came to nothing, as the king trumped him by summoning a similar assembly at the same time, but it shows Simon's understanding of the importance of gaining the support of those outside the baronage, those who were increasingly assuming local power.

In 1262-3, the cause of reform faded, the king reviving charges against Simon, who was basking in the comfortable refuge of northern France. But a series of political accidents and a threat of war with Wales undermined Henry's position. Simon returned to England to take command of the disparate forces opposed to the king, including disaffected Marcher barons, the new earl of Gloucester, alienated followers of the Lord Edward as well as reformers. At no time were reformers a majority among the barons or shire knights. Perhaps only in the church, or at least the university educated elite and the friars, was the cause of reform given the transcendent moral aura which Simon himself attached to it. But from his return to England in April

1263 until his death at Evesham in August 1265, Simon placed the cause of reform at the centre of politics, backed up by his own military skill.

This briefly won for him power in the summer of 1263, when he ably exploited a wave of anti-alien feeling to impose himself on the king's council. But, ominously, he was unable to provide order which was imperative if effective reform, especially at local level, was to be implemented. By early 1264, following the condemnation of the Provisions by Louis IX at the Mise of Amiens (from which Simon, usually so persuasive on such occasions, was absent because of a broken leg), the reformers' plight was desperate. To identify his position with a just cause even more clearly, Simon's troops had begun to wear the white crosses of English crusaders to the Holy Land. But at Lewes in May 1264, whatever the element of divine intervention, it was generalship and luck that gave Simon victory over superior royalist forces. Soon he had negotiated (in the so-called Mise of Lewes) the surrender into his hands of the king, his sons and his brother, Richard of Cornwall. Now master of England, Montfort spent the next six months trying to gain popular support and raising an army large enough to deter a threatened invasion by royalists in France. His role in the summer of 1264 has been likened by his most recent and best biographer to that of Winston Churchill in 1940. Like Churchill, when the invasion scare was over, Simon reaped the political harvest, if only briefly.

The problem for Montfort's regime was its lack of legitimacy. Condemned by popes and the king of France, Simon lived the fiction that he was acting in the name of the king. Apart from the ineffectual title of Steward of England associated with his earldom he lacked formal office. To widen his appeal, as well as implement the Provisions' principles of consultation and justice, he summoned two parliaments in 1264-5, to the second of which, meeting in January, he requested the presence of burgesses from towns and knights from the shires. In the development of parliamentary institutions, this was but a small marker, not an epoch-making initiative. Formal assemblies of prelates and magnates to give advice and consent had been commonplace at least since the reign of King John. Knights had been consulted in national assemblies as early as 1213 and 1227.

Frequently, the main purpose of such assemblies had been to approve taxation, following the principles of *Magna Carta*. The name 'parliament' first appears in official records in 1237, thereafter inconsistently. In 1254, separate or joint assemblies of prelates, magnates and knights were convened, as they were in June 1264 by the Montfort government. The precedent of January 1265, the addition of burgesses, was not commonly repeated until Edward I's reign. For the first effective parliamentary scrutiny of fiscal policy, it is to the assemblies of the end of Henry's reign concerning money for Edward's crusade that the historian must turn. The Provisions of Oxford were clear that control of the executive was in the hands of a council chosen and run by the barons. The significance of the January parliament of 1265 was immediate and political, not visionary and constitutional. There was urgent business to discuss, namely the release of Edward, and the need to extend support for Montfort's narrow factional oligarchy to embrace as wide a section of the local communities as possible.

Simon de Montfort was not the father of parliamentary government, still less parliamentary democracy. However, by the nature of the cause, its clerical support and the lack of baronial sympathy, Simon was forced to become the first populist political leader in English history. He appealed to and won the adherence of freemen and peasants not previously used to the glare of active participation in national politics. Partly through the preaching of the clergy, especially the friars, who seemed more supportive than the laity, Simon's cause of restricting royal prerogative was transformed into a moral crusade for liberty, justice and virtue. Simon was aware of this and played to it.

Whatever his attempts to involve the people of England in a revivalist campaign for political renewal, the reality was increasingly grim. In 1265, Simon's position was gravely weakened by the defection of Gilbert of Clare, earl of Gloucester (March), the invasion of William of Valence, rebellion by the Marcher lords and the escape of Edward (May). Much of the blame for his predicament lay with Simon himself. His excessive patronage of his own sons made him no more palatable to the barons than Henry III. Their own loutish and rapacious behaviour ranked them as no better than the loathed Lusignans. Simon's regime was too narrowly based among the powerful of the realm to survive. Montfort's rule was too partisan and selfish to garner wider sympathy. The single-mindedness that had won him power destroyed him. Over-confident, over-ambitious, avaricious for self and family, unsuccessful in translating principles into policies, Simon did not, as R. F. Treharne believed, add 'greatness' to this period, merely extremism and exaggeration. Except in a few dons' cells, his position was as untenable ideologically as it was politically. Events of 1264-5 had made the compromises sought in earlier years impossible. There were even signs that Simon was toying with transferring the crown from the Angevins to the Montforts, a logical, if desperate recognition of the fundamental flaws in the Provisions of Oxford. In the end, the issue was not about justice but authority. On that score, Simon's pretensions were vapid.

The final act was, appropriately, military. Outmanoeuvred in ideas and politics, this most intellectual and politically adroit ruler was to be defeated by superior military skill and his own tactical blunders in the campaign to secure the Severn in the summer of 1265. His career had come full circle. He had first attracted notice as a commander. His military prowess had been proved from Wales to Syria: his fortifications at Kenilworth were so good that they withstood the longest siege in English history (six months in 1266). When he saw the speed and skill of the army of Edward and Clare springing the trap at Evesham, he exclaimed: 'By the arm of St. James, they come on well: they did not learn that for themselves but from me'. Humility was a virtue Simon de Montfort's spiritual advisers had been pressing on him for years.

Simon's defeat and death at Evesham was appropriate in another way. Through him, England experienced popular violence and civil war unknown for half a century and an aristocratic bloodbath not seen since Hastings. Simon's own harshness rebounded upon him. However civilised and devout, Montfort was eager to resort to war; he massacred Jews with contemporary eagerness; he cared little for the interests of others except on an almost metaphysical level. His Will talks of his regret at his treatment of the poor. Did he think of them when he grabbed for power and ruled through coercion? Or was his no doubt genuine remorse and self-doubt that of which confessions are made: spiritually uplifting personally but of little value to his victims? Like Thomas Becket, he identified his own desires completely with the interest of his cause, a dangerous arrogance, the mentality of the tyrant through the ages. Simon de Montfort was not a hypocrite or a charlatan, but in life he did as little to merit the prayers of those who sought his shrine at Evesham as he did the sordid indignities inflicted on his body. It is hard to avoid admiring the tenacity with which he espoused what he saw genuinely as his duty; it is also hard to ignore how his actions so debased political life that it was acceptable for his killers to send to Lady Mortimer his severed head, hands and testicles.

J. R. Maddicott, *Simon de Montfort*, 1994.

**ELEANOR OF PROVENCE** (*d*.1291; queen of England 1236-72) was the second daughter of Raymond Berengar IV, count of Provence and Beatrice of Savoy. In January 1236, she married Henry III of England as part of the king's attempts to outbid his rival, Louis IX of France, who had married Eleanor's eldest sister, Margaret. The prize was influence in the strategically vital territory controlled by her father. This straddled the routes from France and south-west Germany to Italy and, thus, to the papacy, for over half a century the cockpit of European conflict as Hohenstaufen, Capetian, Guelph and Ghibelline battled for control of the peninsula. The importance of Provence-Savoy was confirmed by the marriages of Eleanor's younger sisters to Richard of Cornwall and Charles of Anjou, who respectively became king of Germany and king of Naples. To England with Eleanor came her uncles, on whom Henry showered favour, in particular Boniface of Savoy, archbishop of Canterbury; William, bishop-elect of Valence and Peter, who became lord of Richmond. Although mainly recruited to help Henry's continental schemes, these Savoyards aroused the dislike and suspicion of native barons and chroniclers who feared their power and aggressive pursuit of rights. Their unpopularity attached itself to the queen. She managed the rare feat of being disliked both by her husband's Lusignan relatives and by the king's enemies, famously the Londoners who, in 1263, attacked her barge. In

France 1263-65, she apparently failed to raise mercenaries for her husband's cause, plunging heavily in debt, not for the first time apparently. In 1276, she took the veil at Amesbury, although retaining property and influence within her family. In 1290, her son Edward I convened a family conference at Amesbury at which he settled matters concerning the marriages of his children and the succession to the kingdom. Eleanor, although on occasion formally acting on her husband's behalf, played no independent political role, but received a poor press for all that.

**ALEXANDER OF HALES** (1170/80-1245) was prominent as a philosopher in the attempt to reconcile newly acquired texts of Aristotle to Christian revelation and as the earliest Franciscan professor of theology at the University of Paris. An Englishman by birth, he followed the conventional path of an ambitious clergyman whose interests went beyond the cure of souls. A prebendary of St. Paul's Cathedral and archdeacon of Coventry, he apparently acquired the wealth necessary to pursue his academic career. Although he remained, according to Roger Bacon, honest, it is unlikely that his ecclesiastical jobs occupied him fully, any more than similar positions engaged men like Geoffrey of Monmouth, Gerald of Wales, Walter Map or Peter of Blois to the exclusion of all else. By the 1220s he was lecturing successfully at Paris where he joined the new Mendicant Order of St. Francis. In about 1231 he helped found the Franciscan school at Paris, becoming its first professor. Although Alexander resigned his Chair in 1238, the establishment of the Franciscans within the University of Paris, then the leading centre of theological studies in northern Europe, was of great significance both for the study of theology and history of the Franciscan Order. Rapidly, the order which had begun as a reaction against the wealth, corruption and compromises of material life became embroiled in fierce academic debates and institutional rivalries both with the traditional university authorities and with the other mendicants, the Dominicans. The Franciscan Order, with its international network and internal discipline, attracted some of the most fertile intellects of the day working on philosophy and theology. Alexander's own most influential work was a *Commentary* on the *Sentences* of Peter Lombard (*d.*1160). The

*Sentences* were a compendium of questions drawn from the Bible and the Church Fathers each of which contained conflicting authoritative opinions about God, Creation, the Incarnation, Redemption and the Sacraments. Lombard resolved the contradictions through dialectic: the question was followed by two answers, one contrary to the other, in the discussion of which opposing statements a solution was reached. This process of inquiry, the so-called *quaestio* technique, became the basis of the scholastic method which dominated philosophical discourse for generations and marked the contributions of some of the most outstanding medieval theologians, notably the Dominican Thomas Aquinas (1226-74). Alexander's *Commentary* incorporated Aristotelian arguments within a rigidly syllogistic framework. Perhaps his greatest influence on thirteenth century thought was exercised through his pupils, outstanding among whom was St. Bonaventura (1221-74), the leading Franciscan theologian of his generation who, as head of the Order, redefined the ideals of St. Francis to accommodate the Order's new and active role in worldly affairs. Alexander's greatest intellectual legacy was the synthetical *Summa Theologica*, a work often, but wrongly, attributed to him, produced at papal request before 1250. The *Summa* reflects Alexander's arguments about God being the source of all ideas and images and, thus, that knowledge is derived not distinctly but from the intellect confronting such divine creations. The *Summa* was a massive work, designed as a sort of philosophical treasury for Franciscans but which, according to Friar Roger Bacon, was heavier than a horse, unusable and ultimately left to rot. Nevertheless, Alexander made a significant contribution to scholastic method and the invasion of Aristotelianism into Christian theology and its triumph over earlier Arabic glosses. This conquest dominated intellectual debate in general, and the study of philosophy and theology in particular, for more than two centuries. Alexander's own adoption of the life of a Mendicant Friar, combining intellectual sophistication with simplicity of living, points to a catalyst which was to produce much of the subtlest thought of the later middle ages. Alexander's achievement was not insular. Like Stephen Langton before him, he acquired his reputation in Paris and his influence embraced Western Christendom.

**ROBERT GROSSETESTE** (*c*.1170-1253; bishop of Lincoln 1235-1253), theologian, natural scientist and church reformer, was one of the most controversial figures in mid-thirteenth century England. Traditionally, it was thought he had studied at Paris and Oxford where he had been elected the first Chancellor of the University in 1214, already a theologian of substance. Recent research by R. W. Southern has shown that this picture is almost certainly false. Instead, a more unusual career emerges, of provincial obscurity and a much later flowering of talent and influence. Born at Stow Langtoft in Suffolk, Grosseteste probably received his early education in Lincoln and Cambridge. Described as *magister* before 1192, he met the chronicler Gerald of Wales *c*.1194/5 who was impressed by his knowledge of law, the liberal arts and medicine. For the next thirty years, Grosseteste was connected with the diocese of Hereford, much of it in the household of Hugh Foliot, archdeacon of Shropshire and later bishop of Hereford (1219-34). During this period, apart from administrative tasks, Grosseteste concentrated on mathematics, astronomy (*i.e.* astrology) and the natural sciences. He may also have done some peripatetic teaching. Lacking the financial support of a benefice, any more permanent academic position was not feasible. Possibly as a consequence of involvement in ecclesiastical attempts to emancipate the young Henry III from baronial control in 1221-3, even perhaps as a result of working for the king himself, Grosseteste, although still only in deacon's orders, received his first benefice, the lucrative rectorship of Abbotsley (Hunts.), in 1225.

This was the turning point of his life. At the age of *c*.fifty-five he now had the financial security to indulge his academic interests. He turned to theology and to teaching in Oxford. He was an instant success. By 1230, he had been elected Chancellor by the secular masters of the university, in the teeth of opposition from the bishop of Lincoln. He was archdeacon of Leicester (1229-32), as well as a prebend at Lincoln cathedral. In 1230 Grosseteste, like many other contemporary intellectuals, had some form of conversion experience which tempted him to join a Mendicant Order. Instead, he contented himself with becoming the theology lecturer for the Franciscans in Oxford. He retained influence in the university, however, in 1234 being entrusted with the hopeless task of expelling prostitutes from Oxford. At this time, he began to learn Greek in an attempt to synthesise Greek philosophy, science and theology with the Latin and Patristic inheritance. He had already come into contact with important secular figures, such as Simon de Montfort with whose expulsion of the Jews from Leicester in 1231 Grosseteste had been closely involved. Nevertheless, despite his long association with the diocese, his election in 1235 to the bishopric of Lincoln, covering, as it did, about one fifth of the population of England, was something of a surprise. If expectations had been of quiet rule by an aged don, they were severely disappointed.

Grosseteste proved himself a courageous and outspoken radical; scourge of lay encroachments and clerical backsliding; opponent alike of king and pope. At the heart of his ministry was a very extended interpretation of the pastoral role of a bishop embracing matters of sin, the welfare of souls, morality and administration: episcopal rights of visitation, pluralities, appointments to benefices, canon law etc. Within his diocese he attempted to impose the legatine decrees of 1237; he insisted on his authority to examine and, if necessary reject any candidate for a benefice; he maintained his right to visit (*i.e.* to investigate and reorganise) monasteries and his own cathedral chapter; he asserted his authority to dismiss and excommunicate errant clergy. On all fronts he made enemies: those patrons, including the king and the pope, whose candidates he rejected; the canons of his cathedral whose autonomy he challenged; the monks whose independence and control of churches he threatened; fellow clergy whose pluralities he condemned. His unorthodox career and his not belonging to the social elite which dominated the English episcopate gave him the freedom to attack many of the cozy habits, such as pluralism, which were accepted even by some contemporary reformers. On the other hand, if he was, in Matthew Paris's words, an 'indefatigable persecutor of monks', he was a patron of friars, notably his Oxford protégé Adam Marsh. He regarded friars as providing spiritual and moral purity lacking elsewhere in the clergy. But even here, he found criticisms as the Mendicants began to adapt their rules to suit their greater secular involvement.

Throughout the Middle Ages, Christian renewal tended to be of two kinds: spiritual revival or institutional reform. Grosseteste attempted both. His hopes for the creation of a truly Godly society were, however, over-ambitious. He wanted an authoritarian Church divorced from the habits of social authority. His policies were doomed to fail. As he grew older, the realisation of this prompted bitterness at his ecclesiastical superiors and an increasingly apocalyptic vision of Christendom's future. In 1250, he visited the pope at Lyons and delivered a blistering attack on the corruption of the church. Although previously a supporter of papal jurisdiction and taxation, the apparently increased venality of papal demands and its cynical exploitation of authority to manipulate the church to its own and its allies' secular advantage, convinced Grosseteste that the curia was the *causa, fons et origo*. The Lyons speech was typically audacious, courageous and fruitless. Increasingly disillusioned, on his deathbed in 1253, he prophesied the dissolution of Christendom. Others in the thirteenth century said much the same thing, but few went as far as the dying Grosseteste in identifying the pope himself as the Antichrist

His wider political influence can be assessed by his large surviving correspondence. He had contacts with the greatest in the land; opinions and advice on all the major issues of the day. His austere refusal to compromise on morality or faith cast him in the role of an Anselm rather than a Langton. He set standards that few were willing or able to meet: a moral arbiter and guide, not a factional leader. Yet, at least in the circle of the pious Simon de Montfort, his influence was great: radical, critical and self-righteous.

It is however as a scholar that he was most renowned. His early scientific interests were founded on the theoretical study of geometry and optics and his own experience and observation (*experimentum*) of the natural world. He extended these techniques of expounding general rules from specific examples when he turned to study Aristotelian philosophy and Scriptural theology in the 1220s. Although his approach was idiosyncratic in not following the usual Paris/Oxford models, his theology leaned heavily on the basic scholastic texts such as Peter Lombard's *Sentences*. Grosseteste, however, placed emphasis on the Bible rather than later glosses. This led to his appreciation of the need to study ancient languages. No less than his scholarly contemporaries, Grosseteste believed in the unity of creation and knowledge. In *De Luce* (*c*.1235-40), his study of optics and light is employed to discuss God's role as creator of the natural world. Experimental science he saw assisting the understanding of scripture and living a Christian life. The new weapon of theology, Greek was used to translate Aristotle's philosophical work *The Ethics*. Grosseteste also believed in addressing as wide an audience as possible: his *Château d'Amour*, a poem in French, provided an outline of Christian theology for a lay audience. Because his approach was so individual, so eclectic, and he himself such a maverick, Grosseteste founded no school. In his declaration of the primacy of the Bible and in his attacks on ecclesiastical corruption he later had a fan in John Wyclif. If he had a disciple, it was Roger Bacon, the troubled Oxford Franciscan: 'Lord Robert . . . was the only one above all men to know the sciences'. But for the rest of educated Christendom there was something rough-hewn, eccentric or, simply, unexpected about Grosseteste's thought. Its originality was, like its author, unsettling and challenging.

R. W. Southern, *Robert Grosseteste*, 1986.

**ADAM MARSH** (*d*. after 1259) was an early Franciscan scholar whose friendships with Robert Grosseteste and Simon de Montfort linked the new Order with innovative academic investigation, ecclesiastical reform and radical politics. His reputation relies chiefly on his surviving correspondence: very little of his academic work remains or has been identified. Marsh appears as a confidant and adviser, not a leader or shaper of the destinies of others. Preferment within the church may have been denied him by his own volition, by his Friar's vocation or by political suspicion of his purist views.

He had the credentials for a successful ecclesiastical career. A nephew of Richard Marsh, bishop of Durham (1217-27), after education at Oxford, where he became a leading Master of Arts, he sustained his position as a wealthy secular clerk and scholar by holding the living of Wearmouth. From this period dates his connection with Grosseteste who became a close friend. The original contact may have been when Grosseteste gathered around him a group of scholars, including Marsh, to translate the newly available Greek philosophical and scientific texts. Marsh possibly encountered the Franciscans in Oxford through Grosseteste who was their patron and regent of the Oxford Franciscans 1229-35. Seeking fresh ways of understanding the temporal world, Grosseteste's group was infected by the new way of religious life offered by the Mendicant Orders. Marsh's secretary abandoned the academic life for that of a missionary friar and this influence may have persuaded Marsh, already a famous teacher, to take the Franciscan habit c.1232.

Such a translation scarcely interrupted Marsh's career. At Oxford he continued to lecture and write on a range of subjects from Biblical commentaries and works on penance to mathematics, languages and natural philosophy (i.e. what passed in the thirteenth century for science). Between 1247 and 1249, he was regent of the friar's school at Oxford, the first of the Order to be so. Roger Bacon, an Oxford near-contemporary and fellow Franciscan, loyally coupled Marsh with Grosseteste as the two leading philosophers of his time. Within the Order, Marsh took a stand against excessive erosion of the original Franciscan ideal of poverty, although accepting the need for secular proctors to handle money for the necessities of life. There was inevitable compromise between St Francis's precepts and the realities of running an international organisation whose functions expanded beyond those of local charity or missionising. Whatever his theoretical position, Marsh's own career pointed up potential contradictions and tensions which were to split the Order in the early fourteenth century and lead to some so-called Spiritual Franciscans, who followed their founder's Rule with pristine severity, being condemned as heretics.

Away from Oxford, he moved freely in the greatest secular and ecclesiastical circles. An observer at the trial of Simon de Montfort for maladministration of Gascony in 1252, Marsh developed an intense admiration for him, acting almost as his secretary as well as spiritual and political adviser. Marsh was one of the earl's executors in 1259. He also facilitated contacts between Simon and Grosseteste, whom he assisted in the administration of the diocese of Lincoln up to 1253. Marsh's influence and abilities were recognised by the king who appointed him to an embassy to France in 1257 to discuss a possible settlement of outstanding territorial disputes. Although exerting much influence as a devout and rigorous friar, Marsh hardly conformed to the pattern of life followed by St Francis. Yet his career was a model of how the new Mendicant Orders could adapt and play a significant role in the wider life of the church and Christendom.

A. G. Little, *Franciscan Papers*, 1943.

**HENRY DE REYNS** (*d.c.*1253) was master of the king's masons and responsible for the rebuilding of Westminster Abbey for Henry III 1245-1253. It was once thought that the undoubted influence on the design of the new Abbey of contemporary northern French Gothic, including Rheims Cathedral, could be attributed to Henry's French origins, but there is no evidence that he was other than English. His name may have derived from the Essex village of Rayne. Alternatively, he may have travelled in France before entering royal service. Although the only direct evidence shows Henry as Keeper of the Works at Wetminster, in charge of paying the labourers and obtaining the materials, including marble and timber, it is probable that he had a hand in devising the architectural scheme. It has been noted that some of the moulding sections at Westminster are almost identical to those at the King's Chapel, Windsor, where Henry may have worked 1239-43. It is also possible that Henry supplied the designs for the abbey at Hailes (1246) built for the king's brother, Richard of Cornwall. From such slight evidence it has been surmised that Henry was the architect of Westminster Abbey. If so, he was a central figure in a project which occupied Henry III's ambitions and treasury for most of his reign as he sought to provide a suitable setting for the shrine of his patron saint, Edward the Confessor, and the relic of the Holy Blood which the king received into the Abbey, then half-demolished and half-built, in a lavish ceremony on the Confessor's Feast Day, 13 October 1247. Such was Henry's importance that he may have been afforded the honour of commemoration in the building he planned. In the Abbey's eastern triforium there is a carved head of a craftsman in the meditative pose used to denote a designer. From the date, it would seem to represent Henry de Reyns.

J. Harvey, *English Mediaeval Architects,* 1987.

**MATTHEW PARIS** (*c.*1200-1259) is one of the most distinguished English historians. Prolific, opinionated, erudite, his chronicles have for centuries shaped views on his period, not least because his prejudices — snobbish, conservative, xenophobic — mirrored those of so many of his successors as historians of thirteenth century England. In 1217, Matthew became a monk at St Alban's, where, with the exception of visits to some important ecclesiastical functions in England and a trip to Norway in 1248, he spent the rest of his life. Although cloistered, Matthew was in no way isolated. St Alban's was a wealthy monastery, conveniently situated on Watling Street within easy reach of London, its guesthouse well-used by the great, the good and the exotic: the abbey hosted Armenians in 1228 and 1252. Among Matthew's informants, many of whom must have stayed at the abbey, were Richard of Cornwall, the king's brother; Hubert de Burgh, the justiciar; Peter des Roches; Robert Grosseteste; and royal officials such as John Mansel. Between 1216 and 1252, Henry III visited St Alban's nine times. In 1247, Matthew attending the ceremonial reception of the Holy Blood at Westminster Abbey, talked to the king who asked him to record all that he had seen and invited him to dinner. On the king's visit to St Alban's in 1257, Matthew hung around the royal guest and dined at his table. The chronicler was obviously something of a celebrity, historiographer to the nobility as well as his monastery.

Matthew's output was prodigious. On the abbey's history he wrote the *Gesta Abbatum (Deeds of the Abbots)* covering the period from the alleged foundation in 793 to 1255 and the *Vitae Offarum (Lives of the Offas)* about Offa of Mercia, the supposed founder of the abbey, and his ancestor Offa of Angeln. For these Matthew, an enthusiastic, if uncritical, believer in thorough documentation, plundered the abbey's archives. His hagiography, which he composed both in Latin prose and, for a lay audience, in French verse, reflected his historical interests, his subjects including St Alban, Edward the Confessor and, for Matthew, the politically correct Archbishops Becket, Langton and Rich, all opponents of royal authority. His masterpiece was the *Chronica majora (Greater Chronicle)*. Begun in 1240, it covered the period from the Creation to 1259. To 1236, Matthew was chiefly dependent on the *Flores Historiarum* of a fellow St Alban's monk Roger of Wendover which Matthew edited and expanded. For the last twenty-three years, however, Matthew was his own source, maintaining an original and almost contemporary account and commentary of events of a range and depth unparalleled in medieval England. His approach was encyclopaedic, cosmopolitan and judgemental. An artist of distinction, Matthew embellished his text with painted heraldic devices, maps (*e.g.* of Palestine; England, Scotland and the world) and numerous vivid marginal line drawings illustrating the narrative. The *Chronica* became bloated by his voracious appetite for information, so around 1250 he began writing shortened versions (the *Flores Historiarum* and *Abbreviatio Chronicarum*); a volume of extracts concerning English history (the *Historia Anglorum*); and a separate book of documents, the *Liber Additamentorum,* which he cross-referenced with the *Chronica majora.* Not only was this a massive historical enterprise, Matthew's original 1236-59 section alone comprising 300,000 words, but much of the actual writing and drawing was done by Matthew himself. On top of this, he found the time to illustrate the works of others.

What prevents this vast enterprise from sinking beneath its own weight is Matthew's readability. This not only turns on the marginal notes and the attractive, almost comic-strip drawings, but also on his style and what he has to say. Matthew's Latin is clear, his narrative easily followed. There are chapter headings, annual summaries of events and neat character sketches of leading figures. He was an early master of the succinct obituary and the telling epigram. Above all, he was an historian, not just a chronicler: he had a definite view on the events he described. His lack of objectivity forms his strength and weakness: it lends intellectual coherence to his work while seducing the reader into accepting his opinions as fact. Like many of his generation,

*Matthew Paris on his deathbed in 1259*
(From the postscript to his Chronica Majora)

surrounded by the seemingly endless conflicts of church, nobles
and king, Matthew had a deep suspicion of any central authority, royal or papal, which appeared to infringe the traditional
rights and habits of locally established hierarchies, noble, clerical or monastic. Although he came to moderate his vilification
of Henry III, perhaps as he got to know the king personally, his
antagonism to the court runs behind all his political analysis.
From Matthew, rather than the documents of government,
derives the familiar picture of Henry III as extravagant, petulant
and easily-led, especially by parasitic Savoyard and Poitevin relatives. As 1258-9 showed, this view was partly shared by some
baronial opponents of royal policy, but it cannot be accepted as
objective. Matthew's fulminations against the papal curia were,
unlike those of Robert Grosseteste, based on institutional self-
interest. Matthew feared papal power because of the possible

encroachments, through patronage of foreigners and taxation, on the freedom (*i.e.* usually, income) of the English church. It is no coincidence that the *Chronica majora* appealed to Elizabeth I's Protestant Archbishop Parker of Canterbury who collected two of Matthew's autograph copies, now at Corpus Christi College, Cambridge. But Matthew's vision of the English church in danger and his insinuation that there was widespread anti-papalism should be treated with caution. Matthew's cynicism at royal and papal motives may appear justified, but not because of Matthew's witness.

Matthew was a traditional Benedictine, proud of an Order somewhat left behind by the new Orders of monks and mendicant friars. The latter were a pet hate: new, ultramontane, and successful. Matthew's political and ecclesiastical model seems to have been that of a Benedictine abbey, autonomous, run by an abbot according to custom and the Rule, with established, immutably defined and mutually recognised obligations to superiors in church and state. This was a central theme of almost all his historical and hagiographical work. What catches the eye may be the descriptions of buffalo; the drawing of the elephant given to Henry III by Louis IX in 1255; the marginal cartoons; the interest in heraldry, art, architecture, and natural science; above all the sheer scale and bulk of the narrative. What cannot be denied is the nature of the literary achievement: the most original and, in the concept of the illustrated chronicle, innovative historical enterprise of its time. Matthew Paris was a historian on the grand scale, amongst Englishmen on a par with Bede, William of Malmesbury, Clarendon and Gibbon. When Matthew's continuator in 1259 claimed he was unworthy to undo the tie of Matthew's shoe, he said no more than the truth. After Matthew, monastic historiography in England, as elsewhere, began to decline. At St Alban's in the fourteenth century there was a revival with Thomas Walsingham, but he was a pale shadow of Matthew Paris.

R. Vaughan, *Matthew Paris*, 1958.

**PETER DES RIVAUX** (*c*.1190-1262) was the son of the powerful Peter des Roches, bishop of Winchester. Born in Normandy, he followed his father in making a career in the service of the Angevin kings of England. A cleric who ultimately held a clutch of lucrative benefices on both sides of the English Channel, Peter's official career centred upon royal finance. It is probably to Peter that the significant reforms of the Exchequer in the 1230s and 1240s should be attributed. Where his father never left the limelight, Peter operated largely away from the glare of political contest.

During the Minority, Peter worked in the royal household. He shared his father's loss of power in 1223 being dismissed as clerk of the Wardrobe. He returned to royal service in the early 1230s and in 1232 became the main instrument of his father's takeover of government. Between 1232 and 1234, Peter effectively controlled the entire financial affairs of the crown, both household and exchequer. Through his offices of treasurer of the household and the Exchequer; keeper of wardships, escheats and the king's small seal; controller of the Mint, ports and the Jews; and, briefly, nominal sheriff of twenty-on counties, Peter, as Matthew Paris put it, had the whole of England under his regulation.

The point of being this financial Poo-Bah was reform. After the civil was of 1215-17, the management of royal revenue had been haphazard. Despite administrative innovations by William of Ely a generation earlier, Exchequer procedures were too cumbersome to be effective. To restore control over raising customary revenue and to maximise its yield required changes at the centre and in the provinces. The political objective was the financial emancipation of the crown from the vested influences of the baronage. Secure and profitable ordinary income would reduce the tensions which had brought the Angevin dynasty to its knees. Magnates would not need to be harassed and the king would not feel exploited or cheated.

Although Peter des Rivaux's extraordinary authority was swept away with the fall of his father's government in 1234, and he himself briefly imprisoned, he was recalled as keeper of the Wardrobe in 1236 and thereafter served the king in numerous posts in the household and the Exchequer until dismissed in 1258 by the baronial reformers, even though many of them had indirectly benefited from the work of Peter and his colleagues over the previous quarter century. The changes had a double thrust. Sheriffs' fiscal role was severely reduced, with separate accounting systems and local agents becoming responsible for the royal demesne, wardships and escheats. Regular commissions investigated the extent of royal rights. At the centre, more intelligible and discrete methods of accounting and keeping records allowed for firmer royal scrutiny and control. Apart from increasing royal profits, the system which emerged during Henry III's personal rule meant the end of extortionate curial sheriffs and heavy-handed general eyres. Sheriffs became more local, their remit more judicial. Although royal rights were vigorously defended, magnates were allowed to enjoy what was theirs broadly unhindered. As the Crown was better able to exploit its own, it had less need to invade what belonged to others: the shires became increasingly what they were to remain, the preserves of the nobility, not the battle ground of royal agents. This highly significant development occurred not through great political upheaval, but partly through the careful and sustained service over decades of increasingly professional administrators of whom Peter des Rivaux, with his brief moment of glory, was one of the most prominent.

**PETER OF SAVOY** (*d*.1268; count of Savoy 1263-8) was one of the brothers of Henry III's mother-in-law. On his marriage in 1236 to Peter's niece, Eleanor of Provence, Henry eagerly employed her uncles to further his expansive international schemes and provide political ballast at home. Peter's elder brother, William, bishop-elect of Valence (*d*.1239), was briefly a dominant figure in royal councils 1236-7. His clerk, Peter d'Aigueblanche stayed in England to become one of Henry's most valued officials and diplomats, as well as bishop of Hereford (1240-68). Another brother, Boniface, became archbishop of Canterbury (1241-70). On Peter were lavished the largest secular rewards, including the honour of Richmond and the wardenship of the Cinque Ports. Knighted by Henry in 1241, Peter, while never abandoning his continental interests, became an influential English courtier and magnate. As such, he attracted the opprobrium of nationalist observers, such as Matthew Paris who invented scurrilous stories of Peter importing bevies of foreign ladies to corrupt English aristocrats. Henry found in Peter a diplomat, whose existing European experience was usefully employed on his behalf. It is a sign of how Henry mismanaged his affairs that Peter was one of the original seven nobles, led by another foreigner Simon de Montfort, who in April 1258 formed a sworn commune to reform English government. Although Peter soon abandoned the opposition, with the rest he had acted out of resentment at the favours given to the king's Lusignan relatives. Reconciled with Henry, Peter was active on his behalf before leaving England in 1262. The following year he succeeded his nephew as count of Savoy. Although resented by insular chroniclers and jealous rivals within the English nobility, Peter's energy, administrative proficiency, wide geographical range of action and military skill earned him the nickname of 'little Charlemagne'. The role that Peter and his Savoyard brothers played in English political life exposed a gulf which divided the cosmopolitan Angevin monarch from the majority of his English nobles. Of these relatives, Peter was possibly the ablest. Whether Henry was wise to promote him, especially in view of his actions in 1258, is less obvious.

**HENRY OF BRACTON** (or **BRATTON** *c*.1208-1268) was until recently considered the author of the greatest English law book of the thirteenth century, *De Legibus et Consuetudinibus Angliae* (*Concerning the Laws and Customs of England*). It now appears more probable that he may, at most, have compiled or transmitted an earlier text. A Devon man, Bracton owed his preferment as a royal clerk and justice to his fellow Devonian, the royal justice William Ralegh, who may also have drawn Bracton to the attention of Henry III's brother, Richard of Cornwall. Bracton was Ralegh's personal clerk in the mid 1230s. By 1240, he was in royal service in the *Coram Rege*, the central royal courts at Westminster. He was a justice-in-eyre, particularly in his native South West, from 1244, and a justice at the *Coram Rege* 1247-51 and 1253-7. Meanwhile, his ecclesiastical career developed profitably, with prebends at Exeter and Bosham, an archdeaconry at Barnstaple and the chancellorship of Exeter in 1264.

Bracton's relationship with *De Legibus* is unclear, although well established by the end of the Middle Ages. Modern research has demonstrated that the prototype of De Legibus was composed before 1236 by a connection of Martin Patteshull, a leading royal justice of the day. It was then revised by a clerk of William Ralegh who clearly had access to the records of Patteshull's cases. It is conceivable that this clerk was Bracton. There were further revisions until some time after 1256 the basis of the surviving, swollen work was produced. Even then, there was no single authoritative text; an epitome was produced in 1292, and two further summaries by the early fourteenth century, one of which, in Latin, was called, obscurely, the Fleta. The composition of De Legibus was, therefore, a process rather than a single creative event. Its origins, though, belong to a generation before Bracton, as the central role in the text of the cases of Patteshull and Ralegh indicate.

The De Legibus was the first attempt to describe English Common Law as it had developed since the procedural reforms of Henry II's reign, in particular the so-called possessory assizes. The task was made possible by the introduction, from the 1190s, of detailed records, kept on rolls, of cases heard before royal justices, either at Westminster or on tour. The formulae for settling civil disputes had begun to be collected from the early thirteenth century, the first law books. But De Legibus goes much further. Its intention was to delineate what English law and custom was and how it worked. Thus the bulk of the work comprises examples of actual cases organised by areas of law, such as possession, right, royal prerogative etc. General principles are adduced from extant case law. This makes the De Legibus unusual in western Europe at the time. Elsewhere, canonists were editing collections of Decretals, judicial decisions exposing general maxims, or compiling Summa of theological orthodoxy. Civil lawyers were either transcribing apparently immemorial customs (as, famously, Philippe de Beaumanoir's Customary of the Beauvaisis) or asserting ideal laws and prerogatives (such as the Emperor Frederick II's Liber Augustalis). The impact of Roman Law is evident in De Legibus but only in so far as the purpose of the work was to collate, systematize and state law as it existed. De Legibus was practical, not abstract, descriptive, not prescriptive. With its emphasis on case law, De Legibus mirrored what was to be one of the most distinctive features of English Common Law down to the twentieth century.

Henry de Bracton, *De Legibus et Consuetudinibus Angliae* ed. & trans E. S. Thorne, who established that Bracton was not the author, 1968-77.

**JOHN MANSEL** (*d*.1265) was one of Henry III's most accomplished and versatile servants, particularly expert in the conduct of foreign policy. From humble origins, educated at court, by 1234 he was employed in the Exchequer. For the next thirty years Mansel acted variously as royal secretary, councillor, keeper of the Great Seal, legal agent, diplomat and ambassador. His rewards were lavish. The clerical son of a cleric, he was a prodigious pluralist, his income from benefices allegedly running into thousands of marks a year. He wore his clerical garb lightly. Until a stone crushed his leg during the Gascon expedition in 1243, Mansel had made a name as a soldier, in Italy in 1238 and again on the 1242-3 French campaign. Unlike other contemporary bellicose clerics (*e.g.* Boniface of Savoy, archbishop of Canterbury), Mansel actually fought, on one occasion unhorsing his opponent, the seneschal of the count of Boulogne. After 1243, he had to content himself with administration and luxurious living. A member of the king's council from 1244, he held the Great Seal 1246-7 and 1248-9, but his main expertise was in foreign affairs. Here his achievement was remarkable, including the treaty and marriage alliance with Castile (1254); the Sicilian agreement with Innocent IV (1254); the election of Richard of Cornwall as King of the Romans (1257); the Treaty of Paris (1259); the papal absolution of the king's oath to support the Provisions of Oxford (1261); and the Mise of Amiens (1264). Mansel became an almost indispensible advisor to the king, reflected in his taking the Cross with his master in 1250 despite recurrent poor health. There were few issues concerning royal interests on which Mansel was not employed. One modern writer has called him 'almost the Wolsey of his age'. Unsurprisingly, he became a focus for the hostility of government critics, such as Matthew Paris and the baronial reformers of 1258-9. In 1263 he was forced into exile by Montfortian rebels, dying abroad two years later. How far he influenced or merely executed royal policy is obscure. Although his skill as a negotiator was, judged by results, exceptional, his own attitudes are hidden. It is intriguing that one of his friends and an executor to his will was Robert Tweng, a veteran nationalist, anti-papal terrorist directly opposed to most of the foreign policy initiatives so smoothly operated by Mansel himself. This alone suggests that there was more to the politics of Henry III's reign than met the eyes of royalist or baronial apologists.

**JOHN OF GLOUCESTER** (*fl.c.*1245-*d.*1260) was Henry III's master mason in the later 1250s. Already a successful mason in the 1240s, during the following decade he was particularly associated with Henry III's grandiose schemes at Westminster, both at the Abbey and the Palace. But his work for the king also included activity at Gloucester, Woodstock, Windsor, Guildford, Merton, Oxford and Old Sarum, largely on secular buildings. The value placed upon him is reflected in his rewards: he amassed property in Gloucester, Oxfordshire, Middlesex, Southwark, Northampton and Surrey. In 1255, he received from the king robes 'such as the knights of the Household receive'. His duties and presumably skills were many: the supervision of the large number of labourers at Westminster; designing the Queen's lodgings at Windsor; general maintenance of the stone fabric of royal dwellings; renewing the drains and sewers at the Palace of Westminster; even constructing lecterns for the king and the Westminster Chapter House. At Westminster, he worked closely with the king's chief carpenter, Alexander (*fl.*1239-*d.c.*1269). Together, they received patents in January 1257 as masters, respectively, of the king's masonry and carpentry. Their positions had earlier been recognised when, in November 1256, they had been ordered to take charge of all royal works in the kingdom because, significantly, the king 'had suffered much damage through causing his works to be carried on by sheriffs and other officers'. Either this can be seen as another encroachment on local power, part of a policy which so irritated the political nation that it led to overt opposition two years later; or Henry, desperately short of money but insistent on maintaining his regality in stones no less than in rhetoric and policy, was determined to avoid the peculation and financial mismanagement inevitable in a localised system of audit and accountability, a problem not unique to Henry III. Whatever the royal motive, John and Alexander set about their new responsibilities by touring the King's works south of the Trent in 1257, viewing not only buildings but the marble quarries at Purbeck. Like many other servants of Henry III, John found that his office was something of a poisoned chalice. The king was nearly bankrupt: in 1259 wages arrears to the Windsor workmen alone had reached £410. It may be that John was expected to cover any immediate shortfall. If so, it ruined him: at his death in 1260 he owed the king 80 marks and the income from his extensive lands was said to reach only two marks a year. This was the grim reality behind the soaring achievement of Westminster Abbey.

J. Harvey, *English Mediaeval Architects,* 1987.

**SIMON STOCK** (*d.*1265), an Englishman who became sixth Prior-General of the Carmelite Order of mendicants, embodies the twelfth century tradition of anchorites, eremitic holy men and women, with the thirteenth century's passion for corporate organisation. Unlike St Francis, however, his vocation was dictated by a physical as well as emotional return to Biblical precept. His life coincided with a brief moment when Western Christendom encompassed the Near East and whose horizons were set at a distance only imagined in the two subsequent centuries. Yet his career also exemplified the retreat from that Eastern dimension as the Order was transformed under his leadership.

Simon's origins are obscure. Possibly born as early as 1166, later legends attribute to him a noble lineage to compare, presumably deliberately, with the archetype of thirteenth century Christ-like holy men, Francis of Assisi. Hagiographic etymology relates his cognomen, 'Stock', to his having spent twenty years in a tree trunk. What is more certain is that at some time in the first half of the thirteenth century Simon went to Palestine and joined a congregation of hermits on Mt Carmel. There existed a long tradition of Christian hermits and monks on the Biblical site of Elijah's cell and his confrontation with the priests of Baal.

In the early thirteenth century, one group of Latin hermits organised themselves under a simple Rule, dedicated to the Virgin Mary. Originally designed for the holy men living on Mt Carmel itself, after the Crusade of Richard of Cornwall (1240-41) the Order was taken up by patrons in the West, not least in England where land grants to members of the Order began in the early 1240s. It was at one of these estates, Aylesford in Kent, that the first General Chapter of the Order was held in 1245 and where, at another Chapter two years later, Simon was elected prior.

As prior, Simon confirmed the translation of the Carmelites from a group of hermits wedded to their eremitic tradition in the Holy Land into an international Mendicant Order. Symbolic of the change was the substitution (only finally accepted in 1286-87) of a simple white habit for the original, somewhat bizarre multi-coloured habit, which, unsurprisingly, had caused some less than flattering comment. In 1248, Simon secured the approval of Pope Innocent IV for a new constitution for the Order and permission for brothers to settle in the West. Almost immediately, the nature and focus of the Carmelites shifted: they became extensive landowners in the West and significant members of the ecclesiastical community; and they began to attend the schools and universities at Oxford, Cambridge, Paris and Bologna. Such innovation met with resistance from traditionalists within the Order and from existing vested interests outside. But it conformed to similar developments in, for example, the Franciscans. To survive and to answer the demand of laymen for fresh outlets for religious patronage and spiritual vocations, simplicity, other-wordly idealism and intimacy with the sites of Holy Geography had to give way to more institutionalised and accessible temporal structures. This Simon's priorship largely set in motion.

**WILLIAM LONGESPEE** (c.1212-1250) rather unexpectedly became one of the most famous Englishmen of the thirteenth century. An unlikely candidate for immortality, William was the son of Ella, countess of Salisbury in her own right (c.1191-1261), founder and later abbess of Lacock abbey (Wiltshire) and William Longespee (d.1226), a bastard son of Henry II. Despite his lineage and the favour of his cousin Henry III, his achievements were less than modest. He campaigned regularly with the king, sharing in the failures in Brittany (1230), Wales (1233) and Gascony (1242-3). He was unable to obtain recognition as earl of Salisbury after his mother took the veil (1237). A companion of his other cousin, Richard of Cornwall, on crusade in 1240, he briefly rose to prominence as leader of a substantial English contingent that joined Louis IX of France's crusade in 1249. Heavily subsidised from central funds for hiring knights and serjeants, William left England, we are told, his saddle-bags stuffed with cash. His availability to lead the English crusaders suggests that he was a very minor political player. The crusade was a disaster. He quarrelled with his French colleagues and was killed at the battle of Mansourah in the Nile Delta (February 1250). Yet whatever his insignificance in life, in death William found apotheosis as an English martyr. At the hands of myth-makers, including Matthew Paris, within two generations William had become a national hero, specifically manufactured to stand in contrast and indictment to the French who were portrayed as panic-stricken cowards. By the early fourteenth century a poem in French detailing William's self-sacrificing heroism was circulating and he featured in the Middle English epic *Richard Coer de Lyon*. William became a symbol and a barometer of a growing literary fashion for nationalist anti-French feeling. William was a specifically English hero, signifying the beginnings of the development of a national consciousness which was to be such a feature of English history in the later middle ages.

S. Lloyd, 'William Longespee II: The Making of an English Crusading Hero', *Nottingham Medieval Studies*, xxxv, 1991.

**WILLIAM,** called of Valence after his birthplace in Poitou (after 1225-1296), the fourth son of Isabella of Angoulême, widow of King John and Hugh of Lusignan, count of La Marche, was the most prominent and disliked of Henry III's Poitevin half-brothers who had their fortunes made in England after their arrival in 1247. William's brothers Guy and Geoffrey were richly rewarded with estates and pensions, while another brother, Aymer, received the richest see in England, Winchester

(1250). For William himself was reserved the largest prize, a wealthy heiress, Joan of Munchesni, who brought with her property worth £700 a year, to which Henry added another £800 worth. For the next decade, William and his brothers continued to enjoy the king's largesse, despite the dwindling scope for royal patronage. By the mid-1250s, William was second only to Richard of Cornwall in preferment and prominence at court. This naturally caused resentment, especially among those like Simon de Montfort who thought they were insufficiently supported. Added insult was the king's explicit protection of his half-brothers from hostile legal action and their own rapacity and violence. They behaved, as indeed they were, above the law. One Norfolk chronicler wrote 'no Englishman could get his right or obtain a writ against them'. The Lusignans were not unique in this: in 1256, Henry included Richard of Cornwall, the earl of Gloucester and his wife's uncle Peter of Savoy in this privilege. However, the Lusignans, through their aggressive exploitation of the king's friendship and immunity, were especially hated. Their apparent monopoly of royal favour turned jealousy into serious political opposition. It is striking that two of those associated in the protection against writs of 1256, Gloucester and Peter of Savoy, were among the first to attack Henry and the Lusignans in 1258. Simon de Montfort's relations with William of Valence had been notoriously bad for years, the earl seeming to blame the Poitevin for much of his disappointment over patronage. However, the crisis of 1258-9 was lent its especially bitter edge by the collective vendetta against the Lusignan favourites who were the first casualties of their refusal to swear to the Provisions of Oxford, being forced into exile. The barons dressed up their factional rivalry by accusing the Lusignans of inciting the king to believe he was above the law. More significantly, the accident of their foreign birth allowed participants and observers alike to characterise the baronial reforms as in some sense a national reaction against malign alien influence. Thus, negatively, William and his brothers contributed to the emergence of national identity among the English political classes. Restored in 1261, William played a leading part in the royalist cause. Escaping after Lewes, he returned with an army in 1265 for the campaign which ended at Evesham. William's career remained attached to the monarchy. He went on crusade with the Lord Edward (1270-3) and continued assiduously to increase his landed holdings thereafter for the rest of his life. William, a lover of tournaments whose passion for his hobby extended to searching out the best horses in Europe, was vain and arrogant, with the love of those spoilt when young of throwing his weight about. That his power derived from no quality of his except the accident of birth was his blessing, but his patron's cross.

**HUGH BIGOD** (*d.*1266) was prominent in the imposition of the baronial programme of reform enshrined in the Provisions of Oxford (1258) and the Provisions of Westminster (1259), acting as justiciar of England from June 1258 to October 1260. His early career is obscure, although by 1258 he had amassed extensive landed interests in Yorkshire and Sussex; had accompanied the king on campaign in Wales in 1257; and served as a negotiator with the French in 1257-8, preparatory to the Peace of Paris (1259). In April 1258, he swore an oath of confederacy with six other magnates, including his brother, the earl of Norfolk, and Simon de Montfort. This group formed the nucleus of the baronial coalition which sought to limit and define royal prerogative in the wake of the financially disastrous Sicilian enterprise; royal manipulation of local justice and administration; and the growing power of the king's Lusignan half-brothers. These were no disinterested framers of a parliamentary constitution. Rather, they were intent on resisting encroachment on their rights and influence to the benefit of the Crown and royal favourites. They did not look forward to a constitutional monarchy but harked back to the days of consensual baronial government during Henry III's Minority (1216-27). At the parliament at Oxford in June 1258, Hugh Bigod was appointed justiciar, a revival of an office closely associated with the Minority, unfilled since 1234. Apart from assuming control of central administration, Hugh's chief and immediate function was to hear pleas and complaints againt royal administration, much of his work being based upon the local enquiries ordered in 1258 and conducted over the following months by the knights of the shire. Hugh drew the plaudits of sympathetic observers as a fearless and efficient judge, impervious to the influence of 'powerful persons'. He also seems to have been impervious to procedural niceties, his itinerary through the south and Midlands in 1258-9 being marked by controversy over his favouring of complainants and his casual treatment of existing rights. Hugh's summary justice may have prompted the return to formal procedures of writs, appeals and recognition of existing liberties, rights and exemptions enshrined in the Provisions of Westminster (March 1259). Hugh's conduct may also suggest that he was not one of the growing number of semi-professional royal justices, his appointment as justiciar owing more to his noble connections and experience of court than to legal expertise: Hugh's role was and remained essentially political. Although partisan against the Lusignan faction, Hugh was not anti-royalist *per se*. In 1259-60, he was regent in Henry III's absence in France, in the spring of 1260 organising resistance to an imagined threat to the king from the Lord Edward. After resigning his office in 1260, Hugh continued as a royal ally except briefly in 1261 when his own territorial position was threatened by the royal resumption of castles. Soon reconciled to the king, thereafter he was loyal, fighting for the king in 1264 and suffering exile after Henry's defeat at Lewes. Hugh's brief career at the top of English politics demonstrates that the tensions of 1258-65 were as much personal and factional as ideological or constitutional. However, all sides had to cope with an expanding political nation, exemplified in the increasing role of the knights of the shire. The failure of baronial reform indicated that it was the crown, not the magnates, which was best able to adapt. The lasting legacy of Hugh's justicarship were the Provisions of Westminster, confirmed by the king in 1263 and forming the basis for the Statute of Marlborough of 1267, a significant episode in the creation of a common law of property, but one guaranteed by royal courts not baronial power.

WALTER CANTELUPE (*d*.1266; bishop of Worcester 1236-66) was a leading partisan of the movement against the rule of Henry III in the 1260s. A close friend and advisor of Simon de Montfort, he was a conservative who, in defence of his views, espoused radical solutions. As so many thirteenth century ecclesiastics, Cantelupe trod the increasingly precarious path of obedience to the universal authority of the papacy and faithfulness to the rights of provincial churches in matters secular as well as spiritual. Thirteenth century dons could — and did — talk in terms of abstract principles. Propagandists could — and did — talk in terms of absolutes. Cantelupe, on the other hand, a clerical man of affairs, was forced to take sides and adopt political positions which earned him defeat and obloquy. The contemporary royalist chronicler Thomas Wykes hit on a general truth when he commented that Cantelupe would have deserved canonisation if he had not supported Montfort. The prizes of this world and the next tend to go to the victors.

The key to unlock the conundrums of conflicting loyalties was the law. Cantelupe acted as a royal justice-in-eyre before becoming a bishop. Thereafter he vigorously implemented canonical instructions for reform, producing his own Constitutions in 1240 and regularly holding diocesan synods and visiting religious houses. As bishop, he was hostile to innovative taxation, papal as much as royal. Increasingly, he became a spokesman for provincial rights, which in the 1250s placed him against the papal taxation of the church in support of Henry III's Sicilian adventure.

In his early career as a bishop he was closely connected with Bishop Grosseteste of Lincoln, a man who suffered fools ill and pious intellectuals highly. Cantelupe's opinions were of significance because of his credentials as a courtier and aristocrat. From 1229 when he collected Archbishop Richard Grant's *pallium* from Rome to 1257 when he was admitted to the king's council, Cantelupe served two masters with skill and success. After 1258, he lent public and startling support to the cause of Montfort and the baronial reformers. In 1263, Cantelupe had been appointed by the pope to raise men and money for a new crusade, itself a recognition of his prominent status in the English church. He turned this authority to novel purpose when, at Lewes in 1264 and Evesham in 1265, he offered Montfort's supporters the sanction of the church. Before the battle of Lewes he granted absolution for their sins to the rebels, a direct echo of crusader privileges. For such partisan use of the consolations of the church and his anti-royalist behaviour, he was suspended after the baronial defeat at Evesham by the papal legate,

Ottobuono. He died shortly after, on 12 February 1266. Cantelupe was a political failure for the simple reason that he, unlike most of his episcopal colleagues, refused to trim. His legalistic views on legitimate rights of local and central powers led him to rebel, and even to espouse a doctrine of Christian resistance more associated with twentieth century Latin America than thirteenth century England. In this he was not the least remarkable English bishop of the period.

**AARON OF YORK** (*d*.1268) was a native of Lincoln who, in the first half of the thirteenth century, built up a substantial financial empire based on York. By 1241, he was one of the two richest Jews in England (the other being worth a relief of 7,000 marks three years later). In his heyday, from the 1220s to 1240s, Aaron was giving personal loans as large as £250; doing business with merchants from Florence, Siena and Bordeaux; leasing property in York to prominent citizens; and helping those with money, such as the Cistercian abbey of Rievaulx, to buy out smaller landowners in financial difficulty. R. B. Dobson has described Aaron in his prime as 'this Croesus of thirteenth century England'. However, by 1255, Aaron was exempted from the Jewish tallage 'his wealth having entirely evaporated'. His fall was a mirror of the fate of English Jewry in the thirteenth century, brought down by the attrition of constant royal tallages and an increasingly hostile social and legal environment. The year of Aaron's bankruptcy was pivotal: a new tallage; a new blood-libel at Lincoln; and Henry III's mortgaging of the whole community to his wealthy brother Richard of Cornwall. Aaron's family kept in business until the end, but suffered increasing financial deprivation and violent persecution. After the expulsion of 1290, the memory of such financial moguls as Aaron of York was preserved only in the names of where they lived and conducted business, as in York's Jewbury and Jubbergate.

R. B. Dobson, 'The Decline and Expulsion of the Medieval Jews of York', *Translation of the Jewish Historical Society of England*, xxvi, 1979.

**BONIFACE OF SAVOY** (*d*.1270; archbishop of Canterbury 1241-70) was the last non-English archbishop of Canterbury, the first since Theobald (1138-61). The eleventh child of Thomas I, count of Savoy, he was the uncle of Henry III's wife, Eleanor. A Carthusian — although hardly an advertisement for that strict and rigorous order — Boniface rose quickly, as well-connected clergy often do, becoming bishop of Belley in 1234. His relationship to Henry III secured his preferment to Canterbury in 1241, but he was consecrated by Innocent IV only in 1245 and not enthroned at Canterbury until 1249. His main concern in these years was as commander of the papal guard, a preference which did not go unnoticed in England. For services to the papacy he received the privilege of collecting all the first fruits(*i.e.* a tax on the revenue of new incumbents) in his province, which added to his unpopularity. When in England in 1249-50, he implemented the decree of the Council of Lyons (1245) instructing archbishops to visit all religious establishments in their provinces, regardless of the rights of their suffragan bishops. Predictably, this met with fierce institutional resistance. On one occasion, the archbishop was so exasperated by the recalcitrance of the canons of St Bartholomew's Priory in Smithfield in London that he personally mugged the subprior. His temperament was perhaps revealed in his wearing a coat of mail under his episcopal vestments during these visitations. He also tended to be accompanied by a gang of Provençal thugs who greatly facilitated collection of money. It was typical that he felt no compulsion to support King Henry in all things, arguing with him over church appointments and with the king's favoured half-brother, Aymer of Lusignan, bishop-elect of Winchester. Boniface's military career continued on the continent in-the 1250s, but from 1256 he began to concentrate on English affairs. In the face of growing hostility to the king's foreign advisors and favourites, Boniface inevitably supported the royalists in the civil conflicts of 1258-65, although he retired to France from 1262 to 1265. After the royalist victory at Evesham in 1265, he returned to England but his power was overshadowed by the Cardinal Legate Ottobuono. In 1270, accompanying the Lord Edward on crusade, Boniface died in his native Savoy.

His career illustrates some of the less edifying aspects of the development since the eleventh century of an international church under the universal authority of the papacy. Boniface owed his position to his birth, was a frequent absentee and treated his see much as a secular lord would a fief or principality: property to be exploited with rights to be protected. In some ways he resembled the forceful aristocratic prelates of the earlier Middle Ages. Yet his promotion was as a papal servant and his insistence on visitation rights mark him as an effective if tactless diocesan, in line with contemporary centralising tendencies at the papal curia. A century ago the historian Mandell Creighton (himself bishop of Peterborough then London) was dismissive: 'Archbishop Boniface did nothing that was important either for church or state in England'. In this he was following the hostile account of Boniface's career in England by the xenophobic Matthew Paris for whom the archbishop represented all that was threatening to the indigenous rights of the English church. Boniface's cosmopolitan interests and outlook would have made him unsympathetic to Paris (and to Bishop Creighton) regardless of what he actually did.

[Mandell Creighton contributed the *D.N.B.* article.]

**THOMAS DOCKING** (*fl.*1230-70), from Docking in Norfolk, was an influential Franciscan scholar and teacher at Oxford University whose career and interests shed light on the preoccupations of contemporary learned circles. He heard Grosseteste lecture to the Franciscans at Oxford in 1229/30, making him one of the earliest of the Mendicants to make an academic career in an English university. By the 1240s, his fellow Franciscan, Adam Marsh was singing Docking's praises as a leading light in the Order at Oxford. He rose to become the seventh Franciscan reader in Divinity at Oxford (1262-5) and a Doctor of Divinity. Active as a lecturer and writer throughout the 1250s and 1260s, Docking is last heard of in 1269. His main works were Commentaries on the Bible which show him to be a discursive exegete, with a then characteristically Oxonian knowledge of natural science and optics, and an interest in morality, theology and contemporary politics. His discussion of a responsible man assuming royal power for the public good may be a reference to Simon de Montfort in 1264-5. Among his lost works was a *Biblical Grammar*. Superficially intractable, Docking's scholarship had a contemporary relevance in its concern with the relationship of the contemplative and active life, one of the great themes of medieval thought. As a Mendicant engaged in the life of a growing university in a city in which national and local politics were never far away, Docking was in a good position to comment. A scholar and teacher whose influence was maintained as much by his pupils as by his writing, he, as much as any, helped confirm the position of the Friars in the forefront of English academic life, and he did so by basing his scholarship upon the Bible. For all the excitement of new discoveries of Aristotle and others, the Bible remained throughout the Middle Ages the great repository of ideas and focus for enquiry. Biblical study was by no means sterile of fresh insights, as was illustrated a century later by another Oxford lecturer on the Bible, John Wyclif.

J. Catto (ed.), *History of the University of Oxford*, vol. i, 1984.

**ROGER BACON** (*c.*1220-1292), nicknamed 'the Marvellous Doctor', was a polymath and encyclopaedist around whom a number of fanciful anecdotes have clustered, some, perhaps,of his own invention. He was suspected (wrongly) of necromancy; to him has been attributed (wrongly) the discovery of gunpowder and spectacles. He liked to see himself as an empirical scientist, but his observations and descriptions were, in keeping with the academic fashion of the time, entirely theoretical. By his own account, he was a prodigiously energetic researcher. Educated in the traditional Liberal Arts (the Trivium: grammar; rhetoric; and logic; and the Quadrivium: music; astronomy; geometry; arithmetic) at Paris in the early 1240s, he lectured on Aristotle before, on returning to Oxford, he began his scientific enquiries. Influenced, perhaps, by the Oxford tradition of Grosseteste, between 1247 and 1257 Bacon studied optics, languages, alchemy, astronomy and mathematics. His empiricism did not extend to experiments in the modern understanding of the term. Thus he described, but did not make, spectacles and, in 1252, provided exact directions for concocting gunpowder, but did not actually assemble the recipe. Like many other academics of the thirteenth century, Bacon, in mid-career, became a Mendicant Friar, joining the Franciscans in 1257. If he hoped the new Order would be open to new ideas, he was misled. Thereafter, he fought a running battle with superiors in his attempts to establish science on the university curriculum and in compiling an encyclopaedia of nature in order to further the cause of Christianity which, in Bacon's lifetime, seemed genuinely threatened by Moslems and Mongols. He managed to interest Pope Clement IV (1265-68) in his project and between 1266 and 1268 he produced three weighty volumes, the *Opus majus*, *Opus minus* and *Opus tertium*, in which he attempted to summarize all human knowledge. Yet he achieved this prodigious feat against the instructions of his Order and was punished for it. But he kept on writing: *c*.1268-72 came the *Communia naturalium* (on natural philosophy); the *Communia mathematica* (on general mathematical principles) and a *Compendium philosophiae*. By the late 1270s, the Order had run out of patience and Bacon was imprisoned for unorthodox teaching, alchemy and heresy. Even this failed to stem his output and he was still writing when he died in 1292. He was buried in the Franciscan church in Oxford. From his own works, Bacon emerges as a man whose erudition was matched only by his self-confidence. Like contemporary theologians, such as Aquinas, he believed that all knowledge could be unified and was, perhaps, rather unfastidious in what he acquired. The boundaries between science and magic, astronomy and astrology, speculation and heresy, empiricism and alchemy were too fluid for his work to escape suspicion. That he was not condemned further is probably explained by the sheer weight and volume of his work: few then or since could possibly have read even a fraction of it. But his personality left its mark in the legends of his learning and his discoveries.

**THOMAS CANTELUPE** (?1218-1282; bishop of Hereford 1275-82), the only Englishman to be canonised in the fourteenth century (1320), was an unlikely candidate for sanctity. Well connected (his uncle Walter was bishop of Worcester), an academic with anti-royalist views, litigious, a greedy pluralist, a misogynist and an anti-semite, Thomas was a fairly typical product of the socially superior and intellectually advanced clergy of the thirteenth century. A red-faced, ginger-haired man with a large nose, throughout his career Thomas's affluence and taste for preferment never interfered with his professional commitment to radical causes, reform in church and state or the friendship of the Mendicant Friars. As a student of canon law at Paris, he lived in style with his own household, apparently even entertaining Louis IX. In 1245, he was granted permission by Innocent IV to hold benefices in plurality. This allowed a secure income without the constraint of duties, a common ploy which sustained generations of civil servants, lawyers and scholars.

Thomas specialised in law. Before Paris, he had studied civil law at Orleans, and he went on to teach canon law at Oxford. In 1262 he became Chancellor of Oxford University. Thomas showed his political allegiances in 1263 when he refused the Lord Edward entry to Oxford, although his most onerous task as chancellor was quelling riots amongst the students and between them and the townspeople. His legal skill was soon employed by the partisans of Simon de Montfort as a baronial commissioner at the Mise of Amiens (1263-4) and, very briefly, chancellor of England in the first half of 1265. After Montfort's defeat at Evesham, Thomas withdrew to lecture on theology at Paris. But his ability, or contacts, saw him back in Oxford in the early 1270s, where he once more became chancellor. His appointment by Edward I as bishop of Hereford in 1275 marked his rehabilitation and was another sign of Edward's policy of partial reconciliation of former rebel sympathisers. His cultivation of Robert Kilwardby, archbishop of Canterbury, may have helped too. By now his benefices brought him an annual income reputed to be £1,000 a year. He was archdeacon of Stafford; a canon at York and London; a prebendary of Lichfield and rector of a clutch of parishes. Later encomiasts suggest that he visited his parishes and was generous with his money. As bishop, Thomas continued his lucrative pluralism, but he also worked hard to raise the standard of his diocesan clergy, although here too there is a whiff of hypocrisy. He dismissed the cathedral precentor for being a pluralist without papal permission: it may have been a coincidence that the precentor had been a rival candidate for the bishopric in 1275. Thomas was also eager in defence of his privileges. It was on the way to Rome to appeal aganist his excommunication by the inflexible Archbishop Pecham for defending his rights as a suffragan that he died at Orvieto on 25 August 1282.

His cult seems to have been started deliberately by his pupil and successor Richard Swinfield (bishop of Hereford 1282-1317) in 1287. A week before Swinfield's carefully prepared translation of Thomas's bones to a new shrine-like tomb, the late bishop performed his first miracle. It was the first of many in a curative cult which grew rapidly. Of all surviving English medieval miracle collections, only Becket's is larger.Swinfield no doubt had one eye on the profits of pilgrimage as well as, presumably, the other on the spiritual advantages of a fresh channel of Divine Grace. Thomas Cantelupe would have  approved.

R. Finucane, *Miracles and Pilgrims*, 1977.

**HENRY OF ALMAIN(E)** (1235-1271) was the eldest son of Richard of Cornwall, younger brother of Henry III. He was closely associated in his father's ventures, particularly in the acceptance of the crown of Germany (*i.e.* Almain(e)) in 1257. Although he initially opposed the Provisions of Oxford (1258), like many  younger nobles he flirted with the baronial critics of royal government. In 1263-4, however, he firmly supported the royalist cause and was captured after the battle of Lewes (1264). In France when Simon de Montfort was defeated at Evesham (1265), his independent political influence grew. He played an important part in organising the crusade with the Lord Edward (1268-70), whom he accompanied to Tunis. However, he did not go with Edward to Palestine, but returned to France, perhaps to protect his cousin's interests with the new king of France, Philip III. At Viterbo, when at prayer in church, he was assassinated by two of Simon de Montfort's sons, Guy and Simon, and his body mutilated in revenge, they claimed, for the death of their father at Evesham. Guy, who actually dealt the fatal blow, was excommunicated and outlawed but managed to survive off his wits with the assitance of various Italian patrons until dying in a Sicilian prison in 1292. Apart from the shock at the removal of a major figure of the new generation of political leaders, Henry of Almaine's murder without heirs made more possible the ultimate reversion of Richard of Cornwall's extremely valuable lands to the crown. This occured with the death of Henry's younger brother, also without heirs, in 1300.

**GILBERT CLARE, EARL OF GLOUCESTER** (1243-95) played a central and disruptive role in the civil wars of the 1260s. Inheriting vast estates in the west country, the Welsh Marches and Ireland after his father's death (1262), Gilbert initially was a strong partisan for the rebellion of Simon de Montfort in 1263-4. Earl Simon knighted Gilbert and his brother shortly before the battle of Lewes (May 1264) After Montfort, Gilbert was the most powerful man in the kingdom during the next year, but relations between the two deteriorated. Gilbert wished for more authority, a greater share of the spoils of victory, and an entirely free hand in policing and defending his lands. Gilbert posed as the defender of the Provisions of Oxford, of which his father had been an initiator, and implied that Montfort's dictatorship was betraying their principles. Here, it is difficult to disentangle selfless ideology from inflated self-importance. In May 1265, Gilbert broke with Montfort, allying with the newly escaped Lord Edward with whom he won the battle of Evesham. His perceived treachery led to bitterness with surviving Montfortians, but relations with the royalists were hardly less tense. A champion of disinherited rebel sympathisers, he protested at the failure to implement the Provisions of Oxford, not seeing that the royalist victory had made them redundant. Gilbert seems to have imagined that he could, under the guise of constitutional moderation and propiety, exercise an independent role in English politics. When his error became apparent, he took to arms in 1267, occupying London before his grievances were submitted to the arbitration of Richard of Cornwall. Although his discontent simmered, he was outwardly reconciled to the regime, taking the Cross in 1268 and promising to travel with the Lord Edward to the Holy Land in 1270 which in the event, despite a threatened forfeit of 20,000 marks, he did not. In 1271, he succeeded in getting agreement to the restoration of the lands of the Disinherited. Thereafter, his political independence emasculated by tight royal control, Gilbert remained loyal to Edward I. Having been divorced from his first wife (a niece of Henry III's, allegedly hypochondriac) in 1271, Gilbert married Edward I's sister Joan of Acre in 1290. This not only tied him more closely to the court, but the stipulation that inheritance of his vast estates was restricted to the descendents of this union, greatly increased the chance of them reverting to the crown (which they did in 1314). Even as late as 1292, Gilbert found himself on trial in a dispute about power in the Welsh Marches, only gaining release and restoration of his lands on agreement to pay of a fine of 10,000 marks. Gilbert, nicknamed the 'Red Earl' because of his colouring, tried to carve out an independent political position for himself from which to negotiate loyalty to the crown. Whatever his private views on the Provisions of Oxford, he used the civil war as a convenient way of extending his own interests, his policy being essentially factional not constitutional. His failure and subsequent humiliations were a function probably of his own political incompetence and certainly of the renewed royal strength after the baronial wars. Increasingly under Edward I, Earl Gilbert appeared something of an anachronism.

# SELECT BIBLIOGRAPHY

This list is intended as suggestions for further general reading. The list is neither exhaustive nor prescriptive for an understanding of the period. Any serious student will wish to read primary sources, but even the casual observer may be inspired by visible relics — the castles, cathedrals, churches, city walls, houses, tombs *etc* — to investigate further. The following may assist.

*Age of Chivalry,* ed J. Alexander & P. Binski (1987).
F. Barlow, *William Rufus* (1983).
F. Barlow, *The English Church 1066-1154* (1979).
F. Barlow, *The Feudal Kingdom of England 1042-1216* (3rd edn 1972).
F. Barlow, *Thomas Becket* (1986).
D. Bates, *William the Conqueror* (1988).
D. Carpenter, *The Minority of Henry III* (1990).
M. Chibnall, *Anglo-Norman England* (1986).
M. T. Clanchy, *From Memory to Written Record: England 1066-1307* (1979).
M. T. Clanchy. *England and its Rulers* (1983).
H. M. Colvin ed, *The History of the King's Works,* vol i (1963).
D. Crouch, *William Marshal* (1990).
R. H. C. Davies, *King Stephen* (1967).
R. H. C. Davies, *The Normans and their Myth* (1976).
D. C. Douglas, *William the Conqueror* (1964).
*English Historical Documents,* Gen ed. D. C. Douglas, vol ii, (1981) & iii (1975).
*English Romanesque Art 1066-1200,* ed J. Drew *et al* (1984).
J. Gillingham, *Richard the Lionheart* (1978).
J. Gillingham, *The Angevin Empire* (1984).
A. Gransden, *Historical Writing in England 550-1307* (1974).
J. Green, *The Government of England under Henry I* (1986).
J. Harvey, *English Mediaeval Architects* (1987).
J. C. Holt, *King John* (Historical Association Pamphlet 1963).
J. C. Holt, *The Northerners* (1961).
J. C. Holt, *Magna Carta and Medieval Government* (1985).
J. C. Holt, ed., *Domesday Studies* (1987).
M. Keen, *Chivalry* (1984).
C. H. Knowles, *Simon de Montfort* (Historical Association Pamphlet 1965).
D. Knowles, *The Monastic Order in England* (1949; 2nd edn. 1963).
D. Knowles, *The Religious Orders in England,* vol i (1948).
J. Le Patourel, *The Norman Empire* (1976).
J. R. Maddicott, *Simon de Montfort* (1994).
E. Miller & J. Hatcher, *Medieval England: Rural Society and Economic Change 1086-1348* (1978).
F. M. Powicke, *King Henry III and the Lord Edward* (1947).
S. Reynolds, *Fiefs and Vassals* (1994).
O. Rackham, *The History of the Countryside* (1986).
R. W. Southern, *The Making of the Middle Ages* (1953).
R. W. Southern, *St Anselm and his Biographer* (1963).
R. W. Southern, *Robert Grosseteste* (1986).
C. J. Tyerman, *England and the Crusades 1095-1588* (1988).
W. L. Warren, *The Governance of Norman and Angevin England* (1987).
W. L. Warren, *Henry II* (1973).
W. L. Warren, *King John* (1961).

# GLOSSARY

**Aid.** An extraordinary grant of tax to the king for which, from King John's reign, it was customary to have the assent of the lay and ecclesiastical magnates, later afforced by representatives of the knights of the shires and burgesses.

**Amercement.** A punishment, levied in money, imposed at the 'mercy', *i.e.* discretion of the king or his justices for minor infringements of regulations, especially fiscal or judicial, or minor offences.

**Assize.** Originally a rule, regulation or law imposed by the king, with the assent of the magnates, which changed or modified customary law (*e.g.* Assize of Arms 1181 on the military obligations of freemen). The term was applied, by extension, to legal procedures resulting from such alterations of the law (*e.g.* assizes of *mort d'ancestor* and *novel disseisin*). Later, the name was given to the courts and judges which heard such pleas. A **Grand Assize** was a procedure introduced in 1179 as an alternative to trial by combat of issues of right to freehold, the case being heard before a jury of twelve knights of the shire. This process was careful and slow. For more rapid solutions to matters of tenure of property, rather than absolute right, quicker procedures were instituted, known as **Petty Assizes**, including *mort d'ancestor* and *novel disseisin*.

**Baron.** A tenant-in-chief of the king, *i.e.* one who held land and titles directly from the king.

**Benefice.** In an ecclesiastical context, a position, office of profit or living; a cure of souls with an income attached. Originally a benefice was a grant of land by a lord to his vassal.

**Carucate.** From *caruca,* a plough, was a measurement of land which could be kept under the plough by a team of eight oxen in a year. This could vary from between sixty and a hundred acres. This formed the basis of a new land tax in 1194.

**Chapter.** In ecclesiastical terms, the governing body of a cathedral, comprising a prior and the priory monks in monastic cathedrals, such as Canterbury and a Dean and canons in cathedrals run by secular clerics, as at York. The name derives from the meetings of these bodies at which it was customary for chapters of the Bible to be read aloud.

**Curialis.** A courtier, hence curial officials, curial sheriffs *etc*, men based at or deriving their authority and influence from their position at the king's court.

**Demesne.** Land farmed directly by a lord or his villeins. The **Royal Demesne** was all land in the kingdom not in church or private hands and from which the king derived rent or other revenue.

**Disseisin.** Wrongful deprivation of possession of land held in freehold (seisin).

**Escheat.** Reversion of a fief to a lord in the absence of an heir or as a result of the holder being declared an outlaw.

**Eyre.** Derived from the Latin *itinere,* to journey. A visitation by the king or his justices, hence justices-in-eyre, to hear pleas. Usually organised on circuits of a number of counties, the system became regular from the 1160s and was an especial feature of the re-establishment of royal power after 1217.

**Familiaris.** A member of a household of a king or magnate, often implying special attachment or closeness without formal office.

**Farm.** Derived from the Anglo-Saxon *feorm* or food-rent. A fixed payment or rent, usually annual. **Sheriff's Farm**: an agreed sum payable annually in composition for the regular royal revenues from the sheriff's county. Anything the sheriff collected above his 'farm' he kept as profit.

**Fealty.** An oath of fidelity sworn, often on the Gospels or relics, to a lord. **Not** to be confused with **Homage**. Fealty could be sworn without any reciprocal undertaking or gift, such as land. Fealty was unilateral. In theory, fealty to the king took precedence over all other obligations, including homage to a lesser lord.

**Fief.** Property, usually a landed estate, occasionally money or rent, held from a lord in return for homage and the performance of services, often military. In England fiefs were normally heritable.

**Fine.** Not necessarily a monetary penalty. Usually in this period a sum paid to the Crown in return for a grant, privilege, concession or merely to avoid the king's displeasure.

**Franchise.** A privilege or right, often of jurisdiction, granted to an individual or group (a town or monastery) by a lord, in England prominently by the king.

**Hide.** An Anglo-Saxon measurement of land, originally calculated as that sufficient to support a household for a year but by the eleventh century a unit of assessment for the geld or land tax, similar in nature to the carucate.

**Homage.** The oath and associated ceremony by which a vassal bound himself to his lord by becoming his man (*homo*) and acknowledged the obligations of holding a fief. Homage implied a reciprocal agreement by the superior to be a good lord. The ceremony, classically, required the vassal to place his hands between those of his lord.

**Honor or Honour.** The estates or group of estates held by the greater tenants-in-chief of the Crown from which they derived their status, prestige and often titles. Within an honor there were often inferior lordships held of the greater lord.

**Hundred.** An administrative sub-division of a shire with its own court.

**Interdict.** Literally a prohibition. Specifically, that by Pope Innocent III in 1208 forbidding any priests in England from performing their priestly functions, including the administration of the sacraments. The only exceptions were the baptism of infants and the hearing the confessions of the dying, both of which were accepted as being matters which could legitimately be conducted by laymen. The Interdict was lifted in 1213.

**Knight's Fee.** An estate or fief technically owing the service and therefore providing for the maintenance of one knight. In practice a unit of assessment of taxes or services.

**Manor.** Ultimately derived from the latin *manere*, to stay, remain, hence to dwell. A unit of territorial and agricultural organisation, generally comprising the lord's demesne and the lands farmed by his tenants. Also a centre used for taxation purposes.

**Mark.** A sum of money equivalent to two-thirds of a pound sterling, *i.e.* 13s 4d.

**Mort d'Ancestor.** A legal procedure developed under Henry II to provide redress for plaintiffs who had been deprived of their rightful inheritance.

**Novel Disseisin.** A legal procedure developed under Henry II to provide redress for plaintiffs who had had their freehold unjustly taken from them.

**Pipe Roll.** The record of the annual audit of the accounts of the sheriffs and others with debts to the crown. The first surviving Pipe Roll is from 1130. From 1155, the series is more or less complete.

**Pleas of the Crown.** Serious crimes, breaches of the peace and certain specific offences which could only be tried by officers of the Crown.

**Relief.** From the latin *relevare*, to take up. A payment to a lord by a tenant on entry into possession of an inherited fief.

**Scutage.** Literally 'shield-money', payment in lieu of military service levied by the Crown on tenants-in-chief according to the number of knight's fees they held.

**Seisin.** The enjoyment of rights and revenues derived from possession of freehold land.

**Serf.** A legally unfree, servile peasant.

**Sheriff.** Originally the Anglo-Saxon shire-reeve, after the Conquest the sheriff was the officer appointed by the king responsible for administering the king's lands and justice in a shire. He was the key royal fiscal and judicial agent in the twelfth century. Thereafter, the sheriff's authority was supplemented or superseded by justices-in-eyre and local commissions established in the thirteenth century. Increasingly, the Exchequer exerted direct control of royal revenues in the localities, further weakening the power of the sheriff.

**Writ.** A written command of the king, after the Conquest both sealed and signed. From the twelfth century, an order to royal officials to initiate legal proceedings in the king's courts. From the 1170s, certain writs were formalized to expedite judicial proceedings under the **Petty Assizes.**

# INDEX

**417**